THE ENVIRONMENTAL DESIGN POCKETBOOK

SOFIE PELSMAKERS

D1323762

RIBA 卌 **Publishing**

The publication of this book has been generously sponsored by:

Levitt Bernstein

GreenSpec®

AfC
ARCHITECTURE FOR CHANGE

© Sofie Pelsmakers, 2012

Published by RIBA Publishing, 15 Bonhill Street, London EC2P 2EA

ISBN 978 1 85946 374 1

Stock code 74334

British Library Cataloguing in Publications Data
A catalogue record for this book is available from the British Library.

Commissioning Editors: James Thompson, Lucy Harbor
Designed and typeset by Phil Handley
Printed and bound by Polestar Wheatons, Exeter, UK
Cover design: Kneath Associates

RIBA Publishing is part of RIBA Enterprises Ltd, www.ribaenterprises.com

This book is dedicated to my late mother, Elsa Dekeersmaeker.

. . . .

Acknowledgements

This book could not exist without generous sponsorship from Levitt Bernstein, GreenSpec and Architecture for Change. This allowed me the privilege of working with my research assistant Georgia Laganakou, who was instrumental in much of the background research and 'number crunching'. Loreana Padron assisted me with substantial image editing and production in the final, manic stages of the manuscript while Hannah Bass was pivotal in co-editing the entire manuscript and clarifying many 'Belgianisms' into English. I also need to thank the University of East London, my previous employer, for providing some teaching relief in the early stages of book research.

I am indebted to several regular reviewers for their input and expertise: Andy Jobling, Brian Murphy, Dan Rigamonti, Melissa Taylor, Peter Sanders and Stephen Choi. I hope this book is worthy of their reputation. Thank you also to my ex-students Cristina Blanco-Lion, Dimitra Kyrkou, Nick Newman, Rob Houmoller and Tugba Salman for their feedback; and Liane Duxbury and Rob McLeod for embryonic discussions about my book idea many years ago. I could not have wished for a more supportive team at RIBA Publishing, and in particular James Thompson, Kate Mackillop, Matthew Thompson and Phil Handley. Thanks also to Lucy Harbor and Susan George in the early stages.

Many amazing people supported, encouraged and inspired me more than they will ever know: David Bass, Dr Fionn Stevenson, Kayla Friedman, Lies Pelsmakers, Mike Thompson, Peter McLennan, Phil Marfleet, Sebastian Moreno-Vacca, Stephen Choi and Sue Glover as well as past students at UEL and current peers at UCL.

Lastly, to Fede, thank you for everything.

The following individuals were instrumental in reviewing and/or contributing to (parts of) the following chapters:

Chapter 1:
Dr Clare Heaviside, Dr Fionn Stevenson, Prof. Mark Maslin, Sandy Halliday, Stephen Choi
Chapter 2:
Dr Federico Calboli, Prof. Mark Maslin, Stephen Choi
Chapter 3:
Georgia Laganakou, Kayla Friedman
Chapter 4:
Brian Murphy, Dr Carol Williams, Dr Federico Calboli, Georgia Laganakou, Nick Newman, Stefano Zucca, Stephen Choi, Veronica Hendry
Chapter 5:
Brian Murphy, Cath Hassel, Georgia Laganakou, Dr Judith Thornton, Nick Grant, Siraj Tahir
Chapter 6:
Dr Andrew Smith, Dr Federico Calboli, Georgia Laganakou, Jessica Eyers, Julia Park
Chapter 7:
Andy Jobling, Brian Murphy, Dan Rigamonti, Dimitra Kyrkou, Dr Federico Calboli, Georgia Laganakou, Joseph Little, Justin Bere, Mark Siddall, Nick Newman, Peter Sanders, Rob McLeod
Chapter 8:
Brian Murphy, Dan Rigamonti, Marion Baeli, Paschal Volney, Stephen Choi
Chapter 9:
Brian Murphy, Georgia Laganakou, Ilona Hay and Levitt Bernstein, in particular: Andy Jobling, Peter Sanders, Sean Hicks and Tony Hall
Chapter 10:
Cristina Blanco-Lion, Georgia Laganakou, Stephen Choi
Chapter 11:
Dr Federico Calboli, Georgia Laganakou, Stephen Choi
Chapter 12:
Dr Andrew Smith, Dr Federico Calboli, Georgia Laganakou, Margo Sagov, Mario Vieira, Paula Morgenstern, Stephen Choi, Tugba Salman

Thank you also to the following professionals for specific advice and help along the way:
Adam Graveley, Ant Wilson, Axel Burrough, Bobby Gilbert, Carine Oberweis, Dave Edwards, David Levitt, David Rimmer, Donald Judd, Gavin Hodgson, Ian Mawditt, Irene Craik, Jo McCafferty, Katleen Pelsmakers, Lori McElroy, Lynne Sullivan, Matthew Goulcher, Mike Fell, Nigel Wakefield, Paul Jennings, Sally Bradforth and Tammy Donohue.

....

About the Pocketbook

The Environmental Design Pocketbook is the culmination of over a decade researching, teaching and practising sustainable architecture.

During this period, there has been great progress through new legislation and through the advance of technology. Yet the fast pace of change and the complexity and variety of solutions can be seen at times as having smothered the decision-making process in a confusing range of information and choice.

This pocketbook is an attempt to cut through that confusion, synthesising the main issues into one single source of practical information. It is written especially with the building industry's key players in mind – architects, designers, clients, contractors, developers and students – in the hope that they can confidently practise what I refer to not as 'sustainable' architecture but simply as 'good' architecture.

Key recommendations are based on the synthesis of simple laws of science and practical building experience. The pocketbook is intended to distil and complement current legislation, guidance and other design manuals as well as to draw emerging research into a single source. However, no single volume can be a substitute for all these other sources; it deals with a rapidly evolving field and cannot attempt to cover everything in depth. So while this book may not have all the answers, key readings are suggested in each section for the reader who hungers for more detail.

As this pocketbook is intended to be useful to you, I look forward to receiving feedback and suggestions from readers via the website www.environmentaldesign pocketbook.com

Sofie Pelsmakers, London, 2012

....

About the Author

Sofie Pelsmakers is a chartered architect and environmental designer with more than a decade of hands-on experience designing, building and teaching sustainable architecture. She taught sustainability and environmental design and led a masters programme in sustainable design at the University of East London. She is currently a doctoral researcher in building energy demand reduction at the UCL Energy Institute and co-founder of Architecture for Change, a not-for-profit environmental building organisation.

In this pocketbook, her practical and academic expertise are synthesised together with her passion and commitment to change and challenge the way we currently design and build. Its focus is on providing practical advice to deliver buildings that quietly mitigate and adapt to climate change using sustainable resources.

CONTENTS

How to use the Pocketbook

....

The book focuses on the environmental aspects of sustainability, with a focus especially on housing developments since most of the available frameworks are directed at this particular sector.

The chapters are structured from the macro to the micro scale. The book concludes with active energy systems, which supports the principle of prioritising 'energy efficiency' and the book's inclination towards passive design principles. It can be read from start to finish or the reader can dip into relevant sections.

- Cross references within the book are clearly marked: ⟶⟿
- Reference to latest legislation and codes is provided in each section.
- CO_2 and energy figures used in the book are estimates. See also clarification note p.317.
- Tables and data are usually provided per m^2 to allow readers to adapt information to their own scenario.
- The UK has been divided into four climatic regions. Where applicable, recommendations take these regions into account.

REGION 1

Edinburgh

Glasgow

REGION 3
Belfast

REGION 2

Manchester

Birmingham

Cardiff

REGION 4

London

Plymouth

Chapter 1
CO₂, climate change mitigation and the building industry

The construction and operation of buildings and cities accounts for around 50% of the UK's CO_2 emissions and is thus a significant contributor to global warming. A reduction in CO_2 is needed to mitigate climate change, and this reduction is the main driver behind many building-specific EU and UK regulations, codes and frameworks.

However, CO_2 emissions are not the building industry's only environmental impact. Other impacts include loss of biodiversity, resource depletion and negative effects on building users' health and well-being.

This introductory chapter gives a brief overview of the main causes of global warming. It looks at climate change mitigation policies and frameworks, particularly CO_2 reduction targets. The chapter also discusses the challenges to CO_2 reduction posed by unpredictable 'human factors' and how building designers can meet them. Finally, a checklist accompanying the RIBA Work Stages is included.

While this chapter sets out climate change mitigation measures, the succeeding chapter covers climate change impacts and adaptation measures.

 Symbol indicates relevance to the Code for Sustainable Homes, EcoHomes & BREEAM.

1.1   FOSSIL FUELS: THE FACTS

Fossil fuels are a finite resource. Easily and cheaply exploited reserves might be nearing depletion and in the future will become prohibitively expensive. But our hunger for fossil fuels not only endangers our financial security; there are grave global environmental implications.

Since the Industrial Revolution in the late 18th century, we have been burning fossil fuels on a gigantic scale. This releases greenhouse gases, the most important of which is CO_2 (carbon dioxide).

While CO_2 is also released through natural processes, in what is known as the 'carbon cycle', these natural CO_2 emissions are offset by CO_2 absorption through other natural processes, ultimately creating a balance. 'Human' CO_2 emissions exceed the capacity of natural reabsorption mechanisms, and this causes climate change. Unabsorbed greenhouse gases create a thick 'blanket' in the earth's atmosphere preventing heat from escaping and leading to global warming.[1]

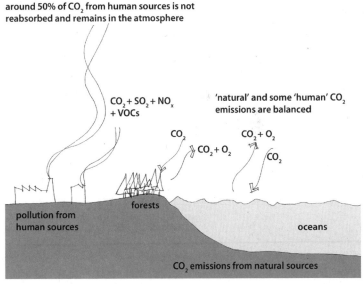

around 50% of CO_2 from human sources is not reabsorbed and remains in the atmosphere

$CO_2 + SO_2 + NO_x + VOCs$

'natural' and some 'human' CO_2 emissions are balanced

CO_2

$CO_2 + O_2$

$CO_2 + O_2$

CO_2

pollution from human sources

forests

oceans

CO_2 emissions from natural sources

Fig. 1.1.1 Human and natural CO_2 emissions

Global warming leads to local climate change. Higher temperatures create rising sea levels and increased evaporation, resulting in unpredictable new weather patterns.

As an island, the UK is particularly vulnerable to heat waves, rises in sea level and changes in precipitation. For predicted climate changes and impacts in the UK, ———⟶ jump to Chapter 2.

There is no dispute that CO_2 levels are rising as a result of human activity. They are changing the planet's climate and will continue to do so until we stop burning fossil fuels altogether.

1.1.1 Why do we burn fossil fuels?

Globally, almost 75% of the fossil fuel burned is used to produce energy.[2] We use this energy for:
- transportation
- industrial manufacturing
- agriculture and food production
- operation of buildings: lighting, heating, cooling

Globally, the average CO_2 emissions are 6 tonnes CO_2e per person per year.[3] In the UK, however, this is closer to 11 tonnes CO_2e per person.[4] To put this into context, 11 tonnes CO_2e is the equivalent of 100 car journeys from London to Edinburgh.[5]

1.1.2 What does this have to do with the building industry?

As well as the energy needed to construct the buildings themselves, buildings and cities require energy to function. This is referred to as 'operational energy' or 'regulated carbon emissions' and includes fossil-fuel-powered systems for transportation, space heating, hot water, lighting, ventilation and cooling. We rely on these systems to use our buildings with comfort. The operational energy of housing alone accounts for 25% of the UK's CO_2 emissions.[6]

The total energy use of occupied buildings is even higher owing to the use of appliances. This is referred to as 'unregulated carbon emissions'.
———⟶ Jump to Section 10.1.1.

It is estimated that around 10% of a building's total carbon footprint comes from the industrial manufacturing of materials and their transportation from extraction to factory and finally to site.[7] These CO_2 emissions are referred to as embodied carbon. ———⟶ Jump to Section 7.1.

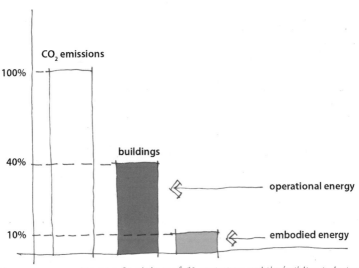

Fig. 1.12 Breakdown of CO_2 emissions and the building industry

Of course, the building industry is not the sole cause of global warming. Although it is responsible for a legacy of energy-inefficient buildings, it still relies on third parties to deliver the materials and fuel needed to construct and run these buildings. At present, this energy is provided mostly by fossil fuels, hence the vast CO_2 emissions in this sector.

Clearly, the building industry cannot solve all the world's environmental problems on its own and any strategies for the built environment should go hand in hand with national energy policies. However, it is an inescapable fact that the building industry is a major culprit when it comes to CO_2 emissions. The pressure is mounting for us to put our house in order. ——➔ Jump to Chapter 7.

1.2   CLIMATE CHANGE: HOW 'BAD' WILL IT BE?

Global warming of around only 0.8–1°C[8] has already caused sea-level rises of 120–220 mm.[9] The EU/UK governments agree that limiting global warming to a 2°C rise is essential.[10] However, global CO_2 emissions are currently rising at the rate associated with the medium or even high risk global warming scenario. Globally we are heading towards a 2–6°C rise by 2100.[11] For the implications, ——⤳ jump to Chapter 2.

Fig. 1.2.1 Medium risk scenario = current trajectory

Climate scenario	Global action undertaken	Global climate change projections
low risk	rapid reduction of global CO_2 emissions by stopping use of fossil fuels	2°C rise by 2050 and 2.9°C rise by 2100
medium risk (current trajectory)	continued use of fossil fuels, but with some renewable energy	2°C rise by 2040 with 4°C rise by 2100
high risk	'business as usual' with no significant reduction and instead heavier reliance on fossil fuels	2°C rise by 2035 with 5–6°C rise by 2100

The medium and high risk scenarios are the most likely to occur. It is these climate projections and recommendations arising from these scenarios which will be used throughout the book.

1.2.1 The uncertainty of climate predictions

Climate prediction models model the different processes that take place on our planet. Future climate modelling uses computer simulations based on past and present climatic data. Necessarily it leaves out uncertainties about future climate change because of the huge number of variables involved.

Human interventions and temperature increases may unbalance natural processes and cause them to release, rather than absorb, CO_2 and other greenhouse gases.[12] This phenomenon could occur with as little as a 2°C global temperature rise and could lead to an additional rise of 1.5°C by 2100.[13]

1.2.2 The UK's mild climate

It is a common misconception that it is the Gulf Stream which gives the UK its mild climate. In fact, the UK is mild mostly because it is an island and because it is exposed to westerly winds from the Atlantic Ocean. Hence in the unlikely event of the Gulf Stream current weakening, the UK would not see any major cooling as a result.[14]

Fig. 1.2.2 UK cities and cities at similar latitude

The cold winters which the UK and most of Europe experienced in 2009 and 2010 were actually caused by changes to air/wind patterns which brought in Arctic weather instead of Atlantic weather.

Our island position may 'protect' us from more extreme temperatures but it does not mean that we would more easily adapt to the impacts of global warming.
⟶≫ Jump to Chapter 2.

Strategies recommended in this pocketbook are based on anticipated increases in temperature. However, in the unlikely event that the UK does experience cooling, passive design recommendations, as presented in the book, are equally useful as future-proofing strategies.

1.2.3 A regional map of the UK

Future climate predictions model 25 km grids across the UK to identify local climate trends, but generalising impacts across the UK is also useful to give an overall understanding of climate change. For example, cities in the south of the UK will be more prone to temperature extremes, while cities in the north will be relatively protected. However, responses to climate change must be tailored to a specific region.

This book uses regional divisions to provide more specific recommendations where relevant. The regions have been divided according to the UK's building legislative divisions: Scotland, Northern Ireland and England & Wales. The large England & Wales region is then further divided to reflect current and predicted temperature differences between its southern and northern regions.

Fig. 1.2.3 The regional divisions used in this book

The reader should also consult specific regional and up-to-date climate data and not simply rely on the rather generalised geographic and climatic regions given here.

1.3   GLOBAL WARMING: WHAT CAN WE DO ABOUT IT?

Global greenhouse gases need to be cut significantly as contractually agreed in the Kyoto Protocol and the Copenhagen Accord. Globally, this means a cut of 50% by 2050 and at least 80% by 2100.[15] Even then there is no guarantee that temperatures will not reach or exceed the 2°C threshold and enter the worst climate change scenario.[16]

1.3.1 Cutting carbon: is that all?

Currently the UK has committed to a 34% cut by 2020 and an 80% cut in carbon[17] emissions by 2050, which is in excess of EU mandatory targets.[18] However, the UK has been, and still is, one of the main contributors to global warming.[19]

The UK supports the adoption of the principles of 'contraction and convergence'. This is a global framework for more equitably reducing greenhouse gas emissions: high-polluting countries should reduce (contract) carbon emissions, while low-polluting countries' emissions increase and converge towards equal per-person emissions globally.

These principles dictate that the UK should actually cut carbon emissions by 85–100%.[20]

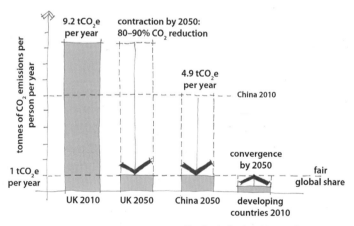

Fig. 1.3.1 *Contraction and convergence*

1.3.2 Cuts of 80%+ in the building industry: how realistic is this?
....

Under EU regulations, all new buildings in Europe need to be 'zero energy' by 2020. This would equate to 100% CO_2 emissions reductions. The UK has introduced a 'zero carbon' framework where buildings neutralise or absorb CO_2 through renewable energy production.

In reality these target cuts will prove unattainable and impracticable to achieve for the majority of buildings.[21, 22] While on-site renewable energy generation can be suitable and useful, on the whole it is not the most effective way to generate energy, nor is it always possible, particularly in urban areas.

⟶⟶⟶⟶⟶↠ Jump to Sections 3.3.3, 10.3.2 & Chapter 11.

1.3.3 What can be achieved in the building industry?
....

Ultimately, we need to stop using fossil fuels entirely, including for the operation of our buildings. But the 100% carbon reduction target is a huge challenge. Achieving it depends on technology, user behaviour[23] and other human factors (Section 1.5). The electrical energy demand is especially difficult to meet from on-site renewable energy alone.

However, a carbon reduction target of at least 40–50% can be achieved simply by building and refurbishing our buildings to much higher insulation and airtightness standards. This would reduce the operational energy required to heat our buildings by at least 80%, leading to 'almost zero space heating buildings'.

⟶⟶⟶⟶⟶↠ Jump to Section 7.5 & Chapter 8.

1.3.4 Myth: 'Whatever we do, it doesn't matter'
....

Meaningful comparisons between the environmental impact caused by different nations can only be drawn on a per-person basis.

For example, in 2007 the global media reported: 'China overtakes US as world's biggest CO_2 emitter.'[24] Why then should reducing CO_2 emissions in the UK make a difference? In fact, China has the largest population in the world (and manufactures huge amounts of stuff for export to us) so it is no great surprise that it has joined the major CO_2 emitters. However, per person China still only emits half as much CO_2 as the UK.[25] Despite other nations increasing their CO_2 emissions, the UK's obligation to contract its CO_2 emissions is clear.

1.3.5 What are we currently doing?

UK climate change policy is mostly driven by EU targets, which filter down in mandatory targets for energy efficiency and for reduction of greenhouse gas emissions in each member state. For the UK, this means a binding 15% CO_2 reduction target for 2020, which is remarkably less than the 20% reduction target for the EU as a whole.[26] The UK has also set voluntary CO_2 reduction targets of 34% and is working towards 'zero carbon' new housing by 2016 and all other new buildings by 2019. ⟶ Jump to Chapter 11.

Policies are largely driven by the following priorities:
- Increase energy efficiency to reduce the need for fossil fuels.
- Understand and adapt to future predicted climate change.
- Consider a cleaner energy supply.

1.3.6 UK general policies, legislation, frameworks and tools: a summary

Climate Change Act 2008 & Climate Change (Scotland) Act 2009
This is a general piece of legislation for developing a world-first low carbon economy in the UK which sets its own binding targets:
- 80% CO_2 emissions reduction target for 2050 with interim targets of 34% by 2020 (based on 1990 levels)
- government obligated to report regularly on climate change risk
- CRC Energy Efficiency Scheme (previously known as Carbon Reduction Commitment): to incentivise companies to reduce operational energy, all companies and public bodies that have an electricity consumption over 6000 MWh per year must purchase carbon allowances for each tonne of CO_2 they emit
- Scotland: a proposed 42% reduction in emissions by 2020 (overall 80% reduction target for 2050 remains).

Energy White Paper 2007
This deals with the promotion of renewables, but initially to bolster the UK's energy security rather than to mitigate global warming. The UK is especially well served by renewable energy sources, particularly tidal and wind.

UK Low Carbon Transition Plan (2009)
This maps out the route to achieve the carbon reduction targets set by the Climate Change Act. It also sets out a vision for the construction industry which includes:
- smart meters for all homes by 2020
- retrofit programme to increase energy efficiency of existing stock
- increase in efficiency to reduce 2008 emissions by 13% for non-domestic buildings and 29% for dwellings by 2020
- all new-build dwellings to be zero carbon by 2016 and all other buildings by 2019
- energy industry to be producing 30% renewable energy by 2020.

The building industry will lead the way until 2012, when it will be joined by the power industry to meet challenging CO_2 reduction targets.

Energy Performance of Buildings Directive (EPBD)
This is the EU's response to its Kyoto obligations. Each EU member state has to comply with it, but has the freedom to choose how it will comply. The Directive applies to new and existing buildings and requires:
- National Calculation Methods (NCM) for assessing the energy performance of buildings: in non-domestic buildings, Simplified Building Energy Model (SBEM), and for dwellings, Standard Assessment Procedure (SAP)
- energy efficiency improvements for large buildings under refurbishment (≥ 1000 m^2)
- Energy Performance Certificates (EPC) to be undertaken when properties are offered for sale or rent; public buildings to display EPC
- minimum energy performance standards for all buildings.

Sustainability of construction works (CEN TC350)
This is an EU standard which covers the social, economic and environmental performance of new and existing buildings, including life-cycle assessment and life-cycle costing. ⟶ Jump to Section 7.1.5.

Planning Policy Statement 22 (PPS22) and 'the Merton Rule'
The Borough of Merton was the first to introduce minimum 10% renewable energy production on site. Any such targets are now referred to as 'the Merton Rule'. Most boroughs have since increased on-site renewable energy production to 20% of the development's total energy needs. Many planning departments translate this as a 10–20% CO_2 emissions reduction, which is not the same as 10–20% on-site energy production. Usually the percentage is explicitly stated in planning conditions.
⟶ Jump to Section 10.6.

Building Regulations

Unlike other European countries, the UK does not regulate total energy consumption within buildings. Instead, UK regulations set limits for:

- building fabric and services such as insulation, thermal bridges and air permeability
- minimum efficiencies for heating appliances, boiler efficiencies, controls and fixed lighting
- maximum acceptable instances of summer overheating.

The Building Regulations are often regarded as 'good practice', but are actually only minimum acceptable standards. The regulations are being revised in 2013 and 2016 as a step towards achieving 'zero carbon'. To comply with Part L1 and Part L2, SAP and SBEM respectively are used.

Standard Assessment Procedure (SAP) and Simplified Building Energy Model (SBEM)

SAP and SBEM are energy consumption tools to predict energy use for dwellings and non-domestic buildings respectively. They are used to ensure compliance with the Building Regulations Approved Document Part L and for the production of Energy Performance Certificates (EPCs). Updates tend to coincide with major revisions to the Building Regulations. SAP is location independent. It is expressed on a scale of 1 to 100, 100 being the best. Dwellings with 100+ rating are net energy exporters. A SAP rating is usually required to submit energy calculations for the Code for Sustainable Homes and EcoHomes. SAP2009 applies from October 2010. A reduced SAP version, RdSAP, is to be used in all regions for refurbishment of dwellings.

 The Code for Sustainable Homes (CSH) and EcoHomes

The CSH underpins the Building Regulations for residential developments in England and Wales, and in Northern Ireland. Scotland uses the code for Sustainable Homes' predecessor, EcoHomes. Both CSH and EcoHomes cover more than 'energy performance' alone, and act as both a design guide and an assessment tool for new dwellings. The sustainability criteria include: energy, water, waste, pollution, management, ecology, health and materials. In EcoHomes there are four standards from pass to excellent. In the Code for Sustainable Homes, there are six levels of compliance, with level six meeting the energy definition of 'zero carbon'. This will become the 2016 compulsory standard for all dwellings. All publicly funded housing has to achieve at least a code level 3 (or EcoHomes 'very good' in Scotland) although code level 4 is required in the London region.[27]

EcoHomes XB

EcoHomes XB is a non-mandatory wider sustainability tool. It is mainly used by local authorities and housing associations to assess and set goals for the refurbishment of existing housing stock. A rating is given from 0 to 100, with 100 being the best.

 BREEAM and LEED

LEED and BREEAM are sustainability rating systems for buildings or larger neighbourhoods. In the UK, neither of these standards are mandatory but they are used to assess, market and set sustainability goals. LEED was developed in the USA, while BREEAM is the UK version for non-domestic buildings. Its ranking is from 'pass' to 'excellent'.

National Home Energy Rating (NHER)

This is a domestic energy rating scheme in the UK. It expresses the estimated total energy use of a dwelling (including space and water heating, cooking, lighting and appliances), on a scale of 0 to 20, with 20 being the most efficient. NHER is location dependent and uses BREDEM (BRE Domestic Energy Model) as its assessment tool. Often it is a requirement for publicly funded housing.

Low carbon building standards

Improved building fabric standards have been developed to reduce carbon emissions beyond what is required by Building Regulations. The Zero Carbon Standard is the only obligatory standard that will come into force in 2016 (new dwellings) and 2019 (all other buildings).

- **Zero carbon standards:** at the time of writing this has only been developed for new dwellings, although definitions to include all buildings are in development. ——⇒ Jump to Chapter 11.

- **Energy Savings Trust 'good', 'best' and 'advanced' practice standards** for new-build housing. Each standard requires improvements over current Building Regulations Part L.

- **AECB CarbonLite programme:** three standards which measure building performance in $kgCO_2/m^2$ per year and require post-occupancy evaluation. Applicable to domestic and non-domestic buildings.
  - Silver Standard: 70% reduction in CO_2
  - Passivhaus standard: 80% reduction in CO_2
  - Gold standard: 95% reduction in CO_2; includes renewable energy production.

- **Passivhaus and EnerPHit standards:** applicable to both domestic and non-domestic buildings. ——⇒ Jump to Sections 7.5.3 & 8.1.

1.4 NOT ALL ENVIRONMENTAL IMPACT CAN BE MEASURED IN CO_2

At present, there is a bias towards 'carbon counting', i.e. measuring or estimating environmental impacts in terms of the quantity of CO_2 emissions. This is because CO_2, although not the most potent pollutant, is – by around 73% – the most significant greenhouse gas contributing to global warming. Other greenhouse gases are expressed as the amount of CO_2 that would have the equivalent global warming potential (GWP) over 100 years. This is referred to as CO_2e (carbon dioxide equivalent).

Fig. 1.4.1 CO_2 and CO_2 equivalent greenhouse gases

Greenhouse gases	CO_2e global warming potential[28]
CO_2	1
methane (CH_4)	21
nitrous oxide (N_2O)	310
perfluorocarbons (PFCs)	6500–9200
hydrofluorocarbons (HFCs)	140–11,700
sulphur hexafluoride (SF_6)	23,900

By focusing on carbon emissions, we risk losing sight of other important environmental impacts. These include waste, water use, material resource depletion, and effects on health and on biodiversity.

Fig. 1.4.2 Environmental concerns, which cannot be measured in GWP or CO_2

Waste	The UK produces 30 million tonnes of demolition building waste and another 30 million tonnes of excavated soil per year.[29] This is disposed of through landfills or in incinerators, both of which contribute to pollution. In the UK, 50% of landfill is associated with the building industry.[30] However, waste incineration can also generate energy. ⟶ Jump to Section 12.7.8.
Material/ resource use (Chapter 7)	Material resources are finite and constantly being depleted. The UK uses 350 million tonnes of new building materials each year.[31] The construction industry accounts for 60% of the UK's timber use.[32] Where this is not managed sustainably, it contributes to deforestation. Indeed, 60% of tropical timber imported into the UK may have been illegally logged.[33]
Water (Chapter 5)	About 40–50% of our water usage is for the operation and construction of buildings.[34] The construction industry impacts on rivers and groundwater indirectly through material/product manufacturing and associated pollution, causing 16% of water pollution incidents in England and Wales in 1997.[35]
Transportation (Chapter 7)	Building materials and goods are transported nationally and internationally. This causes air and noise pollution and devours fossil fuels.
Loss of biodiversity (Chapter 4)	Urbanisation and the deforestation/clearing of 'virgin land' leads to decreased water runoff, alters/degrades the soil structure and destroys natural habitats and ecosystems. Related to local flooding.
Health & well-being (Chapter 6)	Lack of daylight and comfortable heating can adversely affect health and well-being of occupants. The emission of harmful gases from substances such as formaldehyde and VOCs impacts on internal air quality and occupants' health.
Land use (Chapter 3)	Walkable cities, safe streets, proximity to services and amenities, as well as access to public transport, can improve inhabitants' quality of life and reduce car usage.
Economic	The local community can benefit from the training, business and employment opportunities that building developments often bring.
Historic/ cultural/ aesthetics	Our historic and cultural heritage instils a sense of pride, belonging and ownership and is an important local and contextual parameter to consider.
Social well-being (Section 1.5)	Community consultation can make a positive impact on the social well-being of the local community, particularly where they are the users of new spaces and places. Lack of inclusion can lead to disempowered and disenfranchised communities. Post Occupancy Evaluation (POE) is also crucial.

1.5   HUMAN FACTORS IN BUILDING PERFORMANCE

The interaction between the 'human factor' and a building's performance in reality, rather than its predicted performance, is often ill understood or entirely ignored. Best practice should always consider a 'Soft Landings' approach. This is a voluntary framework which engages and guides design team and client from the start of a project to the final handover stage. It incorporates post-completion feedback into the design approach. The five main 'human factors' to consider are as follows:

1.5.1 Stakeholder engagement

This is involving users directly with the decision-making process early on, particularly with regard to the occupant management and operation of the building.

Where client and user are not one and the same, the involvement of building users is recommended where possible. It will be the building managers and users/occupants who will determine how the building is used and what its final carbon footprint will be. Local stakeholders include:
- users/occupants
- design team
- building managers and maintenance teams
- client
- planners, conservation officers, building control and funding agencies
- immediate neighbourhood

1.5.2 Interdisciplinary teams

Early input from environmental consultants and engineers is desirable on all projects. It is crucial on larger and more complex schemes or where there are high environmental design ambitions.

- Interdisciplinary teams bring architects, engineers, environmental consultants and other construction industry experts together from the early stages.
  Close interdisciplinary work leads to better-integrated design. Feedback from previous work should be formally built into these stages using a Soft Landings approach. This reduces the risk of 'abortive' design or the 'bolting on' of eco-design features later in the process.
  See free download at www.softlandings.org.uk.
- Environmental design should never be divorced from the actual building design. Many clients are reluctant to spend money before they have obtained planning application approval. However, it is often too late to make major changes once approval has been awarded.

1.5.3 Software simulations and the real world

Only simple, logical and realistic behaviour should be simulated to predict realistic occupants' patterns and building performance results at design stage. Modelling is not always accurate, so:

- ask the environmental modeller for assumptions to be used
- use knowledge gained about user behaviour from stakeholder engagement (Soft Landings)
- always assume worst-case scenario

Design software can be 'manipulated' to meet required standards and regulations. This should be avoided as it will not reflect the way people use, or behave in, buildings in reality.

Typical unrealistic software assumptions

summer ventilation	An environmental model which relies on the opening and closing of windows to prevent summer overheating is misleading. It makes improbable assumptions; for example, if occupants are out of the house, they would not be able to manipulate windows and blinds.
night cooling	Overestimation of night-cooling potential when, in reality, windows remain closed owing to noise issues or fear of crime.
cross-ventilation	Overestimation of cross-ventilation potential of internal doors when, in reality, they are often closed for privacy and quiet.
electrical usage	Electrical energy needs are often underestimated by simulations which do not rely on user behaviour and instead assume unrealistically low energy consumption patterns. In particular, SAP underestimates the actual electricity consumption by around 25%.[36]

1.5.4 On-site workmanship

Designing energy-efficient buildings will mean little if they fail to achieve these standards in practice or if they jeopardise thermal comfort and affordable bills for occupants.[37] ⟶ Jump to Section 7.4.3 & Chapter 8.

- Identify an 'airtightness champion' on site and within the design team.
- Define the airtight envelope early on and coordinate services with this.
- Undertake a post-completion building performance evaluation to test the success of design intentions.

1.5.5 Building performance and Post Occupancy Evaluation

Post Occupancy Evaluation (POE) is an essential part of the building performance evaluation post-completion. Feedback from occupants about the building's performance must influence the design process.

- Consider a Soft Landings approach from start to finish and integrate post-completion feedback into new designs.
- Appoint a person to be responsible in the team to oversee and coordinate user input and output at different stages of the design and after practical completion.
- Avoid reliance on complex technologies or controls to achieve design performance. Keep building design and controls as simple, logical and usable as possible.
- Provide a user guide (and website for larger projects) which simply explains the controls and services to occupants. Provide immediate handover support to occupants, preferably with an on-site presence for several weeks after handover (Soft Landings).

   Code for Sustainable Homes and EcoHomes credits (Man 1) BREEAM credits (Man 4)
- Include a POE and building performance evaluation as standard practice for at least two to three years after practical completion.
- Ensure that any professional indemnity insurer has agreed to post-completion feedback. Some insurance providers fear that obtaining feedback will lead to insurance claims from the client or users. Ensure that appropriate agreements are drawn up.

In the move towards low carbon buildings, we risk becoming over-reliant on complex new technologies, equipment and controls. Failure to provide the client and users with handover support to help them manage these new technologies will impact negatively on the building's energy consumption, which is significantly determined by the behaviour of individual users.

For example, space heat demand can be up to three times as high in dwellings of the same design and specification.[38] If the measures designed to achieve low and zero carbon buildings are too complex or unintuitive, occupants will simply bypass or remove them altogether.

Typical impacts of occupant behaviour on building performance

smart controls and meters	Occupants will override or ignore them, particularly if too complex to understand or operate. This is why the claims of potential energy saving for smart controls and meters are often unsubstantiated. Smart controls should respond to individual occupants' behaviour.
thermal comfort factor (also referred to as 'take back' or Jevons' paradox)	Because of fuel costs, occupants of heat-leaking dwellings may put up with uncomfortably cool temperatures. In better-insulated dwellings, fuel bills should become more affordable but occupants may then heat rooms to higher temperatures or trade their heating bill savings for higher consumption elsewhere.
energy-saving fixed lighting	Often removed as lampshades are difficult to find and expensive to replace.
summer solar gain control	In hot summers, at the hottest time of day, doors and windows should remain closed with blinds shut. This is how the building has been designed and modelled. However, in reality, occupants prefer a breeze. As a result, hot air enters the building through open doors and windows and, where well insulated, contributes to overheating.
electrical use and hot water	Energy for space heating can be controlled to some extent by the building design, but appliance use and hot water demand are entirely unregulated and determined by the occupant. Regulations do not take into account the cultural diversity and different behaviour of occupants. This unpredictability cannot be allowed for in regulations.

1.6 'GREEN' RIBA PLAN OF WORK CHECKLISTS

Sustainable buildings can be achieved by an interdisciplinary team considering and implementing sustainability from the early stages of design right through to post-completion. The publication *Green Guide to the Architect's Job Book* addresses how to achieve this in detail. The checklists below synthesise the main issues to consider with particular focus on energy and climate change mitigation. However, the *Green Guide to the Architect's Job Book* should always be considered in its entirety.

Work Stage A: appraisal and inception	☑ ☒
Broaden dialogue to include all stakeholders and particularly users. Commit to Soft Landings approach (see Section 1.5).	☐
Obtain client approval for interdisciplinary team to enable early input from energy, environmental and ecological consultants.	☐
Establish workshops to give guidance on strategic issues such as energy, environment and services.	☐
Set realistic targets and priorities. Clarify stakeholders' aspirations and needs, including wider sustainability aspirations related to landscape, water, material/ resource use, biodiversity, indoor air quality and life-cycle costing. ⟶⤷ Jump to Chapters 3–7.	☐
Review climate change impacts and explore suitable site strategies. ⟶⤷ Jump to Chapters 2–5.	☐
Consider energy strategies at neighbourhood scale. ⟶⤷ Jump to Chapters 10 &12.	☐

Work Stage B: feasibility/design brief	☑ ☒
Site investigation to include analysis of constraints and opportunities with regard to solar access/wind/noise/ecology/biodiversity/landscape/urban design/access/views/material use and proposed building location as well as methods of construction and insulation.	☐
Use options appraisal to test approach to site, user and client requirements and above constraints and opportunities.	☐
Use software simulation for initial strategic environmental comparisons between options and initial understanding of energy supply sources.	☐
Confirm assessment methods and frameworks which apply/will be used such as LEED/BREEAM/CSH etc. See Section 1.3.6.	☐
Review climate change impacts and explore suitable building strategies. ⟶⤷ Jump to Chapters 2, 6 & 7.	☐

	□
Formulate and visualise the different environmental responses and strategies to initial targets and priorities set in Stage A, including any wider sustainability aspirations.	□
Ensure that an interdisciplinary team is involved. See Section 1.5.	□
Stakeholder consultation to continue to obtain feedback on different options.	□

Work Stage C: outline proposals/concept	☑ ☒
Confirm and test building location and wider sustainability aspirations, coming out of Work Stages A and B and stakeholder consultation.	□
More detailed building analysis of constraints and opportunities with regard to thermal comfort, daylight, ventilation, zoning of functions, shelter, landscape, materials, services (waste/water/heating etc.).	□
Consider opportunities and obligations for renewable energy.	□
Undertake initial assessment of building performance standards: LEED/BREEAM/CSH assessment as well as construction appraisal.	□
Commit to designing for deconstruction and consider opportunities for Modern Methods of Construction. ⟶ Jump to Section 7.2.1.	□
Environmental modelling: combine initial modelling with more detailed software to understand building performance. Use realistic user assumptions only (Section 1.5).	□
Incorporate measures, with an ecological consultant, to support biodiversity, at both strategic and detailed level. ⟶ Jump to Section 4.4.	□
Stakeholder consultation to continue and include Soft Landings approach as part of procurement process (Section 1.5).	□
Quantity surveyor to undertake initial life-cycle costing for outline proposals over building's projected lifespan. ⟶ Jump to Chapter 7.	□
Review climate change impacts and explore suitable site and building strategies. ⟶ Jump to Chapters 2 and 4–7.	□
Consider sufficient space for construction build-up depths, utility spaces, etc. ⟶ Jump to Sections 6.2 & 7.5.	□

Work Stage D: design development	☑ ☒
Confirm and set specific targets for wider sustainability aspirations and obligations, coming out of previous Work Stages and stakeholder consultation.	☐
Specification of materials and products to analyse and consider environmental impacts. ——⟫ Jump to Section 7.1.	☐
Incorporate detailed environmental modelling analysis in design response, related to daylighting/overheating/heat loss and thermal bridging.	☐
Integrate renewable energy generation requirements and service design.	☐
Commit to support biodiversity, with advice from an ecological consultant.	☐
Appoint an 'airtightness' champion. ——⟫ Jump to Section 7.4.	☐
Review climate change impacts and explore suitable building strategies. ——⟫ Jump to Chapters 2 and 4–7.	☐
Stakeholder consultation to continue and design to be reviewed with respect to services, usability and controls as well as in view of life-cycle assessment and costing analysis.	☐

Work Stages E, F: technical design and production information	☑ ☒
Obtain and undertake research and development with regard to environmental design or innovative approaches. Include biodiversity habitats in building and landscape design. ——⟫ Jump to Section 4.4.	☐
Review climate change impacts and suitable adaptations in detail design. ——⟫ Jump to Chapters 2 and 4–7.	☐
Material and product profiling and sourcing to match sustainability aspirations. ——⟫ Jump to Sections 7.1 & 7.2.	☐
Detailed renewable energy generation and services design.	☐
Detail for deconstruction and freeze services design to allow any prefabrication to commence. ——⟫ Jump to Section 7.1.9.	☐
Ensure thermal bridges and thermal bypasses are minimised through careful detailing. Airtightness champion to review thermal envelope details. Complex junctions to be explained using step-by-step drawings to clarify intent.	☐
Revisit and keep track of client/user aspirations and agreements set out in previous Stages, including any wider sustainability aspirations. Review aspirations in relation to life-cycle assessment and life-cycle costing analysis.	☐
Stakeholder consultation to continue. Include future building managers and maintenance teams.	☐

Work Stages G, H: tender documentation	☑ ☒
In tender documentation, explicitly state the wider sustainability aspirations, biodiversity strategies, environmental benchmarks and renewable energy targets which are to be met.	☐
Design team to review most appropriate construction contract for delivery of the project, particularly in relation to sustainability values.	☐
Specify materials and products accurately where they are essential to meet the overall sustainability vision.	☐
Where 'equivalent' materials may be specified, take great care to list the exact required properties/performance in detail. Equally state where certain materials or products are not acceptable.	☐
Specify that the contractor has to undertake and present for approval a comparative life-cycle assessment and cost analysis where departing from specification.	☐
Specify and check the environmental and social commitment and credentials of the contractor, including Considerate Constructor's Scheme. www.ccscheme.org.uk	☐
Include requirements for an on-site airtightness champion and discuss experience and logistics with shortlisted contractors.	☐
Tender to include stakeholder consultation, building performance and Post Occupancy Evaluation. Specific clauses to set out the contractor's post-practical completion obligations after handover stage (Section 1.5).	☐

Work Stages J, K: on site	☑ ☒
Method statements to delegate responsible person for on-site work such as demolition/waste/water/material storage and reclamation to be provided by (sub)contractors.	☐
Inspect prefabrication units in the factory and on site.	☐
On-site airtightness champion to provide training to employees and to attend and report back at regular site meetings.	☐
Protection of site-ecology and implementation of biodiversity strategy. Ecological consultant to advise prior to site works commencing. ——⟩ Jump to Chapter 4.	☐
Attention to detail on site to be understood by all parties to achieve airtightness standards. ——⟩ Jump to Section 7.4.	☐
Review climate change impacts for on-site construction and implement suitable measures to allow for smooth running on site. Include in critical path. ——⟩ Jump to Chapter 2.	☐

Airtightness and sound testing to be undertaken at earliest opportunity and at key stages in the construction, to highlight failure and rectification measures. If they are left too late it may not be possible to rectify mistakes.	☐
Include building managers and maintenance teams before occupation and involve them (as well as users) in control demonstration and preparation of the user guide and the operation manual (Section 1.5).	☐
Ensure any deviation from the material specification is followed up with a life-cycle assessment and cost analysis, prior to approval.	☐

Work Stage L: post-practical completion	☑ ☒
Demonstrate controls to users/occupants and explain the user manual.	☐
Have on-site management/handover support for the first weeks.	☐
For the first year, provide occupant engagement at start of each season to obtain feedback and fine tune controls/management systems.	☐
Monitor biodiversity and site ecology and provide after-care.	☐
Building performance and Post Occupancy Evaluation to be undertaken at least two years after handover to support building occupant and to review process and design decisions made as well as benefit from lessons learned. (Section 1.5.)	☐
Rectify any drying out/settling cracks to retain airtightness standards.	☐
Undertake a deconstruction drawing and logbook, to include audit of building material standards and reclamation potential. ⟶⟶ Jump to Section 7.1.9.	☐

Work Stages M, N: refurbishment and demolition	☑ ☒
Refer to *Green Guide to the Architect's Job Book*.	☐
Consider reuse and adaptation of building to new uses as priority over demolition or dismantling. Identify opportunities for reclamation/reuse and recycling. ⟶⟶ Jump to Section 7.1.	☐

1.7 UNITS TO REMEMBER

The units used in environmental design can be confusing and difficult to remember, unless used regularly. These pages present the most commonly encountered units, which are used throughout the book, so that the reader can easily compare and use them.

Fig. 1.7.1 Which units to use and what they mean

Unit used	What does it mean?
kWh/m² per year also: kWh/(m²year) kWh/(m²a)	kilowatt-hours per square metre of floor area per year. This is used to express energy usage of a building, particularly for space heat demand, but can also be used for electricity and hot water. Also used for the production of solar energy per square metre of solar panel.
kgCO₂/m² per year also: kgCO₂/a or kgCO₂/(m²a)	kilograms of carbon dioxide (and equivalent gases) per square metre of floor area per year. This is the 'carbon footprint' or CO_2 pollution of the associated energy use of a building or associated CO_2 emissions from the fabrication of building materials. Can also be tonnes CO_2 per year (1 tonne is 1000 kg) and for the whole building can be expressed as kgCO₂/a or kilograms of CO_2 per year.
CO₂e	the greenhouse potential of emissions, considered as if they were all CO_2. CO_2e can be used to measure the global warming potential of gases other than CO_2, a mixture of CO_2 and other gases and even pure CO_2 because one unit of pure CO_2 = 1 unit of CO_2e.
kgCO₂/kWh	kilograms of CO_2 emissions per kilowatt-hour. Used for fuel CO_2 conversion. SAP 2009 fuel conversion factors have been used throughout the book. ⟶ Jump to Section 10.2.
W/m²	to express solar radiation: 1 kWh/ m² per year = 8.76 W/m²
W/mK (k-value)	thermal conductivity: the lower the value, the better the material's ability to insulate. Watts per metre per temperature difference in kelvin or Celsius.
W/(m² K) (U-value)	thermal transmittance coefficient and is the rate of heat transfer through 1 m² element with a 1°C/K temperature difference (watts per square metre of surface per degree temperature difference across it). The lower the U-value, the better insulating it is.
m³/(hr.m²)	cubic metres (volume) of air exchange per square metre of floor area per hour, resulting from a 50 Pa pressurisation test. Used instead of ach-1 (air changes per hour). This means that a volume of 1 m³ of air per hour is exchanged through 1 m² of building element.

pence/kWh	cost per kWh. In the book, 3.7 pence per kWh for gas and 11 pence per kWh for electricity have been used. Future projections can be obtained from: www.decc.gov.uk/en/content/cms/about/ec_social_res/analytic_projs/analytic_projs.aspx

1.7.1 What is the difference between kW and kWh?

- watt (W) or kilowatt (kW) is the power rating of equipment and appliances (1000 watt = 1 kW)
- kilowatt-hour (kWh) is the amount of energy consumed over 1 hour by equipment with a power rating of 1 kW.

For example, if a 20 watt bulb is switched on for 5 hours per day, it demands 0.1 kWh electrical energy. If this bulb is switched on for 5 hours a day for 365 days a year, the total energy consumed that year would be 36.5 kWh.

1.8   FURTHER READING

- Bair (2010) *Sustainable Buildings in Practice. What the users think*, Routledge
- Barlow (2011), *Guide to BREEAM*, RIBA Publishing
- BREEAM 2011 Technical Manual, www.breeam.org/BREEAM2011SchemeDocument/
- CAT, Zero Carbon Britain 2030, 2010
- CEN TC 350, Sustainability of construction works, www.cen.eu/cen
- *Code for Sustainable Homes Technical Guide:* November 2010
- EcoHomes 2006, The environmental rating for homes The Guidance – 2006 / Issue1.2 April 2006
- Edwards (2010), *Rough Guide to Sustainability*, RIBA/Earthscan
- Energy Savings Trust www.energysavingtrust.org.uk
- Gething (2011), *Green Overlay to the RIBA Outline Plan of Work*, www.ribabookshops. com/item/green-overlay-to-the-riba-outline-plan-of-work/10005/
- Halliday (2007), *Green Guide to the Architect's Job Book*, RIBA
- Halliday (1994), Environmental Code of Practice, *Property Management*, Vol. 12 Iss: 1, pp.31–32
- Halliday (2007), *Sustainable Construction*, Butterworth Heineman
- www.unfccc.int/files/meetings/cop_16/application/pdf/cop16_lca.pdf
- www.aecb.net/carbonlite/energystandards.php
- Liddell (2008), *Eco-minimalism, The antidote to Eco-bling*, RIBA
- Mackay (2008), *Sustainable Energy, Without the Hot Air*, UIT Cambridge Ltd. Also from: www.withouthotair.com
- Maslin (2008), *Global warming: A very short introduction*, OUP Oxford
- RIBA, Climate Change Toolkit, Low Carbon Standards and Assessment tools, free from www.architecture.com
- Sassi (2006), *Strategies for Sustainable Architecture*, Taylor & Francis
- Smith (2005), *Architecture in a Climate of Change*, Architectural Press
- Stern Review (2007), *The Economics of Climate Change*, Cambridge University Press, also from The National Archives: www.nationalarchives.gov.uk/webarchive/ and www.hm-treasury.gov.uk/stern_review_report.htm
- Stevenson & Leaman (2010), 'Evaluating housing performance in relation to human behaviour: new challenges', Building Research & Information, 38: 5, 437–441
- Stevenson et al. (2007), The Sustainable Housing Design Guide for Scotland, www.scotland.gov.uk/Topics/Built-Environment/Housing/investment/shdg/
- *The Code for Sustainable Homes: Technical Guide*, 2010
- The Sullivan Report (2007), 'A Low Carbon Building Standards Strategy for Scotland'
- UKCP09: UK Climate Projections, July 2009 www.ukcip.org.uk and http://ukcp09.defra.gov.uk/
- Way, Bordass, Soft Landings Framework (BSRIA BG 4/2009) www.softlandings.org.uk and www.usablebuildings.co.uk
- Zero Carbon Hub, Carbon Compliance for Tomorrow's Homes Topic 4, Closing The Gap Between Designed and Built Performance, 2010

Chapter 2
Design strategies and adaptations for a changing climate

Despite even the best mitigation efforts, our climate is experiencing irreversible changes.

Buildings are usually designed with a lifespan of around 60 years. What we build today will still be standing in 2080 and beyond, and we must design for the climate change predicted during that period. We must also carefully consider our reliance on finite resources which move closer to exhaustion by the day. Only in doing so are we able to fulfil our duty towards clients and building users.

Seasons in the UK, in general, are expected to become warmer. We will see drier summers, wetter winters and more extreme winds and rainfall. Although the increases in temperature are incremental, the actual impact on both the natural and the built environment is significant. As an island, the UK is particularly vulnerable to coastal flooding. Inland, extreme rainfall will increase the risk of urban flash floods and swollen rivers. We are also likely to experience more heat waves and droughts which could pose issues of subsidence and affect the way we cool buildings.

This chapter summarises predicted climatic changes and arising design implications and adaptations, both for site planning, building design and during construction.

 Symbol indicates relevance to the Code for Sustainable Homes, EcoHomes & BREEM.

2.1   A CHANGING CLIMATE: WHAT ARE THE IMPACTS IN THE UK?

By 2080, we expect to have seen temperature increases of up to 2.9–4.3°C in the northern and the southern regions of the UK respectively.[1] Rises in sea level will range from 150 to 900 mm.[2]

In general, each region will see increased rainfall, although overall yearly rainfall increases are deceptively modest. This is because the yearly average evens out significant rainfall decreases in summer (8–26%) and substantial increases in winter (7–32%).[3] In southern regions, reduced cloud cover during summer is likely to contribute to increased solar radiation and higher temperatures as well as more extreme, though rare, rainfall.

The UK is already experiencing a change in climate:
- There has been a 1°C temperature increase since 1970.[4]
- The four hottest years on record were all in the last 15 years: 2006 was the hottest recorded in 350 years.[5]
- In the summer of 2003 a prolonged heat wave hit the country; the UK suffered 2000 heat-related deaths.[6]

Predicted climate changes and impacts in the UK (general)

(based on current trajectory of a global 2°C rise by 2040 and 4°C by 2080)

permanent sea level rise[7]	Loss of agricultural land, displaced people and loss of species. Infrastructure in low-lying land threatened. South of UK more affected by subsiding land movements.[8]
more rainfall in winter and less rainfall in summer	Higher risk of regional flooding in winter and localised urban floods in summer. Prolonged droughts damage planting and lead to increased risk of wildfires. Existing housing stock on clay subsoil will be more prone to subsidence/heave.
extreme rainfall events, not unlike tropical rainstorms	River flooding and localised urban flooding. Threat to underground and ground-floor infrastructure, sewage and clean water supply. Wind-blown water damage due to increased wind pressure.
increased summer temperatures and extremes	Buildings will struggle to provide thermal comfort. Heat-related deaths and illnesses, especially among the old and fragile. CO_2 emissions from summer cooling are likely to increase, exacerbating global warming. Road surfaces will melt with prolonged temperatures over 35°C and other infrastructure will fail.[9]
increased winter temperatures	CO_2 emissions from space heating are expected to decrease but this will not cancel out the predicted increase in cooling energy during summer.

2.1.1 Regional future predicted climate changes: Scotland[10]

Region 1: Scotland	2040s	2080s
sea level	150–390 mm increase	370–750 mm increase
air temperature	An average yearly increase of 1.8–1.9°C. Summer temperatures to increase by around 2°C. Winters to be 1.6°C warmer.	An average yearly increase of 2.9–3.5°C. Summer temperatures to increase by around 3.9°C. Winters to be 2.6°C warmer.
rainfall	Overall yearly increase of 2.7–4.3% in precipitation. A 10% increase in rainfall in winter and the same in autumn. An 8% decrease in summer.	Overall yearly increase of 0.7–1.9% in precipitation. A decrease in precipitation of 15–19% in summer, with increased average rainfall particularly in winter and autumn: 22% and 20% respectively.

2.1.2 Regional future predicted climate changes: north England and north Wales[11]

Region 2: North England and north Wales	2040s	2080s
sea level	190–450 mm increase	440–840 mm increase
air temperature	An average yearly increase of 2°C. Summer temperatures to increase by around 2.2°C. Winters to be 1.8°C warmer.	An average yearly increase of 3.2–4°C. Summer temperatures to increase by around 4°C. Winters to be 2.7°C warmer.
rainfall	Overall yearly increase of 0.7–1.9% in precipitation. Winter precipitation to increase by around 11% and up to 6% in autumn. Summer precipitation to decrease by 12%.	Overall yearly increase of 6–8.7% in precipitation. An increase in winter precipitation of between 18% and 26%, with a smaller increase in autumn (9%). Summer precipitation to decrease by 21–26%.

2.1.3 Regional future predicted climate changes: Northern Ireland[12]

Region 3: Northern Ireland	2040s	2080s
sea level	150–400 mm increase	380–750 mm increase
air temperature	An average yearly increase of 1.8°C. Summer temperatures to increase by around 1.9°C. Winters to be 1.6°C warmer.	An average yearly increase of 2.9–3.6°C. Summer temperatures to increase by around 3.7°C. Winters to be 2.7°C warmer.
rainfall	Overall yearly increase of 1.3–2.3% in precipitation. An increase in autumn (6%) and winter (7%) precipitation and and 8.5% decrease in summer precipitation.	Overall yearly increase of 2.7–4.5% in precipitation. A decrease in precipitation in summer of between 15% and 18%, with an increase in precipitation in autumn (11%) and winter (12–19%).

2.1.4 Regional future predicted climate changes: south England and south Wales[13]

Region 4: South England and south Wales	2040s	2080s
sea level	200–490 mm increase	490–900 mm increase
air temperature	An average yearly increase of 2–2.6°C. Summer temperatures to increase by around 2.4°C. Winters to be 2°C warmer.	An average yearly increase of 3.5–4.3°C. Summer temperatures to increase by around 4.5°C. Winters to be 3.4°C warmer.
rainfall	Overall yearly increase of 1–1.9% in precipitation. A 14% increase in winter precipitation predicted, with 3–4% increases in autumn and 12% decreased precipitation in summer.	Overall yearly increase of 2.3–3.3% in precipitation. An increase in winter precipitation of 24–32%, with small increases in autumn (5%) and 21–26% decreased precipitation in summer.

2.2 A CHANGING CLIMATE LEADS TO A CHANGE IN HOW WE DESIGN

Although the predicted weather conditions will be new to the UK, they are already a fact of life for much of the world. Building precedents in Mediterranean countries, for example, can teach us how to adapt our buildings to cope with increased summer temperatures. And the Netherlands, a country with more than 50% of its landmass below sea level, can teach us how to work with water rather than against it. ──▷ Jump to Chapter 5.

As shown in Fig. 2.2.1, by 2080 summer temperatures in the UK's southern regions will resemble those of the Mediterranean, while temperatures in the north will be similar to those of northern France and the Belgian coastal regions.

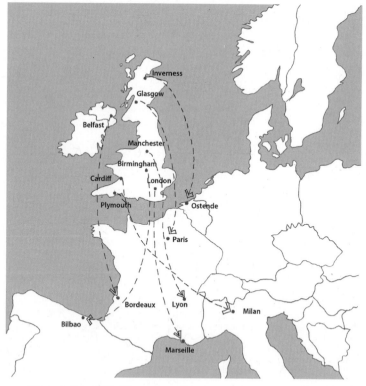

Fig. 2.2.1 Map of UK cities and predicted 2080 future summer climate 'sister cities' (based on approx. summer air temperature comparisons)

2.2.1 Increased summer temperatures: design checklist

Relevant to all regions, but most problematic in urban areas and the south of England. Less significant in Region 1: Scotland.

☑☒

Site strategies: ──▷ Jump to Chapters 3, 4 & 5
- Have 'cool' surfaces (light-coloured or reflective) been specified? ☐
- Are there bodies of water and vegetation to allow for evaporative cooling and shade ideally incorporated into SUDS at city and district scale? ☐
- Does the design allow for good summer ventilation at street level to disperse pollutants? ☐
- Have narrow street and courtyard designs been proposed? ☐

Building scale: ──▷ Jump to Chapters 6, 7 & 8
- Are there passive measures to prevent overheating? (Well-insulated and airtight buildings are still relevant.) Is there provision for solar shading to south, east and west, with inward-opening windows. Does the design include overhanging eaves and large window reveals? ☐
- Does the design provide good natural ventilation, particularly good cross-ventilation and secure night-time cooling? ☐
- Has use been made of thermal mass in exposed surfaces and high floor to ceilings? ☐
- Have you minimised the use of skylights except where overshadowed by surrounding structure to limit overheating in summer? ☐
- Does the specification use light-coloured or reflective external building surfaces, including vegetated roofs and walls? ☐
- Have joints been increased or enlarged to allow for more thermal movement, especially at south facing façades and roofs? ☐
- Increased thermal stress and movement will reduce material durability and performance, particularly on window frames and roof finishes. Has this been taken into account and have reflective layers, stones as ballast and protection layers on roofs with flexible material at upstands been used? ☐
- Have you specified durable window seals and designed recessed windows rather than having windows flush with the external façade? ☐
- Have hot water pipes been well insulated to avoid additional internal heat gains? ☐

During construction:
- Has account been taken of the fact that curing of wet plaster/concrete and other wet trades will be affected? (Cementing/concreting, and/or rendering may be difficult on hot days, which could result in cracking and shrinkage with poor finishes and possible structural weakness. Ideal temperature for maximum strength is 23°C.) ☐
- Is it possible to use prefabricated concrete panels or undertake concrete works in spring/autumn or early mornings and shade the working area from the sun? ☐
- Are the workers being protected from heatstroke? ☐
- Higher productivity may speed up site programme, so have you planned to carefully monitor this for its effect on the critical path? ☐

2.2.2 Increased winter temperatures: design checklist

Relevant to all regions.   ☑ ☒

Site strategies: ⟶ **Jump to Chapters 3 & 4**
- Has shelter been provided from cold northerly and north-easterly winds?   ☐

Building strategy: ⟶ **Jump to Chapters 6, 7 & 8**
- Moderate winter temperature increases mean that current strategies to deal   ☐
  with large heat losses are still relevant, so have you used super-insulation,
  compactness, porches and good airtightness, and maximised solar gain?
- Has thermal mass been used to stabilise day/night-time temperatures?   ☐
- Are you aware that mechanical ventilation systems such as MVHR may be used?   ☐

During construction:
- Do you still need to be concerned about the risk of frost?   ☐
- Increased winter temperatures may speed up site programme, so have you planned   ☐
  to carefully monitor this for its effect on the critical path?

2.2.3 Increased flood risk from sea and rivers: design checklist

Relevant to all coastal regions, especially eastern coasts in UK and cities along   ☑ ☒
river mouths.

Site strategies: ⟶ **Jump to Chapter 5**
- Is the site in a high flood risk zone? If so, avoid development.   ☐
- Has the Environment Agency been consulted about the flood risk designation?   ☐
- Have you responded with strategic planning, such as zoning of functions and   ☐
  programme?
- Is there enough site-wide water retention for sustainable urban drainage systems ☐
  (SUDS) so that we work with water rather than against it?
- Are there strategic escape routes to safe higher ground?   ☐

Building strategies: ⟶ **Jump to Chapter 5**
- Do you need flood-proof building features such as sacrificial basements,   ☐
  elevated ground, stilts or floating structures?
- Have services and infrastructure been located on upper floors, where   ☐
  appropriate, and have you used robust materials on the lower floors?

During construction: ☐
As Section 2.2.5

2.2.4 Decreased summer rainfall: design checklist

Relevant to all regions, but especially Regions 2 and 4. ☑ ☒

Site strategies: ⟶ Jump to Chapters 4 & 5
- Has specialist advice been obtained before removing or adding trees near existing buildings? Is there an increased foundation depth near trees? ☐
- Has landscaping/planting been used that contains a mix of drought-tolerant species as well as native, water-loving species? ☐
- Pressure on water resources: are you collecting water locally and reusing it for landscaping? ☐

Building strategies: ⟶ Jump to Chapter 5
- Has allowance been made for larger roof rainwater collectors to irrigate landscape for longer periods of time? ☐
- Has greywater recycling been considered? ☐
- Has thought been given to the foundation pressures for existing buildings, which may be at risk of subsidence? (Pre-1970 dwellings with foundations of 450 mm or less depth are at particularly high risk of heave/subsidence which will become more pronounced with a changing climate.) ☐
- Has allowance been made for deeper foundations (+0.5 m depth) for new buildings, particularly on clay soils, especially in Region 4, which is mostly clay? Scotland/Region 1 is least affected by subsidence. ☐

During construction:
- Has thought been given to the issue of water shortage during construction, which may affect landscaping schemes and prevent plants from taking root and surviving? ☐

2.2.5 Increased rainfall and extreme weather events: design checklist

Relevant to all regions. Wind-driven rain: Scotland and western UK. ☑ ☒

Site strategies: ⟶ Jump to Chapters 3, 4 & 5
- Can wind buffers be created by use of vegetation and building location? ☐
- Have large-scale SUDS, permeable paving and water retention been used on site to prevent localised flooding? (Increased local water retention is required on clay soils owing to higher risk of flash floods.) ☐
- To avoid slope instabilities is there increased vegetation, particularly on clay soils, as roots protect slopes and absorb water? Do measures include reduced slope angles, the construction of retention or stability measures and additional drainage? ☐
- Is there a tree maintenance plan to contain growth? ☐

Building strategies: ⟶ Jump to Chapters 5 & 7
Roofs
- Are all roof pitches >25°? Have roof penetrations and flush rooflights been minimised? Does the design include large roof overhangs and increased fixing density for roof tiles/slates? ☐
- Has the gutter capacity and/or the number of pipes and outlets been increased? Has the use of internal gutters been avoided? Have flat roof upstands been increased and have they been fully waterproofed with flexible materials? ☐
- Has rainwater harvesting for summer landscaping been employed? ☐

Structure

- Has the design allowed for increased wind pressure, especially above 10 storeys? The design loads may increase by 10%, so have foundations and core walls been increased sufficiently? ☐
- Have cladding systems been designed to stiffen in increased wind pressure? ☐
- Has the decrease in snowfall, particularly in Regions 1 and 2, been taken into account? ☐
- Does the design use robust materials, especially on ground and lower floors, including concrete foundations? ☐
- Has heave been taken into account for existing buildings (pre-1970 dwellings with foundations of 450 mm or less depth particularly), and are deeper foundations (+0.5 m depth) provided for new buildings? (Scotland is least affected by subsidence/heave.) ☐

Windows & walls

- Has attention been given to avoiding water penetration at weak points and junctions, particularly windows and doors? Have you avoided externally flush windows and allowed for recessing all windows with overhanging window sills and providing porches or overhangs to doors? (Windows, doors and rendered surfaces will suffer more than in other EU countries owing to wind-driven rain.) ☐
- Has the design avoided full-fill cavity walls with organic insulation or insulation which performs badly when wet.? (Check NHBC and building regulations approval, particularly in Scotland.) ☐
- Have shutters and other external fixings been designed to avoid cracks and movement joints which may allow wind-driven rain into the fabric? ☐
- Does the design specify lower-movement materials such as light-coloured/reflective surfaces and hardwood in preference to softwood cladding, to minimise the risk of cracking? ☐
- Since higher relative humidity means potential for mould growth, particularly where ill-heated/ventilated, have thermal bridges been avoided? ☐

During construction:

- As working at heights may become difficult or unsafe, has the use of cranes in exposed areas been minimised? ☐
- Has the safety of scaffolding been reviewed, and has water protection for construction elements been provided? ☐
- Has careful consideration been given to the storage of materials to cope with the increased risk of flooding on site and to avoid mould growth by protecting building site/organic materials etc. from damp? ☐
- Has the moving of activities away from the site been considered, e.g. prefabrication in a controlled environment? ☐
- Have plans been made to cope with possible site delays/disruption? ☐
- Does the design deliver construction watertightness as soon as possible? ☐
- Has the winter wet season been avoided for certain trades, such as groundworks, foundation, curing of concrete and other wet trades such as rammed earth? ☐

2.3 THE IMPORTANCE OF FUTURE-PROOFING OUR BUILDINGS

Future-proofing anticipates climate changes and makes plans for adaptation without impacting on CO_2 reduction/mitigation efforts. We need to design now for the future.

Future-proofing does not have to mean spending lots of money right now. Many measures are easily implemented simply by planning ahead and thinking differently about site and building design. Other measures can be implemented in the future if and when climate predictions materialise.

To future-proof, we need to plan ahead. If we know that our buildings may need solar shading, we have to design for this now, even if shading is only installed when it becomes necessary. For example, this means that we need to specify shutter fixings and inward-opening windows right now, which will allow sufficient cross-ventilation when external shutters are fixed in the future. If we do not act now, the cost of coping with climate change in the future will be much greater than the price we would pay to prepare today.[14]

Thinking and planning ahead will mean:
- reduced CO_2 emissions as it will minimise remedial measures and waste of resources
- the cost of climate change mitigation will always be substantially less than any adaptation measures[15]
- occupant comfort at all times
- minimised need for building demolition 50 years down the line

 Code for Sustainable Homes (Sur 1 mandatory, Sur 2), EcoHomes credits (Pol 3, Pol 5) and BREEAM credits (Pol 3)

2.4 ENVIRONMENTAL MODELLING AND CLIMATE DATA

Usually environmental modelling tools will use:
- Test Reference Years (TRYs): historic weather data used mainly for energy consumption purposes
- Design Summer Years (DSYs): historic hotter summer weather data for overheating simulations
- future climate change data for the whole of the UK from: http://ukclimateprojections.defra.gov.uk/
- ready-to-use climate data sets for a selection of UK cities from: www.centres.exeter.ac.uk/cee/prometheus

2.5 FURTHER READING

- Act on CO2, Climate Change and Global Warming, www.nef.org.uk/climatechange/
- Arup, Your home in a changing climate (2008), www.london.gov.uk/lccp
- Beating the Heat, Arup/CIBSE, 2005
- BRE GBG 63, Climate Change: impact on building design and construction, 2004
- BRE, Cooling buildings in London: overcoming the heat island, 2001
- BRE, Digest 486, Reducing the effects of climate change by roof design, 2004
- BRE, Impact of climate change on building, 1998
- BRE, Potential implications of climate change in the built environment, 2000
- BREEAM 2011 Technical Manual, www.breeam.org/BREEAM2011SchemeDocument/
- CIBSE, How to manage overheating in buildings: a practical guide to improving summertime comfort in buildings, 2010
- CIRIA 2005, C638, Climate change risks in buildings – an introduction
- Climate change weather files: www.centres.exeter.ac.uk/cee/prometheus/
- Code for Sustainable Homes Technical Guide: November 2010
- Department for Environment, Food and Rural affairs www.defra.gov.uk/environment/climate/
- Department of the Environment Northern Ireland: www.doeni.gov.uk/index/protect_the_environment/climate_change/
- EA, Using science to create a better place: social impacts of heat waves 2007
- EcoHomes 2006, The environmental rating for homes, The Guidance – 2006 / Issue1.2 April 2006
- Edwards (2010), Rough Guide to Sustainability, RIBA/Earthscan
- Gething (2010), Design for future climate: opportunities for the built environment, Technology Strategy Board
- GLA, 2005, Adapting to climate change: a checklist for development, Guidance on designing developments in a changing climate
- Mackay (2008), Sustainable Energy, Without the Hot Air, UIT Cambridge Ltd. Also from: www.withouthotair.com
- RIBA Climate Change Toolkit, 01 Climate Change Briefing, free download from www.architecture.com/climatechange
- Scotland and Northern Ireland Forum for Environmental Research www.sniffer.org.uk
- Scottish Government: www.scotland.gov.uk/changingclimate
- Stern Review, The Economics of Climate Change, Cambridge University Press, also from The National Archives: www.nationalarchives.gov.uk/webarchive/ and www.hm-treasury.gov.uk/stern_review_report.htm
- The draft climate change adaptation strategy for London, GLA, 2010
- Town and Country Planning Association (2007), Climate Change Adaptation by design
- UKCP09: UK Climate Projections, July 2009. www.ukcip.org.uk and http://ukcp09.defra.gov.uk/
- Welsh Assembly: www.wales.gov.uk/climatechange
- World Business Council on Sustainable Development, www.wbcsd.org
- Zero Carbon Britain 2030
- Zero Carbon Hub (2010), Topic 3 – Future Climate Change, www.zerocarbonhub.org

Chapter 3
Environmental site planning

A building's performance is not only determined by local climate conditions and operational energy efficiency. Site location and urban design approach also have a major impact. Rather than working against the urban grain, we need to work with it by using environmental site planning principles; we can then promote occupant comfort and health as well as minimising operational and transportation energy use.

Instead of endlessly repeating historical patterns, site planning should respond to climate change predictions. This chapter considers the implications of a warmer climate and Chapter 5 discusses flood risk.

It is crucial to get the environmental basics right on the site. Then whoever 'plugs into' the urban grain in the future has a better chance of achieving high environmental building standards.

 Symbol indicates relevance to the Code for Sustainable Homes, EcoHomes & BREEAM.

3.1   ENVIRONMENTAL SITE CHECKLIST

Refer to	Biodiversity	☑ ☒
4.4	Do the proposals enable the existing wildlife and biodiversity to be conserved, protected or enhanced?	☐
3.5.1, 4.4.1	Is there space for the creation of green corridors?	☐
	Site planning	
3.3	Are public transport facilities easily accessible?	☐
3.3	Can the site be located close to community facilities and services?	☐
3.3	Is the development density appropriate? Is the mix of uses and tenure suitable to the locality? Can density be increased around transport nodes, overlooking parks, waterways and other amenities?	☐
3.4	Movement strategy: can new access routes be connected with existing routes?	☐
3.4.1	Prioritisation of pedestrians and cyclists: are there bicycle parking spaces, safe crossings/walkable streets and good connections through the city centre rather than around it?	☐
3.5	Are there easily accessible communal open spaces (within 300–400 m)?	☐
3.6, 3.7	Has the impact of new development on existing community and buildings – traffic/noise/overshadowing etc. – been minimised?	☐
3.7	Have local solar access and average seasonal temperatures been checked and responded to, and is winter solar gain maximised?	☐
3.7.1	Have 'urban breaks' (variety of building heights, providing better solar access and ventilation) been provided?	☐
4.2	Has vegetation been used to reduce air pollution, moderate the urban heat island effect and increase thermal comfort?	☐
	Flood protection (See detailed checklist Section 5.1.4.)	
5	Has a minimum of 5% of the site area been set aside for sustainable urban drainage systems (SUDS)?	☐
	Future-proofing	
3.8	Is there enough space for urban infrastructure, including renewables? Is there enough space for community energy schemes?	☐

3.2 BROWNFIELD: INFILL DEVELOPMENT

A brownfield is a site that has been previously developed. It may be contaminated if its prior use was industrial – docks, gasworks, petrol stations, etc. Most UK cities have policies to protect greenfields (undeveloped land) from development. This pushes developers to use brownfield sites instead. Often brownfields are considered to be of low ecological value compared to rural or suburban greenfields. However, an urban brownfield site which has been derelict for a few years actually provides an excellent habitat for vegetation to grow undisturbed and for wildlife to settle.

Key recommendations

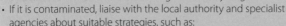

- Undertake site contamination testing at feasibility stage.
- If it is contaminated, liaise with the local authority and specialist agencies about suitable strategies, such as:
  - removing contaminated topsoil from site, capping or chemical cleansing
  - bioremediation – cleansing certain pollutants from soil using plants such as willows and reeds; this method is preferred but it may not remove all pollutants.
- Undertake ecological site survey and identify protected species.
- Undertake site planning to protect as much ecology as possible. Incorporate ecology into new design.
- Introduce plant species to support wildlife habitats.
- Uncontaminated rubble and soil can be relocated to green/brown roofs.

  ⟶ Jump to Sections 7.1.8 & 9.3.

Advantages of developing on brownfields:
- usually central location
- protects the sprawl of cities onto greenfields
- existing infrastructure (roads, energy, water connections)
- sites can be of higher ecological value than greenfields: ecology can be retained if sensitively developed.

Disadvantages of developing on brownfields:
- possible disturbance of valuable biodiversity
- remediation of contaminated land will add to construction costs and may cause delays
- clients often unwilling to do extensive site contamination testing before planning consent has been obtained
- if high biodiversity, it may be difficult to obtain maximum ecology credits under EcoHomes/Code for Sustainable Homes (Eco 1 to Eco 4) and BREEAM (LE 2 to LE 5); in BREEAM, credits can be obtained for developing on brownfields (LE 1).

3.3   DESIGNING FOR URBAN DENSITY

The more compact a city, the more environmentally sustainable it is. However, environmental considerations must go hand in hand with concern for inhabitants' preferences and well-being. People will be driven away from high-density urban areas if they lack spacious, high-quality dwellings and open spaces.

To counter this, high residential densities should always incorporate a range of mixed-use facilities.

The environmental benefits of medium/high density
- uses land efficiently, avoiding sprawl into greenfields
- supports public transport strategies – economies of scale for infrastructure/ numbers of users
- shared and efficient energy/water supply, waste infrastructure and services
- easy access to facilities and public transport
- reduces parking demand and car ownership, which decreases local noise/air pollution and carbon emissions
- enables shared energy strategies such as community/district heating schemes ——➔ Jump to Chapter 10
- energy-efficient building typology: more compact with lower space heating and infrastructure requirements.

Disadvantages
- open space and biodiversity compromised within cities
- perceived overcrowding where insufficient open space is provided
- higher embodied energy due to taller building typology
- potentially compromised access to passive solar gain, daylight and natural ventilation – needs careful design ——➔ Jump to Chapter 6
- urban heat island effect may be exacerbated and make summer cooling more challenging under certain conditions ——➔ Jump to Chapter 4
- zero carbon developments are difficult to achieve at high densities (Section 3.3.3) ——➔ Jump to Chapter 11.

 Credits under EcoHomes/Code for Sustainable Homes (Eco 5)

3.3.1 What are sustainable densities?

Minimum densities of around 80 dwellings per hectare (dw/ha) are recommended. This is a healthy density for public transport use and it supports close walking proximity to community services and facilities.[1] For car-free developments, densities should increase to 200–250 dw/ha (see Section 3.4). Maximum sustainable densities are 400–450 dw/ha. Such high densities should be limited to only part of a development.[2]

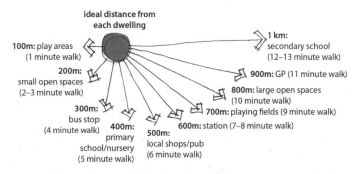

ideal distance from each dwelling

100m: play areas (1 minute walk)

200m: small open spaces (2–3 minute walk)

300m: bus stop (4 minute walk)

400m: primary school/nursery (5 minute walk)

500m: local shops/pub (6 minute walk)

600m: station (7–8 minute walk)

700m: playing fields (9 minute walk)

800m: large open spaces (10 minute walk)

900m: GP (11 minute walk)

1 km: secondary school (12–13 minute walk)

Fig. 3.3.1 Proximity of facilities and ideal distances from each dwelling[3]

Key recommendations

Always accompany sustainable densities with:

- easy access to open spaces and facilities such as GPs, supermarkets and schools
- minimum 15% open space provision – see Section 3.5
- neighbourhoods designed for walking, cycling and good public transport access
- ideally a mix of densities in each development to create variety and open spaces, reduce risk of perceived overcrowding and allow solar access – see Section 3.7
- higher localised densities around transport nodes, overlooking parks, waterways and other amenities
- high four+ storey density developments – may be suitable for communal or district heating plants (at least 200 units in the development)
- a good mix of housing sizes and typologies to support the community through different stages of life.

3.3.2 Regional recommended densities

Each city's Local Development Framework (LDF) (or Unitary Development Plan, UDP) makes recommendations for minimum and maximum densities. These are directly related to city location and public transport access. This is also referred to as PTAL (Public Transport Accessibility Level). The higher the PTAL, the better the public transport access.

Avoid development in areas with little or no public transport access, unless provision is part of the development proposal. Otherwise this will only encourage car usage, increasing pollution and negating any energy savings made by low carbon developments.

The minimum recommended densities are often below 'sustainable' densities. This means that they are unlikely to support good public transport and other facilities. From 30 dw/ha, only bus services are sustainable.[4] The shaded areas in the table below are those densities at which zero carbon developments are likely to be feasible. ——⟶ Jump to Chapter 11.

Fig. 3.3.2 Densities recommended in Local Development Frameworks[5]

Location	Dwelling typology	PTAL	Glasgow	Edinburgh	Manchester	Belfast and Cardiff	Birmingham	Plymouth	London
city centre	flats: 4–6 storeys and taller	high	30–100 max.	50–100+	75	50+	100	150	80–210
suburban	terraced houses & flats; 3–4 storeys	average	75	25–50	75	30–50	50	70	55–145
rural	detached/ semi detached houses; 2–3 storeys	low	<50	<25	40	30	40	40	40–80

3.3.3 Zero carbon versus density paradox

There is a known conflict between zero carbon standards for buildings and large-scale development sustainability. For a development to rely only on on-site renewable energy generation, maximum densities must drop to 35–40 dw/ha. This is below the 'sustainable density' required to support public transport and other facilities. It is also below the density of existing urban areas in the UK.[6] It is difficult to meet zero carbon standards at 'sustainable densities' in urban areas because:

- There are higher energy needs per site area, owing to the large number of residents; at the same time, there is significantly less space to generate on-site energy.
- Renewable energy technologies are particularly inefficient in urban areas; for example, solar panel technologies are at risk of shade, and wind energy is rarely suitable owing to lower and unpredictable wind speeds. ⟶ Jump to Chapter 12.
- A high-density development combined with off-site energy generation may be more appropriate but off-site energy generation may not be allowed as part of the zero carbon definition. ⟶ Jump to Chapter 11.

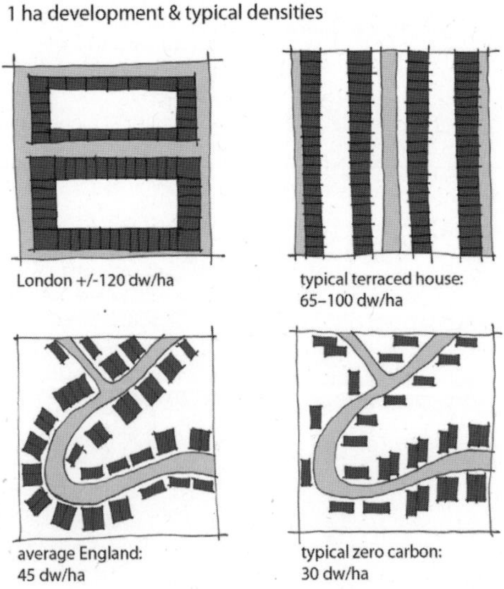

1 ha development & typical densities

London +/-120 dw/ha

typical terraced house:
65–100 dw/ha

average England:
45 dw/ha

typical zero carbon:
30 dw/ha

Fig. 3.3.3 1 ha development and typical densities

If off-site carbon offsetting is used, densities around 50 dw/ha are likely to meet the zero carbon standard. However, such low densities are not recommended as they create sprawl and increased energy use for transport. This negates the buildings' zero carbon status.

Fig. 3.3.4 Feasible zero carbon strategies in relation to development density

Development density	Current feasible zero carbon strategies[7]
rural ≤50 dw/ha max.	Gas boiler with PV and solar thermal panels on individual roofs. If development ≥50 dwellings: communal plant with solar panels on individual roofs may be feasible. Other technologies, such as ground/water source heat pumps, wind turbines, micro-hydro and locally sourced biomass, may also be feasible. ──⇒ Jump to Chapters 11 & 12. Likely to meet zero carbon standards with on-site measures.
suburban >50 and ≤100 dw/ha	Increased Fabric Energy Efficiency Standards (FEES). Individual dwelling approach with PV and solar thermal panels and gas boilers or air source heat pumps. ──⇒ Jump to Chapters 11 & 12 for other suitable technologies. Where ≥50 dwellings in the development: building block approach with shared gas, district heating or CHP. Difficult to meet zero carbon standards with on-site measures only.
urban >100 dw/ha	Increased Fabric Energy Efficiency Standards (FEES), with PV and solar hot water panels on roof and communal gas heating. ──⇒ Jump to Chapters 11 & 12 for other suitable technologies. Unlikely to meet zero carbon standards with on-site measures only.

3.4 DESIGNING FOR CYCLISTS AND PEDESTRIANS

Encouraging residents to walk or cycle not only reduces carbon emissions: it brings streets to life, builds safer neighbourhoods and improves health for city inhabitants. Distances less than 2 km are suitable for walking and cycling, although the average distance people are prepared to walk is 1.25 km (roughly a 15-minute walk). Ideally, local facilities should be located within a 1.25 km radius from residential neighbourhoods. The energy used to access buildings by car can be 30% higher than the energy used to run the buildings.[8]

Fig. 3.4.1 Carbon emissions from different modes of transport

Travel mode	kg CO_2 per km travelled
walking/cycling	0
train	0.07
bus	0.133
car	0.214

Key recommendations[9]

. . . .

- Provide good connections and short routes through the development to facilities, transport and open spaces (max. 300–400 m).
- Conduct wind modelling of long, straight routes to avoid unpleasant wind tunnels. Provide wind breaks or buffers as needed.
- Ensure safe and regular crossings to areas of interest.
- Introduce interesting features along the way, e.g. shops. Design irregular façades and allow for seating areas and arcades.
- Do not randomly place seating in the middle of squares. Place seats in niches, ideally facing the sun, with back protected. This offers protection, security and a good microclimate.
- Provide alternative routes with small squares (20–25 m radius) on the edges of pedestrian routes.[10]
- Avoid squares over 100 m in length.
- Avoid tall, freestanding buildings as they catch wind and direct it downwards. See Section 3.6.1.
- Avoid level differences and stairs; always provide ramps.
- Encourage people to cycle by introducing cycle lanes and parking where possible. Always introduce separate lanes where vehicular speeds ≥ 30 kph (20 mph).[11] Vegetation may act as a barrier. ——⟶ Jump to Chapter 4.

Code for Sustainable Homes credits (Ene 8, Man 1) and EcoHomes credits (Tra 1, Tra 2) and BREEAM credits (Tra 3, Man 4)

3.4.1 Car-free developments[12]

Generally, the single biggest source of urban air pollution is car use. Around 15% of the UK's carbon emissions are related to individual car use.[13] Developments with no car ownership or parking provision may be feasible where the development:

- encompasses minimum 20 dwellings
- has a high density of at least 200–250 dw/ha
- consists of building typology of flats, terraced houses and mostly narrow fronts with 4–6 storey buildings
- is located within 300–400 m radius of regular public transport – local authority classified high Public Transport Accessibility Levels (PTAL)
- is located within 300–400 m radius of mixed use facilities
- includes a car club as part of the development – one car club vehicle replaces on average five individually owned cars[14]
- implements the ten key design recommendations for cycling/walking.

3.5 PLANNING FOR URBAN OPEN SPACES

Green space is particularly important in dense urban areas. It should be an essential part of city and site planning. Protection of open space is also important: any space lost during redevelopment needs to be reallocated elsewhere on the site or in the vicinity.

Urban open spaces are necessary to:
- contribute to the urban dweller's mental and physical health; they have a positive impact on mortality[15, 16]
- store incoming flood waters and protect built-up areas
  ———⟩ Jump to Chapter 5
- contribute to a positive urban microclimate ———⟩ Jump to Section 4.2.1
- support biodiversity. ———⟩ Jump to Section 4.4
- alleviate urban density pressures.

Key recommendations
. . . .

- Consult each region's local development framework and open space standards.
- Allocate minimum 15% of each site to open space provision, of which at least 5% is for sustainable urban drainage systems (SUDS). SUDS can be incorporated creatively to offer both water storage in the event of flooding and open space throughout the rest of the year (e.g. 'water squares'). ———⟩ Jump to Chapter 5.
- Locate open spaces within a 300–400 m (5–6 minute) walk from each dwelling.[17] These parks should include outdoor sports areas/playing fields, wildlife areas and landscaped seating areas. Parks should be at least 2 ha in size.
- Small parks and open spaces under 2 ha are still valuable in densely built-up areas and will be well used by the elderly and people with children.
- An urban grid of about 90 × 90 m with public open space at the centre is the best compromise between wildlife support, accessibility and pedestrian permeability.[18]
- Open spaces are not always purely recreational. They can be squares, allotments, rivers, waterways, ponds and reservoirs and can even be incorporated into buildings.

3.5.1 Plan continuous green corridors

City-scale networks should interlink open spaces to form continuous green corridors which reach from the city centre to the edges. This maximises urban residents' access to large and varied open spaces. Interesting cycle and walking routes can be provided and biodiversity is better supported. Where disruptive new roads and passageways are proposed, undercrofts or green bridges can be introduced to interconnect the spaces. Always ensure greenery is interlinked at macro, micro and building scale.

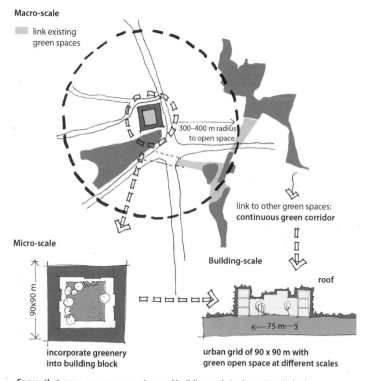

Macro-scale

link existing
green spaces

300–400 m radius
to open space

link to other green spaces:
continuous green corridor

Micro-scale

90x90 m

Building-scale

roof

75 m

incorporate greenery
into building block

urban grid of 90 x 90 m with
green open space at different scales

Ensure that greenery on macro, micro and building scale is always interlinked

Fig. 3.5.1 Scales of open spaces and linking into continuous green corridors at macro, micro and building scale

3.6 CREATING A POSITIVE URBAN MICROCLIMATE

Because of the dense congregation of buildings, people and activities, urban areas have a different local climate from the surrounding countryside. This manifests itself in lower humidity levels, higher air pollution due to lower wind speeds and higher temperatures by 4–7°C which are felt most keenly during summer nights.[19] This is referred to as the urban heat island effect (UHI).

In winter, the local climate is buffered by the heat island effect. However, it can exacerbate overheating in summer. One of the most effective solutions is to increase green space in urban areas as it reduces local summer temperatures yet buffers winter temperatures. ———➤ Jump to Section 4.2.1.

A positive urban microclimate can be created through careful master planning which takes into account local and seasonal wind/solar pathways. There are many parameters to take into account, discussed throughout this book:
- urban surfaces (roofs, streets, buildings) ———➤ Jump to Sections 4.2.2 & 9.3
- vegetation: proportion, type & location ———➤ Jump to Section 4.2
- noise sources ———➤ Jump to Section 4.2.5
- rainfall and water runoff ———➤ Jump to Section 5.6
- flood risk ———➤ Jump to Chapter 5
- wind speed and wind direction (Section 3.6.1)
- solar access throughout the year, taking surrounding buildings into account (Section 3.7)
- other site conditions such as geology and topography.

3.6.1 Designing with the wind
. . . .

Working with the wind is crucial for successful urban environments. The closer the buildings, the more they protect each other from winds, but also the more they reduce each other's solar gain. Buildings too close together will lack summer ventilation and street pollution may not disperse.

In the UK, the winds come from over the Atlantic. The influence of this huge sea mass explains the frequent and heavy rainfall on the western side of the UK. The air from the European mainland is less moderated, temperature-wise, as the North Sea/Channel is too small to have an effect. As a result, the south-westerly prevailing winds are less problematic than the colder north-easterly or south-easterly winds over mainland Europe.

The main wind direction in the UK is from the south-west. In Regions 1 and 3, the prevailing summer wind direction is from the north-east.

Fig. 3.6.1 UK map of dominant wind directions and summer prevailing wind

Key recommendations

Determine wind direction and existing shelter or obstructions. See www.windfinder.com

15–30° | ideal street axis

N

South–westerly main wind direction

For best building ventilation and protection, it is recommended that buildings are skewed by 30° to the prevailing yearly or summer wind direction. Taking into account prevailing south-westerly winds in most UK locations and best winter solar gain opportunities, this means:

- a street axis 15–30° from the west axis, towards west-south-west orientation in most UK locations
- exceptions to this include Edinburgh and Plymouth. Owing to these cities' prevailing wind patterns, they would benefit from a street pattern on the east–west axis.

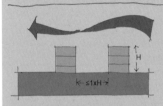

≤1xH

H

Courtyard width should equal height of building if enclosed on all sides. This will provide wind buffering and allow sufficient ventilation and winter solar gain.[20]

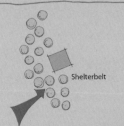

Shelterbelt

Trees and shelterbelts placed to the north-east and skewed by 30° from the main wind direction will protect buildings from cold winter winds.

→ Jump to Section 4.2.3.

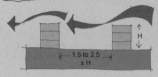

1.5 to 2.5 x H

H

If heights of buildings are greater than their spacing, there is little wind penetration. This can be a problem for dispersal of air-borne pollutants. Spacing of 1.5–2.5 times the building height is recommended for good natural ventilation, daylighting and solar gain.

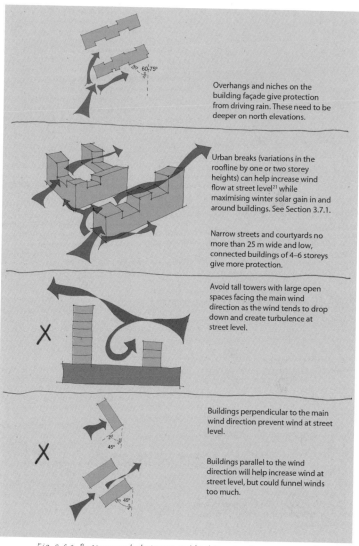

Overhangs and niches on the building façade give protection from driving rain. These need to be deeper on north elevations.

Urban breaks (variations in the roofline by one or two storey heights) can help increase wind flow at street level[21] while maximising winter solar gain in and around buildings. See Section 3.7.1.

Narrow streets and courtyards no more than 25 m wide and low, connected buildings of 4–6 storeys give more protection.

Avoid tall towers with large open spaces facing the main wind direction as the wind tends to drop down and create turbulence at street level.

Buildings perpendicular to the main wind direction prevent wind at street level.

Buildings parallel to the wind direction will help increase wind at street level, but could funnel winds too much.

Fig. 3.6.2 Recommended street and building configuration in relation to prevailing winds

3.7 USING SUNSHINE IN URBAN AREAS

Taking advantage of passive solar gain reduces a building's energy consumption. It also helps to create enjoyable outdoor spaces. Low buildings and open spaces which are oriented to the sun create a positive microclimate in winter. This extends the 'outdoor season' and reduces space heat demand in dwellings by around 15%.[22]

Free heat coming from the sun is important but it is not essential for designing low carbon dwellings. It should not be maximised at the expense of good urban design or if it will jeopardise other factors such as good views, enclosure, existing urban grid, accessibility and security. There's also a risk of summer overheating.
———⟶ Jump to Chapter 6.

Reduced solar gain can be offset by higher fabric energy efficiency standards. Uses such as dwellings, nurseries and housing for the elderly should be prioritised for sites with solar gain.

To illustrate: 1 m² of a double-glazed, unobstructed window facing directly south in Region 4 (South of England and Wales) typically receives an amount of heat energy (190 kWh/m²)[23] from the sun in the course of one year equivalent to the amount released from the body of a single person working within that space. This illustrates that it is not always demanding to offset reduced solar gain by other measures.

In well-insulated buildings, solar gain can provide 10–20% of yearly space heating demand.[24] However, design should not rigidly prioritise southerly orientation. Urban breaks can be a good compromise: they add interest and also aid urban ventilation. See Section 3.7.1.

Key recommendations
....

- Determine sun path and existing shelter/obstructions.
- Design with solar access during February–October in mind but accept that in mid-winter this may not be possible.
- The façade should face directly south, ideally no more than 30° off the east–west axis. However, in most UK locations, after taking prevailing wind conditions into account, this means a predominant west-south-west streetpattern, within 15–30° from the east–west axis. See key recommendations Section 3.6.

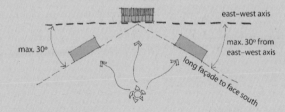

Ideal residential building orientation

east–west axis

max. 30° from east–west axis

max. 30°

long façade to face south

Ideal residential street orientation
See also Figure 3.6.2.

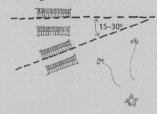

15–30°

Fig. 3.7.1 Urban solar access

- Recommended street spacing is 1.5–2.5 times the building height. In a typical development with 2–4 storey buildings, streets and open spaces have to be 25–30 m wide to prevent overshadowing. However, distances should not be increased to the extent that they create 'rural' wind conditions and over-exposure and jeopardise positive overlooking. Instead, open space width should be:
  - mews: 7–8 m width but maximum 2 storey height
  - typical residential street: 10–15 m
  - squares: 25 m and 4–6 storey height is appropriate.
- Land use on the north–south street axis is ideally suited to commercial or other facilities which do not require solar gain. These east–west facing buildings will also temper the south-westerly winds.
- Alternatively, distant spacing can create squares and open spaces with a side elevation to the south. But this will impact on sustainable building densities and walkability. See Sections 3.3. and 3.4.
- Locate entrances on north/north-east and allow for larger windows and greater floor-to-ceiling heights on the ground floor.
- Introduce urban breaks to increase solar access on street level and between buildings. See Section 3.7.1.
- Plan to allow a view of the sky.

3.7.1 Urban breaks

Urban breaks allow sunlight into buildings, streets and open spaces. They allow air pollution to dissipate from between buildings at street level and increase ventilation both at street level and within buildings. Different building heights also add interest to urban spaces, but this less compact building form needs to be offset with high fabric energy efficiency standards.

If finished in light or reflective surface materials, side elevations of urban breaks can very effectively reflect daylight and sunlight back into spaces.

Key recommendations

- Use them particularly in mews and standard streets (if the street is narrower than 25 m width).
- Use them to provide variety and a useful and accessible roofscape.
- Locate slightly taller buildings to the north-east of the site: this protects from winds without overshadowing. Lower buildings should be on the south with flat or low-pitched roofs. Height difference is ideally only one or two storeys, but less than twice the average surrounding building height to avoid wind turbulence at higher levels.
- The width of the urban breaks should be 3–5 m minimum to avoid wind funnelling and to allow good solar access between and beyond the breaks. They can also be used as open spaces, roof terraces, play areas, etc.
- This also aids good Vertical Sky Component (VSC). (See Section 3.7.3.)

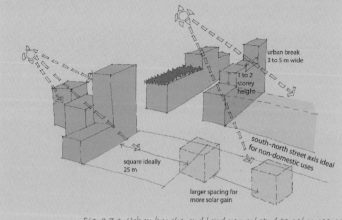

Fig. 3.7.2 Urban breaks and land use related to solar access

3.7.2 Rethinking single-aspect dwellings

Ideally, each building should have two orientation aspects. These should maximise passive solar gain and allow cross-ventilation. Many design and local authority guidelines recommend that single-aspect units should face south or south-west. North-facing single-aspect dwellings are usually not allowed. However, this can lead to excessive solar heat gain, particularly given our increasing temperatures.

Key recommendations

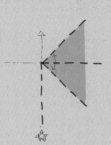

- Depth of plan should never exceed 6 m.
- Single-aspect is only ever suitable for one-bedroom dwellings and buildings not requiring solar gain. It is inappropriate for larger dwellings.
- Increase fabric efficiencies and particularly window performance in single-aspect units.
- Always provide external solar shading unless facing north.
  ⟶ Jump to Chapter 6.
- Where solar gain is undesirable, orient single-aspect buildings or spaces to face east or north.
- In winter, an additional 10–15% (on average) of passive heating energy can be gained by maximising solar gain in single-aspect units.
- Where solar gain is desirable, such as in dwellings (see Fig. 3.7.3):
  - in Region 1, orient single-aspect dwellings south to east
  - in Regions 2, 3 and 4, orient dwellings to south-east and north-east
  - avoid single western aspects to prevent night-time overheating in bedrooms.

Ideal single-aspect orientation

Region 1

Regions 2, 3 & 4

Fig. 3.7.3 Single-aspect dwellings

3.7.3 Spacing for good daylighting: the Vertical Sky Component

The Vertical Sky Component is a measure of daylighting potential. It is expressed as the percentage of daylight falling from an unobstructed sky onto a vertical window, in comparison to the amount of daylight falling onto a horizontal plane under the same sky and at that same point. It is usually measured at 2 m from the ground. Ideally it should be as close to 40% as possible,[25] although this is usually only achieved in rural areas and in high-rise blocks with unobstructed windows. It is indicative of good daylighting in the following conditions (Fig. 3.7.4):
- Region 1 (Scotland): angle h is minimum 22°. This correlates with a vertical sky component of 29%.
- Regions 2, 3 and 4: angle h is minimum 25°. This correlates with a vertical sky component of 27%.

Often this cannot be achieved in urban areas, particularly on lower floors. However, good daylighting can be achieved by:
- angling the window to the sky
- increasing floor to ceiling heights
- increasing height of window
- reflecting daylight with nearby obstructions.

A Vertical Sky Component calculator is available at: www.waterslade.com

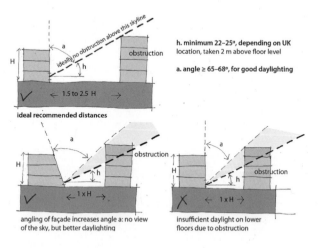

Fig. 3.7.4 Vertical Sky Component diagram and ideal building spacing

Code for Sustainable Homes credits (Hea 1, Ene 9), EcoHomes credits (Hea 1) and BREEAM credits (Hea 1)

3.8	**FUTURE-PROOFING THE SITE**

At the master planning stage, not all environmental considerations can be implemented owing to financial and technological constraints. This doesn't mean that they can't be planned for. Getting the basics right is crucial: it will allow future generations to 'plug into' a sustainable master plan.

In particular, the potential for renewable energy technologies can be designed for today but not implemented until such technologies become financially/technically viable.

3.8.1 Planning for infrastructure

In developments where roads are either being laid out for the first time or being significantly reconfigured, there is an opportunity for new infrastructure and utilities such as:
- dual greywater and mains water pipework provision
- district heating pipework
- sufficient space for plant rooms ——⤳ Jump to Chapter 6
- space for SUDS and longer-term water storage ——⤳ Jump to Chapter 5
- space for innovative waste collection and treatment such as vacuum chutes and on-site waste separation
- space for local waste processing, leading to local energy production (e.g. Biogas) ——⤳ Jump to Chapters 10 and 12
- space and infrastructure for alternative transportation modes, including cycle lanes, car pools and electric car charging points.

3.8.2 Planning for low and zero carbon technologies

Always allow for the future addition of low and zero carbon technologies. It is recommended to:
- orient roof angle due south, taking overshadowing from adjacent buildings into account
- provide primary energy infrastructure so that minimal connections and adaptations will be required
- provide sufficient space for plant rooms

3.9 APPLICABLE LEGISLATION AND GUIDANCE

- BREEAM2011 Technical Manual www.breeam.org/BREEAM2011SchemeDocument/
- *Code for Sustainable Homes Technical Guide*, November 2010
- Department for Communities and Local Government (England, Wales and Northern Ireland)
- EcoHomes 2006 – The environmental rating for homes: The Guidance – 2006/ Issue1.2 April 2006 (Scotland)
- England and Wales: Building Regulations A, C, L
- Northern Ireland: Technical booklet A, C, D, L
- Planning Policy Guidance 17: Planning for open space, sport and recreation 24 July 2002
- PPS1 Climate Change Supplement, 17 December 2007 (England)
- Scotland: Sections 1; 3.1, 3.4, 6 of the Technical Handbooks

3.10 FURTHER READING

- Barton & Tsourou (2000), *Healthy Urban Planning*, Taylor & Francis Ltd
- BRE, Potential implications of climate change in the built environment, 2000
- CE257, Daylighting in Urban areas: A guide for designers, Energy Saving Trust, September 2007, www.energysavingtrust.org.uk
- CIRIA, 2005, C638, Climate change risks in buildings – an introduction
- CLG 2007, 'Improving the flood performance of new buildings – Flood resilient construction'
- Climate Change Toolkit 07, Designing for Flood Risk (RIBA)
- Eco-towns Prospectus, Department for Communities and Local Government 23 July 2007, www.communities.gov.uk
- Erell *et al.* (2011), *Urban Microclimate: Designing the spaces between buildings*, Earthscan, London
- *Facing up to Rising Sea Levels*, RIBA, ICE, www.buildingfutures.org.uk
- Garmory *et al.* (2009), *Landscape Architect's Pocket Book*, Architectural Press
- GLA, 2005, Adapting to climate change: a checklist for development. Guidance on designing developments in a changing climate. Improving the flood performance of new buildings
- Good Practice Guide 245 *Desktop guide to daylighting – for architects*, 1998, Building Research Energy Conservation Support Unit
- Improving the Flood Performance of New Buildings, Flood Resilient Construction, (2007), DEFRA, CIRIA
- Littlefair *et al.* (2000), Environmental Site Layout Planning, BRE
- Llewellyn-Davies (2007), Urban Design Compendium, English partnerships www.urbandesigncompendium.co.uk/
- Pedersen (2009), *Sustainable Compact City*, Arkitektens Forlag
- Pitt review recommendations. Learning lessons from the 2007 floods (June 2009), www.environment-agency.gov.uk
- www.architecture.com/climatechange

Chapter 4
Urban greenery and biodiversity

Biodiversity is an important facet of sustainable building, bringing social, economic and environmental benefits to any development. Not only can energy consumption in buildings be reduced by thoughtful planting, but urban greenery can also improve residents' well-being and provide a crucial habitat for local wildlife.

Provisions for biodiversity need to be carefully thought through, if the benefits are to be maximised. The positioning of vegetation in relation to buildings and green corridors needs to be closely considered, as does the type of vegetation. Native plants are essential for supporting indigenous wildlife habitats, while on the other hand some native plant species will not survive or thrive in a changing climate.

Urban vegetation also contributes to CO_2 sequestration. In addition, the principle of 'food miles' illustrates the carbon reductions that can be achieved by growing food locally.

Symbol indicates relevance to the Code for Sustainable Homes, EcoHomes & BREEAM.

4.1   URBAN NATURE AND BIODIVERSITY BENEFITS

There are many benefits to introducing nature into urban areas:

Social sustainability
- improved quality of life and a more attractive environment
- provides relief from built-up areas and gives human scale
- educational value
- marks the changing seasons with leaf changes and floral displays

Economic sustainability
- areas that are more desirable and can increase property prices by 8%[1]
- reduced energy cost, if strategically located/placed

Environmental sustainability (see Section 4.2)
- creates local microclimate by buffering extreme seasonal temperatures
- absorbs CO_2 – and generates O_2
- traps pollution from car exhausts
- can act as solar shading, reducing cooling energy needs
- buffers noise and wind, thereby reducing energy needs
- absorbs rainwater ⟶ Jump to Chapter 5
- supports wildlife habitats to provide a thriving ecosystem (see Section 4.4).

4.2   EFFECT OF VEGETATION ON ENERGY CONSUMPTION

4.2.1 Impact of vegetation in urban heat islands
. . . .

Urban areas are usually around 4–5°C warmer than the surrounding countryside. While this may be beneficial in the winter, in summer it may lead to overheating in buildings and exacerbate health issues. Reducing CO_2 locally and globally benefits the environment as well as human health, while providing active cooling is likely to increase CO_2 emissions. During the daytime, soil evaporation and the shade from trees creates a 'park cool island' effect, with temperatures in parks 2–3°C lower than the surroundings.[2] The larger the green space, the greater its tempering effect, although this effect can still be felt with spaces as small as 10 m diameter.[3]

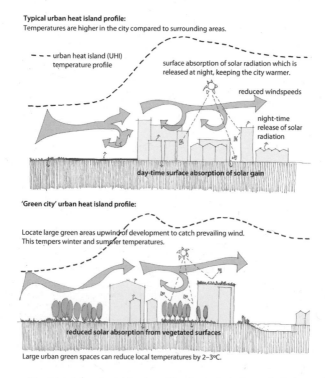

Typical urban heat island profile:
Temperatures are higher in the city compared to surrounding areas.

– – – urban heat island (UHI) temperature profile

surface absorption of solar radiation which is released at night, keeping the city warmer.

reduced windspeeds

night-time release of solar radiation

day-time surface absorption of solar gain

'Green city' urban heat island profile:

Locate large green areas upwind of development to catch prevailing wind. This tempers winter and summer temperatures.

reduced solar absorption from vegetated surfaces

Large urban green spaces can reduce local temperatures by 2–3ºC.

Fig. 4.2.1 Urban heat island profile of a typical city and of a 'green' city[4]

4.2.2 Benefits of green roofs and green walls

A 'cooler' city is one where light surfaces and vegetation are combined to create shade, reflect sunlight and provide cooling through evaporation. Urban vegetation, combined with light and reflective surfaces, can reduce surface temperatures by 10–20°C. There are also winter benefits if the vegetation is evergreen and sufficiently dense.

Solar reflection of different surface materials
(approximate summer surface temperatures °C in brackets)

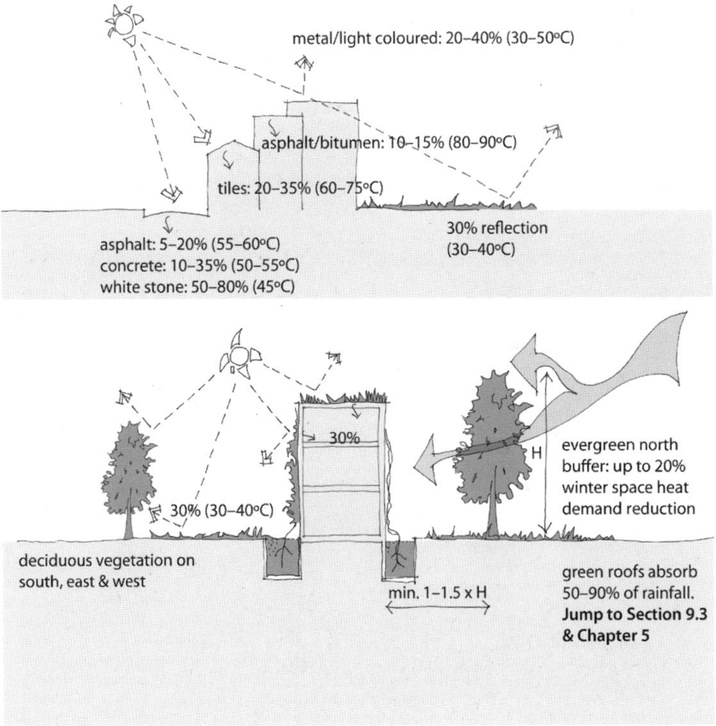

metal/light coloured: 20–40% (30–50°C)

asphalt/bitumen: 10–15% (80–90°C)

tiles: 20–35% (60–75°C)

asphalt: 5–20% (55–60°C)
concrete: 10–35% (50–55°C)
white stone: 50–80% (45°C)

30% reflection
(30–40°C)

30%

30% (30–40°C)

H   evergreen north
buffer: up to 20%
winter space heat
demand reduction

deciduous vegetation on
south, east & west

min. 1–1.5 x H

green roofs absorb
50–90% of rainfall.
**Jump to Section 9.3
& Chapter 5**

Fig. 4.2.2 Typical solar absorption and benefits of green roofs and walls[5]

Key recommendations

- Roofs with a south-west orientation are ideal for food growing and biodiversity. Where exposed to the north-east, they are ideal for biodiversity.[6]
- Several green wall proprietary systems on the market require the plants' root systems to grow horizontally. These systems should be avoided since they require a vast amount of water, energy and resources to keep the plants alive.
- Most vegetation is not suited to growing horizontal roots. Instead, allow plants to naturally grow from the ground or soil upwards.
- Place vegetation at least 400 mm away from walls or buildings to avoid a rain shadow.
- Evergreens, such as ivy, are suitable for buffering north façades.
- Plant deciduous vegetation elsewhere (virginia creeper, wisteria, vines).

4.2.3 Impact of vegetation on wind speeds

Evergreen vegetation can reduce wind speeds in winter. This minimises unwanted air-infiltration, particularly for badly insulated/non-airtight buildings. In summer, however, vegetation should not prevent natural ventilation which relies on wind speeds and air-infiltration through open windows. Year-round natural daylight and solar gain in winter should not be compromised.

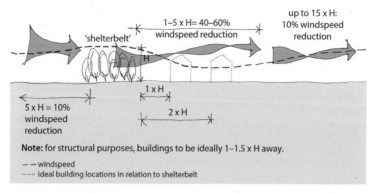

Fig. 4.2.3 Wind speed in relation to distance from trees[7]

There is a clear correlation between the location of a dense, mostly evergreen, 'shelterbelt' and the reduction of space heating demand. This is because the vegetation barrier reduces wind speeds, minimising draughts and heat losses.

Key recommendations

- The closer the building to the shelterbelt, the greater the heating energy reduction. This can be as much as 20% at a distance of 1–2 times the shelterbelt height (H). See Fig. 4.2.3.
- Ideally buildings are located within 2–5 × H.
- Vegetation must be carefully placed: too much shade will mean that buildings and external spaces no longer receive the benefit of free solar gain (see Section 4.2.4). ➔ Jump to Section 3.6
- The shelterbelt width should be 2–5 m where 5 m high, and 10–15 m wide where 25 m high.[8]
- Leaves should cover around 50% of the area, and should be more dense at the bottom than the top.[9]
- Shelterbelts with vegetation of the same height are preferable to shelterbelts which gradually increase in height.[10]

4.2.4 Vegetation as solar shading

Vegetation can be used as summer solar shading. Transparency and solar shading capacity are dependent on the species of tree and how it changes throughout its lifetime. Sufficient solar shading must be provided regardless of vegetation maturity. On average, deciduous trees provide around 80% reduction in summer solar gain but decrease desirable winter solar gain by only 30%. For tree-specific shading factors, ➔ jump to Section 6.5.

Key recommendations

To allow for winter solar gain (see Fig. 4.2.4):
- Locate deciduous trees 1–1.5 times their height away from the building. This reduces winter solar gain by 30%.
- Increasing this distance to 4–5 times the tree height allows for 100% winter solar gain, especially with evergreen trees.

For summer solar shading (see Fig. 4.2.4):
- Trees are ideally the same height as the building they are shading.
- Ideal distances are 1–1.5 times the tree height away from the building, certainly not closer. See Section 4.3.
- More than 4–5 times the tree height away is unlikely to have any summer solar shading effect.

WINTER (Solar gain with deciduous vegetation)

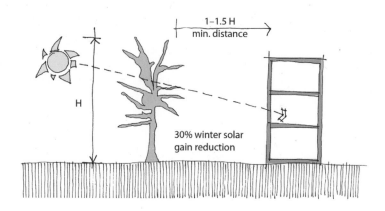

1–1.5 H
min. distance

H

30% winter solar
gain reduction

SUMMER (Solar shading with vegetation)

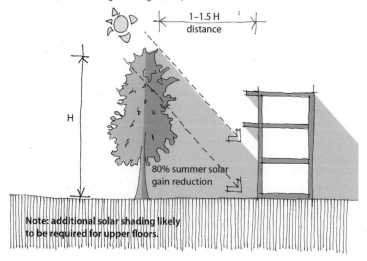

1–1.5 H
distance

H

80% summer solar
gain reduction

Note: additional solar shading likely
to be required for upper floors.

Fig. 4.2.4 Tree distance for winter/summer solar shading impact[11]

4.2.5 Vegetation and noise buffering

Vegetation helps to screen noise but it is not a sufficient noise barrier on its own. This is particularly the case in winter when there are no leaves on deciduous plants. The presence of trees does have a psychological impact: they may visually screen the source of noise and distract from it with the sound of leaves in the wind.[12]

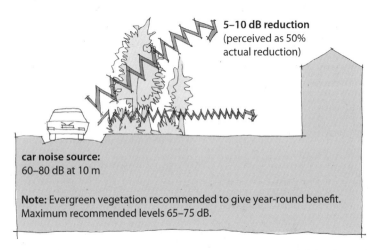

Dense, close-spaced vegetation from ground up. To be placed close to **noise source**.

5–10 dB reduction (perceived as 50% actual reduction)

car noise source: 60–80 dB at 10 m

Note: Evergreen vegetation recommended to give year-round benefit. Maximum recommended levels 65–75 dB.

Fig. 4.2.5 Distance noise source and vegetation and dBA reduction[13]

Noise reductions up to 5–10 dBA can be achieved if dense evergreen vegetation is located near the noise source.[14] Often this is enough to eliminate the noise as a perceived problem.

In selecting planting and location for noise buffering, remember also to:
- select native species which support local biodiversity (see Section 4.5)
- take into account distance between vegetation and buildings with regard to daylight, winter solar gain and structural considerations
- appoint an acoustic consultant if the development is within 20 m of a bus route, 50 m of a major road or 150 m of a railway line, industry or outdoor leisure facility.

4.3   OTHER CONSIDERATIONS FOR THE POSITIONING OF TREES CLOSE TO BUILDINGS

Alongside wind, solar and noise buffering considerations, the protection of the trees and buildings themselves must be considered. A tree protection plan needs to be submitted to the local authorities. However, given the practicalities of construction and site access, this is often not enough to protect on-site vegetation.

Appropriate minimum distances are needed in order to:
- protect the tree with temporary scaffolding during site works and avoid compaction of its roots from excessive traffic
- protect building foundations – distances are dependent on tree species, but generally 1–1.5 times its mature height
- control street level pollution through wind dispersal:[15]
  - allow for at least 1.5 m between crown and building façade
  - allow for 5–8 m between trees
  - mature tree not to be taller than the building

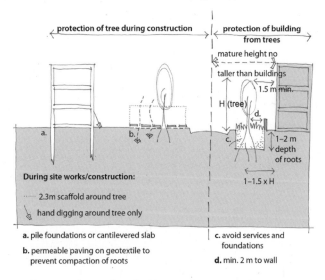

Fig. 4.3.1 Distance of trees from buildings and protection during construction[16]

Code for Sustainable Homes and EcoHomes Credits (Eco 3);
BREEAM credits (LE 2)

4.4   NATURE AND BIODIVERSITY IN URBAN AREAS

Native plant species support a diverse native wildlife. They provide food, shelter and nesting places for small mammals, amphibians, birds, butterflies, bees and other insects.

4.4.1 Continuous green corridors

Most UK cities suffer from biodiversity loss and fragmentation of wildlife habitats. The increase in hard/built-up areas leads to loss of vegetation which provides food and nesting sites.[17]

Most regions and cities have a Biodiversity Action Plan (BAP) which sets out at-risk species and ways to support their habitat. Usually this is by creating habitat corridors which connect smaller green areas with larger, more undisturbed city edge habitat areas. ⟶ Jump to Section 3.5.

Examples of wildlife-friendly green corridors:
  • wild river, pond or lake
  • railway, road and footpath edges
  • wildlife-friendly hedgerows (instead of fencing)
  • parks and meadows
  • back gardens and allotments
  • trees and urban forests
  • green roofs and walls.

Fragmentation occurs when patches of green are interrupted by roads and traffic. This isolates species from their habitat and other food or nesting sources, which affects their breeding gene pool and survival rate.[18]

Well-kept gardens and parks are not always the ideal breeding or nesting places for wildlife. Small areas such as unattended wildflower meadows and steeper or less accessible areas are better suited to providing undisturbed habitats.

Key recommendations: Site
....

- An ecological consultant should be appointed. They will advise on how best to protect and upgrade existing habitat.
- Define important and locally protected species and ways to support their habitat. Consult local and regional Biodiversity Action Plans. www.ukbap.org.uk
- Alleviate the impact of urban fragmentation: retain and strengthen/ extend existing habitat edges and increase density of greenery. Larger open spaces support a larger and more stable wildlife population.[19]
- Create continuous green habitat corridors on site, linking to larger habitats within the city and beyond.
- Interlink green corridors to provide safe crossing points for wildlife and allow dispersal of seeds and plants.[20] (Use undercrofts/green bridges to connect.)
- Specify a diverse planting selection and leave some areas/edges undisturbed.
- To avoid disease/pests and to support biodiversity, select plants from a maximum 30% of the same family, 10% of same genus and 20% of same species.[21] Always aim to select native species. Where exotic plants are chosen, ensure that they support native wildlife and do not have an invasive growth that would be a potential threat by spreading and out-competing native flora (see Section 4.5).
- Minimise light pollution/street lighting. Keep lighting away from ponds, tall trees, hedges and green corridors. Lighting should be low wattage/UV emission with bulbs protected and directed downwards.[22]
- Consider safety, accessibility and maintenance of green spaces for city inhabitants.[23]
- Consider hedges instead of constructed fences to reduce the embodied energy of landscaping.

Code for Sustainable Homes and EcoHomes Credits (Eco 1 to Eco 4); BREEAM (LE 1 to LE 5)

Key recommendations: Building

- Birds nest and bats roost in the cracks and roof voids of existing buildings. This opportunity for nesting will disappear with our current drive towards higher airtightness standards in both new and existing buildings.[24]
- We need to turn the negative impact of development into a positive support for biodiversity by creating habitat opportunities and migration routes in the landscapes and buildings we design.
- In addition to continuous green corridors at the city/site master planning scale, intentional nesting and roosting areas should be provided in the walls and roofs of buildings. These must be incorporated while maintaining high Fabric Energy Efficiency Standards (FEES). ──➔ Jump to Section 9.3.
- There are a large number of proprietary wall and roof nesting and roosting products available. Be sure, however, to specify UK-manufactured products to support native species nesting and roosting and to fit with UK standard construction/material dimensions.[25]

The following pages list species currently considered a top priority for habitat support.

4.4.2 Amphibians – detailed design recommendations

Species	Recommendations
frog, toad 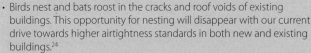 great crested newt, smooth newt	• Create more ponds, ideally surrounded by tall herb plants.[26] Improve the quality of existing ponds – decrease the levels of nitrogen and tree shading. • Use diverse plant species, but decrease invasive plant species.[27] • Ensure management of wildlife along canals by leaving wildlife edges undisturbed/inaccessible and by marking toad crossing points on roads.[28]
	Provide one water feature/pond per dwelling where individual housing, or a larger one per development.

4.4.3 Birds – detailed design recommendations

Species	Recommendations
house sparrow	• Increase suitable habitat through creation of brown roofs,[29, 30] green walls and native shrub specification (see Sections 4.2.2 and 4.5). • Increase nesting places in roofs and elsewhere.[31] • Position nesting boxes 2 m above ground, ideally facing east and 1.5 m apart.[32] • A range of manufactured systems can be embedded into walls.[33] **Provide one nesting space for every 40 buildings.[34]**
black redstart	• Increase suitable habitat through creation of green and brown living roofs.[35] • Allow for typical brownfield features, such as remnants of stony ground, vertical structures and ledges.[36]
starling	• Provide nesting and roosting opportunities at least 3 m above ground. • Place boxes 1.5 m apart. Position them on east-facing walls to prevent overheating.[37] **Provide one nesting space for every 100 buildings.[38]**
skylark	• Retain or introduce grassland, pasture, hedgerows and green/brown roofs.[39]
linnet	• Create green roofs.[40] • Leave the natural build up of moss and sedums on roofs and other surfaces where possible. • Allow for plant diversity.[41] **Provide one nesting space for every 20 buildings.[42]**
swallow	• Create more nesting opportunities inside roof spaces, particularly in outbuildings. • All that is required for access is a small opening 60 mm high and 80 mm wide. • Nests are used every year between April and September – construction activity should not disrupt during this time.[43] • Distance the nesting boxes to avoid house martins colonising them.[44] **Provide one nesting space for every 50 buildings.[45]**
peregrine falcon	• Provide nesting ledges on tall buildings of 20+ metres. • Ideally position north-east facing and with some protection from prevailing winds.[46] • Peregrines hunt the feral pigeon population. **Provide one nesting/roosting space for every medium-sized development and two for a large development.[47]**
nightjar	• Restore mossland. • Use peat-free substitutes. • Control invasive plant species such as birch.[48]

song thrush	• Likely to nest in gardens. They eat worms and snails, so limit pesticide use. • Provide tall, thick hedges for cover and nesting opportunities. • Plant wild, seed-producing plants.[49]
barn owl	• Create nesting places in tall buildings, at least 3 m above ground. • Position them facing away from prevailing winds and towards open grassland.[50] • Increase habitat in suburban and rural areas.
	Provide two nesting/roosting spaces for every medium-sized development and three for a large development.[51]
swift	• Increase nesting opportunities in roofs, eaves and under tiles. • Minimum height of 5 m for nesting boxes or access points in roofs 65 mm (w) x 30 mm (h). • Ideally position facing east and avoiding direct sun to prevent overheating.[52] • A range of manufactured systems can be embedded into walls. • Nests are used every year between April and July,[53] so avoid building work during this period.

4.4.4 Mammals – detailed design recommendations

Species	Recommendations
bats 	• Avoid use of pesticides and chemicals in roof timbers.[54] (see National Trust guidelines for safe chemicals). • Create roosting places and provide bat boxes in roofs and gardens at 2–7 m height, ideally facing south.[55, 56, 57] • A range of off-the-shelf systems can be embedded into walls and roofs.[58] • Introduce/retain broad leaf trees.
	Provide one roosting space for every 20 buildings; one for every five public buildings for horseshoe bats and bats requiring flight space to enter.[59]
hedgehog	• Hedgehogs will avoid areas frequented by badgers. • Provide a wildlife corner with piles of leaves and wood. • Avoid using slug pellets and insecticide. • Avoid any netting. • Use ramps to create access to raised ponds.[60] • Avoid nest disturbances and site works October to April.
water vole	• Protect waterside habitats and conserve wetlands.[61] • Ensure management of wildlife along canals.[62]

4.4.5 Insects – detailed design recommendations

Species	Recommendations
butterflies	• Create brown roofs or roof wildflower meadow – even up to 20 storeys high. • Provide suitable habitats of grouped plants with sequential flowering. • Leave areas of grass undisturbed and uncut, particularly in urban areas.
	Provide a diversity of flowering plants in each development, such as a wildflower meadow, either on the roof or at ground level. To be located in sun.
stag beetle	• Create heaps of dead wood in shaded areas of parks and gardens. • Avoid wood chipping of felled trees.
bee, bumble bee, solitary bee	• Provide wild flowers and sedum on vegetated roofs.[63] • Plant nectar-rich crops with sequential flowering throughout the year. • For solitary bees position undisturbed wood piles and bundles of bamboo (4 mm sections) in sunny areas.[64]
	Provide a diversity of flowering plants in each development, such as a wildflower meadow, either on the roof or at ground level. To be located in sun.

4.5   LIST OF PLANT SPECIES TO ATTRACT BIODIVERSITY

Often the seeds and flowers of exotic plants are useless to our native wildlife. Exotic plants should only be used in combination with native species. Sadly, around 70% of the UK's garden plants are exotic and this has had a negative impact on pollinating insects such as bees, bumble bees and butterflies.[65]

At the same time, not all native plant species will thrive and continue to support wildlife in the hotter and drier summers predicted for most of the UK.

Key recommendations

· Landscape irrigation requires large amounts of water.
  Rainwater harvesting is recommended. ⟶ Jump to Section 5.6.
· Usually energy is used to pump rainwater. It is more energy-efficient to design landscapes which include drought-resistant species as well as native moisture-loving species.
· Generally, plants whose leaves are small, glossy, grey-coloured, leathery or hairy can withstand drought and heat better.
· Always check local soil conditions and plant suitability.
· In wetter Scotland and Northern Ireland, it is appropriate to use mostly native drought-resistant species (see Fig. 4.5.1).
· In the drier south-eastern UK areas, however, these native species should be combined with more drought-tolerant Mediterranean plants (see Fig. 4.5.2).

Below is a list of suitable native and non-native plant species, which support UK wildlife habitats.

Fig. 4.5.1 2080 predicted climate & recommended plant species for Regions 1 & 3

Region 1 & 3 (Scotland & Northern Ireland)	2080 predicted climate: 15–20% less rain in summer and 20–25% more in winter		

Specify native planting, with increased specification of more native drought-resistant species. Plants listed below are all beneficial to native wildlife.

Native drought-resistant species		Native trees ranked in order of biodiversity benefit	Native shrubs, climbers, flowers	
honeysuckle	yew	oak	bramble	violet
ivy	broom	willow	dogwood	wood anemone
roses	heather	alder	gorse	mallow
juniper	privet	hawthorn	hazel	wild marjoram
sea holly	buckthorn (rhamnaceae)	blackthorn fruit trees	wild angelica bluebells	meadow saffron

Fig. 4.5.2 2080 predicted climate and recommended plant species for Regions 2 & 4

Region 2 & 4 (Wales & England)	2080 predicted climate: 25–30% less rain in summer and 25% more in winter		

Specify plant species as Region 1 & 3, but combine with more drought-resistant Mediterranean species (those listed below are suited to UK wildlife & winter conditions).

buddleia	echinops	phlomis	fennel
boston ivy	escallonia	potentilla (rosaceae)	oregano
virginia creeper	geranium	exotic rose	rosemary
ceanothus	san-guineum	(i.e. asia/persia)	sage
caryopteris	helichrysum	St John's wort	thyme
cistus	honeysuckle	santolina	chamomile
clematis	jasmine	sea holly	
cotinus	juniper	sedum	
	lavender	snapdragon	

Place drought-resistant plants in areas that receive most sunshine, with native plants nearer to buildings to allow shade and ease of watering. Only water native species – water them in the morning using harvested rainwater. Water 'deep' (i.e. large amounts of water infrequently, rather than daily sprinkling).

4.6 CO_2 ABSORPTION OF URBAN/SUBURBAN TREES

Planting and protecting urban trees is crucial for CO_2 absorption: the older the tree, the more carbon sequestered over its lifetime. In a large, mature urban tree, this is on average 110 tonnes of CO_2 over its lifetime. This is why timber is such a sustainable building material and why we need to protect trees during construction and development (see Section 4.3). Note that forest trees absorb less CO_2: greater competition for space means that they do not grow as large as urban trees.

Broadleaf trees, particularly fast-growing ones, absorb more CO_2 than coniferous trees (coniferous trees may even increase CO_2 in a warming climate). Native broadleaf trees generally also support a wider range of biodiversity (see Fig. 4.6.1 & 4.6.2). As they are deciduous, they can provide summer shading but still allow winter solar gain (see Section 4.2.4).

Excellent CO_2 absorbers such as the London plane are non-native and limit UK wildlife. This is actually the main reason why they are popular as urban street trees: nesting wildlife foul the pavement or cars parked underneath, which is less of an issue with non-native trees. Non-native trees should always be combined with UK native species.

Urban trees need to live for at least 5–10 years before their initial planting and 'maintenance' embodied carbon is paid back.[66]

When a tree dies, a strategy for its removal needs to be put in place. Mulching or burning will release all of the sequestered CO_2 back into the atmosphere. Landfill retains most sequestered CO_2.[67] However, if the tree is harvested for use in building/ other industries, around 80% of the tree's sequestered carbon can be retained[68] (see Fig. 4.8.1).

Fig 4.6.1 CO₂ absorption accumulated in trees, taking survival rate into account[69]

Tree species	After 60 years	Over a lifetime	Listed in order of biodiversity ranking
		tonnes CO₂	
broadleaf, slow growing: oak, beech, hornbeam	1.8	123 (oak: 350 yrs old)	Oak is the best UK tree for supporting native wildlife, but is not a good street tree. Beech and hornbeam are average.
broadleaf, moderate growing: hawthorn, maple, most fruit trees, silver birch	4	118 (maple: 250 yrs old)	Very good, particularly birch and hawthorn. Birch reaches 50–80 years; fruit trees 20–50 years. Note that birch is not drought-tolerant.
conifer, slow growing: Scots pine	1.4	49 (250 yrs old)	Good wildlife support: mainly birds and small mammals such as protected red squirrel.
broadleaf, fast growing, native: willow, alder, elm, ash, poplar, linden (small-leaf lime tree)	7.1	123 (200 yrs old)	Willow is particularly good but, like poplar, it is not a good street tree (invasive roots). Other species listed are average. Linden is a good pollution-resistant street tree. Elm trees are sensitive to Dutch elm disease.
conifer, fast growing: Douglas fir (non-native), pine	5.9	126 (200 yrs old)	Average wildlife support: mainly birds and small mammals such as protected red squirrel. Usually found in urban parks rather than on streets.
conifer, moderate growing: European spruce (Christmas tree), cedar	3.2	120 (250 yrs old)	
broadleaf, fast growing, non-native: London plane, horse chestnut, sycamore	7.1	123 (200 yrs old)	Limited support for native wildlife, particularly the London plane. Sycamore supports aphids and so attracts birds and bats. (All non-native trees; London plane is a particularly good street tree.)

Fig 4.6.2 CO_2 sequestration rates by tree type (cumulative total by age of tree)[70]

	Broadleaf trees speed of growth			Pine/conifers speed of growth		
	Slow	Moderate	Fast	Slow	Moderate	Fast
	oak, hornbeam, beech	hawthorn, maple, silver birch, most fruit trees	horse chestnut, London plane, sycamore, willow, alder, elm, ash, poplar, linden	Scots pine	European spruce, cedar	Douglas fir, pine
Age	Total accumulated CO_2 absorption (kgCO_2)					
1	5	8	11	3	4	6
5	22	39	63	13	23	37
10	60	115	192	36	72	123
15	119	237	403	74	155	273
20	199	409	706	129	277	497
25	303	634	1106	202	443	804
30	433	916	1611	295	658	1204
35	589	1258	2225	409	924	1703
40	772	1663	2954	548	1246	2307
45	984	2132	3801	710	1627	3024
50	1225	2668	4771	898	2069	3860
55	1496	3274	5868	1112	2577	4819
60	1799	3951	7097	1356	3154	5911

4.7   CO$_2$ ABSORPTION OF SHRUBS AND OTHER PLANTS

Shrubs and other plants also absorb CO$_2$. However, they are regularly pruned (to contain growth) and are usually short lived (5–15 years). As wood from shrubs cannot be harvested for long-term uses, the biomass of the dead/discarded shrub is usually composted or chipped and burned. This is why shrubs and other plants are carbon neutral: they will eventually release the CO$_2$ they absorbed over their relatively short lifetime.

Green roofs and grass areas tend to be long lived. Owing to regular cutting and specific soil behaviour, a carbon equilibrium is reached whereby the plant growth is equal to the plant decomposition.[71] This means that their contribution to CO$_2$ absorption is minimal and they should be considered carbon neutral.[72]

4.8   CO$_2$ REDUCTIONS FROM URBAN AGRICULTURE/FOOD GROWING

Seasonal vegetable plants grow fast and absorb CO$_2$ during this process. However, they die at the end of each season and all of this absorbed CO$_2$ is released back into the atmosphere. Vegetables are therefore carbon neutral. The only exception to this are fruit trees: they last 20–50 years and their wood can be used for building interiors. A typical cherry tree will absorb around 400 kgCO$_2$ over its lifetime, while apple and pear trees sequester around 2.5 tCO$_2$. They are particularly suitable in gardens where fruit can be harvested by users.

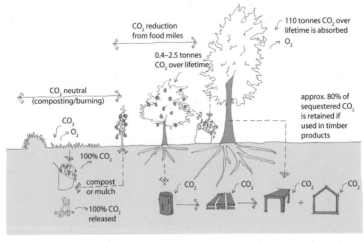

Fig. 4.8.1 CO$_2$ absorption from different urban vegetation

4.9   CO$_2$ REDUCTIONS FROM 'FOOD MILES'

Some 8% of the UK's total carbon emissions is associated with food consumption; 2.5% is from fruit and vegetable consumption.[73] In London alone, 10 million tCO$_2$ emissions yearly are food related.[74] This means that, annually, each household contributes around 1000 kgCO$_2$ from fruit and vegetable consumption and around 2000 kgCO$_2$ from meat, dairy and other processed foods.

Clearly, some CO$_2$ reductions can come from 'food miles' savings. This means growing seasonal food at or near its place of consumption instead of importing it from faraway regions. However, urban food growing is limited in its CO$_2$ reductions, as meat, dairy and other processed foods have the largest CO$_2$ impacts. This is illustrated by a 'fractional' vegetable shopping basket and its modest carbon reductions of 79 kgCO$_2$ per household per year (see Fig. 4.9.1).

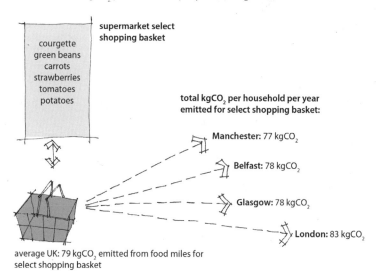

supermarket select shopping basket

courgette
green beans
carrots
strawberries
tomatoes
potatoes

total kgCO$_2$ per household per year emitted for select shopping basket:

Manchester: 77 kgCO$_2$

Belfast: 78 kgCO$_2$

Glasgow: 78 kgCO$_2$

London: 83 kgCO$_2$

average UK: 79 kgCO$_2$ emitted from food miles for select shopping basket

Fig. 4.9.1 Food mile reductions from a select 'fractional' shopping basket in different regions. Based on typical average UK consumption patterns[75]

4.9.1 Which vegetables can be grown in urban gardens?

For small gardens: aubergine, beets, broccoli, cabbage, carrots, courgette, English peas, garlic, green beans, lettuce, onions, radishes, spinach, tomatoes. All herbs.

For bigger gardens or allotments: as above, plus cantaloupes, cauliflower, cucumbers, mustard, okra, potatoes, pumpkins, runner beans, southern peas, sweetcorn, sweet potatoes, squash.

4.9.2 Typical urban food-growing yields and carbon reductions[76]

On average, 1 m^2 of land provides approx. 0.85 kg of food per year, grown in a typical suburban garden or allotment.[77] Of this yield, 90% occurs in summer. Figure 4.9.2 lists five vegetables that account for 85% of a typical yield of an urban allotment and can lead to food miles reductions of 1.5–1.6 kgCO$_2$ per m^2 of urban arable land.

Fig. 4.9.2 Typical urban food growing yields and carbon reductions

Five urban growing vegetables – approx. nr. plants	Typical Region 1 yearly 'top five' yields on a 100 m^2 plot	Approximate yearly CO$_2$ reductions from food miles savings if grown locally (garden/allotment)[78] kgCO$_2$ per year	Typical supermarket country of origin[79]
courgettes (8 plants)	40 kg	3	Spain (rail + road)
squash (6 plants)	18 kg	59	Greece (air + road)
tomatoes (in cold greenhouse) 25 plants	14 kg	61	Canary Islands, Spain (air + road)
runner beans (20 plants)	8 kg	34	Nairobi, Kenya (air + road)
chard/pak choi (15 plants)	5 kg	0.3	Spain (rail + road)
yearly total	85 kg	157 kgCO$_2$	
yearly CO$_2$ reduction:		• 1.5–1.6 kgCO$_2$ reduction per m^2 of urban food growing • 1.85 kgCO$_2$ is reduced per kg of locally grown food	

4.9.3 Composting bins: size guide

An average UK household wastes around 5 kg of organic matter per week. This takes 6–9 months to break down (leaves take 1–2 years).[80, 81]

Compost bin sizes:
- per household, 200–300 litres minimum, with ideally 750 litres[82] (0.2–1 m³)
- for larger developments, allow minimum 100 litres per person (10 m³)

Place communal composting facilities within 30 m from building/site entrances and provide small kitchen containers. Do not place near windows, doors or any ventilation intake.

 Code for Sustainable Homes (Was 1 mandatory to Was 3 and Man 1)
EcoHomes credits (Man 1 and Mat 4), BREEAM credits (Wst 3)

4.10   APPLICABLE LEGISLATION AND GUIDANCE

- Biodiversity Action plans (BAP), Habitat Action Plan (HAP), Species Action Plan (SAP)
- BS 5837 (2005) 'Trees in Relation to Construction'
- CIRIA, C567/C502 & C503
- Conservation (natural habitats) Regulations 1994 & Nature Conservation & Amenity Lands Order 1985; The Conservation (natural habitats) Regulations 1995 and Environment Order 2002 (Northern Ireland)
- Natural Environment and Rural Communities Act 2006 (England & Wales)
- NPPG4, Natural Heritage & PAN 60 Planning for natural heritage (Scotland)
- PAS 2010:2006: Planning to halt loss of biodiversity
- PPS2, Planning and nature conservation (Northern Ireland)
- PPS9, Biodiversity & geological conservation (2005) (England)
- RSPB (1997), Good practice aid for prospective development
- TAN5 nature conservation and planning (Wales)
- The nature conservation Act 2004 (Scotland)
- Wildlife and Countryside Act 1981 (as amended) and Wildlife NI Order 1985 (Northern Ireland)

4.11   FURTHER READING

- Beer & Higgins (1999), *Environmental Planning for Site development*, Taylor and Francis
- Defra, 2005, The Validity of Food Miles as an Indicator of Sustainable Development Final Report
- Erell (2011), *Urban microclimate, designing the spaces between buildings*, Earthscan Ltd
- Filipi (2008), *The dry gardening handbook, plants and practices for a changing climate*
- Goddard (2009), *Scaling up from gardens: biodiversity conservation in urban environments*, Trends in Ecology and Evolution, Elsevier
- Hessayon (2009), *The green garden expert*, Expert Books
- McMahon & Signoretta (2009), *Urban Design – Health & The Therapeutic Environment*, Architectural Press
- Natural England, Standards for accessible Urban Greenspace (ANGST)
- Natural History museum – native plant finder by postcode: www.nhm.ac.uk/nature-online/life/plants-fungi/postcode-plants/
- Santamouris (2000), *Energy and Climate in the Urban Built Environment*, James & James Ltd
- Steel (2009), *Hungry City, How food shapes our lives*, Random House
- Trees in Towns 2, 2007 (Dept of Communities and Local Government)
- UKGBC (2009), Biodiversity and the built environment.
- US Department of Energy, 'Method for calculating Carbon Sequestration by trees in urban and suburban settings'
- Vernont et al. (2009), *Landscape Architect's Pocketbook*, Elsevier
- Viljoen (2005), CPULS: *Continuous Productive Urban Landscapes, Designing Urban Agriculture For Sustainable Cities*, London, Elsevier
- Williams (2010), *Biodiversity for Low and Zero Carbon Buildings: A Technical Guide for New Build*, RIBA Publishing

Chapter 5
Water and flooding

Environmental design must work with water rather than against it. This is a primary consideration which will become even more important in a changing climate:
• Increased flooding due to extreme rainfall events is anticipated.
• At the same time, increased periods of drought and water shortages are expected.

Careful consideration is no longer a luxury: where to build, which building typology, how much land to set aside for water storage and which surface finishes are more resilient are now vital decisions for design. Allowing water run-off to soak-away on site instead of connection to sewers is nearly always the preferred option.

Water efficiency inside buildings is also starting to be regulated. Water-efficient appliances, rainwater harvesting systems and greywater recycling will eventually become embedded in building design. However, not all such systems are sustainable: it is energy intensive to treat and pump water around, and the embodied energy of the system can be significant.

Hence, careful building-specific design specification is required to avoid increasing carbon emissions in the quest to save precious water. Usually, connection to mains water supply and sewers is the most suitable option.

 Symbol indicates relevance to the Code for Sustainable Homes, EcoHomes & BREEAM.

5.1 FLOOD RISK AND LIVING WITH WATER

There are around 1.85 million dwellings at risk from flooding in England and Wales alone. In England, 11% of dwellings are built in flood risk areas, most of which are in London.[1] The factors contributing to increased flood risk are:
- pressure to build on new land, which decreases permeable surfaces
- runoff from hard surfaces
- increased intense rainfall events due to climate change.

Flood risk is expressed as the likelihood that a flood will occur in a given year. There are four flood zones, ranging from zone 1, the lowest risk, to zone 3b, the highest. Zone 1 is at risk of flood less than once every 1000 years and all development is suitable, while in zone 3, or zones with a risk of flooding more than once every 75 years, it is usually impossible to insure dwellings.[2]

Flooding is likely to affect more people in a changing climate,[3] particularly near coastal areas and rivers and in the south of the UK, where the landmass is slowly sinking.[4] The threat inland is changing too: climate change will alter the intensity and duration of rainfall, resulting in more urban and flash flooding. In response, we need to work with water rather than against it:
- Each site needs a flood risk assessment.
- At least 5% space needs to be made for water storage and provision of water flow channels (see Section 5.3).
- At building scale, building adaptations and different typologies need to be considered (see Section 5.2).

5.1.1 Sources of flooding

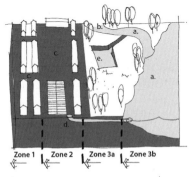

a. **Tidal flooding: sea/rivers**
b. **Fluvial flooding**
   River capacity exceeded from rain/snow
c. **Pluvial flooding**
   Rainwater or snow melting/flash floods
d. **Sewer flooding**
   At risk during storms, where combined sewers are used
e. **Other causes**
   From groundwater or blockage of man-made infrastructure

Zone 1   Zone 2   Zone 3a   Zone 3b

Fig. 5.1.1 Sources of flooding (for zones, see 5.1.2)

5.1.2 Land use planning based on flood zones
....

The four flood zones relate to the probability of sea and river flooding. They do not take into account existing defences or the risk of local flash floods.[5] Certain flood risk zones are unsuitable for development as it would place peoples' lives and property at risk.

Key recommendations
....

- Submit a site-specific flood risk assessment (FRA).
- Include sustainable urban drainage systems (SUDS), particularly for developments of 1 ha+ owing to changes in land permeability (see Section 5.3).
- Housing developments are ideally located in zones 1 or 2.
- Housing can be located on upper floors in zone 3a but should never be built in zone 3b.
- Flood risk can be checked for sea-level rises and impact on land at http://flood.firetree.net/ and at each region's Environment Agency www.environment-agency.gov.uk/flood for England and Wales, www.dardni.gov.uk/riversagency for Northern Ireland and www.sepa.org.uk/flooding for Scotland.

Land use planning based on flood zones

low flood probability (zone 1)	• less than 1 in 1000 annual probability of river/sea flooding • all uses appropriate; only zone appropriate for basement dwellings and emergency services
medium flood probability (zone 2)	• 1 in 1000 to 1 in 100 annual probability of river flooding and/or less than 1 in 200 annual probability of sea flooding • suitable for less vulnerable uses such as shops, leisure, assembly halls, restaurants, workshops and storage
high flood probability (zone 3a)	• more than 1 in 100 annual probability of river flooding and/or greater than 1 in 200 annual probability of sea flooding • suitable for defence, open spaces, marinas, sewage and water infrastructure; avoid ground-floor dwellings and locate residential uses higher than less vulnerable uses as in zone 2
functional floodplain (zone 3b)	• more than 1 in 20 annual probability of flooding; this is land which regularly floods and acts as a water storage area • can be developed with limited uses but should be avoided where possible, but do not reduce flood plain storage if developed • mainly suitable for open space and outdoor recreation as well as marinas, sewage and water infrastructure • warning and evacuation plan required

5.1.3 Flood mitigation: building typologies that work with water

A. Sacrificial basement/ ground floor

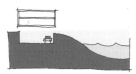

A raised ground floor with water retention in the basement (storage/car park) area, with residential at first floor. Suitable in zones 1 & 2.
This typology can lead to poor-quality street levels and security issues. Better to put workshop uses with less vulnerability on ground floor and vulnerable uses above to create active frontages. Move all equipment etc. above flood risk level. See Section 5.2.

B. Building on stilts

Useful in a flood inundation area; but still needs protection from breakwaters to avoid debris damaging stilts structurally. Suitable in zone 3a. Difficult in an urban environment: issue with the undercroft and aerial walkways, usually lacking surveillance and ownership, leading to poor-quality street level and security issues. Lift or ramps required. Nothing can really grow under the stilts, to utilise as open space. Workshop/community infill space could be useful.

C. Floating buildings

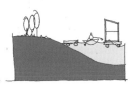

Ground floor rises with water levels up to around 5.5 m. Usually built with EPS polystyrene slabs, with concrete screed over, to achieve floating ground floor base. Suitable in zone 3a/3b. Good for areas where inundation can be controlled. Building on water avoids the need to reclaim land. Services to be encased in flexible pipework to allow vertical movement of buildings. Connection to a floating pier and mooring posts required. Most suited to smaller buildings. Usually low thermal mass buildings, which may lead to issues of summer overheating. Not many UK precedents, but more common in Netherlands.

D. Flood-resilient or 'wet-proofed' buildings

'Wet-proofed' buildings are designed with possible future flooding in mind and with minimal damage to the property when this happens. This may be achieved through the use of water-resistant materials for floors, walls and fixtures and the siting of electrical controls, cables and appliances at a higher than normal level. If the lowest floor level is raised above the predicted flood level, allow ramp access for disabled users. Suitable in all zones. See Section 5.2.

5.1.4 Flood design response: checklist for site development

Developments should only be built in areas of low flood risk. Even where sites are not at risk of river or sea flooding, the development itself will change the permeability of the land. This will impact on storm water runoff and local flooding conditions.

Flood design response checklist	☑ ☒
Flood risk assessment (FRA)	
At feasibility stage, has account been taken of future climate change impacts, including floodwater volume and height over a 100-year period?	☐
Has a flood risk assessment been done at initial feasibility stage? (This is usually required when submitting a planning application.)	☐
Have the local and regional authorities and environment agencies been consulted at feasibility stage? Refer to Planning Policy Statement 25: Development and Flood Risk (PPS25).	☐
Land use planning (see Section 5.1.2)	
Have more vulnerable uses been located in safe zones 1 and 2?	☐
Have ground floors been reserved for non-residential uses such as workshops?	☐
Are there safe escape routes and refuge areas on higher ground?	☐
Has infrastructure been located at higher levels?	☐
Are there raised areas, walls and barriers that could slow floods and 'defend' the site?	☐
Flood risk reduction: landscape/site response (see Section 5.3)	
Has at least 5% of the site area been allowed for flood plain areas with floodwater storage capacity? (These large open spaces also have biodiversity and recreational value.)	☐
Have water flow channels been designed into the landscape?	☐
Are there SUDS for water attenuation – min. 5% of site area?	☐
Has planning permission been obtained, where more than 5 m² of front garden area is to be paved with impermeable surfaces (for new and existing developments)?[6]	☐

Mitigation: building typology (see Section 5.1.3)	
Is the ground floor above flood risk level?	☐
Has the building typology been adapted to minimise damage: sacrificial basements and ground floors, stilts or floating buildings?	☐
Are all habitable rooms raised above the flood risk height?	☐
Have the buildings been designed to be flood-resilient? (This is particularly suitable where the risk is of a low flood water depth rather than flood inundation.) See Section 5.2.	☐

Code for Sustainable Homes credits (Sur 1 mandatory and Sur 2), EcoHomes credits (Pol 3 and Pol 5) and BREEAM credits (Pol 3)

5.2   FLOOD-RESILIENT BUILDING DESIGN

Flood-resilient buildings are 'wet-proofed', designed with future flooding in mind. Property damage may be minimised by raising the ground floor above the predicted flood level. It may also be minimised through the use of water-resistant materials for floors, walls and fixtures and the siting of electrical controls, cables and appliances at a higher level than normal.[7] If the floor level is raised, restricted mobility access must be considered.

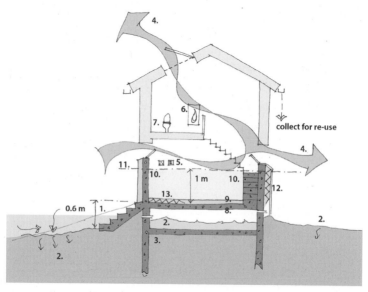

Fig. 5.2.1 A flood-resilient building: design strategies to 'wet-proof' – numbers relate to key recommendations below

Key recommendations (Fig 5.2.1)
....

- Raise ground floor above risk level. Provide ramped access and ensure compliancy with Lifetime Homes. (1)
- Provide permeable external surfaces. Include temporary flood water storage with access and outward slope if located under ground floor. Must have ability to flush out polluted water. (2)
- Concrete ground floor construction resists pressure with zero to limited damage. (3)
- Good cross-ventilation aids quick drying. (4)

Services
- Protect infrastructure and services: electrical sockets, utility meters, electrical controls, thermostats and appliances should be located at least 1 m above flood risk level. Underfloor pipework and services should be encased with rigid closed cell insulation. (5)
- Heating: locate boilers on first floor or at least 1 m above flood level; avoid underfloor heating on the ground floor. (6)
- WC and drainage: use non-return gate valves to prevent back-flow. (7)

Floors
- Ground floors: solid concrete at least 150 mm thick, resistant to uplift forces. Suspended floors generally not recommended, unless a flood storage area is provided. Unprotected steel reinforcement may corrode. If the risk is high, use stainless steel or galvanised mild steel and inspect after flooding. Damp-proof membranes: polyethylene 1200 gauge + taped 300 mm overlap or liquid applied. (8)
- Floor finishes and skirting: hard-wearing materials which are water-resistant and easy to clean (e.g. ceramic/stone or concrete tiles, sand/cement screeds). Use water-resistant grout and tooth-combed adhesive. Avoid timber finishes. Mortar below in flood zone: 1:3 (cement/sand). (9)

Walls
- Ground-floor walls: use impermeable materials and easily cleaned finishes up to 1 m above flood level, e.g. water-resistant renders, engineering bricks and tiles, cement renders and plaster. Stairs should have same water-resistant finish up to 1 m above flood level. Avoid plasterboard unless sacrificial, but sacrificial construction should be avoided where possible. (10)
- Internal partitions: avoid hollow construction. Use solid unperforated brick or dense aggregate concrete blocks. Avoid timber-framed walls. Avoid timber panel products and other wood board finishes; steel-framed walls are more suitable than timber-framed, but the finishing layers will be sacrificial. Avoid hollow core doors. (11)

Insulation
- Wall insulation: best combined with external renders or partial-fill cavity. Avoid full-fill cavity. Use non-organic and water resistant (rigid, closed cell/surface, non-porous) insulation, such as XPS or PUR, phenolic foam and cellular glass. (12)
- Ground insulation: place above slab to reduce water impact. (13)

 Code for Sustainable Homes credits (Sur 2), EcoHomes credits (Pol 5) and BREEAM credits (Pol 3)

5.3 RAIN GARDENS AND SUSTAINABLE URBAN DRAINAGE SYSTEMS (SUDS)

Water run off is usually diverted to storm water sewers. The UK's increased risk of urban flooding is compounded by swollen mains sewers and increased impermeable surfaces in our urban areas as well as a changing climate. In dense urban areas, only 3–25% of rainwater percolates to the soil. This depletes the groundwater table and puts mains sewers under pressure to carry this water away.[8] This can lead to localised 'flash floods'. Sustainable urban drainage systems, or 'rain gardens', intercept the water runoff and retain it temporarily before slowly releasing it back to the mains sewers.

Key recommendations

....

- SUDS do not always prevent flooding, but delay inundation and reduce damage to infrastructure.
- SUDS exist at different scales. They can act as public open spaces and help support biodiversity.
- Usually around 5–10% of a site, in the lowest lying terrain, should be earmarked for water retention.[9]
- SUDS are ideally a hybrid of systems (see Fig. 5.3.1). Typically around 500–850 m³ should be allowed for per hectare of land (see Section 5.3.1).
- All systems are dependent on soil condition and regional rainfall.
- Environment Agency and planning authority approval need to be obtained.
- Often issues of adoption are encountered with local authorities.

Fig. 5.3.1   Summary of sustainable urban drainage systems (read with Fig. 5.3.2)

		Biodiversity?	Urban?	Suburban?	Rural?
Building-scale interventions					
Green roofs (a)	reduce water available for harvesting/runoff by 50–90%. ⟶ Jump to Chapter 9	✓	✓	✓	✓
Rainwater harvesting (b)	minimal flood prevention. See Section 5.6	X	✓	✓	✓

	Biodiversity?	Urban?	Suburban?	Rural?
Streetscape interventions: limited and temporary storage				
Permeable paving (c) a hard surface (often 'open pavers') interspersed with vegetation and with drainage layer below, usually gravel or water collecting channel				
• always recommended for large car park areas, private pavements/roads and outdoor spaces • outflow to larger basin required	X	✓	✓	✓
Filter drain/ditch or channel (d) either open water channels or trenches filled with stones/gravel, usually at bottom of inclination/slope – safety issue with open water channels				
• suitable along road, car parks and public open spaces as well as overflows of lawn area • can be planted to increase biodiversity • size 5–15% of land area (0.5 m deep)[10] • outflow to larger basin required	X	✓	✓	X
Larger development/neighbourhood scale interventions				
Soakaway and swales (e) lined underground trenches (1.5 m deep) which do not store water but allow it to soak directly into soil or run off into a larger collection pond or sewer				
• unsuitable in clay soils • swales are vegetated/grassed • size: 2–5% of land area[11] • outflow to soil or pond required	✓	X	✓	✓
Ponds and wetlands (reedbeds) (f) a biological ground system with vegetation and reeds				
• always wet, designed to take more water in heavy rainfall • higher maintenance but good for treating roadside pollution • usually used as the final destination for flood waters or to slowly release to mains sewers • size 3–5% of land area (0.6–1 m deep)[12]	✓	X	✓	✓
Retention pond/basin (g) temporary water storage under or above ground in hard landscape				
• outflow required with slow release to other systems • usually dry, but can be designed to be permanent water basin and to hold more in extreme events • size >1% of land area (5 m deep)[13]	X	✓	X	X

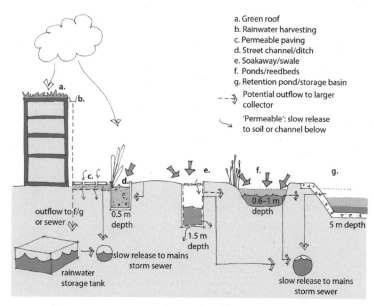

a. Green roof
b. Rainwater harvesting
c. Permeable paving
d. Street channel/ditch
e. Soakaway/swale
f. Ponds/reedbeds
g. Retention pond/storage basin

- - -> Potential outflow to larger collector

'Permeable': slow release to soil or channel below

outflow to f/g or sewer

0.5 m depth

1.5 m depth

0.6–1 m depth

5 m depth

rainwater storage tank

slow release to mains storm sewer

slow release to mains storm sewer

Fig. 5.3.2 Sustainable urban drainage systems diagram –
read with Fig. 5.3.1 (p.106–7)

5.3.1 How much water needs to be collected to prevent flooding?

The drainage system size will depend on many factors, including:
- average yearly rainfall and extreme events
- runoff coefficient of land or surface to be drained (see Fig. 5.6.3)
- soil type and permeability

SUDS calculator: http://geoservergisweb2.hrwallingford.co.uk/uksd/sudsguidancedocument.htm

On-site water storage volume per hectare of urban development.
(Based on city's soil conditions and rainfall events. Based on hybrid of long-term and short-term attenuation and 3% permeable surfaces.)

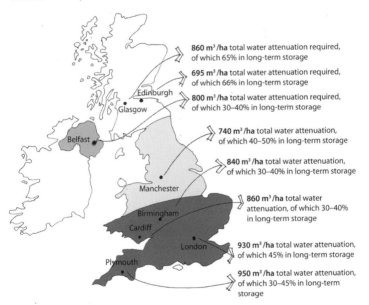

860 m³/ha total water attenuation required, of which 65% in long-term storage

695 m³/ha total water attenuation required, of which 66% in long-term storage

800 m³/ha total water attenuation required, of which 30–40% in long-term storage

740 m³/ha total water attenuation, of which 40–50% in long-term storage

840 m³/ha total water attenuation, of which 30–40% in long-term storage

860 m³/ha total water attenuation, of which 30–40% in long-term storage

930 m³/ha total water attenuation, of which 45% in long-term storage

950 m³/ha total water attenuation, of which 30–45% in long-term storage

Note: Above volumes are 'worst case scenario' figures. For 25% urban permeability, reduce storage volume by 30% and by 15% if no long-term attenuation provided.

Fig. 5.3.3 Regional water attenuation volume, based on 1 ha urban development

Code for sustainable homes credits (Sur 1 mandatory), EcoHomes credits (Pol 3) and BREEAM credits (Pol 3)

5.4 HOUSEHOLD WATER USAGE: HOW MUCH DO WE USE, AND WHAT IS ITS CO$_2$ IMPACT?

On average, each person uses around 150 litres of water per day,[14] while the carbon footprint of water usage is around 130 kgCO$_2$ per household per year.[15] However the energy required for water supply and wastewater removal and treatment accounts for only 11% of water's carbon footprint.[16]

Even greater carbon emissions are associated with hot water provision, which accounts for around 60% of domestic water usage. Heating water contributes around 1000 kgCO$_2$ per household per year.[17] This brings the carbon footprint of a typical household's water consumption to 1130 kgCO$_2$ per year.

Figure 5.4.1 gives a detailed regional breakdown of water usage and carbon impact per person. Note that unmetered households tend to consume 15–20% more water. Only unmetered data for Northern Ireland was available.

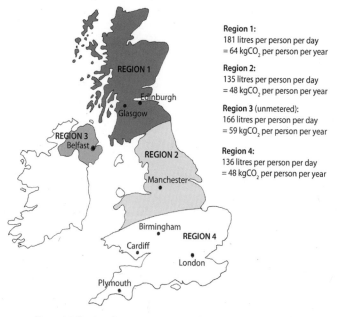

Region 1:
181 litres per person per day
= 64 kgCO$_2$ per person per year

Region 2:
135 litres per person per day
= 48 kgCO$_2$ per person per year

Region 3 (unmetered):
166 litres per person per day
= 59 kgCO$_2$ per person per year

Region 4:
136 litres per person per day
= 48 kgCO$_2$ per person per year

Fig. 5.4.1 Regional water use per person per day and annual CO$_2$ impact

5.4.1 How is water used in a household?

Fig 5.4.2 Water consumption breakdown and CO$_2$ impact

average uses[18]	%	litres per day per person	household kgCO$_2$ per year
toilet flushing	30	45	40
personal washing – baths and taps	13	19.5	17
personal washing – shower[19] (based on a 5 min shower)	20	30	25
clothes washing	13	19.5	17
drinking water	4	6	5
washing up (mostly hand wash)	8	12	10
outdoor	7	10.5	9
other	5	7.5	7
CO$_2$ impact of water supply and treatment.[20]		150	130 kgCO$_2$ per year per household
Additional 1000 kgCO$_2$ per household per year for energy needed to heat hot water			1000 kgCO$_2$
Total per household per year			1130 kgCO$_2$

5.4.2 Toilets and water consumption

Around one-third of all water is used for toilet flushing. Figure 5.4.3 shows how this can be reduced by 50% or more if inefficient cisterns of 9 litres per flush are replaced, for example, with dual-flush WCs. If the WC cannot be replaced, water consumption can still be reduced by 10–30% by placing a 'save a flush' bag or bottle in the cistern.[21]

Fig. 5.4.3 WC water consumption and kgCO$_2$ emissions per household per year[22]

	typical WC pre-1991	low/dual flush WC	WC with recycled basin water[23]	vacuum WC[24]	compost WC (tank size 1 m^3)
litres per flush	9	4/2.5	4.5/3	1.5	0–2.5
approx. purchase cost	–	£100	£455	£1175	£1350
kg/CO$_2$ emissions annually[25]	40	17	8.3	6	0

5.4.3 Shower or bath? How much water and CO$_2$ do they use?

The average bath uses 80 litres of water. Compared to a bath, 5 minutes in a standard mixer shower reduces CO$_2$ emissions and water use by around 65%. Carbon and water savings are of course compromised if showers are used for longer.

Key recommendations

- Always specify water efficient appliances as a priority over recycling systems. See Section 5.5.
- Specify thermostatic shower mixers.
- Specify more compact baths with lower water capacity.
- Avoid power showers.
- Avoid electrically heated showers. Although they achieve modest water savings, their total CO$_2$ emissions are higher than for a standard shower.
- Never specify outdoor spas (they use up to 1500 litres of water).
- Design must strike a balance between water savings and CO$_2$ emissions, and in particular where small water efficiencies are achieved and higher CO$_2$ emissions result from electrical energy use.

Fig. 5.4.4 kgCO$_2$ from shower/bath usage

Personal washing and carbon emissions
(CO$_2$ emissions from water supply, wastewater treatment and water heating)

	bath large	bath standard	power shower 16 litres per min	bath small/ corner	shower electric[26]	shower standard[27]
max. capacity (overflow) in litres	250	225	–	140–165	–	–
usage based on 5 minute shower (litres)	100	88	80	65	24	30
kgCO$_2$ per single usage	0.92	0.86	0.75 (500W pump)	0.63	0.33	0.25
kgCO$_2$ per year per household	806	753	657	552	289	219

Above figures are based on one bath/shower per person per day. In reality, usage patterns are likely to be a hybrid of bath and shower. As showers are likely to be used 60% of time, this would lead to a carbon footprint of 400 kgCO$_2$ per year per household for personal washing. If water needs to be pumped to provide sufficient pressure, add approximately 1% of the space and water heating demand.[28]

5.4.4 Appliances and tap types: water usage and CO$_2$ emissions

Hot-fill appliances
Hot-fill appliances achieve around 30% carbon savings.[29] These are appliances which, rather than electrically heating water, use preheated water. In the UK market, hot-fill dishwashers and washing machines are difficult to find.

Washing machines
Most washing machines are at least A-rated and use no more than 7 litres of water per kg of washing, compared to older models which use three times as much water. Carbon reductions of 40% can be achieved by washing at 40°C instead of 60°C.[30]

Fig. 5.4.5 Typical energy saving washing machines (7 kg capacity)[31]

litres per cycle	kWh per cycle	total CO$_2$ emissions (water supply, treatment and heating) based on average 270 cycles/year[32]
49	1.225	171 kgCO$_2$ per household per year

Dishwashers

Most dishwashers are at least A-rated and use less than 12 litres of water per cycle. This typically saves around 70% of water compared to hand washing. However, a dishwasher emits around 25% more CO_2 than hand washing owing to its high electrical load (Fig. 5.4.6). Specify hot-fill and best-performing appliance (A+rated).

Fig. 5.4.6 Typical energy-saving dishwashers – water usage and CO_2 emissions[33]
(cold-fill appliance; hand washing based on a daily wash)

per household per year	dishwasher[34]	hand washing
water used	3000 litres	10,500 litres
energy consumed[35]	237 kWh (average electricity)	441 kWh (gas)
carbon impact per household per year[36]	126 kgCO₂	92 kgCO₂

Taps

Standard taps use around 6 litres of water per minute. Specify water-efficient taps in order of recommendations:

- spray taps: 30–65% water saving, cost from £50
- self-closing: 20–50% water saving by timing water flow, cost £50
- automatic shut-off taps: sensors need energy, cost £200

Increasing water efficiency

The Building Regulations require increased water efficiency. To achieve maximum credits in the Code for Sustainable Homes, internal water use must be reduced to 80 litres per person. One way of achieving this is by using water-efficient appliances throughout and providing a shower in place of a bath. Alternatively, it can be achieved through rainwater and greywater recycling although, depending on the systems used, this could increase CO_2 emissions (see Sections 5.5 and 5.6).

The Code for Sustainable Homes water calculator has been criticised by a number of professionals who do not consider it a useful design tool and only use it to meet planning requirements.[37]

Code for Sustainable Homes, EcoHomes (Wat 1 and Wat 2) and BREEAM credits (Wat 1 to Wat 4). Use water calculator from
www.thewatercalculator.org.uk/calculator.asp

5.5 DEALING WITH WASTEWATER AND FOUL WATER: GREYWATER AND BLACKWATER

Each person produces around 150 litres of 'blackwater' or 'foul water' per day. This comes largely from the toilet, and includes 55 grams dry weight of solid waste.[38] A typical household produces 40 m³ of foul water per year, containing nearly 50 kg of dried solid matter.

Around 90 m³ of 'greywater' is produced per household per year. Greywater is the cleaner wastewater from baths, washing machines, showers and sinks, but usually not kitchen sinks/dishwashers owing to contamination.

5.5.1 On-site wastewater treatment systems: greywater and blackwater

Usually, greywater and blackwater are flushed away to the nearest sewage plant for chemical treatment. However, they can be intercepted and recycled on site. The water can be reused for toilet flushing, reducing mains water consumption. Treatment is usually required prior to reuse. There are several on-site blackwater treatment systems (see Figs. 5.5.1 and 5.5.2).

Key recommendations

- Be aware that many grey and blackwater treatment systems are not as sustainable or appropriate as they are claimed or perceived to be; hence why specialist advice is always required. For example, on some sites with the right soil conditions and with a natural 1–2 m fall, vertical reedbeds may be suitable; while on others they are not.
- In particular, living machines are highly energy intensive and may need to be heated to protect plants from frost and are therefore inappropriate in most situations.
- Always obtain specialist design advice, which takes into account site-specific systems; sized for the specific waste water effluent output, space availability, specific site/soil conditions, required quality of effluent, maintenance requirements, etc.
- Consult Environment Agency/planning/Building Regulations.
- On-site blackwater treatment is not recommended in urban areas.
- Mains connection and sewage removal, wherever they are available, are the preferred blackwater treatment system.
- Where no direct sewer connection is possible, a septic holding tank is often most suitable as primary treatment.
- Always size for the maximum number of people.
- Ensure it is free of flood risk.

Fig. 5.5.1 On-site wastewater treatments, including reedbeds

System sizes below are for a household of up to four persons unless otherwise stated*	Urban?	Remote sites?	High upkeep?	Costly?	Mainstream?	Biodiversity?
Primary treatment (initial breaking down of solid organic matter)						
Compost toilet (a) waterless toilet that allows natural process of waste into compost; WC content (blackwater) is collected from a compost WC into a 1 m³ tank						
• allow 1 m² clear space in front of the tank • end product: ~500 litres of humus per year to cover ~30 m² of bare soil; humus cannot be used near vegetable plants which are eaten raw • not recommended in public/urban buildings as input control is difficult (i.e. use of damaging cleaning products etc.)	X	✓	✓	✓	X	X
Holding tanks (b) tanks that gradually separate solids and sludge from wastewater so it can pass to secondary treatment or sewage						
septic tank: periodical sludge removal with outflow into sewer/secondary treatment; size of tank min. 2.7 m² + 180 litres per additional person; check monthly	X	✓	X	X	✓	X
settlement tank: frequent sludge removal; size of tank min. 1 m³; connect to secondary treatment	X	✓	✓	✓	✓	X
Living machine[39] (for all stages, large scale) vegetation placed on hydroponic tanks that treat and recycle wastewater through natural processes						
energy-, maintenance- and cost-intensive hence often unsuitable; total area required for 15 households: 100 m²; may be suitable for educational purposes and where effluent <200m³/day	X	✓	✓	✓	X	✓
Secondary and tertiary treatments (further breaking down to clean water)						
reedbed (c),[40] (also referred to as constructed wetlands) a biological ground system that treats and recycles wastewater through the natural processes of vegetation and reeds placed in a sunny location						
vertical flow: 0.6–1.5 m deep; size 2 m² per person if greywater only, reducing to 0.8 m² if 100+ people; if blackwater 5 m² per person. Outflow to horizontal reedbed, pond or tank	X	✓	✓	✓	X	✓

horizontal flow: usually tertiary treatment; size: 5–10 m² per person for blackwater; greywater: 1 m² per person with 6 m² minimum size	X	✓	X	X	✓	✓

* to be read with key recommendations page 115.
* some systems can also be used for greywater recycling only; if this is the case, system sizes can be reduced by 30%.
* always obtain specialist and site-specific advice.

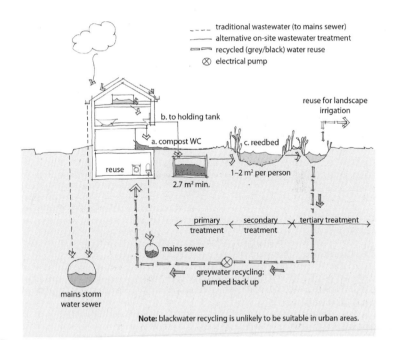

_ _ _ _ traditional wastewater (to mains sewer)
——— alternative on-site wastewater treatment
▭▭ recycled (grey/black) water reuse
⊗ electrical pump

reuse for landscape irrigation

b. to holding tank

a. compost WC

c. reedbed

reuse

2.7 m² min.

1–2 m² per person

← primary treatment ← secondary treatment ← tertiary treatment

mains sewer

greywater recycling: pumped back up

mains storm water sewer

Note: blackwater recycling is unlikely to be suitable in urban areas.

Fig. 5.5.2 Alternative on-site wastewater treatments (read with Fig. 5.5.1)

5.5.2 On-site greywater recycling

Recycled greywater can be used for non-potable and non-bathing uses, preferably toilet flushing or landscape irrigation.[41] Greywater must either be used immediately to prevent any bacteria build-up, or it must be treated and stored before usage. The CO_2 emissions produced by pumping and cleaning water can even be greater for greywater recycling than for water taken from the mains, while offering only marginal water reductions, yet require additional space, money and energy (see Fig. 5.5.4).

Short retention system (a)

Biological roof system (b)

Reedbeds can also be used for treatment of blackwater (rural) (c)

Biomechanical greywater system (large scale) (d)

Greywater harvesting with heat recovery (large scale) (e)

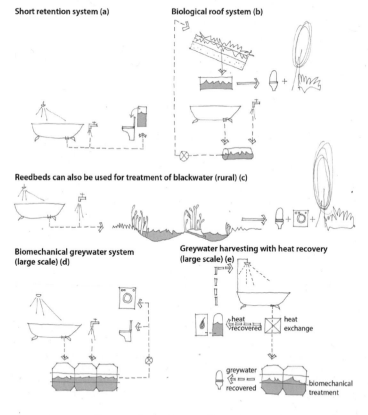

Fig. 5.5.3 Greywater recycling systems and recommendations
(read in conjunction with Fig. 5.5.4)

Fig. 5.5.4 Summary of greywater harvesting systems[42]

System	Design notes (system size and CO_2 impact based on a four person household and overall typical water usage, based on low flush toilets)	CO_2 reduction?	Urban?	Rural?
short retention system (a)	collection from shower/bath directly to cisterns for flushing; needs min. 2.3 m ceiling height; individual dwelling system, 0.1–0.2 m² storage	-12%	✓	✓
biological roof system (b)	green roof water recycling system;[43] the green roof module measures 8 m² and is 1 m deep; it can recycle greywater for 30–45 people but is untested; 1 m² roof area per four persons	-3%	✓	✓
reedbed (biological ground system) (c)	water is passed through a UV-filter to kill any remaining bacteria; some water loss through evaporation and plant usage; large areas required: 6–8 m²; individual or communal system; see also Fig. 5.5.2	-3%	X	✓
bio-mechanical systems (d)	an enclosed biological system using bacteria to break down organic matter; size 40 m² with 3 m ceiling for 150 households; likely to increase CO_2 emissions	increase: +15%	✓	✓
bio-mechanical with heat recovery (e)	as above, although CO_2 savings possible; additional space required for hot water tank; may be suitable for communal greywater recycling	-20 to 30%	✓	✓

 Code for Sustainable Homes, EcoHomes credits (Wat 1, Wat 2) and BREEAM credits (Wat 1, Wat 2, Ene 8)

In most situations, 100% of WC flusing demand can be met from bath/shower water, which is 18–30% total water saving per household (lower figure for water-efficient WCs). Once the systems' embodied energy is included, greywater recycling is likely to increase overall carbon emissions in most situations.[44] Greywater recycling should not be regarded as a panacea for both water saving and CO_2 reductions (see Section 5.5.3).

5.5.3 Not all greywater recycling systems are energy-efficient

Key recommendations

- Reducing water use is always a priority over recycling it.
- Always obtain specialist and site-specific design advice to balance site suitability, cost, energy use, maintenance and space requirements.
- Beware that many greywater systems are not a panacea for achieving water and carbon reductions, and may increase carbon emissions (see Fig. 5.5.4), particularly once embodied energy is taken into account.
- In most situations, specifying water-efficient appliances with a mains connection is the most appropriate 'greywater strategy'.
- If installing greywater systems, the best use is toilet flushing: greywater from the bathroom basin and the shower/bath could meet a household's entire toilet flushing need, saving 18–30% of potable mains water. Usually, a minimum size of storage tank of 100–200 litres per household is required.[45]
- Depending on site conditions, short retention systems, reedbeds or communal biomechanical systems with heat recovery may be suitable (see below).

Greywater and landscape irrigation
Greywater is more alkaline than rainwater. When using greywater for landscape irrigation, the following are recommended:
  – Use ecological cleaning and washing products; avoid bleach.
  – To avoid bacteria build-up, do not store water for too long.
  – Use only on established plants in unlimited soil, not in pots.
  – Reduce fertiliser usage.
  – Do not use on vegetable plants and small herbal plants.
  – Monitor plants and stop watering with greywater if they stop flourishing.

Some suitable plants for greywater irrigation
  – honeysuckle, juniper, rose, oak tree, rosemary

Biomechanical greywater harvesting with heat recovery
A greywater system can be combined with heat recovery. Usually, warm shower and bath water is lost down the drain. However, proprietary systems can recover heat from this water and return it to the building at a base temperature while also collecting, storing and treating the wastewater. This only works at a large scale, and requires regular maintenance and additional space and money. The heat recovery offsets some of the energy needed for biomechanical treatment.

- A net CO_2 reduction of 1.1–1.6 $kgCO_2$ per 1000 litres of shower/bath water recycled.[46]
- Useful for large buildings with high warm water usage, such as student halls, hotels and large domestic buildings.
- Requires large hot water storage tank and separate greywater tank systems.

Heat recovery systems without greywater recycling also exist. These are more compact and suitable for single domestic use:

- Around 2–2.5 $kgCO_2$ per 1000 litres of shower water is saved compared to a shower system without heat recovery; this is around 70–100 $kgCO_2$ reduction per year per household.
- They only work with shower water, not baths; as water is drained, heat is recovered to provide base heat to the shower system as it is running.

Calculations are complex. A calculator can be downloaded from the SAP website: www.sap-appendixq.org.uk/page.jsp?id=4

5.6   COLLECTING AND USING RAINWATER

The 2–3°C temperature rise predicted by 2040/80 will mean that the air will be able to contain approximately 20% more water.[47] This will lead to heavier rain than we are used to. Rainwater can be harvested for toilet flushing, landscape irrigation and washing machines.

Harvesting also reduces the strain on storm water or combined sewers. Rainwater tanks are usually sized to store 5% of yearly collected rainwater. However, given the changing climate, storage tanks should be increased to bridge dry spells.

Although yearly total predicted rainfall is only expected to vary between −1% and +1% by 2080, the seasonal changes will vary significantly. Across the UK, winter rainfall is predicted to be 30–50% greater than the proportion of summer rainfall.

CO_2 reductions may be achieved, depending on which systems are used. A water harvesting calculator can be downloaded from: www.rainwaterharvesting.co.uk/calculator.php

 Code for Sustainable Homes, EcoHomes credits (Wat 1, and Wat 2) and BREEAM credits (Wat 1, Wat 2, Ene 8)

5.6.1 Rainwater harvesting systems and CO_2 implications

For a typical household, rainwater recycling can reduce CO_2 emissions by 15–40%, and even up to 100% with a gravity-fed system.[48] CO_2 reductions are dependent on the rainwater system used, how much rainwater can be collected versus the amount needed and how much pumping is required to get the rainwater to the place of reuse. This will cost more.

The CO_2 reductions do not, however, take into account the embodied energy of the rainwater tank, pipes or pumps. Once this is included, it is often found that rainwater harvesting systems reduce mains water consumption but at a higher carbon cost.[49]

Key recommendations

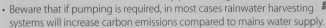

Different strategies are appropriate depending on specific water demand and the ratio of roof availability per building.

- Beware that if pumping is required, in most cases rainwater harvesting systems will increase carbon emissions compared to mains water supply.
- Always prioritise simple water butts without pumps to collect rainwater for landscape irrigation, even if they may not be equally rewarded by assessment systems.
- Calculate water tank size in accordance with steps in Section 5.6.2/3.
- For internal domestic rainwater reuse, the following is recommended:
  - To maximise the water savings from the capital cost of additional pipework, prioritise strategies which can cover all of the water demand.
  - Internal water demand is building and occupant specific. Reusing rainwater for internal purposes only makes sense where a large percentage of demand can be met.
  - Rainwater is of too high a quality to be used for toilet flushing.
  - Rainwater harvesting for internal use has a larger financial and carbon payback where there is greater rainfall, e.g. in Cardiff or Glasgow.
  - Similar principles apply for non-domestic building uses, but always obtain professional advice.

For individual dwellings (see Fig 5.6.1):

- For landscape irrigation, install a simple rainwater butt without pumps. A simple gravity-fed system may be suitable, either directly collected from the roof, or taken to the ground and into a tank, from which it is pumped up into a header tank then gravity-fed down to the washing machine.

For larger dwelling blocks (see Fig 5.6.2): less roof area is available per household and only a small percentage of a household's water needs will be met from rainwater. This makes rainwater dual pipework costly for little return.

- Rainwater recycling is recommended for landscape irrigation only, particular in drier regions.
- Specify an indirect feed system with break tank.

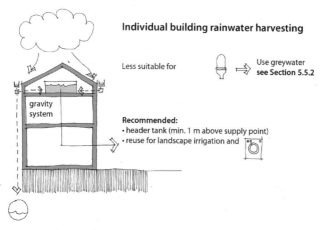

Individual building rainwater harvesting

Less suitable for → Use greywater **see Section 5.5.2**

gravity system

Recommended:
• header tank (min. 1 m above supply point)
• reuse for landscape irrigation and

Fig. 5.6.1 *Recommended rainwater harvesting system for individual, small-scale building*

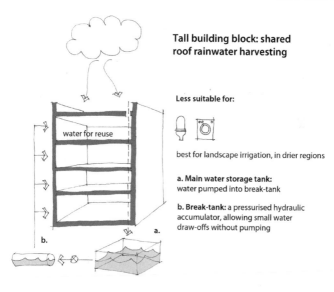

Tall building block: shared roof rainwater harvesting

Less suitable for:

best for landscape irrigation, in drier regions

a. Main water storage tank: water pumped into break-tank

b. Break-tank: a pressurised hydraulic accumulator, allowing small water draw-offs without pumping

water for reuse

b.

a.

Fig. 5.6.2 *Recommended rainwater harvesting system for tall multiple-use building block*

5.6.2 Step 1: How much rainwater can be collected per year?

Fig. 5.6.3 Surface type and water runoff coefficients

Possible rainwater collected per year (in litres) =
Yearly rainfall (mm) × roof collection area (m²) × 90% efficiency × percentage runoff coefficient (see below)

Runoff or drainage coefficients are affected by the rainwater collection surface and how much water is lost, evaporated or absorbed. Rainwater collected from pavements will be of poorer quality than water collected from roofs.

Surface type	Runoff coefficient[50]
pitched roof	90%
flat roof	80%
green roof extensive 50 mm	50%
green roof intensive 150 mm	40%
green roof – deep substrate (300–900 mm)	10–30%
smooth pavement with small joints	85–90%
rough pavement with wide joints	50–70%
gravel road	15–30%
vegetated area – soil	0–10%

5.6.3 Step 2: Determine appropriate storage tank size

Rainwater tanks are normally sized to store 5% of the yearly collected rainfall. However, a larger proportion of collected rainwater should be stored to bridge increasing dry spells. It makes sense to store winter rain to be used over longer, drier summer periods. This will require a rainwater tank sized to hold 15–20% of the yearly collected rainfall.

- For a typical terraced house, this should be minimum 3000 litres for WC and household usage and at least double that for landscape irrigation. However, typical proprietary rainwater butts hold much less than this (around 150–300 litres of water only).
- Large buildings need to derive their rainwater storage tank size according to the above steps.

Fig. 5.6.4 Rainwater harvesting tank sizes

Rainwater reuse purpose	Rainwater tank sizing
WC and other household uses	traditionally 5% of the annual rainfall, collected (as calculated in Step 1, see Section 5.6.2), but instead 15–20% recommended of annual rainfall
landscape irrigation only	large tank, located on lower floors or buried to collect 50% of 2080 winter rainfall calculated in Step 1 (Section 5.6.2) and as per predicted average 2080 rainfall in Fig. 5.6.5

2010 yearly regional rainfall (predicted 2080 yearly rainfall change in brackets)

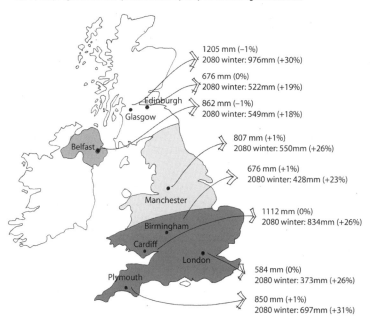

1205 mm (–1%)
2080 winter: 976mm (+30%)

676 mm (0%)
2080 winter: 522mm (+19%)

862 mm (–1%)
2080 winter: 549mm (+18%)

807 mm (+1%)
2080 winter: 550mm (+26%)

676 mm (+1%)
2080 winter: 428mm (+23%)

1112 mm (0%)
2080 winter: 834mm (+26%)

584 mm (0%)
2080 winter: 373mm (+26%)

850 mm (+1%)
2080 winter: 697mm (+31%)

Edinburgh
Glasgow
Belfast
Manchester
Birmingham
Cardiff
London
Plymouth

Fig. 5.6.5 UK regional rainfall map

5.6.4 Rainwater pipes – location and sizing recommendations

Always consult local building regulations regarding rainwater pipes and distances between pipes. For future climate change scenarios, oversize pipes by 30%. In general:

- Min. 68 mm rainwater pipe as standard; depending on slope and roof area, this may be increased up to 150 mm.
- A pipe in the middle of the roof can take twice as much water runoff as a pipe at one end; gutter should be min. 100 mm.
- Green roofs may require fewer rainwater pipes.
- Avoid internal gutters and burying rainwater pipes in walls;
  however, if this is necessary:
  - allow access panels at 1350 mm height × 300 mm wide
  - insulate pipework to prevent condensation and reduce thermal bridging
  - specify non-organic wall insulation or insulation which is not affected by water ingress (e.g. XPS)
  - check gutters are free from blockages at regular intervals, i.e. at least quarterly.
- Pipes for drains/sewers should be 100 mm for a single dwelling or 150 mm for multiple dwellings.

5.7   APPLICABLE LEGISLATION AND GUIDANCE

- BS 6920 and BS 6297 – septic tanks and soakaways
- BS 8515 rainwater harvesting and BS 8525 (greywater recycling)
- Building Regulations, part G and H for England and Wales
- Building Regulations Scotland, part SLD3
- Environment Agency – England and Wales
- Environment and Heritage Service (Northern Ireland)
- Pollution Prevention Guideline (PPG) 5: Works in, near or liable to affect
- Scottish Environment Protection Agency
- The Flood and Water Management Act 2010 (Commencement, No. 3 and Transitional Provisions) Order 2011
- Water Quality Regulations and Private Water Supplies Regulations (Northern Ireland) 1994
- Water Supply (Water Fittings) Regulations 1990, England and Wales
- Water Supply (Water Quality) Regulations 1990, Scotland
- Watercourses. www.environment-agency.gov.uk

5.8   FURTHER READING

- AECB Water Standards, Vol. 2, Delivering buildings with excellent water and energy performance, 2009
- Boardman et al. (2005), *40% house*, Environmental Change Institute
- BRE (2000), Good Building Guides GBG 42 Part 1 and 2 Reedbeds
- Burkhard et al. (2000), Ecological Water and Wastewater Management for New Housing, Technical, Economic and Social Considerations, www.rgu.ac.uk
- CIRIA (2000), C522: Sustainable urban drainage systems – design manual for England and Wales; and The SUDS Manual – 2007 (CIRIA C697)
- CIRIA (2001), C539: Rainwater and greywater use in buildings – best practice guidance
- Clarke et al. (2009), Quantifying the energy and carbon effects of water saving, full technical report, (EST/EA)
- Energy and Environment Programme, Environmental Change Unit (1997), 2 Mt Carbon Report, University of Oxford, www.eci.ox.ac.uk
- Environment Agency (2010), Harvesting rainwater for domestic uses: an information guide
- Grant et al. (2000), *Sewage Solutions, Answering the Call of Nature*, Powys: Centre for Alternative Technology Publications
- Hall (2008), *Green Building Bible Volume 1 and 2*, Green Building Press
- Kwok et al. (2007), *Green Studio Handbook*, Architectural Press
- NHBC (2010), A simple guide to sustainable drainage systems for housing, 2010
- Parkes et al. (2010), Energy and carbon implications of rainwater harvesting and greywater recycling, Environment Agency, www.environment-agency.gov.uk
- Randall (2003), *Sustainable Urban Design, An Environmental Approach*, Spon
- The Water and Energy Implications of Bathing and Showering Behaviours and Technologies, April 2009
- www.environment-agency.gov.uk
- www.waterwise.org.uk

Chapter 6

The internal environment: space, warmth, light and air

Two key drivers are making consideration of a building's internal environment ever more vital: the changing climate and the increased thermal performance of the fabric from which the building is built.

The fact that we are operating in a changing climate can no longer be ignored. If buildings are not designed to cope, temperature-related health issues will become a significant problem and it is therefore critical that issues such as thermal comfort, natural ventilation, winter solar gain and summer solar shading are considered early on by the designer.

Equally, increased airtightness standards, controlled ventilation and even the impact of building fabric on space standards all mean that a careful approach is required to avoid compromising the quality of the internal environment.

 Symbol indicates relevance to the Code for Sustainable Homes, EcoHomes & BREEAM.

6.1   INTERNAL ENVIRONMENT

Internal environment – checklist		☑ ☒
Space allowance		
6.2	Is sufficient indoor space provided, taking into account Lifetime Homes requirements? Space for waste, recycling and composting?	☐
6.2.4	Do wall thicknesses reflect increased fabric efficiency standards?	☐
6.2.5	Space for utilities: is a 'technical' or plant room provided?	☐
Thermal comfort		
6.3	Are internal spaces responding to the sun path?	☐
6.6.2	Has the design provided natural ventilation? (cross-ventilation preferred)	☐
3.7.2	Ideally, there should be no single-aspect dwellings, but if there are, do they face S to SE in Region 1; and SE to NE in other regions?	☐
6.6.1	Is there sufficient exposed thermal mass with night ventilation?	☐
6.5.2	Is daylight maximised, i.e. shallow plan?	☐
Fig. 6.5.9	Are ceiling heights min. 2.9 m ground and 2.7 m first floor?	☐
Fig. 6.6.3	Have you specified windows that allow opening, even with vertical shutters closed, for example inward-opening windows, sliding/sash?	☐
6.6.2	Have you allowed for good night cooling, particularly where thermal mass is provided?	☐
6.5.1	Is solar shading provided? This should be horizontal on south and vertical on east and west.	☐
6.5.2	Is privacy retained while maximising daylighting?	☐
Flood protection		
5.1/5.2	Have you considered future-proofing strategies?	☐
Internal air quality		
6.6.2, 6.7	Have you provided good natural ventilation in summer and ventilation with heat recovery (HVR) in winter?	☐
6.8	Have you specified finishes and materials that do not emit gas?	☐

6.2 DWELLING SPACE STANDARDS: MINIMUM DWELLING AND ROOM SIZES

Housing standards and minimum dwelling and room areas are subject to government and local authority guidance. Figure 6.2.1 synthesises these standards and recommendations, with a focus on Lifetime Homes.[1] Lifetime Homes are adaptable to meet occupants' changing needs, from families with small children to people with reduced mobility in later life.

All dwelling and room areas given are recommended minimum areas. These will need to increase where plots are irregular, where access is difficult or where additional WCs, en-suite bathrooms and utility rooms are provided. To allow for good daylighting and natural ventilation, the depth of plan should not exceed twice the ceiling height if openings are on one side (and four times if openings on both sides) – see Sections 6.5 and 6.6.

Fig 6.2.1 Minimum recommended dwelling areas relating to bedrooms and person occupancy *(1B2P stands for a 1 bedroom, 2 persons dwelling)*

Minimum dwelling areas	1B2P	2B3P	2B4P	3B5P	3B5P	5B7P
dwelling size – flat	48–50 m²	61 m²	70 m²	86 m²	95 m²	—
dwelling size – two-storey house	—	74 m²	83 m²	96 m²	105 m²	122 m²

Fig 6.2.2 Minimum room areas according to bedrooms and person occupancy[2]

Minimum room areas	1B2P	2B3P	2B4P	3B5P	3B5P	5B7P
living/dining kitchen room	22 m²	24 m²	26 m²	28 m²	30 m²	32 m²
living room min. width	2.8 m			3.2 m		
bedrooms	11.5 m² double/twin bedrooms and 7.5 m² single bedrooms, with at least one bedroom also for home office: add 1 m² for that bedroom. Min width: 2.75 m for double bedroom and 2.3 m for single bedroom.					
storage internal	1.5 m²	2 m²	2.5 m²	3 m²	3.5 m²	4 m²
storage external	1–2 m² where flats or with garden respectively			1.5–2.5 m² where flats or with garden respectively		

Code for Sustainable Homes credits Hea 4 (Lifetime Homes requirements)

6.2.1 Space standards for waste, recycling and composting

- All external waste and recycling facilities should be located within 5 m of an external door.
- All internal waste recycling facilities should have a dedicated space in or near the kitchen.

Fig. 6.2.3 Space for waste and recycling[3]
(1B2P stands for a one bedroom, two persons dwelling)

standard household waste	• min. 100 litres (based on 1B2P) – approx. space required 476 × 536 × 866 mm • add 70 litres for each additional bed space
recyclables where local authority collection	• internal storage requirement of minimum 30 litres – approx. space required 470 × 300 × 440 mm
recyclables with no local authority collection	• 30 litres internal • 180 litres external – space required 1060 × 400 × 820 mm • or 60 litres internal if no external space where flats – approx. space required 665 × 350 × 660 mm
composting	⟶ Jump to Section 4.9.3

6.2.2 Outdoor space requirements

Fig. 6.2.4 Minimum outdoor space requirements per person

	1B2P	2B3P	2B4P	3 bed +
min. balcony size	5 m²	6 m²	7 m²	8 m²
communal space per dwelling	2 m²	3 m²	4 m²	5 m²

- Depth of balconies: 1.5–1.8 m maximum. South-facing balconies ≥ 1.5 m are likely to block desirable winter solar gain to windows below.
- For communal/public open space requirements, ⟶ jump to Section 3.5.

Code for Sustainable Homes credits (Was 1, Hea 4 mandatory, Ene 9, Hea 3, Man 1) EcoHomes credits (Tra 4, Mat 4, Hea 3, Man 1) and BREEAM credits (Wst 3 mandatory, Man 4)

6.2.3 Solar spaces and conservatories

Sun spaces should face within 30° of south with façades at a 30–40° sloping angle from vertical and roof slope of 30–40°. Solar spaces need to be designed with caution. They tend to be too cold in winter and too hot in summer. Residents often regard them as extended living space and heat them, thereby increasing space heating demand. Solar spaces often also reduce daylighting to living spaces beyond.

6.2.4 Sufficient space for wall thicknesses

Increased regulations require additional insulation as part of the drive towards low carbon buildings. ——⟩ Jump to Chapters 7 & 8. Allow sufficient external wall zones:
- external wall zone of 400–470 mm if brick/blockwork
- 300–350 mm if framed construction.

6.2.5 Space for utilities: 'the technical room'

Internal utility spaces or 'technical rooms' are becoming more important as we rely increasingly on low and zero carbon technologies and MVHR. Internal technical room areas are not included in recommended minimum dwelling/storage room areas and thus require additional space:
- size per dwelling: typically 3–5 m²
- size per dwelling can be reduced to 1 m² of internal utility space, if communal/district energy systems are used; an additional 1 m² per dwelling then needs to be allowed for the communal plant room

6.2.6 Bicycle spaces

To encourage cycling, provide secure cycle storage for each dwelling (ideally one bicycle space per person). Ensure minimum 2 m manoeuvring space in front of the storage area. For urban and street design for cycling, ——⟩ jump to Section 3.4

Fig. 6.2.5 Storage requirements for bicycles

Cycle storage space in shed		Proprietary system – mostly for communal cycle proprietary storage enclosures	
1 cycle	2 m × 750 mm	4 cycles	2 m × 1200 mm
2 cycles	2 m × 1500 mm	6 cycles	2 m × 1800 mm
4 cycles	2 m × 2500 mm	10 cycles	2 m × 3000 mm

 Code for Sustainable Homes credits (Ene 8), EcoHomes credits (Tra 2) and BREEAM credits (Tra 3)

6.3   IDEAL ROOM ORIENTATIONS: RECOMMENDED ZONING

For thermal comfort in multi-storey houses, living spaces are ideally located on the upper floors and bedrooms on the lower floors. People prefer lower temperatures for sleeping and this 'upside down living' configuration makes use of the natural stratification of rising warm air. It is particularly suitable for maisonette arrangements with no garden, but it may not always be desirable for security and accessibility purposes. When designing 'upside down living' arrangements, be sure to adhere to Lifetime Homes and Building Regulations.

Less drastic arrangements than 'upside down living' can significantly increase residents' thermal comfort:

Key recommendations

- Maximise winter solar gain and control summer overheating.
- Avoid single-aspect dwellings. ——⟩ Jump to Section 3.7.2.
- Orient living areas, where higher temperatures are tolerated, to south and south-west.
- Orient sleeping and cooking to east and north-east; always avoid south and west aspect for bedrooms in Regions 2, 3 and 4 to avoid night-time overheating; bedrooms can be located to south and south-east in Region 1.
- Corridors, entrance, technical rooms and services such as bathroom and WC should ideally face north.
- Always provide lobbies where front doors are directly exposed to the outside.

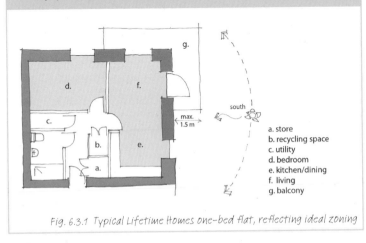

a. store
b. recycling space
c. utility
d. bedroom
e. kitchen/dining
f. living
g. balcony

Fig. 6.3.1 Typical Lifetime Homes one-bed flat, reflecting ideal zoning

6.4 THE CONCEPT OF THERMAL COMFORT

Thermal comfort is the expression of satisfaction with the surrounding thermal environment, usually whether it is (too) hot or (too) cold.[4] Each person's comfort level is different and it is influenced by many environmental factors besides air temperature alone. Other factors include humidity, air velocity (draughts), temperature of surrounding surfaces (radiant temperature) and each individual's metabolic rate and clothing.[5] However, most people will experience satisfaction within a similar range.

Extreme thermal discomfort can lead to thermal stress. This causes medical conditions which may even prove fatal, particularly in the elderly and infirm. Thermal stress occurs in cold winters and increasingly during hot summers.

Key recommendations

- Relative humidity is 40–70%. Over 70% can lead to mould growth which aggravates asthma and allergies.
- Warm feet and a cool head can be achieved with underfloor heating; occupants experience discomfort if the temperature at foot level is below 19°C or is 3°C lower than the temperature at head level
- Ideal internal temperatures are 20–24°C in winter and 22–27°C in summer. See Section 6.5.
- Ensure adequate ventilation to keep internal CO_2 concentrations below 1000 ppm; with windows closed, levels are usually below 800 ppm.[6] Levels above this are not hazardous but may make a room feel stuffy, and over 5000 ppm is considered to affect concentration and respiration.[7]
- To retain winter internal air quality, use whole house ventilation with heat recovery (VHR) if airtightness ≤3 m^3/(hr.m^2). See Section 6.7 and ⟶⟩ Jump to Section 7.4.
- Internal air movement to be ≤ 0.1–0.3 m/s:[8] occupants experience discomfort near cooling/air outlets, which can reach 3 m/s.
- 'Adaptive comfort': user control allows each person to achieve thermal comfort by adapting the internal environment, for example, the opening/closing of windows/blinds and adjusting heating/cooling controls.

6.4.1 A changing climate increases summer thermal stress

Internal temperatures below 12°C[9] and above 35°C increase cardiovascular stresses. The impact of such temperatures varies from person to person. Above 35°C also increases risk of respiratory diseases, especially where local air pollution is high.[10] While cold-related deaths may drop in a warmer climate, the death toll from heatwaves will increase, as witnessed during the 2003 heatwave in Europe.

It is not the increased temperatures per se that are dangerous – after all, there are many countries with far hotter climates. It is the irregularities in temperature and the intensity and duration that people in the UK are unaccustomed to.[11] Our buildings are often ill-adapted, with indoor air temperatures exceeding external temperatures.

Fig. 6.4.1 Designing for thermal comfort: design strategies now and in the future

Scotland and northern England and Wales (Regions 1 and 2)	
2010 climate	**2080 predicted climate**
cold climate with strong winds, low solar radiation and low temperatures for most of the year	temperate climate with mild winters and warmer summers; increased frequency of heatwaves; significant summer temperature increases in Region 2
Ideal 2010 building response	**2080 climate change solution/response**
tightly sealed construction, high insulation; maximise solar gain; pitched roofs to discard snow and rain as quickly as possible, combined with attenuation	the same as ideal building response plus: Region 1: careful zoning of rooms and good cross-ventilation to avoid summer overheating Region 2: as Region 3 and 4, 2080 climatic response

Northern Ireland and south England and Wales (Regions 3 and 4)	
2010 climate	**2080 predicted climate**
temperate climate with mild winters and summers; overheating in summer can occur	temperate climate with mild winters and warm summers; increased frequency of heatwaves; overheating in summer a regular occurrence unless appropriate site response
Ideal 2010 building response	**2080 climate change solution/response**
well-insulated and airtight construction which maximises solar gain in winter; careful zoning of rooms to avoid summer overheating	the same as ideal building response plus: • increased insulation and airtightness • external shading, especially south and west • high ceilings • light-coloured external materials • exposed thermal mass and night ventilation • good cross-ventilation

For wider site and building adaptation strategies, ——⟶ jump to Chapters 2 and 3.

6.5. DESIGNING FOR HOTTER SUMMERS

Design should maximise winter solar gain without risking summer overheating.

If buildings are ill-adapted to extreme temperatures, residents may resort to the ad hoc installation of air-conditioning units. Air-conditioning could increase a typical dwelling's operational energy by 20–37% in carbon emissions by 2080.[12] Air-conditioning units also increase local external temperatures as they dump the heat outside. To avoid risking human health and exacerbating local and global warming, our buildings must be designed with warmer summers in mind.

Fig. 6.5.1 Recommended summer comfort temperatures and overheating thresholds[13]

Summer comfort	When overheating occurs
living room: 25°C	peak temp of 28°C, where 1% (or approximately 30–60 hours of yearly occupied time) over 28°C
bedroom: 21°C	peak temp of 25°C, where 1% (or approximately 30–60 hours of yearly occupied time) over 26°C
offices and schools: 25°C	peak temp of 28°C, where 1% (or approximately 20 hours of yearly occupied time) over 28°C

- Design naturally managed buildings. These are buildings where internal temperatures will vary according to external temperatures and conditions.
- To provide thermal comfort, such buildings rely on 'passive measures' and on 'adaptive comfort': for example, occupants adapt their clothing and adapt the opening and closing of windows and shutters.
- Designing a naturally managed building is about tempering the external environment within acceptable limits. The perceived difference between inside and outside conditions can be more important than the actual temperatures.
- Thermal insulation and increased airtightness minimise winter heat losses but also increase heat gains in summer. Overheating occurs when heat gets trapped in a well-insulated building.
- Internal temperatures in naturally ventilated buildings will never be as low as in actively air-conditioned buildings.
- Top-floor units and single-storey unshaded units are most likely to overheat as they are exposed to full solar radiation.
- Elderly people are particularly at risk from increased thermal stresses.[14]
- Buildings must demonstrate that they do not overheat to meet regulations.[15]

Key recommendations

Naturally ventilated buildings require a hybrid of passive measures if they are to prevent overheating without increasing cooling-related carbon emissions:

- design site layout, streets and external spaces with environmental considerations in mind ⟶⟩ Jump to Sections 3.6 and 3.7 (1)
- increase urban vegetation: park areas are 2–3°C cooler than surrounding streets[16] ⟶⟩ Jump to Section 4.2 (2)
- external materials with high reflectancy/albedo ⟶⟩ Jump to Section 4.2 (3)
- design airtight and well-insulated buildings to buffer external temperatures ⟶⟩ Jump to Chapter 7 (4)
- solar shading that does not compromise good daylighting (5)
- high ceilings and shallow plan buildings (6)
- exposed thermal mass with summer night cooling (7)
- good cross-ventilation, particularly at night, is the most effective of all passive 'cooling' strategies (8)
- specify efficient electrical appliances to minimise heat generation
- specify efficient heating systems and insulated pipework.

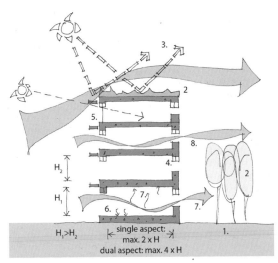

Fig. 6.5.2 Key strategies to prevent overheating (numbers relate to 1–8 above)

6.5.1 Solar shading without compromising good daylighting

Solar shading should be designed to allow solar gain during the colder months while reducing summer solar gain.

- Good solar shading design should not reduce daylighting so much that electrical lighting is needed.
- Solar shading is as an integral part of sustainable building design in the UK's more southern Regions 3 and 4 (Northern Ireland and southern England and Wales).
- From 2040 buildings in Region 2, northern England and Wales, will be likely to require solar shading elements.
- From 2080 in Region 1, Scotland, solar shading may also be provided as 'future proofing' with retrofit measures in Regions 1 and 2 (see Section 6.9).

Key recommendations (read in conjunction with Fig. 6.5.3)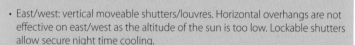

- South: deep reveal windows and horizontal shading. The total shading depth should be around 50% of the window height and maximum 1.5 m to allow winter solar gain.

- East/west: vertical moveable shutters/louvres. Horizontal overhangs are not effective on east/west as the altitude of the sun is too low. Lockable shutters allow secure night time cooling.

- SE/SW: combination of horizontal overhangs and vertical 'fins'.

- External shading devices are the most effective as they deflect solar radiation before it enters the building. South façades are the easiest to provide with solar shading without compromising daylight. Overhangs, eaves or horizontal louvres can be utilised. On east/west façades, external movable louvred shutters provide the best solar shading, while also providing good solar gain during winter. The louvres allow for ventilation and some daylight penetration. If they are closed at night, they also provide best night-time winter heat loss reduction. Shutters for reducing heat loss should be 40 mm thick and insulated.[17]

- Internal shading devices are less effective as they absorb part of the solar radiation. However, they can still significantly reduce summer solar gains. They may be easier to operate than external shading devices, but there is a danger that curtains and venetian blinds are continuously closed: this reduces both summer and desirable winter solar gain by around 50% and daylighting by 50% or more. Light-coloured blinds are much more effective.

- Building form can provide shading. Ensure that daylighting is not compromised. ⟶⟫ Jump to Section 3.7.3 for Vertical Sky Component.
- Courtyards can provide shading and cooling. Width of courtyard should equal the building height.
- Avoid outward-opening windows. Always specify sliding or inward-opening windows to allow external shutters to be (retro)fitted.
- Up to 80% summer solar gain can be reduced by trees. ⟶⟫ Jump to Section 4.2.4 and Fig. 6.5.4.
- Ideally, architectural solar shading should be made from reflective/light-coloured surfaces.[18]
- Ensure night-time cooling: solar shading alone cannot provide indoor thermal comfort; it should always be combined with secure night-time cooling. Inward-opening/sliding windows and external shutters are recommended. See Fig. 6.5.3 and Section 6.6.
- Be aware of solar control/tinted glazing: it reflects sunlight by around 30% even in winter, when solar gain is desirable. Moreover, it cuts daylighting by 50%. It can cause glare as it reflects sunlight into external spaces and surrounding buildings.

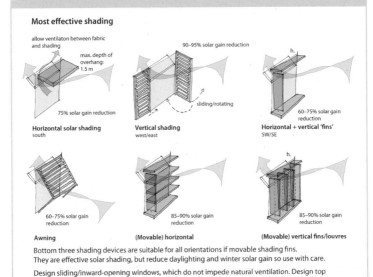

Most effective shading

allow ventilaton between fabric and shading

max. depth of overhang: 1.5 m

75% solar gain reduction

Horizontal solar shading
south

90–95% solar gain reduction

sliding/rotating

Vertical shading
west/east

h.

60–75% solar gain reduction

Horizontal + vertical 'fins'
SW/SE

60–75% solar gain reduction

Awning

85–90% solar gain reduction

(Movable) horizontal

h.

85–90% solar gain reduction

(Movable) vertical fins/louvres

Bottom three shading devices are suitable for all orientations if movable shading fins. They are effective solar shading, but reduce daylighting and winter solar gain so use with care.

Design sliding/inward-opening windows, which do not impede natural ventilation. Design top inward-opening 'hopper' windows for night cooling (h.).

Fig. 6.5.3 Solar shading

Solar shading from trees

Deciduous trees can provide solar shading in summer and allow solar gain in winter. The tree's transparency changes throughout its lifetime, and this needs to be taken into account when planting for solar shading purposes. Allow for temporary solar shading until the tree is mature.

- particularly useful on east and west
- upper floors will usually still require architectural solar shading
- distance from tree to building is crucial ———⟶ Jump to Sections 4.2 and 4.3

Fig. 6.5.4 Tree solar shading in summer/winter dependent on tree species[19]

Species + max. height	Sunlight blocked in summer	Sunlight blocked in winter
Average tree (height in brackets)	**80%**	**30%**
London plane (30–35 m)	80–90%	35–55%
maple tree (20–35 m)	75–90%	20–40%
birch (15–30 m)	75–85%	12–52%
beech (18–30 m)	85–95%	17%
oak (23–30 m)	65–85%	20–30%
horse chestnut (22–30 m)	70–90%	27%

Fig. 6.5.5 Solar altitude/angles of main UK city locations[20]

City location	Maximum solar altitude angle	Maximum solar altitude angle	Equinox solar altitude angle
	21 June, 1 pm	21 December, 12 pm	21 March, 12 pm and 21 September, 1 pm
Edinburgh	58	11	34
Glasgow	58	12	35
Belfast	59	12	36
Manchester	60	13	37
Birmingham	61	14	38
London	62	15	39
Cardiff	62	15	39
Plymouth	63	16	40

6.5.2 Daylight
. . . .

Good daylighting depends on:
- amount of daylight available (from an overcast sky)
- external obstructions and reflectance
- internal reflectance of room finishes
- proportion of window opening
- location of window opening
- depth of plan.

Daylighting is usually expressed as 'daylight factor' (DF). The daylight factor is the internally available daylight, expressed as a proportion of the daylight available externally at the same time. This is usually taken at different points inside and depends on external available daylight as well as window size and reflectance of surfaces.

$$DF = \frac{\text{internal daylight} \times 100}{\text{external daylight}}$$

- Minimum daylight factor is 1.5–2% in habitable rooms.
- Recommended daylight factor is 5%. This achieves good daylighting standards and reduces the need for electrical lighting in overcast conditions.[21]

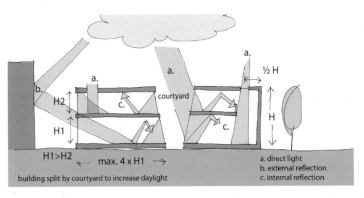

Fig. 6.5.6. Daylight rules of thumb

 Code for Sustainable Homes credits (Hea 1, Ene 9) EcoHomes credits (Hea 1) and BREEAM credits (Hea 1)

Recommendations for designing spaces with good daylight factor are provided on the following pages.

Key recommendations

Window room area – total window area should be no smaller than 10% and ideally around 20% of the floor area. It should be no greater than 40% on south and 32% on other orientations to prevent over-heating.[22] When windows are on one wall only, make window width 35% of the wall length.[23]

Shallow plan – natural daylighting and natural ventilation can be achieved with floor plan depths up to 2 × floor-to-ceiling height, if the façade width is fully glazed. This means the depth of plan should be 6 m maximum with a single-sided window and façade fully glazed (based on a 3 m floor-to-ceiling height). Maximum 12 m if dual aspect.

Introduce lightwells and courtyards in deep plans – this can provide daylighting and fresh air where depth of plan is greater than 12 m.

Limit roof light areas – roof light area maximum 12% of floor area to reduce excessive heat losses in winter and solar gains in summer. Where spaces are only rooflit, the distance between rooflights should be 1 × ceiling height (H) with ½ H at external wall boundaries/corners. Provide solar shading.[24] See Fig. 6.5.6.

Maximise view of the sky – vertical sky component Jump to Section 3.7.3.

Window glazing specification – triple glazing gives greater comfort because its surface temperature is closer to the internal air temperature. Consider triple glazing specifically on north, east and west façades. Double-glazed windows may be more appropriate on south façades, as increased winter solar gain can offset the heat loss. Modelling this before specifying is recommended. For low E glazing and definition of Ug, Jump to Section 7.3.2.

Fig. 6.5.7 Window specification and light transmittance[25]

Window specification	Daylight transmission	Solar transmission (Ug = direct heat from the sun)
single glazing	88%	83%
double glazing	77–80%	65–76%
double-glazed tinted	29%	39%
triple glazing	70%	40–60%

Internal reflectance of daylight – light-coloured finishes internally reflect daylight and improve daylighting conditions.

Fig. 6.5.8 Reflectance factors of different internal finishes[26]

Internal finishes	Approximate daylight reflection
white paint (glossy)	85%
wood finish – light colours	40%
carpet-cream	40%
yellow brick	30%
carpet-dark	10%
black paint (glossy)	5%

Lightshelves – when light is too bright, glare can be caused, which makes it difficult to look into the direction of the light. This is often the case with low-angled light from east and west and in winter. Glare can be avoided by:[27]
• avoiding single-aspect rooms
• light-coloured materials to reflect light more uniformly
• splayed and light-coloured window reveals
• use of adaptable solar shading
• use of lightshelves.

Lightshelves are horizontal solar shading devices which, if used with glazing above, can deflect some sunlight back into the room at ceiling level, providing diffuse daylighting deep into the space. Lightshelves are particularly useful in non-domestic situations, where daylighting is desirable but winter solar gain is not. In these situations, the overhanging lightshelf can be deep and should be equal to the height of the lightshelf above the intended work surface.[28] This works well with high ceilings.

High ceilings – in the UK, standard new dwelling ceiling heights are around 2.35–2.5 m. More generous ceiling heights allow for better daylighting with the introduction of taller windows, particularly on lower floors, although this will increase construction costs. Always combine high ceilings in well-insulated dwellings with exposed thermal mass. See Fig. 6.5.9, p.146.

Fig. 6.5.9 Recommended ceiling heights

Dwelling floor/level	Recommended floor-to-ceiling heights
ground floor	2.9–3.0 m
first floor and above	2.7–2.8 m
minimum floor-to-ceiling heights	2.3 m, but where MVHR used, increase this to 2.65 m to allow for service ducting without encroaching on floor-to-ceiling heights

More generous ceiling heights allow for:
- taller windows to bring daylight deeper into plan without compromising privacy
- natural stratification with hot summer air rising well above head height
- better night cooling, allowing a 300/400 mm zone above patio windows/ doors to have smaller 'hopper' windows which open for secure night cooling
- service ducting which does not breach minimum floor-to-ceiling heights – particularly important with increased MVHR units
- use of ceiling fans for temperature peaks – ceiling fans can give the feeling of a 2°C temperature reduction by increasing air movement and aiding natural ventilation[29]
- mechanical systems or top window winders which may need to be used to reach to the openable top window
- a greater volume of air, which may lead to higher winter space heating demand although thermal mass can help balance this out.

Privacy, daylighting and solar shading

Environmental design basics include high-performing glazing and solar shading to maximise winter solar gain and prevent summer overheating. However, these principles must also take into account user behaviour and site constraints which may impact on a sense of privacy and security.

Protect privacy while maximising winter solar gain and daylighting:

- Hierarchy of outdoor spaces: provide privacy strips of minimum 1.2 m depth. These are soft edges such as low walls and semi-private areas in front gardens. Communal front spaces should be softened with flower beds which also provide security and privacy to the ground floor units.
- Increase ceiling heights and window heights on ground floor and on the upper floors of exposed units.
- Avoid floor-to-ceiling windows on ground or where visible.
- There is a real risk that curtains will be drawn most of the time, reducing solar gain and daylighting by 50% or more. Provide a mixture of appropriate boundary plants and window boxes.
- Design window division and curtain or blind installation to allow the lower part to be protected with moveable curtains and privacy screens, while allowing the top part to remain open to sun/daylight.
- Balcony design: use etched glazing/semi-transparent but reflective surface finishes for balcony enclosures.
- Avoid solid vertical shutters as these might remain closed throughout the year for privacy reasons. Provide external louvred shutters which can be split in two parts, allowing the bottom part to be closed. Lower shutters can have smaller louvred openings to increase privacy.
- Lockable louvred shutters on ground level are particularly good for providing secure night time-ventilation.

6.6   NATURAL VENTILATION, COOLING AND THERMAL MASS

Natural ventilation and thermal mass can passively cool buildings. However, unwanted summer solar gain must be dealt with before considering passive (or any active) cooling. See Section 6.5.

6.6.1 What is thermal mass and what are its benefits?

Thermal mass is a material's capacity to store heat from surrounding air or surfaces. Usually, the denser the materials, the better their thermal capacity. Thermal mass in continuously used buildings has the capacity to moderate day and night temperatures. This achieves operational carbon savings and greater thermal comfort year-round.

Exposed concrete ceilings and thermal mass walls are the best performers. However, the embodied carbon is high and may never be paid back through operational energy savings. Thermally massive buildings can provide summer cooling of 3–5°C and can decrease summer cooling energy demand by 7–17% as well as winter heating demand by 9–32%.[30] Lightweight buildings without thermal mass should only be specified for intermittent use, such as holiday homes. Thermal mass can be introduced into lightweight buildings as ceiling, floor and wall finishes. See Fig. 6.6.2 and ——⤙ jump to Section 7.2.7 for a more comprehensive list. For thermal lag, ——⤙ jump to Section 7.3.6.

Using thermal mass externally
The external environment can also benefit from thermal mass:
- External thermal mass can be used to moderate external microclimates. This extends the 'outdoor season', allowing outdoor spaces to be used for longer.
- External mass surfaces should be light-coloured to reduce absorption. This minimises contribution to the urban heat island effect.
   ——⤙ Jump to Section 4.2.1.
- Brick, concrete, blocks and stone are best for maintaining airtightness. They suffer less thermal movement and are less prone to cracking.

Trombe wall
A Trombe wall is a thermal mass wall, usually around 150–300 mm thick, placed behind south-facing glazing. Its wall area should not exceed 20% of the floor area which it heats.[31] It stores daytime solar gain and releases it back at night when residents most benefit from the heat. However, it can exacerbate summertime overheating, hence is most suitable in Region 1.

Key recommendations

- A large surface area is more important than the thickness of thermal mass, and should always be combined with good night-time ventilation (see Section 6.6.2).
- Around 5–8 m² of 50 mm masonry thermal mass is effective in a 10 m² space.[32] Thermal mass > 150 mm depth is not hugely beneficial.

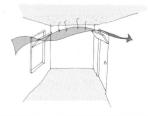

Thermal mass should always be combined with secure night-time ventilation.

Note: 'Hopper' windows/panels above window and door to allow for security and privacy.

Fig. 6.6.1 Thermal mass recommendation

- A structurally heavyweight building is not necessarily heavyweight in effective thermal mass: its structural mass needs to be exposed.
- High thermal mass materials such as concrete, brick and stone are also recommended for flood-resilient design. ——⊗ Jump to Section 5.2
- Prioritise retrofitting externally solid-walled properties with external insulation. Internal insulation covers up the internal thermal mass brick walls. External insulation will also avoid difficult thermal bridging. ——⊗ Jump to Chapters 8 and 9.
- Thermal mass may delay the need for mechanical cooling systems by another 40–60 years.[33]
- Many modelling tools are not able to accurately model the behaviour of thermal mass in relation to heating or cooling energy demand.[34] Manual calculations are more accurate. A thermal mass calculator can be downloaded free from www.concretecentre.com.[35]

Material specifications

- Specify high thermal mass materials throughout; ensure that they are also flood resilient for lower floors. ——⊗ Jump to Section 5.2.
- Internal exposed concrete for ceilings – painted or wet plastered.
- Specify hard flooring surfaces such as solid timber or stone.
- Avoid plasterboard over thermal mass materials as it insulates the thermal mass; use in-situ plaster, which also increases airtightness.
- Water is the best thermal mass with lowest embodied carbon, hence its use as a seasonal heat store. ——⊗ Jump to Section 10.4.1.

Thermal mass and embodied carbon

Figure 6.6.2 indicates that high thermal capacity materials (particularly brick and concrete) significantly increase embodied energy. The additional embodied carbon is estimated at 3–5 tonnes of CO_2 for a 100 m² house,[36, 37] which would take around 19–25 years to pay back from operational heating energy savings alone. However, thermal mass may have other benefits such as increased thermal comfort, and it is often more flood-resilient.

Fig. 6.6.2 Typical materials and their thermal mass capacity and embodied carbon

Materials	Specific heat capacity J/kgK	Density kg/m³	Effective heat capacity Wh/m²K	Embodied carbon kgCO₂ per 1 m²
water (150 mm depth)	4200	1000	175	0.15
cast concrete (150 mm depth, e.g. exposed ceiling)	1000	2000	83.3	33.6
heavyweight concrete block (140 mm depth)	840	2240	73.1	31.3
calcium silicate blocks (100 mm) e.g. Silka	1000	1850	51.4	24
brick wall (102 mm depth)	800	1873	42.4	43.3
gypsum block (100 mm)	840	950	22	11.4
solid timber flooring (25 mm depth)	1200	650	5.4	14.6
natural stone (10 mm depth)	700	2600	5	1.5
ceramic tiles (10 mm depth)	800	1900	4.2	11.2
wet plaster (10 mm depth)	1000	1330	3.7	1.6
plasterboard (12.5 mm depth)	840	950	2.7	3.8
phase change materials (PCM) minimal depth	70	855	0.09	n/a

Phase change materials

Phase change materials (PCMs) provide heat capacity by changing phase in response to the environment (i.e. by freezing, melting, vaporising or condensing). They usually contain minuscule particles of paraffin which change from solid to liquid state if temperatures reach a certain threshold (usually 23–30°C). In doing so, the PCM absorbs heat from the surroundings, providing a cooling effect. The heat is later released as the surroundings cool and the paraffin changes back to a solid. The thermal mass of most PCMs is low – 3% for plasterboard and <1% for concrete – thus they should not be relied upon for significant temperature moderation. Instead, they should be specified as a way to top up the capacity of existing thermal mass. For dwellings, PCMs with melting point around 25–26°C should be specified. Products include aluminium-clad panels containing paraffin and paraffin capsules mixed with plaster and paint. The impact of PCMs on indoor air quality is unknown.

6.6.2 Natural ventilation

Natural ventilation is best achieved in shallow, dual-aspect spaces with a network of openings through which fresh air enters and stale air is expelled. In dwellings, ventilation is required to remove humidity, while in offices, this is mostly to remove smells. However, in winter, open windows lose valuable warm air. This is why ventilation with heat recovery (VHR) is often used in winter (see Section 6.7).

In summer, good natural ventilation is the key to reducing internal temperatures and extracting odours. Using natural ventilation to cool a building at night is particularly effective, especially when combined with thermal mass (see also Section 6.6.1). But remember that ventilation is only a cooling source if the air is cooler outside than inside.

Key recommendations

Don't underestimate the importance of site layout for natural ventilation.
——⟶ Jump to Section 3.6.

 Natural ventilation requires floor plan depths up to 2 times floor-to-ceiling height with openable windows on at least one side. If the area or number of openable windows increases or, for example, stack effect is used, the depth of plan can increase up to 5 times floor-to-ceiling height.

 **Cross-ventilation** is the free flow of air between two window openings. For air to flow freely, temperatures need to be minimum 2°C cooler outside than inside.

Size of openable window area: minimum 5% of room floor area where window tilt angle is more than 30° (and 10% of room floor area where window tilt angle is 15–30°).[38] The window tilt angle is the openable angle of the window.

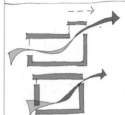 **Stack effect** uses the natural stratification of rising warm air and requires top and bottom openings. The intake openings must be minimum 1.2 m below the air outlets. Clear flow between rooms is required. For multi-storey stack effect ventilation, the stack inlet should be 3–4% of floor area and with matching outlet area. Stack ideally 2–3 m above highest roof point.[39]

- Secure night-time ventilation should occur near the ceiling where hot air has risen and thermal mass needs cooling. Allow for window winders to open top-level windows easily.
- Window design: small top openings such as inward-opening 'hopper windows' are ideal. They can be opened separately from larger openings lower down. Take care with potential rain penetration.
- Internal door design: it is important to have opening panels/shutters between rooms, e.g. above doors, to allow for a good cross flow between rooms with a retained sense of privacy. These openable panels can be glazed. They will need to meet Building Regulations requirements for fire protection.
- In noisy urban areas, acoustically attenuated panels may replace these hopper windows on the external façade. They can also be specified between rooms.
- In offices and non-domestic uses, care needs to be taken so that night-time air movement does not trigger intruder alarms falsely.

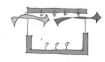

Night cooling: night-time natural ventilation is the most effective way of cooling building spaces during summer, particularly when combined with thermal mass. For night cooling to be effective, a minimum 7–8°C difference between day- and night-time temperatures is required. This is usually the case in the UK.

Designers need to be realistic about noise in cities when providing night cooling for bedrooms. Acoustically attenuated wall or window openings may be considered. Failure to provide night cooling will create great thermal discomfort once thermal mass capacity is saturated.

Code for Sustainable Homes credits (Hea 1 and Hea 4, Man 4). EcoHomes credits (Man 4) and BREEAM credits (Hea 2 and Hea 6)

Realistic ventilation rates[40]

Window type	Cross-ventilation (air changes per hour)	No cross-ventilation (air changes per hour)
trickle vents	0.1–0.2	0.1
hopper window 50 mm opening	0.8–1	0.5–0.6
fully opened window	6–8	4–6

Ventilation building management systems

To avoid reliance on occupants' behaviour, a building management system (BMS) may be used to control windows and shutters. Sensors control motors which automatically open and close windows/shutters to modify internal conditions in relation to external conditions. It is important that the controls can be easily overridden by the occupants, but equally important that they have a full understanding of how the system works. BMS is uncommon in dwellings.

Window design

Windows tend to open outwards in the UK. The key benefit is that they are usually more weathertight and do not intrude on internal space when opened. However, outward-opening windows are often incompatible with vertical external solar shading devices and secure night-time ventilation. See key recommendations on page 155.

Key recommendations

- Inward-opening windows should be specified, particularly on east/west orientations where use of vertical solar shading will be required.
- Horizontal central pivoting windows (see Fig. 6.6.3a) are best for natural ventilation and are ideal on north and south. Where combined with vertical shutters, ensure that a 15–30° opening angle can be accommodated in the wall depth and take into account use of space/placement of furniture.
- Alternatively, specify windows that do not jeopardise internal space and provide good ventilation, such as sash or sliding windows (see Fig. 6.6.3b and c).
- Ensure good draught stripping for vertical sash windows (see Fig. 6.6.3b). Large triple-glazed sash windows may be too heavy to operate.
- Inward-opening hopper windows are ideal for night cooling. Recommended for each window (see Fig. 6.6.3 – detail 'd'). Most internal doors benefit from an equivalent solid top door panel to ventilate at night while retaining privacy.
- A balance is to be achieved between heat loss, daylighting and solar gain. Ideal total window area should be 70:30 south to north, if winter solar gain is desirable.
- Windows should be sized as 10–20% of the floor area, with the higher percentage in the more northern regions in the UK.

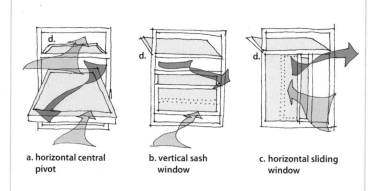

a. horizontal central pivot

b. vertical sash window

c. horizontal sliding window

Fig. 6.6.3 Window design for best natural ventilation and night cooling (read in conjunction with key recommendations)

6.7 VENTILATION WITH HEAT RECOVERY (VHR), INCLUDING PASSIVE STACK VENTILATION AND MVHR

In winter, stale air is often ventilated through window trickle vents and/or 'accidentally' through fabric gaps and cracks, but with airtightness standards increasing to ≤3 m³/(hr.m²), fresh air needs to be provided by other means.
——⟶ Jump to Section 7.4.

Simply by extracting stale air and using it to preheat fresh air supply, VHR can remove contaminants, smells and CO_2 while providing oxygen and a base heat.

The volumes of air never mix but pass over each other in metal ducts, effectively exchanging heat. VHR can be specified for kitchen and bathroom extracts only, and does not have to be whole building ventilation. VHR can happen mechanically or passively and windows can be opened as normal if need be.

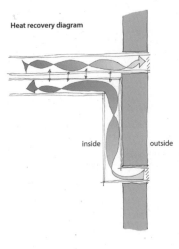

Heat recovery diagram

inside   outside

Ventilation with heat recovery can be utilised locally for computer server rooms or bathroom and kitchen extracts. It can also be used for a 'whole house' or 'whole building' approach. This is particularly the case if airtightness standards are ≤3 m³/(hr.m²), because the accidental provision of fresh air through gaps and cracks is no longer sufficient to provide good indoor air quality and remove humidity. The better the fabric efficiency of a building, the greater the suitability for heat recovery. Where airtightness standards are ≤1 m³/(hr.m²), ventilation with heat recovery negates the need for traditional heating systems. Generally the required 'top-up' heating is provided via air-to-air heating or much smaller localised radiators/heaters.
——⟶ Jump to Sections 7.4 and 7.5.

Fig. 6.7.1 Heat recovery principle

For heat recovery from shower and bath waste water, ——⟶ jump to Section 5.5.3.

Key recommendations

....

- It is crucial that design, installation and commissioning is undertaken with care.
- Ventilation with heat recovery is always recommended to reduce heat losses with air extraction, as in bathrooms and cooker hoods.
- Insulate all ductwork.
- Allow more generous floor-to-ceiling heights to accommodate ductwork (see Fig. 6.5.9).
- Building Regulations stipulate minimum heat recovery efficiencies of 66–75%. In field trials, heat recovery units performed significantly worse than specified.[41] Specify heat recovery units with much greater efficiencies than those stipulated by the regulations – 90% or above.
- Advise clients and occupants that filter cleaning is required every few months to prevent mould spores from growing. Install filter where it can be easily replaced. Schedule two- or three-yearly inspections and filter replacement as part of ongoing maintenance. At the same time, record occupants' satisfaction.
- Internal doors to have a gap underneath in accordance with Building Regulations (usually 10 mm).
- Users must have a clear manual and easy-to-use humidity on/off switches. Inlets and outlets should be located where they cannot be covered by furniture and be less useful.
- Ventilation intakes should be placed away from pollution sources and cold draughts/winds. Ventilation outlets should be placed away from seating areas to prevent draught/discomfort.
- Heat recovery is usually used for around nine months of the year, and is not needed in summer. Hence a summer bypass is required so that no heat exchange and/or any mechanical ventilation takes place.

Passive stack ventilation (PSV) with heat recovery

Passive stack ventilation does not require operational energy. It works with the wind. This means that when there is no wind there is no fresh air supply or heat recovery. It is usually not recommended as the sole means of whole house ventilation or heating.

- It is ideal for localised extraction of air, e.g. in bathrooms and kitchens, where there is access to wind at roof level.
- Air intake and out-take are combined, usually in the form of a windcowl which moves depending on the wind direction. This means that the windcowls and connecting ductwork need to reach to the roof level. Ductwork can be complex in flats and multi-use buildings. Fire dampers will be required around ductwork between separating floor levels.

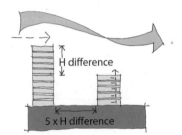

Passive stack ventilation is suitable if the building is the tallest in the vicinity, and at least 75% higher; or if taller buildings are in the vicinity, they need to be placed away by five x buildings' height difference.

Fig. 6.7.2 Passive stack ventilation

Passive stack ventilation can also be used without heat recovery.

Mechanical ventilation with heat recovery (MVHR)

Localised extracts can recover heat through mechanical rather than passive means. This uses electrical energy. Therefore MVHR should only be used in super-insulated and airtight buildings. It is always recommended in buildings with airtightness ≤3 m³/(hr.m²) (some argue from < 5m3/(hr.m²) to control humidity).[42] If airtightness standards are less than 1 m³/(hr.m²) and with space heat demand of ≤15 kWh/m² per year, such as in the Passivhaus standard, no traditional radiators or gas-heating system may be required if there is whole house ventilation with MVHR.

The UK has a humid climate and the jury is still out on MVHR winter performance. However, in other EU countries, occupant satisfaction with thermal comfort and air quality has been good. MVHR units can also filter incoming air. This is beneficial in inner city areas and near polluted areas and major roads.

> ### Key recommendations
>
> - It is crucial that design, installation and commissioning is undertaken with care.
> - Whole house MVHR is suitable if airtightness standards are ≤5m³/(hr.m²) and recommended where ≤3m³/(hr.m²).
> - An automatic 'boost' function with manual override is important for moisture control at peak times in UK dwellings.
> - Specify MVHR with ≥ 90% efficiency (≤1W/l/s).
> - Cleaning of filters every three to six months.
> - If the dwelling is built to Passivhaus standard, the MVHR unit contributes around 80 kgCO₂ per year to the atmosphere. However, a total carbon reduction of 300–350 kgCO₂ per year is achieved from 'free' space heating.[43]
> - The MVHR unit should be located within the warm thermal envelope, and for a dwelling has approximate dimensions 950 mm (h) × 780 mm (w) × 590 mm (d).

- The exhaust outlet should be situated at least 1 m horizontally and 1.2 m higher than the air intake. Inlets should be located away from pollution.
- MVHR can work even more efficiently where combined with earth pipes or ground ducts (see below).

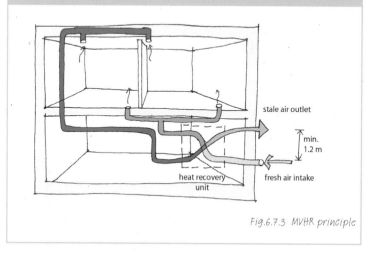

stale air outlet

min.
1.2 m

heat recovery
unit

fresh air intake

Fig.6.7.3 MVHR principle

More effective MVHR and summer cooling systems
• Ground ducts/earth pipes

The earth is at a constant temperature of 10–15°C. By drawing external air through 1.5–2 m deep ground ducts, the air is heated before it reaches the MVHR unit, making heat exchange more effective. Buildings can be cooled this way in summer, bypassing the MVHR unit. The ground ducts precool the air by 5–10°C.[44] For dwellings, a 40 m duct run is usually sufficient. Ducts are laid a metre apart at a gradient of 2% to discharge any summer condensation.
——⟩ Jump to Section 12.8.8 for ground source heat pumps.

• Indirect adiabatic cooling

Instead of bypassing the MVHR unit in summer, the extracted air is humidified before it passes through the heat exchanger. This cools the fresh air from outside.
——⟩ Jump to Section 12.8.13 for evaporative cooling.

6.8 POLLUTANTS AND THE INDOOR ENVIRONMENT

Good indoor air quality is maintained through ventilation. In an airtight construction the ventilation is often lower than in traditionally constructed buildings. This means certain internal materials may impact on health.

Making buildings more airtight means there is less air infiltration to dilute pollutants. Symptoms may be headaches, itchy eyes, blocked nose, loss of concentration, dizziness, exacerbated asthma and allergies.

Most of this pollutant 'off-gassing' from new materials will disappear after two years. However, because of the regular cycle of replacement and upgrading, the potential impact on residents is nevertheless significant. The careful specification of material finishes is crucial.[45]

Key recommendations

Stipulate alternative standards, finishes and fixing methods with little or no additional financial cost:

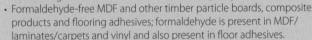

- For flooring look out for EU EMICODE label – specify EMICODE EC1
- Formaldehyde-free MDF and other timber particle boards, composite products and flooring adhesives; formaldehyde is present in MDF/laminates/carpets and vinyl and also present in floor adhesives.
- Avoid carpet finishes: they are a source of dust, high in pollutants and exacerbate allergies and asthma.
- Always specify tongue and grooved solid timber finishes or mechanical fixings as this also enables deconstruction; avoid glues.
- Volatile organic compounds (VOCs) are also present in cleaning products, fabric softener and car exhausts so specify low VOC or solvent-free paints, timber preservatives and glues.
- The designer has no control over what occupants acquire, but in the occupants' user manual, give advice about internal air quality and health risks from furniture bought.

Some pollutants come in from outside: NOx, SO_2, dust, lead. This can be controlled by:

- external vegetation to trap dust particles.
- good airtightness to minimise pollutants entering uncontrolled. MVHR with filtering will help. Ensure that inlets are located away from main busy roads and pollution sources.

Fig. 6.8.1 Typical internal finishes and possible recommended alternatives

Typical Internal finishes	Recommended alternative finishes
Flooring	
carpet with PVC backing	timber, carpet with woven or latex backing, wool carpets without moth insecticide treatment
PVC/vinyl/laminated floor	rubber and linoleum with low VOC glues, ceramic, stone, solid non-glued timber
cork	solid non-glued timber or cork without (acrylic) sealant
parquet/engineered /glued timber	solid timber floor with mechanical fixing or tongue and grooved; some manufacturers have minimised off-gassing – always obtain advice
Walls/ceiling	
solvent-based paint; oil	water-based acrylic paints with low VOC, but matt paints are better than glossy finishes; paints with natural-based pigments still emit VOCs, although often reduced
vinyl	always avoid – see above for alternatives
wall paper	wet plaster and low VOC paint finish
plasterboard	wet plaster; avoid plywood, unless formaldehyde free
timber particleboard and MDF	specify formaldehyde-free MDF and timber boards
treated timber	only treat where necessary; specify low VOC content, borate-based, and finish with water-based sealants or natural beeswax/oil
phase change materials	exposed structural concrete thermal mass and thermal mass finishes (see Fig. 6.6.2)

6.9 FUTURE-PROOFING: NOW AND IN THE FUTURE

Buildings must always function efficiently and provide a comfortable space for occupants, so certain environmental approaches are required right from the start. However, other strategies can be implemented later as the climate changes. The table below gives an overview of which strategies are essential now, and which can be planned for to allow future adaptations.

Which strategies can be done later, instead of now? (✓ = can be done later; x = do now)	Regions 1 and 2	Regions 3 and 4
Maximise building orientation to take advantage of free solar gain.	X	X
Design shallow plan buildings to maximise natural daylighting and ventilation.	X	X
Provide high floor-to-ceiling heights.	X	X
Provide structural thermal mass.	X	X
Provide thermal mass finishes (design heavyweight construction now, even if not initially with exposed surfaces – for example, plasterboard can be removed from internal thermal mass walls and replaced with in-situ plaster; pipes and services will need to be relocated).	✓	X
Use phase change materials.	✓	✓
Provide green spaces between buildings (for adaptation, transform hard landscape into green space).	✓	X
Green roofs and walls (for adaptation, design current structure for possible future load increases).	✓	✓
Solar shading (for adaptation, design space for future structure/fixings).	✓	X
Provide inward-opening windows.	X	X
Specify light-coloured and reflective surfaces.	✓	X
Night cooling (for adaptation, windows may need to be replaced to allow for night cooling, unless inward-opening hopper windows are specified at initial design stage).	✓	X
Low carbon cooling (for adaptation, in initial design, provide compatible heat distribution systems such as underfloor heating and ground ducts).	✓	✓

6.10 APPLICABLE LEGISLATION AND GUIDANCE

- BRE Information Paper 17/03, Impact of horizontal shading devices on peak solar gains through windows
- BREEAM2011 Technical Manual www.breeam.org/BREEAM2011SchemeDocument/
- British Coating Federation www.coatings.org.uk
- BS 5707:1997 Specification for preparations of wood preservatives in organic solvents
- BS 8206-2:2008 Lighting for buildings – Part 2: Code of practice for daylighting
- BS EN 13141-9:2008 Ventilation for buildings. BS EN 13779:2007 Ventilation for non-residential buildings
- BS EN 13829:2001 Thermal performance of buildings. Determination of air permeability of buildings. Fan pressurization method
- BS EN 15217:2007 Energy performance of buildings. Methods for expressing energy performance and for energy certification of buildings
- BS EN 15239:2007 Ventilation for buildings. Energy performance of buildings. Guidelines for inspection of ventilation systems
- BS EN 15251:2007 Indoor environmental input parameters for design and assessment of energy performance of buildings addressing indoor air quality, thermal environment, lighting and acoustics
- BS EN 599-1:2009 Durability of wood and wood-based products
- Centre for Window and Cladding Technology (CWCT), Standard for systemised building envelopes, 2006
- CIBSE Guide A, Environmental design 2006
- CIBSE Guide B, Heating, ventilating, air conditioning and refrigeration, 2005
- CIBSE Guide F, Energy efficiency in Buildings 2004
- CIBSE TM23: Testing buildings for air leakage 2000
- Code for Sustainable Homes Technical Guide, November 2010
- Code for Sustainable Homes, Impact assessment, December 2009
- Comfort (CIBSE Knowledge Series) 2006
- DFP Technical Booklet F1: 2006 – Conservation of fuel and power in dwellings, N. Ireland
- EcoHomes 2006, The environmental rating for homes The Guidance – 2006 / Issue1.2 April 2006
- EST (2006), Energy efficient ventilation in dwellings – a guide for specifiers
- ISO16000-25 Indoor air – Part 25: Determination of the emission of semi-volatile organic compounds by building products – Micro-chamber method
- Technical Booklet K: 1998 Ventilation, N. Ireland
- Technical Guidance Document F, Ventilation, 2009, Ireland
- Technical Handbooks 2011 – Domestic Energy Section 6 and Section 3 – Environment, Scotland
- The Building Regulations 2000, Ventilation, Approved Document F 2010 Edition
- The Building Regulations 2010 Conservation of fuel and power, Approved document L: Criterion 3, England and Wales; Scotland

6.11   FURTHER READING

- Baker Laporte et al. (2001), *Prescriptions for a healthy house, a practical guide for architects, builders and homeowners*, New Society Publishers, Canada
- CE257, Daylighting in Urban areas: A guide for designers, Energy Saving Trust, September 2007, www.energysavingtrust.org.uk
- CIBSE, How to manage overheating in buildings, Practical guide to improving summertime comfort in buildings, 2010
- Evans (2011), *Guide to the Building Regulations*, RIBA Publications
- Good Practice Guide 245 Desktop guide to daylighting – for architects, 1998, Building Research Energy Conservation Support Unit
- Hacker et al. (2005), Beating the Heat: keeping UK buildings cool in a warming climate. UKCIP Briefing Report. UKCIP, Oxford,
- Harrison et al. (2000), BRE Building Elements, Building services, Performance, diagnosis, maintenance, repair and the avoidance of defects
- www.lifetimehomes.org.uk/
- Levitt (2011), *The Housing Design Handbook*, Routledge
- Martin and Goswami (2005), *Solar Energy Pocket Reference*, Earthscan
- NHBC (2009), Indoor air quality in highly energy efficient homes – a review
- Stevenson and Williams (2007), Sustainable Housing Design Guide for Scotland, Communities Scotland

Chapter 7
The building fabric

Taking steps to reduce a building's operational carbon footprint usually requires an increase in its embodied carbon footprint, owing to the increased amount of insulation material required. This 'investment' in a higher carbon footprint will soon pay off if the building is carefully designed and constructed for long life, ease of maintenance, deconstruction and reuse.

Materials and construction methods may be chosen according to:
- aesthetics
- costs
- availability
- robustness
- material performance, e.g. acoustics and structural strength

When specifying the fabric of a sustainable building, the designer should also prioritise:
- life-cycle assessment and embodied carbon of materials, including designing for deconstruction and reuse
- thermal performance
- air, vapour and water permeability
- impact on internal air quality

This chapter explores the latter in more detail. The focus is on mainstream building techniques and materials suitable in the UK.

 Symbol indicates relevance to the Code for Sustainable Homes, EcoHomes & BREEAM.

7.1 THE ENVIRONMENTAL IMPACT OF BUILDING MATERIALS

7.1.1 Material specification overview – checklist	☑ ☒
Does the design specify timber from sustainable sources with chain of custody only? (See Section 7.2.2.)	☐
Have uPVC products been avoided, particularly for internal finishing and windows? (Otherwise internal air quality will be compromised and embodied carbon is high.)	☐
Have you specified standard products/modules and components to reduce off-cuts of waste on site (e.g. standard sizes such as brick and timber dimensions)?	☐
Have you designed for deconstruction and reuse? (See Section 7.1.9.)	☐
Does the design specify materials with low embodied carbon? (See Sections 7.1.2 and 7.2.7.)	☐
Where specifying materials with high embodied carbon, have you ensured that they are excellent at reducing operational carbon emissions?	☐
Have you sourced heavy mass materials locally: within a 50–100 km radius?[1]	☐
If the specification permits the substitution of equivalent products or materials, have you used careful performance specifications to avoid substitution of inferior products or materials?	☐
Have you specified products and materials only after supply chain of responsible/local sourcing has been established?	☐
Does the design specify prefabrication (MMC) for lightweight materials/ components without compromising decrement delay? (See Section 7.3.6.)	☐
Have you specified reclaimed materials and products? (See Section 7.1.8.)	☐
Have you specified ICE EU demolition protocol for waste minimisation on site, and submitted a statement to the local authority (usually with planning application)?	☐
Have you taken care not to order materials too far in advance? (Disappearance, wastage and risk of damage would otherwise be greater.) Have you considered just-in-time delivery?	☐
Structural elements, roofs, walls and floors take up the largest percentage of budget and carbon emission, so have you focused on reducing these, particularly as they are often not replaced?	☐

Have you specified hygroscopic materials as internal finishes, particularly in bathrooms, wetrooms and kitchens, to help moderate relative humidity naturally?	☐
Have you specified materials that do not jeopardise internal air quality? ⟶ Jump to Section 6.8.	☐
Have you specified constructions with exposed thermal mass materials? ⟶ Jump to Section 6.6.	☐
Have you avoided compromise on airtightness detailing, thermal bridging and avoiding thermal bypasses? (See Sections 7.3 and 7.4.)	☐

7.1.2 Embodied carbon

Embodied energy is a hidden, theoretical energy. It is the energy used to construct a building and the materials with which it is made. It can also be expressed as embodied carbon by multiplying the energy used to produce the materials by the carbon intensity of the fuel used. Embodied energy is usually expressed as MJ/kg of material, and its embodied carbon is expressed as $kgCO_2$ per kg or per m^3 of material. If a manufacturer runs their operations with renewable energy, the embodied carbon of a material is significantly reduced but its embodied energy remains the same.

Plant- or tree-based materials can be carbon negative or act as a 'carbon sink'. This means that they store carbon. This is usually not included in embodied carbon assessments, but it is a crucial consideration.

7.1.3 Whole-life carbon footprint

The total carbon footprint of any building is the sum of its operational carbon footprint and the carbon footprint embodied in the materials and their construction. This embodied carbon accounts for about 10% of a building's total carbon footprint, but depending on building typology this can be much higher. It can increase to as much as 30–40%[2] as fabric thermal performance improves because:
- reduced operational energy increases the relative proportion of the embodied energy
- better-performing buildings tend to need more materials and technologies to achieve a lower operational energy demand.

For example, walls built to Passivhaus standards are 8% thicker than Building Regulations walls and have at least 10% increased embodied carbon. However, the Passivhaus standard reduces the operational carbon by 70% and saves around 1 tonne of carbon for every year of the building's lifespan.[3]

Embodied carbon of a material usually encompasses the carbon from energy used to extract, process and manufacture material until the point that it leaves the factory gate. This is referred to as 'cradle to gate'.

'Cradle to cradle' extends this definition to include routine maintenance – replacement of components, future deconstruction and reuse at the end of the material's first life. This is the ideal approach. However, at present this is difficult to quantify and it depends on each site's location, so embodied carbon figures are usually quoted as cradle to gate only. Many buildings currently operate on a 'cradle to grave' principle as they are simply demolished and landfilled. (See Fig. 7.1.1.)

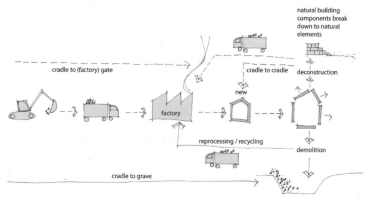

Fig. 7.1.1 Cradle to gate, cradle to grave and cradle to cradle

Key recommendations

- Improving building energy performance standards usually requires more materials or more components. This can require an increase in a building's embodied carbon. However, overall low-energy demand buildings have lower CO_2 emissions over their lifetime, and therefore a reduction in operational energy should be a priority over a reduction in embodied carbon since this will reduce carbon emissions now and until the end of the building's lifespan.[4]
- Truly low energy and low carbon design should consider the impact of its materials by undertaking an LCA study. (See Section 7.1.5.)
- Be careful not to mix embodied energy/carbon data from different sources and only ever use country-specific sources. Different sources of data use different methods and boundaries of calculation. Inconsistencies will be reduced as the industry responds to EU legislation such as TC 350.
  → Jump to Chapter 1.
- Intelligent logistics: sourcing materials locally can lower the embodied energy, transport emissions and transport congestion. (See Fig. 7.1.2.)

7.1.4 How to calculate the embodied carbon of a material

Embodied carbon figures used in this book are from the Inventory of Carbon and Energy (ICE), undertaken by Bath University based on cradle to gate principles.

Calculating the embodied carbon (EC) of a material

EC = volume of material × density of material × $kgCO_2$/kg*

Volume (m³)	Density (kg/m³)	kgCO₂(e)/kg	Embodied carbon of component kgCO₂
0.102 m³	× 1873 kg/m³	× 0.227 kgCO₂/kg	= 43.3 kgCO₂

* From the ICE database: example taken is for 1 m² of brick wall at 102 mm depth (mortar cement:lime:sand 1:1:6)

Transportation distances to site increase the embodied carbon further and can be calculated separately.

0.013 kgCO₂   0.029 kgCO₂   0.124 kgCO₂   0.587 kgCO₂

Fig. 7.1.2 Transportation mode and $kgCO_2$ per tonne of material per km travelled[5]

171

7.1.5 Life-cycle assessment and life-cycle costing

• **Life-cycle assessment (LCA)** considers the environmental impact of a material or product over its lifetime – from cradle to grave. This includes energy and carbon used for extraction, transportation and manufacture. It also includes other impacts such as resource use, pollution, waste and toxicity to air, water, land, humans and ecology. Finally, it includes maintenance, demolition and recycling, waste disposal or deconstruction and reuse.

• **Whole life costing (WLC) or life-cycle costing (LCC)** follows on from this, but just looks at the financial implications of materials over their lifetime. For example, maintenance and replacement are included as a proportion of the total building cost and operational costs.

Whole-life costing

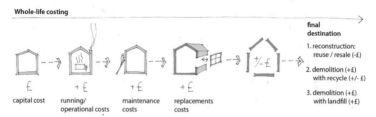

final destination

1. reconstruction: reuse / resale (-£)
2. demolition (+£) with recycle (+/- £)
3. demolition (+£) with landfill (+£)

£ — capital cost
+ £ — running/ operational costs
+ £ — maintenance costs
+ £ — replacements costs

Fig. 7.1.3 Whole-life costing

• **Building lifespan** is normally 60 years. Commercial property is often designed for shorter periods. Buildings designed for a longer time span will usually cost more to construct. In reality, buildings are used and maintained for longer than the design life. Housing can achieve 125 years or more. Typically, 3% yearly maintenance costs are incurred for large housing.[6]

7.1.6 BRE Green Guide to Specification

The BRE Green Guide to Specification uses life-cycle assessment to evaluate construction build-ups from the least environmentally impacting (A+) to the worst (E). Only the most common conventional specifications for creating building elements are included. The most heavily weighted impact category is embodied carbon ($kgCO_2$/kg).

Impacts such as water and resource extraction, ozone depletion, human and eco toxicity and waste disposal are also included.

The guide is used to obtain EcoHomes, Code for Sustainable Homes and BREEAM material credits. It cannot be ignored when designing to CSH levels 5 and 6 or to BREEAM/EcoHomes very good and excellent.

 Code for Sustainable Homes credits (Mat 1 mandatory), EcoHomes (Mat 1 and BREEAM (Mat 1, Mat 2)

7.1.7 Recommended specification distances

Sourcing material and products locally reduces the transportation fuel, emissions and congestion incurred in bringing materials from factory to site.

Key recommendations

- Reuse any materials from on-site demolition.
- Aim to source all materials as close to the site as possible.
- Aim to source all virgin, primary or new materials within a 100 km/ 70 mile radius.[7]
- Aim to source heavy and bulky materials close to the site.
- Reclaimed materials as well as lightweight virgin materials can justifiably be sourced from further away, although the closer they are sourced, the lower the environmental impact.[8]
- Avoid importing from outside the UK unless EU procurement rules apply.
- EU procurement rules apply for government-funded projects of above €3 m. Where the specification permits the substitution of equivalent products or materials, careful performance specifications and careful checking are required to avoid substitution of inferior materials.
  More info at www.europroc.eu.
- Avoid importing from outside the EU unless WTO rules apply. Require chain of custody or audit trails.
- Consider social labels, e.g. Fairtrade and Rugmark.
- Internet databases allow materials and manufacturer search according to distance from site address.
- Even where building materials can be sourced locally, do still check the environmental credentials.

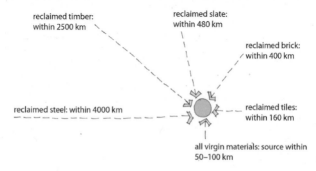

reclaimed timber: within 2500 km

reclaimed slate: within 480 km

reclaimed brick: within 400 km

reclaimed steel: within 4000 km

reclaimed tiles: within 160 km

all virgin materials: source within 50–100 km

Fig. 7.1.4 Recommended maximum material sourcing distances

7.1.8 Reclaimed/recycled materials

Existing buildings' materials and components can be utilised in a second life. In order of preference:

- reuse of buildings without demolition or deconstruction
- 'soft stripping' of finishes, removable fixtures and equipment
- deconstruction for reuse on-site
- deconstruction for reclamation for reuse off-site.

The latter two avoid sending waste to landfill and needing to manufacture new materials. They are preferable to 'downcycling', which reduces a material's quality and/or value:

- demolition for recycling in situ such as hardcore or concrete crushing
- demolition for recycling off site, which usually involves on- or off-site segregation for reprocessing.

Reclamation and reuse of building materials should not be more expensive but it will impact on the programme as it is usually a labour-intensive process carried out by hand.

Key recommendations

- Plan time for deconstruction and reclamation of materials. Lead time/ critical path may be affected for larger projects and with greater quantities of reclaimed materials.
- Allow extra time during construction to source materials.
- Minimise over-ordering. Where material is over-ordered, designers should make use of excess elsewhere.
- Use careful secure storage of materials on or near site, especially where large quantities need to be held.
- Reclaimed materials used for structural purposes (e.g. steel or timber columns and beams) will need to undergo strict testing and assessment by an insured expert to ensure structural integrity.
- Agree use of reclaimed materials with client, contractor and building insurer and ensure contractual agreements are in place (collateral warranties).

Some sources to obtain reclaimed materials from

- www.wrap.org.uk/rcproducts
- www.aggregain.org.uk
- www.salvomie.co.uk
- www.eastex.org.uk
- www.lassco.co.uk
- www.salvo.co.uk
- www.bremap.co.uk
- www.greenspec.co.uk

Typical materials and suitable products for reclamation[9]

Steel
- Most new steel has a 40–60% recycled content, but recycled steel is still high in embodied carbon and energy owing to its high melting temperature.
- Reclamation for reuse is always best.
- Can be dismantled, but bolts need to be carefully removed for health and safety reasons.
- Blast clean and prime for new finishes where needed.
- Redundant bolt holes generally should not affect the strength.
- Building Regulations need to be satisfied if used elsewhere structurally.
- Steel framed buildings are cost-effective in reuse: 35–50% cheaper than new.
- Designs should permit numerous steel sections as they may come from several different buildings.[10]

Concrete
- Concrete framed buildings can only be deconstructed if they are prefabricated and designed with joints for deconstruction purposes.
- Concrete frames crushed on site are referred to as recycled concrete aggregate (RCA). Other in-situ concrete is usually downcycled as crushed concrete for hardcore and green roofs etc.
- For in-situ structural concrete, 20% recycled aggregate or RCA is allowed.[11]
- Precast concrete floor plates could be reclaimed as long as no screeds were applied during first life.
- Applicable standards:
    - BS 8500-1: 2006 (it includes recycled aggregate standard)
    - WRAP, protocols for production of aggregates from inert waste, 2005.

Timber
- When timber is reused, it reduces nearly 80% of its environmental impact compared to virgin timber.[12]
- However, timber products are often downcycled into chipboard.
- Reclaimed studs and joists are usually cheaper and of better quality as they tend to be older, slower-grown timber. Timber beams come at a premium.
- Beams for structural purposes will require strength grading.
- Reclaimed timber flooring is easily available and tends to be cost neutral. It can have aesthetic advantages when reclaimed.
- Applicable standards:[13]
    - BS 4978 (softwoods) and BS 5756 (hardwoods)

Bricks

- Brick and block can be reclaimed where lime mortar has been used.
- Availability is good but it is not always cost-effective, unless high-quality new bricks are substituted with reclaimed bricks.[14]
- Applicable standards:
  - BS 3921:1985 (1995)

Other materials

- Roof slates, ceramic tiles and pavers, granite sets and kerbs are easily available.
- Avoid use of reclaimed railway sleepers in vegetable-growing planters.
- Reclaimed concrete pavers are very cost-effective.

Architectural fittings

- All easily available: sinks, baths, taps, iron, stone, timber, timber doors, radiators.
- Reclaimed doors are cheap but difficult to find matching styles in quantity.

Services

- M&E services such as fans and other equipment.
- Any electrical goods will require electrical safety testing.

Fig. 7.1.5 Embodied carbon reduction of reclaimed materials[15]

Reclaimed material	kgCO$_2$/kg reduction (recycled)	kgCO$_2$/kg reduction (reclaimed)	kgCO$_2$/m² reduction from reclaimed unless stated otherwise
aluminium	1.69	8.24	depends on end product use
steel and steel fencing	0.44	1.37	~6 kgCO$_2$ per m run (depending on amount of steel used)
timber beams/joists	n/a	0.58	353.8 kgCO$_2$/m³
timber hardwood flooring	n/a	0.58–0.86	14.6–8.8
timber door	n/a	n/a	~15 kgCO$_2$ (depending on type of wood used)
common brick	n/a	0.23	483 kgCO$_2$/m³ (~0.55 kgCO$_2$ per brick)
slate roof tile	n/a	0.058	1.7
terracotta/clay tile	n/a	0.45	8.5
granite stone	n/a	0.64	16.6

 Code for Sustainable Homes credits (Mat 1 mandatory, Mat 2, Mat 3, Was 2, Man 3), EcoHomes credits (Mat 1, Man 3) for use of reclaimed timber floorboards, bricks and roof tiles (slate/clay) and BREEAM (Mat 1, Mat 3, Wst 1 mandatory, Wst 2)

7.1.9 Designing for deconstruction and reuse

The most significant contributor to construction waste is material and product packaging, followed by timber, plastic products and concrete.[16]

Yet materials could be reused if the building is designed for easy dismantling. Designing for deconstruction and reuse can be financially beneficial at the end of a building's life owing to diminishing landfill capacity, increased landfill costs and taxes, and escalating waste treatment. The resale value of components can also be taken into account.

 Code for Sustainable Homes credits (Was 2 and Man 3 mandatory), EcoHomes credits (Man 3) and BREEAM (Wst 1 mandatory)

Designing for deconstruction – checklist	☑ ☒
To make future continuing use of the building easier, have you designed internal spaces free from structural columns to allow a flexible plan and layout, and have you avoided loadbearing structural internal walls to remove for future building use adaptation?	☐
Have you separated cladding and finishes from main structural elements, and specified lightweight materials and components as they are easier to dismantle?	☐
Have you used bolting or clamping instead of welding steel?	☐
Have you specified fixing mechanically with screws rather than nails; using low-tack or weak glues, friction or compression; using flooring with tongue and grooved jointing with fewer fastenings?	☐
Is the concrete frame designed to be prefabricated with joints to allow for deconstruction?	☐
Can you create and maintain a paper trail for structural timber and its strength and grading, including specification of gluelam and other engineered timber products?	☐
Have you used lime mortars instead of cement mortar for brick and blocks to enable reclamation and reuse of the parts, and stronger lime mortar mixes to suit exposure?	☐
Have you avoided painting or staining timber and galvanised steel?	☐

Have you avoided internal paint finishes, suspended ceilings and plasterboard? Where acceptable, try to specify finishes that can be left as they are (such as exposed blockwork). If finished internally, have you used clay or lime plaster?	☐
Have you used standardised/modular design, responding to standard manufacturing sizes to avoid off-cut waste?	☐
Have you specified prefabricated lightweight components without compromising on acoustic mass, thermal lag or thermal mass?	☐
Have you specified durable materials in preference to treatment and protection?	☐
Have you considered health and safety issues for deconstruction – i.e. how will someone do this safely?	☐
Have you undertaken a health and safety assessment of proposed deconstruction strategies, with special consideration for upper floors and the structural elements, in accordance with the Construction Design and Management (CDM) Regulations?	☐
Have the building owner and demolition (sub)contractor agreed the ownership of, and income from, any potentially sold materials recovered from site, if not reused on site?	☐
Have you complied with the ICE Demolition Protocol and Site Waste Management Plan Regulations? This includes an audit of which parts, and how much, of the proposed building and materials can be reused or reclaimed.[17] This is usually mandatory for planning permission and under the Code for Sustainable Homes. Useful checklist from www.ice.org.uk and specifications from www.greenspec.co.uk.	☐

7.1.10 APPLICABLE LEGISLATION AND GUIDANCE

- BIP 2026:2003 Whole life-cycle costing. Risk and risk responses
- BS ISO 15686-5:2008 Buildings and constructed assets, Service life planning, Life cycle costing
- ISO 14040:2006 Life cycle assessment – Principles and framework
- ISO 14044:2006 Life cycle assessment – Requirements and guidelines
- KIT 200 Standardized method of life cycle costing for construction
- PD 156865:2008 Standardized method of life cycle costing for construction procurement. Supplement to BS ISO 15686–5.
- BS 8902:2006 Responsible sourcing sector certification schemes for construction products
- BS 8903 Principles and framework for procuring sustainably

7.1.11 FURTHER READING AND GUIDANCE

- Addis (2004), Design for Deconstruction, CIRIA
- Addis (2006), Building with Reclaimed Components and Materials
- An environmental profiling system for building materials and components, 2009, BRE
- Anderson et al. (2009), The Green Guide to Specification, www.bre.co.uk/greenguide
- BS 6817 Code of Practice for Demolition
- Coventry et al. (1999), The reclaimed and recycled construction materials handbook, CIRIA
- Cycle Assessment Procedure for Eco Materials (CAP'em), www.capem.eu
- Design Handbook for Reuse and Recycling, Earthscan
- EU Procurement Rules version 2, OGC and GPP
- Hammond and Jones (2011), Inventory of Carbon and Energy (ICE), version 2 database, Bath University
- www.greenspec.co.uk/dismantling-re-use.php
- www.greenspec.co.uk/reclaimed-materials.php
- Hurley et al. (2001), Deconstruction and reuse of construction materials, BRE
- Institute of Civil Engineers (ICE), Demolition Protocol
- Practical solutions for sustainable construction, Reclaimed building products guide, Waste and Resources Action Programme www.wrap.org.uk/
- Reclamation-led Approach to Demolition, BioRegional Development Group, July 2007
- Ryan (2011), Traditional construction for a sustainable future, Spon Press
- Sassi (2006), Strategies for Sustainable Architecture, Taylor and Francis
- Stevenson and Morgan (2005) Design for Deconstruction book, SEDA Design Guides for Scotland: No. 1
- www.wrap.org.uk/construction

7.2 TYPICAL MAINSTREAM MATERIALS AND CONSTRUCTION METHODS

7.2.1 Modern methods of construction (MMC)

Modern methods of construction are also referred to as off-site construction, prefabrication and modular construction. Many materials are prefabricated: from brick and blockwork to windows and doors.

- 'Volumetric' or 3D prefabrication, e.g. plant rooms, bathroom/kitchen pods, student housing and hotel bedrooms and services as well as apartments and retail units. They are entirely fitted out in a factory-controlled environment, transported to site and craned into place.
- Panelised prefabrication: roof, wall and floor panel systems which, when put together, form rooms and buildings. This is more suitable where there is a larger variety of layouts.
- Pre-assembly: modular components, such as solar shading, balconies, decking and partitions, are made and preassembled in the factory for rapid placement or connection on site.

Benefits of off-site manufacture and on-site assembly

- better working conditions: weather, access, stability and safety
- reduced damage and loss of materials
- better supervision and quality control
- potentially easier to reuse off-cuts
- easier assembly and deconstruction

Risks of off-site manufacture and on-site assembly

- structural design must address progressive collapse
- lightweight components have little or no thermal mass capacity
- prefabricated components could mismatch with on-site in-situ work

---

Key recommendations (continued overleaf)

- Decide early in design process to use prefabrication.
- Continuous close coordination between designers, service and structural engineers as well as manufacturer and contractor.
- Freeze the design at RIBA Work Stage F to allow for manufacturer to complete design and manufacture.
- Use modular design, responding to standard manufacturing sizes with as few deviations as possible. This allows for repetition and economies of scale as well as simple fabrication and site installation.
- Generally, minimum of 20 identical units make volumetric prefabrication economically viable.

- Maximum size of prefabrication units is dependent on lorry size, route and road/access widths, etc. Units should ideally be no greater than 2.9 × 12 m, although under special circumstances 4 × 15.8 m could be used.[18] For just-in-time deliveries, holding bays and road closures should be pre-organised, especially in urban sites.
- Transportation energy and emissions become greater with distance. Balance the factory distance from site with other environmental benefits.
- Units may be too large to be stored on site.
- Performance of prefabricated components is crucial to ensure the overall building meets its final design intent.
- Use high thermal mass finishes to increase inherently lightweight low thermal mass units: for example, clay or lime plaster, particleboards, stone or timber floor finishes. See Section 7.2.7 and ⟶⟶⟶ Jump to Section 6.6.1.

7.2.2 Timber

Timber, if used in construction, retains the majority of the carbon that it absorbed in its lifetime. For forest trees, this is estimated at around 1.5–1.8 $kgCO_2$ per kg of wood,[19] and the figure is higher for urban trees. ⟶⟶⟶ Jump to Section 4.6. UK sustainably grown softwoods include cedar, larch, Douglas fir and pine. Sustainable hardwoods are beech, ash, maple and birch. Chestnut and oak are also sustainable hardwoods but both are acidic which can initially stain nearby finishes.

Key recommendations

These recommendations apply to all timber products, including timber processed boards, furniture and temporary timber uses such as concrete formwork and site hoardings.

Sourcing
- Reuse timber wherever possible, including formwork and hoardings.
- Consider using reclaimed timber and timber products first and source it locally from National Community Timber Recycling Network (NCTRN).
- Specify virgin timber:
  - locally grown timbers with UKWAS or FSC certification
  - if FSC is not available, consider PEFC
  - do not specify any endangered species
- Ensure that the timber species characteristics are suitable for the intended application.
- Accept that timber species availability will continuously change owing to sustainable forestry practices and reclamation availability.
- Be aware that harvesting timber is seasonal and there may be a delay in supply.

- Avoid specifying imported tropical hardwoods, even from certified sources, to avoid associated transportation pollution.
- Use solid timber rather than timber panel products which have high embodied energy and high embodied carbon.
- Use plywood rather than OSB or particleboard to minimise use of binders and adhesives.
- Avoid mixing synthetic binders with natural fibres. Cradle to cradle (C2C) principles indicate that natural and technical cycles are difficult to separate at the end of the first life.
- Some timber engineered flooring can have minimal off-gassing. Check manufacturer's health and safety data sheets.
- See www.trada.co.uk for timber properties.

Treatment

- Unseasoned, untreated, unfinished durable species can last the life of the building if correctly selected, applied, detailed and specified.
- Internal timber does not normally need preservative treatment. It can be finished with beeswax and/or natural oils.
- Specify timber species of appropriate durability instead of using preservative. This will help to:
  – avoid toxic off-cut waste ending up in landfill
  – avoid toxic timber being used in energy generation.
- Sole plates in timber frame are normally treated in the UK but careful detailing can avoid this. Elsewhere in Europe, timber used in 'breathing construction' does not receive treatment.
- Exposure to sunlight and weather gradually bleaches timber. If a particular species has been chosen for its colour, it should be stained or coated every 3–5 years to prevent bleaching.
- If using preservative:
  – avoid creosote and consider borate-based preservatives instead. It is prohibited for use near food/play areas etc.[20]
  – avoid chromated copper arsenate (CCA) such as Tanalith, and consider alkaline copper quat (ACQ) instead (e.g. Tanalith-e).

Other

- To avoid staining, provide temporary protection until the tannin in acidic timber subsides.
- Where used externally, design water shedding details such as generous overhangs to avoid discoloration caused by water.
- Use tongue and grooved or mechanical screw fixings (rather than nails or glue) for flooring and cladding. This maximises the potential for reuse.
- Any wood boards should be specified without formaldehyde glues and solvent-free adhesives.
- Raise all wooden materials off the ground during site storage. Allow for ventilation by cross-stacking.

7.2.3 Use of structural timber

- Use of timber as structure comes in a variety of forms, including:
  - solid or laminated timber
  - solid wood structures (SWS)
  - timber stud loadbearing panels (TSLP) made on or off site
  - pre-insulated or insulated in situ (ISPS)
  - structurally insulated panel system (SIPS)
  - post and beam or portal frame
  - glued cross-laminated timber panel systems (CLTP).
- Always confirm with client and building insurer that timber construction/ structural elements are appropriate because of fire risk.
- Risk of fire is greatest during construction: undertake additional health and safety assessment and measures such as installing temporary sprinklers, informing the fire brigade and avoiding partial handover and occupation of timber-framed sites.[21]
- Timber loadbearing structures above four storeys were not permitted until recently in the UK owing to fire and access issues. Some clients may reject them too.
- Closed timber panels, including any openings for windows and doors, can be pre-made in the factory and swiftly erected on site. This speeds up weathertightness for further external cladding and internal finishing.
- Unlike many processed timber composite panels, timber frame is easy to deconstruct and reuse.
- All timber systems require external outer faces, cladding or rainscreens such as brick, timber weather boarding, or tiles and rendered board and rainscreen cladding.

A. Timber-framed construction

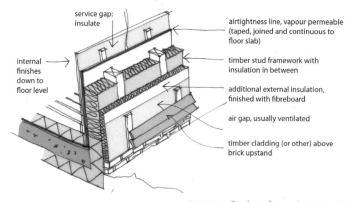

service gap: insulate

airtightness line, vapour permeable (taped, joined and continuous to floor slab)

internal finishes down to floor level

timber stud framework with insulation in between

additional external insulation, finished with fibreboard

air gap, usually ventilated

timber cladding (or other) above brick upstand

Fig. 7.2.1 Timber-framed construction

- **Advantages**
  - can have great structural strength
  - high insulation capacity can be achieved with relatively thin wall construction, ~300–350 mm (see Fig. 7.2.1)
  - 1.45 kgCO$_2$/kg embodied carbon reduction can be achieved from using timber studwork instead of, for example, galvanised steel studs[22]

- **Disadvantages**
  - can be carbon intensive when treated with preservative
  - achieving good U-values requires a complex build-up with two layers of insulation (one in the timber stud zone and another on the external face)
  - a lot of carpentry required: typical 38 × 89 or 38 × 140 mm timber studs at 600 mm centres for two-storey house
  - limited storey height

B. Structurally insulated panels (SIP)

SIPs are prefabricated panels with rigid PUR insulation between (OSB) sheets on both sides.

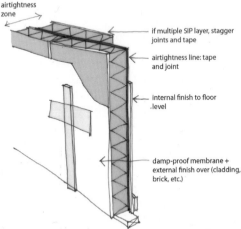

airtightness zone

if multiple SIP layer, stagger joints and tape

airtightness line: tape and joint

internal finish to floor level

damp-proof membrane + external finish over (cladding, brick, etc.)

Fig. 7.22 Structurally insulated panels (SIPs)

- **Advantages**
  - loadbearing and non-loadbearing walls and roofs
  - U-values: ≤0.20 W/m²K with 110 mm PUR insulation (k-value 0.023 W/mK)
  - potential for reclaimed and recycled components (OSB panels)
  - whole panels could be reclaimed and reused
  - speedy erection on site
  - lightweight: 25 kg/m²
  - up to 7.5 m long[23]

- **Disadvantages**
  - size dictated by the OSB 1200 mm wide panels
  - thickness: 100–250 mm
  - must specify double staggered panels to improve thermal performance
  - thermal bridging at joints where timber frame is used for structural elements
  - possible off-gassing from formaldehyde glues and insulation
  - only up to three storeys high
  - likely to have higher embodied energy and carbon than timber-framed construction
  - glued components unlikely to be recycled

C. Glued cross-laminated timber panel systems

These are structural engineered timber prefabricated panels of solid cross-laminated timber. Unlike SIP panels, there is no integral insulation. Additional insulation is always required.

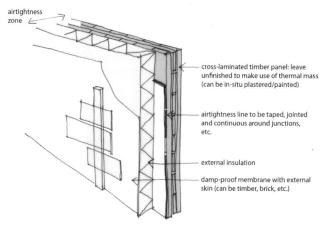

airtightness zone

cross-laminated timber panel: leave unfinished to make use of thermal mass (can be in-situ plastered/painted)

airtightness line to be taped, jointed and continuous around junctions, etc.

external insulation

damp-proof membrane with external skin (can be timber, brick, etc.)

Fig. 7.2.3 Glued cross-laminated timber panel systems

- **Advantages**
  - application: loadbearing walls, floors and roofs up to nine storeys, although theoretically this can be higher (20+)
  - thickness: 60–600 mm
  - size: <3 m high × 13 m long
  - good thermal mass if left exposed (1600 J/kgK)
  - good sound and fire resistance (up to 1 hr)
  - can be specified with formaldehyde-free glues
  - airtight and vapour permeable
  - speedy erection on site
  - can be deconstructed and has high reuse potential
  - carbon sequestration in wood
  - can be airtight with plywood core

- **Disadvantages**
  - additional insulation required
  - embodied energy is increased owing to processing and transportation
  - heavy for transportation to site
  - unlikely to be recycled owing to glued components

D. Timber frame with hemp-lime surround (hempcrete)

Hempcrete is a composite material which consists of hemp and hydraulic lime as a binder with some cement for a faster set and some aluminium for aeration.

Depending on the proportional mixes, it can be used
- as an insulating render or plaster or to create insulated solid mass walls
- with the addition of aggregate solid mass floors and roof slabs – referred to as hempcrete.

Hempcrete is non-loadbearing and is usually cast around a timber loadbearing structure, with timber panels acting as the shuttering to create a solid mass construction.

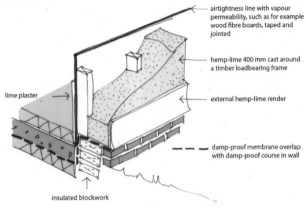

airtightness line with vapour permeability, such as for example wood fibre boards, taped and jointed

hemp-lime 400 mm cast around a timber loadbearing frame

lime plaster

external hemp-lime render

damp-proof membrane overlap with damp-proof course in wall

insulated blockwork

Fig. 7.2.4. Hemp-lime typical wall diagram

- **Advantages**
  - hempcrete is a carbon sink, absorbing around 100 kg CO_2 per m^3 [24]
  - good thermal insulation properties (k = 0.07–0.12 W/mK)[25]
  - any thickness to suit U-value
  - good thermal mass capacity (1700 J/kgK)
  - moisture permeable and hygroscopic
  - air permeability: ≤2.5 m^3/(hr.m^2) can be achieved[26]
  - 1 hr fire resistance[27]
  - suitable for clay or lime plaster and render; can be used to repair historic buildings
  - can be recycled to produce more of the same
  - fast monolithic simple construction
  - little training required
  - 20 m^3 hempcrete a day can be cast per labourer/machine[28]

- **Disadvantages**
  - non-loadbearing on its own: needs to be cast around a timber frame or other structure
  - thick walls to maximise thermal properties
  - proprietary products contain some cement and aluminium oxide, but still a low carbon material
  - specialist spray equipment and applicator required
  - needs protection from water penetration
  - takes around four weeks to fully cure, although the temporary shuttering can be removed after 24 hours; external rendering can take place after 6–8 weeks
  - not all systems have automatic building control approval

Key recommendations

- No additional insulation is required if walls are at least 400 mm thick. However, its full performance may not come into effect immediately.
- If exposed to water, place off the ground, usually on a brick or concrete plinth with damp-proof course. Needs weather protection such as lime render, cladding or brickwork with lime mortar (if no lime mortar, ventilated cavity required).
- No additional vapour barriers/breathing membranes are required owing to the high vapour permeability of hemp-lime. Impermeable water vapour barriers should be avoided.
- Timber frame requires no treatment as the lime has an antiseptic function.
- Shuttering should be untreated and smooth, e.g. plywood or OSB.
- Permanent shuttering should be 9 mm plywood; can be left exposed on the internal face only.[29]
- There should be no difficulty in obtaining Building Regulations approval. However, always undertake discussion with relevant local authority building control officers at the early stages. Automatic approval across the UK has been given for a few methods, with more systems in the process of obtaining accreditation. See: www.limetechnology.co.uk

7.2.4 Solid mass structural systems

Solid mass structures are a mixture of materials, which when put together form a solid structure. They tend to be structurally loadbearing and heavy, compacted constructions.

The systems discussed are rammed earth and concrete. Characteristics they have in common are:

- good thermal mass capacity if left exposed ——$>$ Jump to Section 6.6
- on-site works must be protected from water penetration
- avoid casting in winter and when temperatures are $\geq 30°C$
- cast in spring/summer to allow for sufficient drying out and finishing by autumn.

A. Rammed earth

Rammed earth is a solid wall structure with soil rammed into a shuttering framework. Rammed earth walls can be loadbearing, if wall thicknesses are increased. However, rammed earth is not usually used as loadbearing structure as it needs protection from rain. This is usually achieved by constructing a permanent loadbearing roof enclosure.

- **Advantages**
  - can be loadbearing
  - low embodied energy and carbon, if soil is sourced on site
  - without added cement it can break down to soil again
  - good hygroscopicity for passive humidity control
  - thermal conductivity k: 0.64–1.28 W/mK
  - good thermal mass capacity: 868–880 J/kgK
  - usually left exposed – can be very aesthetically pleasing

- **Disadvantages**
  - structural limitations
  - always needs protection from rain and water penetration
  - subject to moisture and thermal movements
  - insufficient thermal insulation capacity on its own, hence requires additional insulation
  - most UK soil cannot be used without additives
  - takes specialist skills to develop recipe with site soils
  - extensive and slow manual work

Key recommendations
....

- Use a mixture of sand, gravel and clay (12% clay ideal but up to 30% is workable).
- Chalk can be used in place of clay; additional features such as flints can be accommodated in the mass wall.
- Use a (cement/lime) stabiliser for structures in excess of two storeys,[30] and where local soil is unsuitable, as in south-east England (too much clay). Using cement/lime increases the embodied carbon.
- Suitable soil can also be imported to site but this should be avoided.
- Loadbearing walls are only recommended where soil is sourced locally, owing to increased quantity of soil required.
- Usually used for internal walls, typically 300–450 mm thick, or as a cavity wall where insulation is required.
- Rammed earth walls can be prone to moisture and thermal movement if directly exposed to the sun.
- Avoid all vapour-impermeable finishes: leave exposed, render/plaster with lime or clay, or finish with clay or mineral paints.
- Externally exposed rammed earth walls always need to be protected from water penetration with either large overhangs or external cladding such as timber fixed on battens directly into the rammed earth wall.
- Always needs to be raised off the ground by at least 400 mm: use a brick or concrete footing with a damp-proof course as wide as the wall to avoid water damage.

B. Concrete

Concrete is a mixture of cement, aggregates and water. It is either poured in situ or precast and transported to site. Prefabricated elements usually weigh less as they can be cast with integral insulation or voids. Structural concrete contains very high levels of embodied carbon, principally because of the energy-intensive manufacture of its cement constituent and steel reinforcements (even though around 90% of the steel is recycled).[31] Another impact is the corrosion of reinforcement bars in the concrete. This reduces the lifespan and significantly increases the maintenance and therefore embodied carbon of concrete.

- **Advantages**
  - loadbearing
  - appropriate for buildings of great height and width
  - good fire resistance
  - only reclaimed where prefabricated and designed for deconstruction
  - for thermal conductivity, embodied carbon and heat capacity, see Section 7.2.7
  - curing only takes about a week

- **Disadvantages**
  - high environmental impact owing to cement content, aggregate extraction, steel reinforcement bars and temporary formwork (see checklist below)
  - bad thermal insulation capacity; always requires additional insulation
  - usually downcycled into crushed concrete hardcore or recycled into RCA recycled concrete aggregate

Checklist: how to reduce the environmental impact of concrete	☑ ☒
Concrete mix	
Can the cement proportion be reduced?	☐
Are you using additive-free cement (including organic resins and additives)?	☐
Can you specify Portland pozzolana instead of pure Portland cement?	☐
Have you considered ground granulated blast-furnace slag (GGBS) cement as a cement replacement?	☐
Or pulverised fuel ash (PFA) as a cement replacement?	☐
For coloured concrete, have you avoided aniline-based pigments and instead specified high-quality mineral pigments?[32] (Tubular translucent aggregates make translucent concrete.)	☐
Have you used secondary aggregate, recycled aggregates, recycled concrete aggregate (RCA), ideally crushed brick (e.g. from site demolition) or plastic/ glass waste? Have you ensured that the aggregate is not from polluted or toxic sources? (Building Regulations allow ≤ 20% RCA in structural concrete.)	☐

Reinforcement

Have you minimised requirement for steel reinforcement bars with post-tension concrete?	☐
Have you considered alternative reinforcement such as 15 mm glass/plastic fibres? This reduces the amount of steel reinforcement required and so reduces corrosion risk, although it cannot be recycled.[33]	☐
Could you use smooth, round steel reinforcement bars as these are easier to separate for recycling?	☐
If using glass aggregates, have you checked that you have specified GGBS cement to minimise risk of reaction?	☐
Have you considered reinforced plastic, stone or fibre?	☐
Have you considered concrete reinforced with chopped recycled tyre wire?	☐

Formwork/shuttering

Can you reuse shuttering for other building materials (internal/external cladding, (sub)flooring, etc.)?	☐
Could you use non-petroleum-based shutter finishes, such as vegetable oil?	☐
Are you using FSC timber shuttering in preference to steel (unless it can be reused)? Timber gives a rougher finish texture, although some treated plywoods can achieve finishes as smooth as steel.	☐
Have you specified plywood which is formaldehyde-free and FSC sourced?	☐
Have you avoided specification of bamboo ply formwork, as it is imported from China or Brazil? (If unavoidable to use, specify from plantations, not forests.)	☐

Thermal mass

Can you use concrete's excellent thermal mass qualities by exposing it or by in-situ plastering it with dense, non-insulating plasters? ⟶ Jump to Section 6.6	☐

Construction detailing

Have you avoided exposed external concrete floor slabs and walls?	☐
Have you detailed exposed concrete well to avoid rainwater runoff stains?	☐

Deconstruction/recycling

Have you specified prefabricated concrete elements with mechanical fixings and clear deconstruction joints?	☐
Have you avoided using in-situ cast concrete because it cannot readily be reused? (It needs to be landfilled or crushed as RCA or hardcore.)	☐

7.2.5 Brick and brick slips
....

Brick with block construction is widespread in the UK, mainly owing to the availability of suitable soil for local brick manufacturing.

Bricks have a longer lifespan than any building. Therefore it is crucial to design for the deconstruction and reuse of bricks, although at present only around 6% of demolished bricks are reclaimed.[34]

- Around 65% of a typical brick wall's embodied carbon is attributed to the bricks and around 20% to the inner concrete blockwork. This is due to the high firing temperatures used to create bricks (around 500–1000°C).
- Hence the reclamation of brick and blockwork is crucial: lime mortar should be used to enable reclamation.
- Brick slip cladding can be used instead of bricks, either mechanically fixed or glued to insulation. This way, thinner external walls are achieved with the same thermal performance. See Fig. 7.2.5.

Solid brick
- **Advantages**
  - good useful thermal mass capacity if internally exposed
  - can be loadbearing if one brick thick or greater
  - can be reclaimed and reused if lime mortar is used
- **Disadvantages**
  - high embodied energy due to firing temperatures and high embodied carbon depending on fuel used
  - if cement mortar is used it can only be downcycled into crushed aggregate

Brick slips, glued to insulation
- **Advantages**
  - 20 mm brick slips bonded and mortar jointed on site to create rigid insulation
  - embodied energy/carbon reduced by 48% compared to solid brick
  - speedy construction on site; limits the need for wet trades
- **Disadvantages**
  - highly processed material (bonded to petrochemical insulation)
  - glues and processed insulation may lead to off-gassing and health issues
  - use of glues makes reuse and recycling difficult
  - limited choice of (rigid) insulations
  - inflexible around complex junctions
  - limited to use below 5–6 storeys only

Brick slips, mechanically fixed
- **Advantages**
  - around 12–15 mm brick slip, usually profiled and individually clicked into a metal 'tray'
  - use of lime mortar is possible; joints are then filled with mortar: 1:1:6 cement:lime:sand
  - mechanical fixings allow for deconstruction; ensure manufacturer approves increased lime content
  - embodied carbon reduced by 40% compared to solid brick
  - flexibility to move bricks until mortar jointed
  - use up to 21 storeys
- **Disadvantages**
  - likely to be more expensive
  - fixing and mortar jointing of the façade is from the top down, rather than from the bottom up as with traditional brickwork construction; protect windows and other façade elements

Fig. 7.2.5 Comparison of different brick constructions with inner leaf blockwork wall and phenolic insulation in between

Brick construction method (U-value 0.15 W/m²K)	Wall thickness (mm)	Approximate embodied carbon kgCO₂/m²	Can it be reclaimed/ recycled (if lime mortar used)?
traditional brickwork	417	73	✓
glued brick slips	330	38	✗
mechanical brick slips	330	43.7	✓

7.2.6 Lime and cement mortar, render and screeds

Both lime and cement renders can be used for mortar joints between bricks and blockwork. Lime can also be mixed with water to create lime plaster. Lime is environmentally a better choice than cement because it is produced using lower temperatures and reabsorbs some CO_2 during curing. Hydraulic lime sets under water and contains impurities, while non-hydraulic lime, or pure lime, needs air to set. Both can be rapidly applied as spray-on renders to concrete, brick and blockwork. With both applications, but particularly lime, do not undertake during winter and allow for natural drying. Avoid draughts or forced heating.

Fig. 7.2.6 Comparison of cement and lime

Type	Advantages	Disadvantages
cement mortar, render and screed	Strong and quick to cure, allowing for speedier work. Thinner application for renders.	High embodied carbon. So strong that it makes the reclamation of bonded materials difficult, time-consuming and sometimes impossible. High vapour impermeability. Cracks with thermal movements and is left prone to water ingress. Movement joints are therefore required.
lime mortar, render, screed, plaster	Mortar: usually 1:3 or 1:6 lime to sand. Materials that it has bonded to can be deconstructed and recycled easily. Will reduce and 'heal' cracks so no movement joints required. Vapour permeable so works well in breathable construction.	Less strong. Curing takes longer. Usually requires 3–5 days between render coats.

7.2.7 Typical material properties: technical data

Material (depth material in mm)*	Density kg/m³	kgCO$_2$/ kg[35]	kgCO$_2$ per m² of surface area	Specific heat capacity J/kgK	Effective heat capacity Wh/m² K	k-value (thermal conductivity) W/mK
Walls						
brick, general clay 102 mm (outer brickwork) mortar cement: lime:sand 1:1:6	1873	0.227	43.3	800	42.4	0.84
brick, general clay 102 mm (outer brickwork) mortar lime:sand 1:6	1875	0.221	42.2	800	42.5	0.84
brick, general clay 102 mm (inner brickwork) mortar cement: lime:sand 1:1:6	1873	0.227	43.3	800	42.4	0.62
brick, general clay 102 mm (inner brickwork) mortar lime:sand 1:6	1875	0.221	42.2	800	42.5	0.62
mortar cement: lime:sand 10 mm 1:1:6	1900	0.163	3	920	4.8	0.72
mortar lime:sand 10 mm 1:6	2005	0.027	0.54	950	5.3	0.63–0.72
rammed earth (general soil) 300 mm	1460	0.023	10	880	107.1	1.28

Material (depth material in mm)*	Density kg/m³	$kgCO_2/$ kg[35]	$kgCO_2$ per m² of surface area	Specific heat capacity J/kgK	Effective heat capacity Wh/m² K	k-value (thermal conductivity) W/mK
rammed earth (cement stabilised soil 8%) 300 mm	1900	0.082	46.7	868	137.4	0.64
concrete block (light density 8 N/mm²) 140 mm	600	0.059	4.9	840	19.6	0.19
concrete block (medium density 10 N/mm²) 140 mm	1400	0.073	14.3	840	45.7	0.51
concrete block (high density 13 N/mm²) 140 mm	2240	0.100	31.3	840	73.1	1.63
aerated concrete block 140 mm	400	0.24	13.4	1000	15.5	0.16
cast concrete 28/35 Mpa 250 mm	2000	0.112	56	1000	138.8	1.3
high density concrete 250 mm	2100	0.194	101.8	840	122.5	1.7
reinforced concrete 1% steels 250 mm	2300	0.202	116.1	840	134.1	1.9
gypsum block 100 mm	950	0.12	11.4	840	43.1	0.35
calcium silicate blocks (Silka) 100 mm	1850	0.13	24	1000	51.3	0.91
hempcrete 300 mm	330	—	—	1700	46.7	0.07–0.12

Material (depth material in mm)*	Density kg/m³	$kgCO_2$/ kg[35]	$kgCO_2$ per m² of surface area	Specific heat capacity J/kgK	Effective heat capacity Wh/m² K	k-value (thermal conductivity) W/mK
Floors and roofs						
aerated concrete (slab) 250 mm	500	0.24	30	840	29.1	0.16
screed (cement: sand 1:4) 75 mm	2100	0.171	26.9	650	28.4	1.4
asphalt (8% binder) 10 mm	1550	0.076	1.1	1600	6.8	1.2
bitumen 10 mm	1700	0.43	4.3	1000	4.7	0.2
built-up roofing felt 10 mm	960	1.65	15.8	1000	2.6	0.16
clay tiles 10 mm	1900	0.45	8.5	840	4.4	0.85
concrete tiles (fibre cement panels uncoated) 10 mm	350	1.09	3.8	1300	1.2	0.082
aggregate general (gravel or crushed rock) 100 mm	2240	0.0048	1	920	57.2	1.3
soil 50 mm	1460	0.023	1.6	880	17.8	1.28
soil 150 mm	1460	0.023	5	880	53.5	1.28
soil 300 mm	1460	0.023	10	880	107	1.28
typical copper (tube and sheet) 0.5 mm	8600	2.6	11.1	390	0.4	384
recycled copper (tube and sheet) 0.5 mm	8600	0.8	3.4	390	0.4	384
aluminium 1 mm	2700	8.24	22.2	880	0.6	230

Material (depth material in mm)*	Density kg/m³	kgCO₂/kg³⁵	kgCO₂ per m² of surface area	Specific heat capacity J/kgK	Effective heat capacity Wh/m² K	k-value (thermal conductivity) W/mK
recycled aluminium 1 mm	2700	1.69	4.5	880	0.6	230
zinc 0.7 mm	7000	2.88	14.1	390	0.5	113
lead (61.5% recycled) 1.32 mm	11340	1.57	23.5	130	0.5	35
lead (100% recycled) 1.32 mm	11340	0.54	8	130	0.5	35
Surface finishes						
thermal mass panel Energain 5.26 mm	855	—	n/a	70	0.09	0.14–0.18
gypsum plasterboard 12.5 mm	800	0.38	3.8	840	2.3	0.25
limestone 10 mm	2180	0.087	1.8	720	4.3	1.15
granite 10 mm	2600	0.64	16.6	820	5.9	3.49
slate 10 mm	2950	0.058	1.7	750	6.1	1.72
fibreboard (high density) 10 mm	880	1.05	9.2	1340	3.2	0.12
fermacell 12.5 mm	1200	—	—	1000	4.1	0.32
ceramic tiles 8 mm	1900	0.74	11.2	850	3.5	1.2
sandstone 25 mm	2600	0.058	3.7	700	12.6	1.2
plywood 18 mm	700	1.07	13.4	1420	4.9	0.15
softwood timber (sawn) 25 mm	610	0.58	8.8	1420	5	0.13

Material (depth material in mm)*	Density kg/m³	kgCO₂/kg³⁵	kgCO₂ per m² of surface area	Specific heat capacity J/kgK	Effective heat capacity Wh/m² K	k-value (thermal conductivity) W/mK
hardwood timber (sawn) 25 mm	680	0.86	14.6	1200	5.6	0.15
OSB oriented strand board 18 mm	650	0.96	11.2	1700	5.5	0.13
chipboard 18 mm	800	0.84	12	1300	5.2	0.12
MDF 18 mm	500	0.72	6.4	2600	6.5	0.15
external rendering (cement: sand 1:3) 12 mm	1300	0.208	3.2	1000	4.3	0.5
plaster (in situ) 10 mm	1330	0.12	1.6	1000	3.7	0.79
Insulation						
cellular glass (glass foam) 282 mm	135	—	—	—	—	0.048
cellulose 230 mm	42	—	—	—	—	0.039
cork 235 mm	160	0.19	7.14	1800	18.8	0.04
fibreglass (glasswool) 235 mm	12	1.35	3.8	—	—	0.04
flax (insulation) 224 mm	30	1.7	11.4	—	—	0.038
mineral wool (quilt) 212 mm	30	1.28	7.6	710	1.2	0.036
rockwool 222 mm	23	1.05	5.3	710	1	0.038
sheep's wool 248 mm	14	—	—	1000	0.9	0.042
phenolic foam 106 mm	30	2.98	9.47	1400	1.2	0.018

Material (depth material in mm)*	Density kg/m^3	kgCO$_2$/ kg^{35}	kgCO$_2$ per m^2 of surface area	Specific heat capacity J/kgK	Effective heat capacity Wh/m^2 K	k-value (thermal conductivity) W/mK
polystyrene expanded 206 mm	25	3.29	16.9	1400	2	0.035
polyurethane rigid 135 mm	30	4.26	17.25	1470	1.6	0.023
urea formaldehyde foam 235 mm	10	2.76	6.48	1400	0.9	0.04
woodwool (board) 590 mm	500	0.98	249	1000	81.9	0.1
wood fibre, soft insulation panels 341 mm	255	—	—	—	—	0.058
straw 590 mm	370	0.01	3.7	1000	60.6	0.1
sawdust 658 mm	—	—	—	—	—	0.059

* Material depth used to calculate effective heat capacity and embodied carbon per m^2 of surface area (kgCO$_2$/m^2)

7.3   THERMAL PERFORMANCE: KEEPING THE HEAT IN (AND OUT)

7.3.1 Super-insulation: k-values, R-values and U-values

Thermally insulating materials do not readily allow heat to pass through them. They reduce space heat demand by delaying the transfer of heat from warm to cold spaces. This reduces the operational energy and carbon footprint of the building. All materials have the capacity to delay heat transfer to some extent; the UK Building Regulations identify good thermal insulators as having a low k-value. 'Super insulated' buildings are defined by the intelligent use of materials, design and construction detailing that contributes to significantly reduced heat losses from the building fabric:

- **k-value** or **λ-value** (W/mK) is the thermal conductivity, which gives the rate at which heat is conducted through materials. The lower the figure, the better the insulation.
- **R-value** (m²/WK) is the thermal resistance of a material/construction layer and is simply the thickness of a material divided by its k-value. The greater R, the better its thermal resistance.

$$R = \frac{\text{thickness (m)}}{\text{k-value (W/mK)}}$$

- **U-value** (W/m²K) is the thermal transmittance coefficient and is the rate of heat transfer through 1 m² of an element with a 1°C temperature difference. The smaller the U-value, the better the element is at resisting this heat transfer. U-values are calculated as follows:

$$\text{U-value} = \frac{1}{\text{sum of R-values}}$$

7.3.2 Windows, g-values and BFRC ratings

The thermal transmittance of windows is more complex: heat is lost through the frame, glazing and seals, but some of this is offset as heat is also gained from the sun through the glazing.

- **Thermal performance:**
  - Uf = U-value through the frame alone
  - Ug= is the U-value of the glazing pane in the middle of the glass
  - Uw= overall U-value of the window, including Uf and Ug

Often manufacturers give one U-value (the optimistic Ug) without indicating what it refers to. Always clarify this before selection or specification.

- **g-value** is the solar energy transmittance and gives the total heat gain through the window compared to the solar radiation of an opaque wall. The higher the g-value, the more solar gain it allows. ——→ Jump to Chapter 6, Fig. 6.5.7. (Single glazing tends to have the best g-value – around 80–85% – but lowest Uw value.)
- **Low emission (low-E)** glass coatings are coatings of metal oxide which permit daylighting and the sun's radiation, but block heat from leaving the room.
- **Ventilation equivalent and free area:** this relates to the window's background ventilation, including trickle vents. Free area is the actual size of the opening of the trickle vent. Building Regulations refer to equivalent area, which measures the air flow performance of the trickle vent. Two different trickle vents, for example, can have the same free areas but not the same flow rate/equivalent area.
- **The British Fenestration Rating Council (BFRC)** rating attempts to take into account both heat losses and heat gains in kWh/m² per year. It gives a window a single rating from A to G based on its overall Uw-value and g-value. Apart from BFRC A-rated windows, most windows have a yearly heat loss. Note that this is a theoretical calculation and in reality the heat losses/gains will entirely depend on the orientation and location in the UK. It is likely that even an A-rated window on a north wall will still lead to heat losses and no heat gains.

BFRC rating	kWh/m² per year	Approx. max. U-value (W/m²K) [36]
A	≥0	1.2–1.4
B	0 to −10	1.4–1.6
C	−10 to −20	1.6–1.8
D	−20 to −30	1.8–2
E	−30 to −50	2–2.2
F	−50 to −70	2.2+ Note: no longer Building Regulations approved
G	less than -70	

7.3.3 Insulation materials

Insulation materials can be divided into three broad categories: organic (plant derived), mineral derived and petrochemical derived insulation materials.

- Usually the best performing insulations (in terms of k-values) have the highest embodied energy and/or carbon. However, as less material is needed, this is partially offset by reduced space heating or cooling demands (if the same wall thickness is used).
- Radiant barriers, or reflective foil insulations, reflect heat back with an aluminium foil backed onto a petrochemical or mineral derived insulation with k-values around 0.033 W/mK. Their effectiveness is debated.[37]
- Plant-based materials have many environmental and performance benefits such as good acoustic and hygroscopic characteristics. They often have lower embodied carbon. However, they are not always the best at delaying heat transfer (i.e. they have higher k-values). Much greater wall thicknesses are usually required where they are used. It is always recommended to choose an insulation material with low k-value as well as low environmental impact. See Figs 7.5.1 and 7.5.2.

 Code for Sustainable Homes credits (Pol 1) and EcoHomes credits (Pol 1), BREEAM (Mat 4)

7.3.4 Summary of different insulation materials

Mineral based insulations	
Such as?	rock, slag and glass mineral fibre, cellular glass, aerogel
Advantages	• average insulation properties – medium k-values in the range of 0.036–0.05 W/mK although aerogel is excellent (0.013 W/mK) • vapour permeable apart from glass foam and aerogel • usually contains recycled waste products, diverting from landfill • good fire resistance, can be recyclable and often reusable, except mineral fibre • rot resistant but performance diminished if saturated
Disadvantages	• average embodied energy • can contain formaldehyde – specify with care • rock, slag and glass mineral fibre are not hygroscopic; increased moisture in masonry cavity construction affects the k-value and reduces insulation capacity, therefore increase any full-fill cavity insulation thickness by 25-30%[38] • cellular glass is suitable for high-impact areas, such as foundations, floors and green roofs • aerogel insulation is often fixed to internal finishing boards, such as plywood or plasterboard, which makes recycling and reuse more difficult

Petrochemical derived insulations	
Such as?	expanded polystyrene (EPS), extruded polystyrene (XPS), polyurethane (PUR), polyisocyanurate (PIR) and phenolic foam
Advantages	• good insulation properties – k-values in the low range of 0.028–0.04 W/mK although PUR/PIR and phenolic foam can be very good (0.018–0.022 W/mK) • can be recyclable (apart from phenolic foam) and often reusable • good fire resistance, although not always suitable with rainscreen cladding • rot resistant • most are closed cell or closed surface – suitable in damp conditions, e.g. masonry cavity walls • suitable for high-impact areas, apart from some EPS products – check specification
Disadvantages	• high embodied energy – partially offset as less insulation is required for the same fabric performance standard • old CFC- and HCFC-based insulation has to be treated as hazardous waste and is not suitable for reuse • EPS thermal insulation capacity may be reduced by moisture[39] • off-gassing, particularly phenolic foam ⟶ Jump to Section 6.8 • vapour impermeable so cannot be used in breathable constructions, although some breathing grades are appearing in the market • closed cell/surface insulation should not be considered for timber-framed construction; moisture will only be able to escape through the timbers which will then require treatment

Organic (plant /animal) based insulations[40]	
Such as?	cellulose, straw, flax, hemp, coconut, cotton, sheep's wool, cork, woodwool/fibres, etc.
Advantages	• hygroscopic (see Sections 7.4.6 and 7.4.7) •.usually low, zero or negative embodied carbon • often waste or by-products • recyclable and often reusable if not fixed with glue • can be airtight, with high acoustic performance • suitable in breathing, timber-framed constructions • high density materials have high thermal lag properties (see Section 7.3.6)
Disadvantages	• not always good k-value – 0.038–0.040 W/mK • hemp does not have excellent thermal insulation capacities at around 0.07–12 W/mK, but is normally used in thick constructions and has high thermal lag value (see Section 7.2.3 D) • rots if exposed to high relative humidity and water • not recommended on lower walls in flood risk areas • not normally suitable for wet construction, e.g. masonry cavity walls, as full or partial fill insulation • not suitable for high load areas such as foundations, floors and green roofs • a breather membrane is required if adjacent to a ventilated cavity • some insulations are heavily processed to provide treatment against fire/rot/fungal attack, etc.; this increases the environmental impact and can lead to off-gassing ──⇥ Jump to Section 6.8

7.3.5 Thermal bridging and thermal bypasses

An area-weighted U-value takes into consideration the combination or layering of materials used to create a build-up. It should include adjustments for thermal bridges.

Thermal bridges are areas with reduced insulation or locally higher U-values, allowing significant heat losses and potential for local surface condensation and mould growth. It is estimated that up to 25% of internal heat can be lost through thermal bridges.[41] In a typical house, the heat lost can be as much as 15 kWh/m^2 per year, while on a Passivhaus this is reduced to around 1–5 kWh/m^2 per year.[42]

There are different types of thermal bridges:
- Repeating thermal bridges tend to be evenly distributed in the thermal envelope, e.g. steel cavity wall ties, mortar in insulated blockwork, studs and additional structural timber components in panel constructions.
- Non-repeating thermal bridges or linear thermal bridges are intermittent and usually occur around openings and where materials with different k-values make up the thermal envelope, e.g. around windows and other openings but also cantilevered balconies.
- Geometrical thermal bridges result from the shape of the thermal envelope. They can be two- or three-dimensional, depending on how many planes intersect, e.g. wall/roof and wall/floor junctions. Corners are particularly sensitive as they have a greater external surface area exposed than internal surface area.

Thermal bypass is an indirect heat loss caused by air bypassing insulation and infiltrating into construction cavities. This occurs particularly in separating party walls and floors. Party wall bypasses are addressed in the latest Building Regulations in England and Wales and Scotland.

Heat losses through walls are often 50–350%[43] higher in reality than designed owing to thermal bridging caused by thermal bypasses:
- partially insulated voids and cavities
- ventilated partial fill cavities with open cell or fibre insulation
- ill-fitting insulation which allows air circulation around it
- pierced vapour barriers, wind or airtightness membranes
- cavities in separating party walls.

Key recommendations

- The thermal insulation and airtightness barrier should follow each other in a continuous line.
- No gaps or breaks should occur in the thermal insulation and barrier material.
- Thermal bridges at ground-floor and foundation junctions, particularly with pile foundations, are difficult to resolve.
- Take extra care around material and component junctions and junctions with airtightness membranes.
- Treat separating party walls and floors as external fabric elements.
- Refer to the Energy Saving Trust's Enhanced Construction Details (ECDs) and robust details elsewhere for best practice examples.
  —⇾ Jump to Chapter 9.
- Thermal bridging adjustment factors for various junctions can be obtained from BRE IP 1/06. This is an essential part of energy performance modelling and required for SAP/SBEM.
- Area-weighted U-values may be given by manufacturers or can be calculated. Always check with Building Regulations whether manufacturer's data is acceptable.
- A thermal bridge heat loss coefficient is expressed as Ψ(W/mK). This should ideally be below 0.01 W/mK, although as high as 0.04 W/mK is common around windows.[44] In a Passivhaus, thermal bridging below 0.01 W/mK is considered thermal bridge free.

7.3.6 Thermal lag or decrement delay[45]

Thermal lag or decrement delay refers to the time it takes for heat generated by the sun to transfer to the inside of the building envelope. Materials with higher rates of decrement delay have:
- a low thermal conductivity, i.e. k-value
- combined with a high specific heat capacity/thermal mass – see Section 7.2.7 and —⇾ Jump to Section 6.6
- a high density

This can be useful in the design of lightweight buildings, where materials with high thermal lag can limit overheating. Insulation materials such as cork, cellulose fibre and wood fibre board provide a good thermal lag, whereas materials such as low-density mineral fibre, polyurethane and polystyrene do not.

7.4   AIRTIGHTNESS

- Air leakage, air permeability and air infiltration all express the amount of air exchanged through 1 m² of thermal envelope. The terms are synonymous. They are given in $m^3/(m^2.hr)$ at 50 Pa which is the standard UK convention of expressing airtightness. The air leakage index excludes the solid ground floor area from the thermal envelope.
- Airtightness standards are acceptable standards of air infiltration defined by the Building Regulations or other standards such as Passivhaus. Again this is expressed as $m^3/(m^2.hr)$ or as air changes per hour (ach-1), which is the EU standard of expressing airtightness.
- The airtightness zone is the notional line of airtight construction. This can be achieved:
  - with monolithic construction of airtight materials
  - with an airtightness membrane over permeable materials
  - by taping all joints in airtight boards or materials and by lapping and taping membranes at junctions.

Since poor airtightness is often the result of gaps in joints and at junctions between elements, it is important that the airtightness line is continuous and laps are well sealed. The line of airtight construction is usually located on the inner leaf of the external construction elements, but can be located on the warm side of the inner leaf or on the cold side of the inner leaf. Both have advantages and disadvantages, hence the reference to an 'airtightness zone'. Ideally, the airtightness line is located one-third into the airtightness zone on the warm side of the construction.

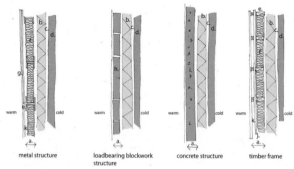

metal structure	loadbearing blockwork structure	concrete structure	timber frame

Legend:
a. airtightness zone
b. insulation zone
c. partial fill or full fill cavity
d. rainscreen: cladding, brick finish, etc.
e. metal section/timber frame

f. flexible insulation in between frame
g. double layer plasterboard or other internal finish
h. blockwork with in-situ plaster finish
i. concrete with in-situ plaster finish
j. fibreboard, vapour permeable
k. service gap; ideally filled with (fire-resistant) insulation

Fig. 7.4.1. Typical zones of airtightness clearly shown on design and construction drawings

7.4.1 Definitions[46]

- **Air permeability** refers to a material's ability to permit air to pass through it. Materials with open cells, open fibres or an open surface exhibit this characteristic. For example: rock, slag, glass mineral fibre, most plant-fibre-based insulation and sheep's wool.

- **Vapour permeability** refers to a material's ability to permit moisture (water vapour) to pass through it. Materials which can absorb or release moisture exhibit this characteristic, for example: rock, slag, glass mineral fibre, most plant-fibre-based insulation and sheep's wool. Cement, glass and metals are not vapour permeable.

- **Hygroscopicity** refers to a material's ability to absorb and release water vapour without reducing its thermal performance.

- **Interstitial condensation** occurs when moisture-laden air diffuses into a vapour-permeable material and reaches the 'dew point' within the material. At this point, it condenses into water. Interstitial condensation is problematic when it remains undetected, threatening structural damage such as timber decay, or degrading the effectiveness of insulation.

- **Moisture mass** acts like thermal mass but with moisture. This is a material's ability to absorb excess moisture in the air, such as any condensation, and to release it when conditions improve. For example: unfired clay bricks, rammed earth, clay plaster and clay finishes.

- **Vapour-open construction** is a breathing construction (usually timber-framed) that allows moisture to pass through. It depends on a number of requirements:
  - vapour permeable but airtight inside
  - only hygroscopic thermal insulation
  - more vapour permeable but wind-tight outside.

- **Vapour-closed construction** is the conventional approach to timber-framed construction, which attempts to stop vapour passing through. It depends on a number of requirements:
  - vapour-resistant barrier inside
  - most types of thermal insulation
  - vapour-permeable breather membrane outside
  - choose vapour-proof membranes inside to make airtight vapour check and use vapour-permeable membrane outside to make breather membrane. The 1:5 rule applies (five times more resistant inside than outside).

- **Vapour barrier** is a vapour-resistant barrier to stop the movement of water vapour through construction. In the UK they have been renamed 'vapour check' because they generally leak at service penetrations and joint laps. Examples include polyethylene sheet and OSB boards.

7.4.2 Which airtightness level and how to achieve it

Uncontrolled ventilation through cracks and gaps in the construction can cause up to 15% of heat loss.[47] The current Building Regulations allow a hole or crack the area of one side of a 20 pence piece per m² of fabric. For low carbon buildings, such as the Passivhaus standard, this hole is reduced to the equivalent of a 5 pence piece per 5 m² of fabric surface.[48]

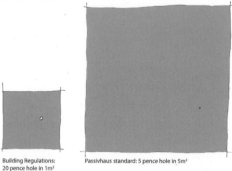

Building Regulations:
20 pence hole in 1m²

Passivhaus standard: 5 pence hole in 5m²

Fig. 7.4.2 Visualisation of different airtightness

Key recommendations

- Airtightness for all building types should be ≤3 m³/(m².hr).[49]
- Increasing airtightness requires 'controlled ventilation' to minimise build-up of moisture, CO_2 and other indoor air pollutants.
  → Jump to Sections 6.7 & 6.8.
- When airtightness levels are further reduced to 1 m³/(m².hr), with appropriate insulation, no conventional space heating system is required.
- The airtightness line can be on the cold side of the inner leaf of the construction element. This protects the airtightness line from penetrations, but is more difficult to construct and rectify.
- Often the airtightness line is the final internal finish, such as in-situ plaster. This may be interrupted by skirting or at light and power service plates and light fittings. The airtightness line is also likely to be broken as soon as the occupant nails into the wall.
- Therefore, the airtightness line should be separated from the internal finish with a services gap, such as on timber-framed walls, or ideally moved further into the wall construction, around one-third into the warm construction side.
- Ideally all service and skirting voids should be filled to prevent heat loss.

7.4.3 Don't we need gaps and cracks for good air quality?

In short, no. Around 0.5–1.5 air changes per hour per dwelling will achieve good air quality and avoid high humidity levels/condensation.[50] This is around 1–3 m³/(m². hr) and is 3–10 times better than the current Building Regulations requirement of 10 m³/(m².hr). Most existing buildings have even greater uncontrolled air leakage from building fabric. This leads to draughts, lack of thermal comfort and unwanted heat losses, and provides much more fresh air than is needed.

7.4.4 The reality of achieving increased airtightness standards

Studies have found that a large proportion of buildings regularly failed to achieve the Building Regulation standards with regards to airtightness.[51] Rectifying failed buildings and poor performance is more onerous and expensive than getting the principles right from the beginning. ──⟶ Jump to Section 1.5.

7.4.5 How can good airtightness be achieved?

- close attention to detail with a clearly marked airtightness line on the drawing board
- an understanding of airtightness by all stakeholders, particularly the contractor and installers
- airtightness testing carried out on the building fabric before finishes are applied, then finishes can be changed in the future without destroying the airtightness of the whole building
- making a building airtight at the finishes is challenging as it requires sealant along virtually every junction
- leaks can be detected with smoke wands and these leaks can be fixed during the works
- purpose-made sealants, adhesives, tapes and grommets help to complete the airtightness line after the initial design, specification and workmanship on site
- inherently airtight finishes are: in-situ plaster and concrete, rendered brick and blockwork, taped OSB and membranes

See Checklists on pages 214–215.

Airtightness checklist: design stage	☑ ☒
Have you appointed an airtightness champion in the office to liaise with the airtightness site champion?	☐
Have you provided clear airtightness drawings which indicate the line of air barrier separating between the heated and unheated spaces? Air and/or wind barrier must be continuous.	☐
Have you treated separating 'party' floors and walls as external elements?	☐
Have you designed more compact, simpler form buildings?	☐
Have you adopted a whole house/building airtightness approach (rather than floor by floor)?	☐
Have you provided entry lobbies/vestibules to external doors? This reduces heat losses by around 1 kWh/m²a.[52]	☐
Have you considered self-supporting balconies rather than cantilevered balconies (cantilevering penetrates the thermal envelope)? (However, this may conflict with Secured By Design.) Have you provided thermal breaks if cantilevered? ——⊱ Jump to Chapter 9, detail 7.	☐
Have you specified high-performing windows and external doors with good weather seals and draught excluders? (Avoid letterboxes in doors unless with draught excluder.)	☐
Have you specified construction and external materials which minimise cracking and excessive movement? ——⊱ Jump to Chapter 2.	☐
Have you reduced joint numbers and specified larger tiles and panels?	☐
Have you avoided or minimised sockets, light fittings and switches on external walls? Have you specified on internal partitions only or specified airtight sockets? (Tape carefully to internal membranes if used in airtightness zone.)	☐
Airtightness membranes are not always necessary, so have you thought how airtightness can be achieved through layer build-ups and (taping) junctions?	☐
Have you specified airtightness membranes that are also vapour permeable? Have you considered using an airtight 'intelligent' membrane, which allows vapour to move from the inside to the outside in winter and from the outside inwards in summer only (to release any wind-driven rain from the construction)?	☐
Have you kept the airtightness line away from internal finish to avoid damage from second fixings (hanging picture frames etc.)?	☐
Have you issued drawings showing services penetrations which need to be sealed? Have you included a specification of how to make it airtight, and how it will be tested and rectified?	☐

Airtightness checklist: on site/during construction	☑ ☒
Have you taken account of the fact that the as-built standard will need to meet or exceed the standard design to meet zero carbon compliance?	☐
Have you appointed an airtightness champion on site to liaise with the office champion?	☐
Has each junction between walls/ceilings/doors/windows and walls and floors been taped on the internal side before linings and finishes are applied?	☐
Have you used tape instead of foam sealants to seal junctions, and rubberised gaskets and tape around services? (Foam sealants tend to perform during the airtightness testing but fail soon after.)	☐
Have you overlapped and sealed joints to manufacturers' recommendations or relevant standards? And taped leaky butt joints between panels?	☐
Have you used in-situ plaster to seal blockwork and avoided plasterboard?	☐
In-situ plaster may shrink and minor gaps may appear after 18 months, so have you specified that they be refilled and that the airtightness be inspected?	☐
Has in-situ plaster been taken all the way to the top of the unfinished floor slab? And have floor/wall junctions been sealed with tape before installing floor finish and skirting boards?	☐
Plasterboard fixing is not easy to make airtight, so have you sealed blockwork walls and floors before work commences? And used low-VOC adhesive or plaster ribbons along joints and across tops and bottom of walls? And taped around plasterboard edges, including behind fitted furniture?	☐
Have you sealed gaps around all service penetrations with grommets or airtightness tape – including soil vent pipes, ventilation openings, gas and water services coming into the building, recessed wall or ceiling lights, switches and power sockets, drainage points, etc.? Have they been sealed before fitting kitchen and sanitary units and appliances?	☐
Service penetration: have you left sufficient space between each pipe in the same opening to seal with grommets, gaskets or tape?	☐
Have you taped around floor joists if supported in a cavity wall, or used a joist sealing box and sealed it to the masonry?	☐
Have you undertaken airtightness testing before applying finishes (this minimises the cost and disruption of making good afterwards)? Have you ensured that internal finishes do not compromise the airtightness barrier?	☐
Have you undertaken incremental smoke testing during the works and before any final finishes are applied? (Many leaks can be detected and fixed as the work progresses.)	☐

7.4.6 Airtightness is good, but what happens to water vapour?

There are two main sources of vapour in buildings; opinion is divided as to their relative importance and the solutions.

1. The vapour produced internally by humans and human activities: breathing, cooking, bathing, machine-washing and tumble-drying all raise the internal humidity. Cold room surfaces can create condensation which can lead to mould growth. If relative humidity values go above 70%, mould growth is likely. This causes discomfort, potentially asthma and, in the worst cases, toxicity and uninhabitable buildings. Hygroscopic internal finishes will temporarily absorb some water vapour and later release it when conditions improve, avoiding the risk of condensation. Internal vapour-permeable finishes can be useful to even out fluctuations in bathrooms, kitchens, etc. However, this is insignificant compared to bulk ventilation through MVHR or simply opening windows.[53] As the climate changes, hygroscopic internal finishes may become more important. Specific materials are mentioned in Section 7.4.7.

2. Humidity in construction comes from water added to materials or absorbed from the atmosphere, flooding and simple defects which allow water ingress. Water or vapour can do damage within the construction unless ventilated away and/or allowed to evaporate out through the surfaces. Damage includes rotting of timber and of organic insulations, corrosion of materials and loss of thermal insulation capacity in some insulations.

It is for these reasons that a hygroscopic construction is important.

Key recommendations

There are two approaches to water vapour: vapour-closed or vapour-open (breathing) construction. (See above and definitions in 7.4.1.) The construction industry tends to build vapour-closed constructions. The two approaches should not be combined.
- Opting for a vapour-open construction requires:
  – the material layers to 'breathe' while also achieving good airtightness via careful detailing; air leakage comes from bad connections and joints
  – water vapour to be able to travel through the entire construction without causing interstitial condensation.
See checklist overleaf.

Vapour-open construction checklist: design stage	☑ ☒
Having first decided whether to adopt vapour-closed or vapour-open construction, have you then designed and specified accordingly?	☐
Have you chosen vapour-open membrane or insulation boards inside to make airtight vapour-permeable membrane on the inside and a wind-tight, waterproof, vapour-permeable (open) membrane on the outside? (The 1:5 rule applies – five times more resistant inside than outside.)	☐
Are the airtightness membranes also vapour permeable? Have you considered using an airtight 'intelligent' membrane which allows vapour to move from the inside to the outside in winter and from the outside inwards in summer only (to release any wind-driven rain from the construction)?	☐
Are timber constructions highly vapour permeable? (condensation potentially causes damp and rot)	☐
When using full-fill cavity, have you ensured that inorganic but vapour-permeable insulation is specified, which does not significantly lose thermal insulation capacity when moist? Have you increased the thickness of insulation by around 25% in masonry cavity walls to compensate for modification in k-value at raised moisture content?	☐
Have you ensured that masonry cavity walls have water-repellent cavity insulation materials, whether partial or full fill?	☐
Have you ensured that masonry cavity walls have closed cell, closed fibre or closed surfaces to avoid thermal bypass? Alternatively, have you used a breather membrane to the cavity face of the insulation?	☐
Are rainscreens ventilated behind and through cladding joints?	☐
When considering wooden composite boards on internal (warm) side of the insulation, have you used vapour checks, which work well as an airtightness layer in timber constructions?	☐
Have you thought of using internal unfinished timber which is appropriate for all constructions as it is vapour permeable, hygroscopic and has some thermal capacity?	☐
Have you used a vapour barrier to internally insulate existing solid brick or blockwork? Or will sufficient care be taken to avoid interstitial condensation by other means?	☐
Where repairing existing lime mortar, could you use lime mortar pointing rather than cement mortar pointing?	☐

7.4.7 Hygroscopic material qualities

Hygroscopic materials allow the movement or storage of water. Water vapour is absorbed temporarily by these materials and then released back when the relative humidity in the space lowers again.

Hygroscopic insulations maximise their k-values when they absorb moisture from its airspaces.

Internal material finishes and hygroscopic characteristics

high hygroscopic materials (high capacity to **absorb** water vapour and regulate internal relative humidity)	unfired clay bricks, mortar, plaster & finish, timber, natural plant and wood fibre insulations, lime plaster & lime mortar, cellulose fibre insulation, unfinished cork never finish with varnish: instead finish with beeswax or lime wash to retain permeability
medium hygroscopic materials (limited capacity to **absorb** water vapour and regulate internal relative humidity)	cement, fired bricks & exposed concrete blockwork, plasterboard, limestone and composite woods such as plywood and particle board
impervious materials (no capacity to **absorb** water vapour or regulate internal relative humidity)	ceramics, metal, glass, dense concrete and bricks, mineral fibres, plastics & rubber, asphalt, bitumen, petrochemical derived insulation such as EPS, EXPS, PUR/PIR and phenolic foam and mineral insulation

Fig. 7.4.3 Hygroscopic characteristics of materials

7.5   WHICH FABRIC PERFORMANCE STANDARDS?

Airtightness and insulation standards in the UK are defined by each region's Building Regulations. They are moving towards zero energy buildings with more stringent construction standards.

Key recommendations

- Always build to the best airtightness and insulation standards that can be afforded. The Building Regulations' requirements are the lowest allowable standards and should always be exceeded, particularly since as-built standards are worse than on paper. ⟶ Jump to Section 1.5.
- It is more difficult, costly and disruptive to upgrade a building to higher standards after it has been built. Eventually, of course, this will have to happen to most under-insulated buildings. ⟶ Jump to Chapter 8.
- Zero energy buildings can be regarded as low energy buildings or Passivhaus, if renewable energy provides the remainder of the building-related energy needs.
- Building fabric insulation, airtightness and thermal-bridge-free standards need to be maximised before any renewable energy generation is considered. This will minimise the size of expensive equipment required and ensure significant CO_2 reductions over the building's life.
- The cost of increased insulation and airtightness standards can be offset by smaller, more efficient heating or cooling plant and reduced long-term running costs.

7.5.1 Building Regulations standards for housing

At present, the Building Regulations set standards according to required airtightness rates and maximum U-values per building component. Northern Ireland has the least advanced U-value targets and Scotland the highest fabric efficiency standards.

In England and Wales no distinction is made between northern and more southerly regions. This results in around 20% higher heat load demands in the colder northern regions for the same dwelling type. Building Regulations also set minimum efficiency standards for MVHR. —⟶ Jump to Section 6.7.

Building Regulations (residential buildings)	Region 1 (Scotland 2010)	Region 3 (Northern Ireland 2010)	Regions 2 and 4 (England and Wales 2010)
What are the maximum U-values (W/m²K) in each region?			
walls	0.25	0.35	0.30
party walls	0.20	—	0.20
exposed floors	0.20	0.25	0.25
roofs	0.18	0.25	0.20
windows, doors, roof lights	1.8	2.2	2.0
What is the maximum air permeability (at 50 Pa)?			
m³/(hr.m²)	max.10 m³/(hr.m²) To achieve this, design for: 8 m³/(hr.m²)		
What is the typical average heat load demand of an east–west facing terraced house, built to each region's standards?			
	Region 1	Region 3	Regions 2 and 4
Space heat demand kWh/m² per year	75	71	60 (Region 4) 75 (Region 2)

- Orientation is not taken into account, even though the same terraced house facing north–south would have a 3–5% reduced space heat load demand.
- For an apartment, reduce heat load demand by around 10% to reflect reduced heat losses from the more compact building plan and volume.
- For existing dwellings, —⟶ Jump to Chapter 8.

7.5.2 Zero carbon fabric energy efficiency standards for housing

All EU countries are obliged to regulate towards zero energy buildings by 2020. The UK's zero carbon buildings drive is part of this: from 2016, all new dwellings (and from 2018–19 all other buildings) must meet Code for Sustainable Homes level 6, or 'zero carbon'.

Instead of regulating maximum fabric U-values, maximum Fabric Energy Efficiency Standards (FEES) are set. These determine a yearly maximum space heat demand per m^2 floor area. Wales, Scotland and Northern Ireland are also setting goals and definitions of 'zero carbon'. These have not been released at the time of writing and so this book uses the English standards of maximum 39 kWh/m^2 per year for flats and terraced houses with up to 46 kWh/m^2 per year for all other dwelling types. ——⟶ Jump to Chapter 11.

- A fabric performance standard similar to Passivhaus is recommended to achieve 'carbon compliance', particularly in the UK's northerly regions.
- At present the Fabric Energy Efficiency Standard is calculated at design stages via SAP software, which uses only one UK climate.
- It is recommended that U-values are regionally adapted, as suggested below.

Recommended regional fabric standards to achieve zero carbon space heat load demand of 39–46 kWh/m^2 per year (residential buildings)				
Maximum recommended U-values (W/m^2 K)	Region 1 (Scotland)	Region 2 (north England and north Wales)	Region 3 (Northern Ireland)	Region 4 (south England and south Wales)
all walls (W/m^2K)	≤0.15	≤0.15	≤0.18	
roofs (W/m^2K)	≤0.11	≤0.13	≤0.15	
floors (W/m^2K)	≤0.15	≤0.15	≤0.18	
windows (W/m^2K)	≤1.2	≤1.5	≤1.6	
airtightness (m³/hr.m²)	≤1	≤2	≤3	
MVHR? 90% efficiency	✓	✓	✓	

- 2–3 kWh/m^2 per year reduced heat load demand if south facing.
- MVHR, with minimum 90% efficiency, is required with airtightness values ≤3 m³/hr.m². This will reduce yearly space heat load demand by a further 50%. ——⟶ Jump to Section 6.7.

 Code for Sustainable Homes credits (Ene 1, Ene 2, mandatory for levels 5 and 6) and EcoHomes credits (Ene 1, Ene 2), BREEAM (Ene 1, mandatory)

7.5.3 Passivhaus and EnerPHit standards for all buildings

Building to the best energy standards is recommended as it will:
- make compliance with zero carbon targets easier and more cost-effective (i.e. fewer active technologies required to offset the remaining carbon emissions) ——→ Jump to Chapters 11 and 12
- allow for a passive performing building throughout its lifetime
- reduce energy bills for occupants
- improve thermal comfort.

The Passivhaus standard is an energy efficiency standard successfully applied to many domestic and non-domestic buildings and currently well tested in Germany and other EU countries. It requires a building to be super-insulated and airtight to reduce space heat load demands to such a low level that a conventional heating system is no longer required. The EnerPHit standard deals with upgrading existing properties and recognises the difficulty of achieving strict airtightness standards retrospectively. Design and assessment is done via software, Passivhaus planning package (PHPP), although it is usually not accepted under the UK Building Regulations where SAP dominates. ——→ Jump to Chapter 1.

	EnerPHit	Passivhaus
space heating demand kWh/m² per year	25	15
primary energy demand kWh/m² per year	120	
airtightness (ach-1)	1.0	Max. 0.6 (around 1 m³/hr.m²)
fabric U-values W/m²K	maximum 0.15	
window U-values W/m²K	maximum 0.8	
ventilation	MVHR (min. 75% efficiency) or preheated ventilation air by other means ——→ Jump to Section 6.7	
space heating system	usually via warm air systems; however, can be via other low-surface temperature heating systems ——→ Jump to Section 10.4.1	
hot water heating and electricity provision	no requirement, although solar panels may be suitable ——→ Jump to Chapter 12	
cost implications	around 40% additional capital cost; payback around 10 years[54]	5–10% additional capital cost,[55] depending on site, climate, scale of development etc.; payback around 20–25 years

Key recommendations
....

- 2.5–3 times less heating energy is needed in a Passivhaus compared to the UK recommended zero carbon standard. However, the electrically powered MVHR increases the running costs and carbon impacts. Electricity is more expensive and carbon intensive than grid gas, unless 'clean' carbon-free renewable energy provides this additional electrical demand. ——$ Jump to Section 6.7 & Chapter 12.
- Building orientation is likely to become less important with higher fabric efficiency standards: around 1–2 kWh/m² per year winter space heating demand from the sun, depending on orientation in a low energy building. Although this appears insignificant, proportionally it is important as it accounts for up to 13% of a low-energy building's space heat demand.
- Solar shading in summer is likely to be required. ——$ Jump to Section 6.5.

Recommended regional fabric standards to achieve the Passivhaus space heat load demand

Maximum recommended U-values (W/m²K)	Region 1 and Region 2 (Scotland, north England and north Wales)	Region 3 and 4 (Northern Ireland, south England and south Wales)
all walls	≤0.14	≤0.15
roofs	≤0.10	≤0.15
floors	≤0.12	≤0.15
windows	≤1	≤1
airtightness	≤1 m³/(hr.m²)	≤1 m³/(hr.m²)

7.5.4 Yes, you can open windows in a Passivhaus!
....

Windows can be opened in 'tightly sealed constructions'. However, in winter most occupants find that they do not need, or want, to do so.

- In winter, mechanical ventilation with heat recovery (MVHR) system filters and preheats incoming fresh air. ——$ Jump to Section 6.7.
- If a window is opened for a long period of time in winter, temperatures will drop internally and it will take longer (with additional energy input) to increase internal temperatures. Thermally massive internal finishes can reduce this effect.
- In summer, and during warm periods, windows are opened for natural and night ventilation. The MVHR is usually switched off.

7.5.5 Future-proofing: why does super-insulation still make sense in 2080?

Even with the 2080 'worst case scenario' climate change, super-insulated buildings are very much appropriate to the UK climate.

Average yearly space heat demand may be reduced by 40–50% by 2080, but there will still be a heat load demand. Even where buildings are built to Passivhaus fabric standards or similar, the heat load will not be reduced to zero.

The prevention of summer overheating will be necessary when designing to, or better than, current Building Regulation standards, in all regions but Scotland. ——➢ Jump to Section 6.5. Strategies to reduce winter heat losses such as super-insulation and good airtightness also help to reduce summer heat gains.

		Region 1 Scotland	Region 2 north of England and Wales	Region 3 Northern Ireland	Region 4 south of England and Wales
Approximate yearly space heat load demand kWh/m² per year					
Building Regulations	2010	74	72	70	58
	2080	45	38	43	31
zero carbon standard	2010	39	39	39	39
	2080	37	30	30	24
Passivhaus standard	2010	15	15	15	15
	2080	11	8	8	6

7.5.6 Super-insulation: how much to use

- Construction U-values of 0.1–0.15 W/m²K are recommended. This reflects the Passivhaus and other similar standards' approach to fabric efficiency.
- Depending on insulation type, different thicknesses are required to meet such high standards. In most cases, insulation depths of at least 200–250 mm are required. See Figs 7.5.1 and 7.5.2.
- If not concerned with other environmental impacts, the insulation thickness can be reduced to around 100–135 mm if high-performing insulations such as phenolic foam and polyurethane are specified.
- Insulation depths increase significantly for straw, wood fibre and wood wool. However, these have the added benefit of their thermal lag properties in lightweight construction walls and most roofs.

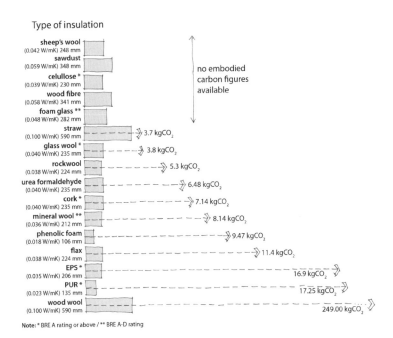

Type of insulation

sheep's wool
(0.042 W/mK) 248 mm
sawdust
(0.059 W/mK) 348 mm
celullose *
(0.039 W/mK) 230 mm
wood fibre
(0.058 W/mK) 341 mm
foam glass **
(0.048 W/mK) 282 mm

no embodied
carbon figures
available

straw
(0.100 W/mK) 590 mm → 3.7 kgCO$_2$
glass wool *
(0.040 W/mK) 235 mm → 3.8 kgCO$_2$
rockwool
(0.038 W/mK) 224 mm → 5.3 kgCO$_2$
urea formaldehyde
(0.040 W/mK) 235 mm → 6.48 kgCO$_2$
cork *
(0.040 W/mK) 235 mm → 7.14 kgCO$_2$
mineral wool **
(0.036 W/mK) 212 mm → 8.14 kgCO$_2$
phenolic foam
(0.018 W/mK) 106 mm → 9.47 kgCO$_2$
flax
(0.038 W/mK) 224 mm → 11.4 kgCO$_2$
EPS *
(0.035 W/mK) 206 mm → 16.9 kgCO$_2$
PUR *
(0.023 W/mK) 135 mm → 17.25 kgCO$_2$
wood wool
(0.100 W/mK) 590 mm → 249.00 kgCO$_2$

Note: * BRE A rating or above / ** BRE A-D rating

Fig. 7.5.1 Relative thicknesses of insulation types with embodied carbon (kgCO$_2$) for a typical brick/block construction to achieve an overall U-value of 0.15W/m^{2}K

Note: Calcium silicate blocks, which have a better thermal insulating performance than concrete blockwork, can reduce wall thicknesses by around 30 mm and achieve the same U-value of 0.15 W/m^{2}K as in Fig. 7.5.1. However, this may increase embodied carbon. See Section 7.2.7.

7.5.7 Typical wall construction thickness and embodied carbon to achieve high fabric energy efficiency (Passivhaus or equivalent)

Notes to be read in conjunction with Fig. 7.5.2:

- Wall sections to the left are based on a typical brick/blockwork wall with U-value 0.15 W/m²K.
- Wall sections on the right are timber framed walls with 140mm mineral wool in between studs + additional 'other' insulation to achieve U-value 0.15 W/m²K. Other insulation varies and is as listed.
- EC= embodied carbon: $kgCO_2$ of 1m² wall surface based on the above.
- Note that some of the insulations are non-breathable and may not be suitable for use in timber-frame and other vapour-open constructions. (See Section 7.4.6.)

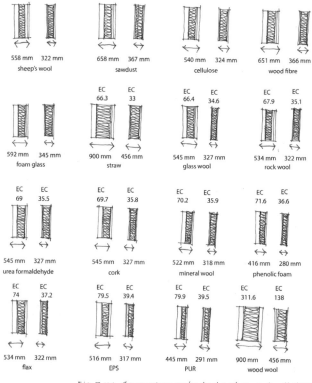

558 mm / 322 mm sheep's wool	658 mm / 367 mm sawdust	540 mm / 324 mm cellulose	651 mm / 366 mm wood fibre
	EC 66.3 / EC 33	EC 66.4 / EC 34.6	EC 67.9 / EC 35.1
592 mm / 345 mm foam glass	900 mm / 456 mm straw	545 mm / 327 mm glass wool	534 mm / 322 mm rock wool
EC 69 / EC 35.5	EC 69.7 / EC 35.8	EC 70.2 / EC 35.9	EC 71.6 / EC 36.6
545 mm / 327 mm urea formaldehyde	545 mm / 327 mm cork	522 mm / 318 mm mineral wool	416 mm / 280 mm phenolic foam
EC 74 / EC 37.2	EC 79.5 / EC 39.4	EC 79.9 / EC 39.5	EC 311.6 / EC 138
534 mm / 322 mm flax	516 mm / 317 mm EPS	445 mm / 291 mm PUR	900 mm / 456 mm wood wool

Fig. 7.5.2 Comparison embodied carbon and wall thickness to achieve U-value 0.15W/m²K

7.6 APPLICABLE LEGISLATION AND GUIDANCE

- BRE Digest 306 Domestic Draught proofing: Ventilation Considerations
- BRE IP 1/06 (Assessing the Effects of Thermal Bridging at Junctions and around Openings)
- BRE, GBG 67, part 1 to part 3; Achieving Airtightness, 2006
- BREEAM2011 Technical Manual www.breeam.org/BREEAM2011SchemeDocument/
- BS 7386: 1997 Specification for draught strips for the draught control of existing doors and windows in housing (including test methods)
- BS EN 12152 – Airtightness and BS EN 13829 – Airtightness testing
- BS EN 13162 to BS EN 13170 – Insulation
- BS EN 13187 Thermal performance of buildings. Qualitative detection of thermal irregularities in building envelopes. Infrared method
- Building Regulations 2000, Ventilation, Approved Document F, 2010 Edition
- Building Regulations 2010, Conservation of fuel and power, Approved document L, England and Wales; Scotland CIBSE Guide A Environmental design 2006
- CIBSE Guide B, Heating, ventilating, air conditioning and refrigeration- 2005
- Code for Sustainable Homes Technical Guide, November 2010
- DFP Technical Booklet F1: 2006 – Conservation of fuel and power in dwellings, DFP Technical Booklet F2: 2006 – Conversation of fuel and power in buildings other than dwellings, N. Ireland
- EcoHomes 2006, The environmental rating for homes, The Guidance – 2006, Issue 1.2 April 2006
- May (2005), Breathability: The Key to Building Performance, NBT
- Technical Handbooks 2011 – Domestic Energy Section 6, Scotland

7.7   FURTHER READING

- Berge (2009), *The Ecology of Building Materials*, Elsevier 2009
- Bevan and Woolley (2008), *Hemp lime construction, A guide to building with hemp lime composites*, IHS BRE Press
- BRE 2008, Simple ways to make it happen www.bre.co.uk/filelibrary/rpts/ sustainable_construction_simpleways_to_make_it_happen.pdf
- BRE, Designing quality buildings, 2007
- BRE, GBG 67, part 1 to part 3, Achieving Airtightness, 2006
- BRE, Ventilation, airtightness and indoor air quality in new homes, 2005
- Borer, P. and Harris C. *The Whole House Book: Ecological Building Design and Materials, 1998.* Centre for Alternative Technology (CAT)
- Building Research Energy Conservation Support Unit. Energy Saving Trust Refurbishment site guidance for solid walled houses – walls, 2000.
- BRECSU Good Practice Guide 297, DOE, London
- Building Research Energy Conservation Support Unit, Energy Saving Trust
- CIBSE, Guide A, Technical Handbooks, 2011
- Haryott, et al. (1998), The Long-term Costs of Owning and Using Buildings, The Royal Academy of Engineering, UK
- Hegger et al. (2008), Energy manual, sustainable architecture, Birkhauser
- Hemp Lime Construction Products Association (HLCPA) www.hemplime.org.uk/
- Little, Lime-hemp: a potential solution to a concrete problem, Construct Ireland magazine, Sept 2005, Issue 11, Vol 2.
- May (2005), Breathability: The Key to Building Performance, NBT
- Morgan (2006), Design and Detailing for Airtightness, SEDA Design Guides for Scotland: No. 2
- NHBC, A Practical Guide to Building Airtight Dwellings, 2009
- Watts (2007), *Pocket Handbook*, RICS
- Stirling (2001), Good Building Guide GBG 45, Insulating ground floors, BRE
- www.greenspec.co.uk

Chapter 8
Retrofit of existing housing stock

There are around 26 million dwellings in the UK,[1] 80% of which will still exist in 2050.[2] At present, these dwellings represent around 27% of the UK's CO_2 emissions.[3]

Around 7.6 million are solid walled properties.[4] One solid walled property needs about the same amount of space heating as eight dwellings of the same size built to current Building Regulations. This illustrates both the necessity and the potential impact of retrofitting the existing housing stock.

Yet, so far, less than 1%[5] of solid walled dwellings have been insulated, and no UK regulations deal with the refurbishment of existing housing stock. However, the 2008 Climate Change Act aims to make the entire UK housing stock zero or low carbon by 2050.[6]

By simply refurbishing to much higher insulation and airtightness standards, carbon reductions of at least 40% can be achieved. This would reduce the operational energy required just to heat our buildings by at least 80%.

 Symbol indicates relevance to the Code for Sustainable Homes, EcoHomes & BREEAM.

8.1 WHICH STANDARDS FOR RETROFITTING THE EXISTING HOUSING STOCK?

Existing housing should benefit from the highest fabric energy-efficiency standards that can be afforded – ideally to at least zero carbon standard. ⇢ Jump to Section 7.5.2.

The highest theoretical carbon savings are achieved by upgrading to the Passivhaus standard. In the UK, it is beneficial to retrofit to the required U-values of the Passivhaus standard, and the successful implementation of the full Passivhaus standard in refurbishments is currently being monitored from a thermal comfort and running costs point of view.

Existing housing stock legacy and CO$_2$ savings of other standards. Based on a typical two-storey, 100 m² mid-terrace Victorian house

Building Standard (mid terrace house)	Space heat demand (kWh/m² per year)	CO$_2$ impact from space heating	CO$_2$ impact of space heat demand for 7.6 million houses[7]	% CO$_2$ reduction if Victorian house upgraded to higher standards
solid wall Victorian – UK average	380[8]	7500 kgCO$_2$ per year	57 million tonnes of CO$_2$ per year	—
Part L New dwellings (Region 4)	60	1200 kgCO$_2$ per year	9 million tonnes CO$_2$ per year	84% reduction
zero carbon fabric energy efficiency	46[9]	900 kgCO$_2$ per year	6.8 million tonnes CO$_2$ per year	88% reduction
EnerPHit standard (Section 7.5.3)	25[10]	1300 kg CO$_2$ per year[11] or 500 kgCO$_2$ if gas	9.8 or 3.8 million tonnes CO$_2$ per year if electricity or gas respectively	93% space heat reduction 83–93% total CO$_2$ reduction depending on fuel used
Passivhaus standard (Section 7.5.3)	15	780 kgCO$_2$ per year[12] or 300 kg CO$_2$ if gas	5.9 or 2.3 million tonnes CO$_2$ per year if electricity or gas respectively	96% space heat reduction 90–96% total CO$_2$ reduction depending on fuel used

8.2   RECOMMENDED RETROFIT MEASURES CHECKLIST

Measures in order of carbon reduction and financial payback	☑ ☒
Have you installed 300 mm loft insulation? (It needs to have high thermal lag characteristics under pitched and flat roofs.) ——⤳ Jump to Chapter 7.	☐
Have you specified draught-proofing, particularly around service switches, sockets and pipe penetrations, behind skirting boards, around windows and doors? ——⤳ Jump to Chapter 7.	☐
Owing to high levels of airtightness, have you considered strategies for dealing with internal moisture and pollutants at the start of the project? This can be dealt with by either:	☐
• installing cost-effective masonry cavity wall insulation, if there is a 50 mm cavity (polystyrene beads or blown mineral wool are recommended; avoid urea formaldehyde spray foam because of internal air quality issues; needs to be combined with internal or external insulation to further reduce space heat demand), or:	☐
• insulating externally (reduce insulation around window reveals; specify new window sills and carefully detail roof overhang: verge and eaves extension gutters are available), or:	☐
• installing internal wall insulation, which is usually more disruptive (adapt services, windows doors, rooflights and their frames and architraves; refit skirting boards, floors and all electrical cabling; ideally replace ceilings and insulate below or above ceiling joists to avoid thermal bridging).	☐
Assuming that the above fabric efficiencies are in place, have you installed new central heating thermostats or thermostatic radiator valves and smart controls?	☐
Have you replaced the boiler with a smaller SEDBUK A-rated boiler and/or other monitoring and control technologies? ——⤳ Jump to Chapter 12.	☐
Floor insulation is disruptive, but if there are suspended timber floors, have you considered lifting floorboards and placing insulation between floor joists, maintaining existing ventilation – but not blocking airbricks and sleeper walls? If this is not possible or if it's a concrete floor, have you considered insulating above, adapting and refitting skirting boards, and adapting door frames and architraves? (A new floor finish will be required.)	☐
Have you repaired or improved existing windows and shutters? Or added secondary windows? Or replaced windows and doors with triple glazing or double-glazed argon-filled BFRC A-rated windows? Have you insulated and sealed around windows and door frames?	☐
Have you installed MVHR for whole house ventilation if sufficiently airtight (≤ 3 m³/hr.m²)? Otherwise, have you used local MVHR for cooker hood and bathroom extracts? ——⤳ Jump to Chapter 6.	☐
Once fabric efficiency has been optimised, have you then considered any renewable energy system?	☐

8.3 WILL IT STILL BE NECESSARY TO REFURBISH EXISTING PROPERTIES IN A WARMING CLIMATE?

Yes, for three reasons:

1. Upgrading to zero carbon standards and above continues to make climatic sense. Even in 2080, we will still require space heating.
2. In 2080, for each unrefurbished Victorian house, an equivalent 13 houses can be heated if they are upgraded to the zero carbon standard of 39–46 kWh/m² per year. Future climate change alone is likely to reduce space heat demand in the region of 30%. However, the environmental impact of the existing housing stock is still significant. These unrefurbished houses will also fail to provide affordable bills or thermal comfort to occupants.
3. Insulating the building fabric also helps to protect our internal environment from overheating. Fabric improvements will future-proof our buildings from a changing climate, both in the likelihood of temperatures rising, and in the unlikely worst case scenario of temperatures decreasing.

 Jump to Chapters 1 and 2.

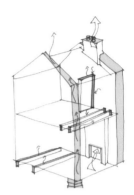

Fig. 8.3.1 Typical weak points in existing housing, which are difficult to resolve

Fig. 8.3.2 Theoretical predicted space heat demand of a typical dwelling in 2080 with warmer/cooler scenario

	Space heating demand 2010	Predicted space heat demand 2080 (high emissions scenario)[13]	Unlikely UK cooling scenario and predicted increased space heat demand
	kWh/m² per year		
existing Victorian terrace	380	265 (30% reduction)	estimated 35–50% increase in space heating demand in worst case scenario if temperatures were to decrease[14]
zero carbon standard	46	29 (35% reduction)	
Passivhaus standard	15	9 (40% reduction)	

8.4   THE REAL COST OF RETROFITTING THE EXISTING HOUSING STOCK

For a modest two-storey semi-detached house (100 m^2), 'passive' fabric improvements of walls and windows to Passivhaus U-value standards can cost up to £38,000. This does not include replacement or upgrading of active heating systems, pipework, etc.[15] A whole house ventilation system will be necessary once airtightness standards are ≤3m^3/hr.m^2. MVHR needs to be sized, installed and commissioned with care. ———➔ Jump to Section 6.7. A full upgrade to Passivhaus standard would cost around £75,000 (±10%).[16]

- Cavity wall insulation gives the quickest payback in just three years, but to meet higher Passivhaus standards it has to be 'topped up' with additional internal or external wall insulation, simultaneously reducing thermal bridging. Retrofitting cavity wall insulation may not be as effective as initially thought.
- Most measures, apart from loft insulation and cavity wall insulation, have a higher payback than 5 years.
- Replacing windows will immediately enhance thermal comfort and increase sound insulation. However, payback is 15+ years for the cheapest double glazing and around 25+ years for triple glazing.

8.5 THE GREEN DEAL

Under the UK Government's Green Deal, upfront costs of up to £10,000 in energy efficiency improvements may be met through low interest loans on a 'pay as you save' basis from autumn 2012. Energy savings have to be equal to or greater than the sum borrowed over a 25-year period (or less, dependent on the useful lifespan of interventions). However, it is clear that this funding will not go very far in meeting the ambitious 80% CO_2 reductions required.

Green Deal £10,000 budget: what it might buy	
£10,000 retrofit – larger dwellings	**£10,000 retrofit – two-storey terraced houses**
1. loft/floor insulation and cavity wall insulation where cavities exist	1. loft/floor insulation
2. boiler replacement and heating controls	2. boiler replacement and heating controls
3. draught-proofing behind and around skirting, windows, doors and other fabric services penetrations	3. external wall insulation

Some funding for the capital cost of low and zero carbon technologies may also be available. ——⟶ Jump to Section 10.7.

8.6. REDUCED STANDARDS FOR A REDUCED COST

Taking costs, regional climate and different dwelling types into account, initial research[17] has shown that on average the maximum amount people are willing to spend on retrofitting is a budget of £25,000,[18] and that space heating demands of between 33 and 117 kWh/m^2 per year could be achieved within this budget. These space heating demand reductions are based on theoretical savings. Often occupants tend to 'take back' energy bill savings by for example increasing internal temperatures or heating more rooms. ⟶ Jump to Section 1.5.5.

Recommended regional space heating demands and U-value standards with a £25,000 budget

Recommended maximum space heat demand	Region 1 Scotland	Region 2 north England and north Wales	Region 3 Northern Ireland	Region 4 south England and south Wales	Maximum U-values
	kWh/m^2 per year				W/(m^{2}K)
pre-1920 two-storey terraced, solid wall	78	73	65	61	all elements: 0.2 windows: <1.6
pre-1920 three-storey terraced, solid wall	95	90	81	76	walls: 0.35 roofs and floors: 0.3 windows: <1.6
pre-1920 two-storey semi-d, solid wall	117	110	100	93	all elements: 0.25 windows: <1.6
two-storey semi-d, cavity wall	42	40	35	33	all elements: windows <1.0 (triple glazing)
	most post 1930s dwellings with additional internal/external wall insulation				

Recommended maximum airtightness to achieve the above:
4–5 ach-1 or max. 6 m^3/(hr.m^2)

Note that the above recommendations may be below Building Regulations recommended standards where Part L 1B applies (i.e. substantial conversion or change of use). The reader should consult the appropriate regulations.

8.7 EXISTING DWELLINGS AND APPLICABLE REGULATIONS

- All national regulations require higher U-value for new thermal elements in extensions than in entirely new-build elements (under Part L1 A, new dwellings).
- This is to allow for high-performing extensions to make up for the rest of a house that is vastly underperforming.
- Air permeability of 10 m³/(hr.m²) is required for new parts, but there are no limits at present for the rest of the house.
- Trade-offs between poorly performing thermal elements may be allowed if they are compensated for with other, better-performing elements.
- Buildings may opt out of the standards if the payback of measures undertaken will exceed 15 years, or if too much of the internal floor space will be jeopardised.
- Historic buildings may also opt out.

8.8 APPLICABLE LEGISLATION AND GUIDANCE

- BREEAM for Domestic Refurbishment (2011), BRE
- BS ISO 21931-1, Sustainability in building construction. Framework for methods of assessment for environmental performance of construction works, Part 1, Buildings
- Building Regulations Approved Documents: Parts L, F and J, England and Wales
- EcoHomes XB, http://www.breeam.org/page.jsp?id=275
- SLD Section 3 and Section 6, 2010, Scotland
- Northern Ireland: DFP Technical Booklet Technical Booklet L and K, F1: 2006, AMD4/5, updated 2010, Northern Ireland
- rdSAP 2009

8.9 FURTHER READING

- BCIS, The Greener Home Price Guide, RICS
- BREEAM for Domestic Refurbishment (2011), BRE
- Construction Products Association. *An introduction to low carbon domestic refurbishment*, 2010
- Cook G. (2009), *Energy Efficiency in Old Houses*, Crowood Press
- Decrement Delay: www.greenspec.co.uk/decrement-delay.php
- Energy Savings Trust CE83/CE53/CE184/CE291/CE309: www.energysavingtrust.org.uk
- GreenSpec www.greenspec.co.uk/housing-refurb-retrofit.php
- Griffiths N (2007), *Eco-House Manual*, Haynes
- Hunt and Suhr (2008), *Old House Handbook, A Practical Guide to Care and Repair*, Frances Lincoln
- Liddell et al. (2008), Design and Detailing for Toxic Chemical Reduction in Buildings, SEDA Design Guides for Scotland: No. 3
- Morgan (2006), Design and Detailing for Airtightness, SEDA Design Guides for Scotland, No. 2
- RIBA, *Climate Change Toolkit, Principles of Low Carbon Design and Refurbishment*, free from www.architecture.com
- Sinn and Perry, Housing, The environment and our changing climate, Chartered Institute of Housing Policy, 2008
- SPAB: www.spab.org.uk/
- Stevenson and Morgan (2005), Design for Deconstruction book, SEDA Design Guides for Scotland, No. 1
- The Carbon Trust – www.carbontrust.co.uk
- The Green Deal – www.decc.gov.uk
- The National Refurbishment Centre – www.rethinkingrefurbishment.com/
- The Warm Front – www.warmfront.co.uk
- Thorpe D (2010), *Sustainable Home Refurbishment*, Earthscan
- www.existinghomesalliance.org.uk
- www.greatbritishrefurb.co.uk

Chapter 9
Key details

This chapter contains key details to illustrate good practice concerning insulation placement, airtightness zones and minimising thermal bridging. These details include some typical retrofit junctions as well as green roofs. The airtightness recommendations and principles in Section 7.4 need to be applied to all of the details at both design and construction stage.

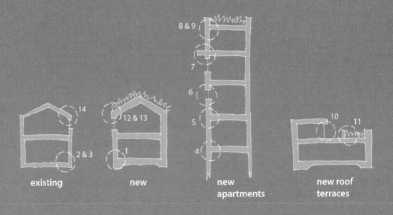

Fig. 9.1 The locations of key details 1–14 on both new and existing buildings

 Symbol indicates relevance to the Code for Sustainable Homes, EcoHomes & BREEAM.

9.1   FOUNDATIONS, FLOORS AND WALL JUNCTIONS

Detail 1: Super-insulated brick-blockwork wall and concrete floor and foundation

design considerations	• avoid full-fill cavities unless specification of water-repellent, closed cell or closed surface insulation and over-specify insulation thickness by 25–30% • if partial-fill cavity: 50 mm clear air gap with retention clips on ties, between brick outer leaf and water repellent, closed cell or closed surface insulation, or include breather membrane in cavity ——⟫ Jump to Section 7.3 • ensure no misalignment, sagging or air gaps between insulation, especially at corners and between airtight barrier and insulation
advantages	• robust ground floor in case of local flash floods ——⟫ Jump to Section 5.2 • where lime mortar specified, can be deconstructed after its first building life for material reuse • suitable with underfloor heating
disadvantages	• thermal bridging of brickwork onto concrete slab but loadbearing thermal insulating strips are available to build into wall, e.g. cellular glass and foamed plastics
suitable insulation?	• **wall:** rigid, water-resistant insulation below damp-proof membrane (DPM); above DPM: hydrophobic insulation • **above foundation:** rigid dense mineral wools are ideal to support screed; use increased insulation depth of minimum 70 mm where underfloor heating • **foundation:** ideally protected by compatible DPM with high-density loadbearing, XPS, incompressible and water-resistant EPS, PUR and cellular glass – all on blinded consolidated hardcore on undisturbed, level subsoil. Use reduced thicknesses with overlap to achieve total insulation thickness; insulation to have sufficient compressive strength to cast floor on and high resistance to groundwater and chemical attack (place on damp-proof membrane where high risk). If clay subsoil, insulation under slab to be compressible to allow for soil movement
thermal mass?	✓ good thermal mass if blockwork with in-situ clay, lime or cement plastering and if floor finish with good thermal mass ——⟫ Jump to Section 6.6
vapour permeable?	✓ if wall layers are specified with good vapour permeability ——⟫ Section 7.4.6

how to minimise thermal bridges	• a course of loadbearing thermal insulation or blockwork required at the base of the inner skin blockwork and outer brickwork • cladding panels instead of brick allow a continuation of foundation insulation (so no loadbearing thermal insulation or blockwork required in outer leaf) • install insulation above and under the slab and ensure a continuous line of insulation • brick wall ties will cause localised thermal bridging and should be calculated; stainless steel, reinforced mineral or plastics are better than galvanized steel wall ties • seal between floor and skirting board with flexible sealant • ensure that all insulation abuts tightly against each other and against blockwork/concrete structure
embodied energy?	• high embodied energy and embodied carbon due to use of heavyweight materials and cement content, unless reclaimed bricks and blocks are specified and/or lime mortar. • to reduce, specify secondary, recycled or manufactured aggregate (up to 20% content) and ordinary Portland cement replacement for concrete mix —⟶ Jump to Figure 7.2.5 and 7.2.6
BRE Green Guide	**floor:** solid concrete floor rating ranges from B to E; B-rating for recycled aggregate and where timber instead of screed **wall:** all blockwork cavity walls are A+; cladding or render on loadbearing masonry ranges from A+ to B rating, but can be as low as E if UK slate is used on steel supports; A+ cladding where supported by timber battens, including UK slate, concrete tiles, fibre cement, treated timber. Although uPVC weatherboarding receives a BRE A+ rating, this should be avoided

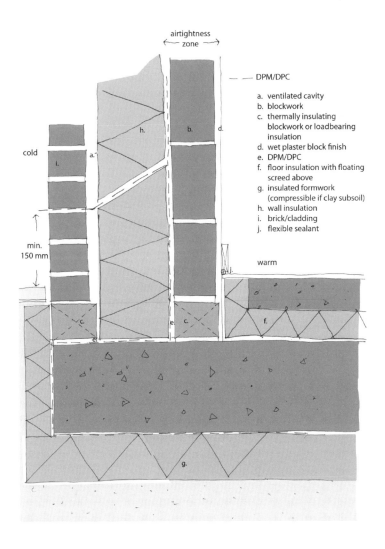

airtightness
← zone →

- - DPM/DPC

cold

min.
150 mm

warm

a. ventilated cavity
b. blockwork
c. thermally insulating
   blockwork or loadbearing
   insulation
d. wet plaster block finish
e. DPM/DPC
f. floor insulation with floating
   screed above
g. insulated formwork
   (compressible if clay subsoil)
h. wall insulation
i. brick/cladding
j. flexible sealant

Detail 1: Super-insulated brick-blockwork wall and concrete floor

Detail 2: Retrofit of a typical Victorian solid brick wall with external insulation and floor insulation between joists

design considerations	• suitable for solid walled buildings, where no town and country (T&C) planning restrictions exist to externally insulate • minimum 150 mm external insulation with render or cladding based on EPS insulation ──⟹ Jump to Chapter 7 • roof overhangs to be increased to over-sail additional external insulation • proprietary verge, eaves and window sill extension products are available • DPM from foundation to turn up to the wall and lap with any DPC to avoid water rising up • DPC usually injected, electro-osmosis or inserted • always retain ventilation below floor joists and do not obstruct airflow or block up airbricks
advantages	• external insulation minimises thermal bridging • retention of thermal mass and internal architectural features • less disruptive than internal insulation • opportunity to insulate any hot water pipes while lifting floorboards
disadvantages	• check with local T&C planning/conservation officers at early stages if permitted • expensive • structural damage more difficult to spot once installed • aesthetic implications
insulation between floor joists	• disruptive as it requires lifting of the floorboards, installing netting and then placing insulation in between joists
thermal mass?	✓
vapour permeable?	✓ if wall layers are specified with good vapour permeability ──⟹ Jump to Section 7.4.6
how to minimise thermal bridges	• wall insulation to be extended minimum 200 mm downwards from ground level • airtight strips or tapes to be applied to junction between joists and wall/foundation • remove skirting, seal any gaps, refit skirting • flexible sealant between floor and skirting • floor insulation to be tightly packed between joists, in contact with floorboards above

suitable insulation	· **wall:** usually EPS, XPS or phenolic foam, but rock mineral fibre and dense wood fibre also suitable · **wall at and below ground level:** water repellent, watertight, frost resistant, robust, impact resistant; insulation required, e.g. cellular glass · **timber floor:** usually flexible mineral fibres; preferably not plastic foams unless vapour barriers are introduced, $\longrightarrow$ Jump to Section 7.3.4
anything else?	ideally refurbishment happens at city block or street scale; this is to avoid thermal bridging and party wall thermal bypasses and for economies of scale

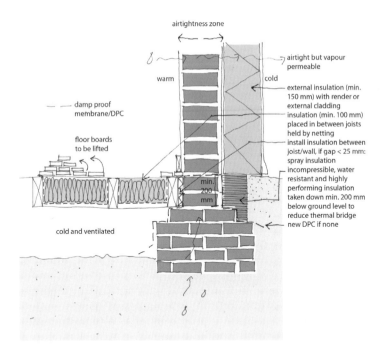

airtightness zone

airtight but vapour permeable

warm

cold

external insulation (min. 150 mm) with render or external cladding

damp proof membrane/DPC

insulation (min. 100 mm) placed in between joists held by netting

floor boards to be lifted

install insulation between joist/wall, if gap < 25 mm: spray insulation

min. 200 mm

incompressible, water resistant and highly performing insulation taken down min. 200 mm below ground level to reduce thermal bridge

cold and ventilated

new DPC if none

Detail 2: Retrofit of a typical Victorian solid brick wall with external insulation and floor insulation between joists

Detail 3: Retrofit of a typical Victorian solid brick wall with internal insulation and floor insulation above joists

design considerations	• requires adaption of all electrical cabling/radiators and sockets; is less expensive but usually only justified where a major refurbishment needs to take place • more disruptive and jeopardises internal floor areas, complicated if bathrooms, kitchens and stairs are at external walls • consult local authority/conservation officer and English Heritage where listed building • DPM from foundation to turn up to the wall and lap with any DPC to avoid water rising up • DPC usually injected • increased thermal bridge junctions compared to external wall insulation • airtightness zone best placed away from internal finishes to avoid penetration from internal fixtures
insulation above floor joists	• disruptive and requires adaptation of doors, frames, architraves and skirting boards • not recommended combined with external insulation owing to larger thermal bridging • similar principles for insulation of solid concrete floors • retains ventilation below floor joists
suitable insulation?	• **wall:** minimum 80 mm insulated XPS plasterboard with vapour barrier backing; undertake interstitial condensation calculations. • **floor:** minimum 50 mm rigid, low k-value insulation, usually mineral fibre or petrochemical and dense wood fibre boards ⟶⟩ Jump to Section 7.3.4
thermal mass?	X
vapour permeable?	✓ as Detail 2
how to minimise thermal bridges	• extend/return internal insulation by 1000 mm where internal walls meet external walls • consider placing insulation into ceiling joists with new ceiling on first and any upper floors • specify high performance insulation, usually of reduced thickness, around window and door openings, well sealed and taped
anything else?	internal insulation can be combined with insulation between floor joists – see Detail 2

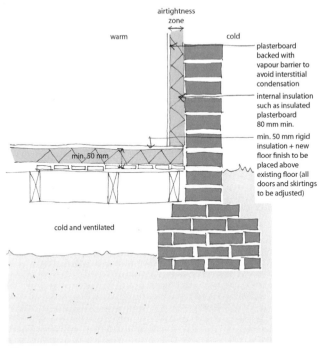

airtightness zone

warm

cold

plasterboard backed with vapour barrier to avoid interstitial condensation

internal insulation such as insulated plasterboard 80 mm min.

min. 50 mm rigid insulation + new floor finish to be placed above existing floor (all doors and skirtings to be adjusted)

min. 50 mm

cold and ventilated

Note:
– detail similar for solid concrete floor
– internal insulation can be combined with floor
  insulation between joists

Detail 3: Retrofit of a typical Victorian solid brick wall with internal insulation and floor insulation above joists

Detail 4: Reduced thermal bridging at concrete pile foundation

design considerations	• to use for taller buildings or where built on made-up ground/ unstable subsoil or inadequate loadbearing capacity subsoil • turn DPM from pile foundation up to the wall and lap and seal joints to avoid rising damp up
advantages	as Detail 1 • significant structural strength
disdavantages	as Detail 1 • significant thermal bridging of pile foundation
suitable insulation?	as Detail 1
thermal mass?	✓ if internally exposed thermal mass ⟶⟫ Jump to Section 6.6
vapour permeable?	✓ if wall layers are specified with good vapour permeability ⟶⟫ Jump to Section 7.4.6
how to minimise thermal bridges	• always install insulation above and under the slab and ensure a continuous line of insulation. • minimum 100–150 mm insulation on ground • return foundation insulation down to pile foundations, by around 1 m, or until the thermal bridge ≤2 × wall U-value • seal between floor and skirting board with flexible sealant • ensure that all insulation abuts tightly against blockwork/concrete structure
embodied energy?	as Detail 1
BRE Green Guide	**floor:** solid concrete floor rating ranges from B to E, B-rating for recycled aggregate and where timber instead of screed **wall:** can be A+

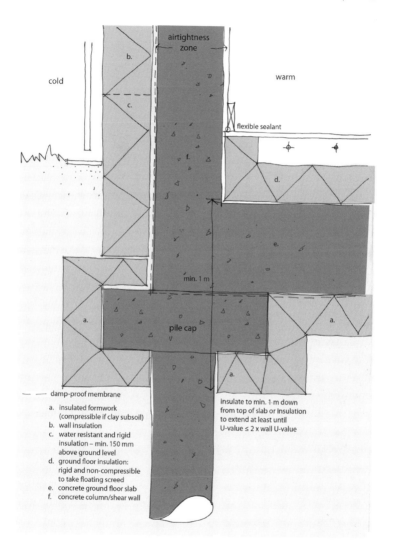

- damp-proof membrane
  a. insulated formwork
     (compressible if clay subsoil)
  b. wall insulation
  c. water resistant and rigid
     insulation – min. 150 mm
     above ground level
  d. ground floor insulation:
     rigid and non-compressible
     to take floating screed
  e. concrete ground floor slab
  f. concrete column/shear wall

insulate to min. 1 m down
from top of slab or insulation
to extend at least until
U-value ≤ 2 x wall U-value

Detail 4: Reduced thermal bridging at concrete pile foundations

Detail 5: Exposed solid concrete separating floor/ceiling

design considerations	• if wall cladding, fix at 600c/c at slab edge; insulation at floor slab edges requires thermal and fire stopping capacity • prefabricated slabs can be specified with soffit finish ready to receive paint; if cast on site, usually an in-situ plaster finish is required – use a dense plaster, not a lightweight insulating plaster • where underfloor heating, no impact-sound-reducing layers such as rubber underlays can be specified between screed and floor finish, as this will reduce heat transfer to room above • services such as gas/water/electrics to be brought into the building via the corridor, and then distributed via hollow internal walls to rooms beyond. Electrical conduits can be cast into the formwork. Corridor and bathroom ceilings to be finished with plasterboard or other finish to allow for these services, but all habitable rooms to be finished with in-situ dense plastered or painted exposed concrete
advantages	• the cost of exposing concrete floor soffit surfaces, including the casting-in of electrical conduits, can be offset by the material saving and on-site manual labour saving of not having a plasterboard ceiling
disadvantages	• cost and time of higher-quality concrete finishes if left exposed • early fixing of services design required to coordinate concrete casting
suitable insulation?	• to achieve good acoustic separation between flats, and particularly with an exposed concrete soffit in the unit below, a high impact-absorption insulation to be specified (minimum 50 mm); this will also act as thermal insulation between units and insulates – where used – the underfloor heating system from the unit below (so it does not heat up the slab soffit below)
thermal mass?	✓ do not dry line/plasterboard over the exposed surface in the main habitable spaces, as this removes the thermal capacity of the structure from exposure to indoor warm air; apply dense plaster instead ⟶⟩ Jump to Section 6.6
vapour permeable?	✓ if wall layers are specified with good vapour permeability ⟶⟩ Jump to Section 7.4.6
how to minimise thermal bridges	• where reduced depths in front of slab edges, columns and shear walls, specify a low k-value insulation
embodied energy?	as Detail 1
BRE Green Guide	**separating floor:** from A (precast only) to E **wall:** can be A+

anything else?	carpet floor finishes to be avoided, unless compatible with underfloor heating, as the transfer of heat can be impeded, hence carpet + underlay ≤2.5 Tog

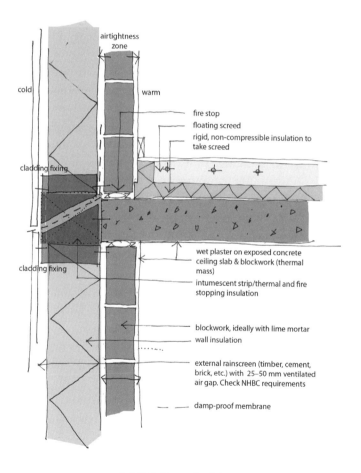

Detail 5: Exposed solid concrete separating floor/ceiling

9.2   WALL AND WINDOW JUNCTIONS

Detail 6: Typical window head/sill

design considerations	• avoid placing windows in line with the external façade: thermal bridging and significant exposure to the elements which is to be avoided with increased wind driven rain ———⤳ Jump to Section 2.2.5 • align windows and doors with thermal insulation in walls • allow for min. 100 mm above window head to allow for fixing of curtain rails • specify top inward-opening hopper windows to allow for night cooling ———⤳ Jump to Section 6.6.2
advantages	• protected window placement
disadvantages	• proprietary window reveals and sills required • careful fixing and taping of joints required – care on site required, which is time-consuming
suitable insulation?	• insulated plasterboard and thin low k-value insulation around window opening • high-performing, rigid insulation in wall cavity for robust window frame fixing • openings taped and jointed carefully to achieve airtight layer
thermal mass?	✓ if blockwork and exposed floor soffit are in-situ dense plastered ———⤳ Jump to Chapter 6
vapour permeable?	✓ if wall layers are specified with good vapour permeability; ensure compatible with full-fill cavity insulation
how to minimise thermal bridges	• a course of thermal blockwork or rigid/loadbearing insulation under the window sill • all internal openings lined with insulated plasterboard or other rigid, high-performing insulation • flexible sealant to close window frame/insulation junctions as well as window sill/wall junctions • minimum 70 mm overlap between window frames and insulation cavity • ensure cavity closing rigid insulation is in contact with window
embodied energy?	• high embodied energy and carbon where uPVC windows – ideally, timber or timber composite windows specified (softwood to be treated with water-based stains)
BRE Green Guide	windows rating ranges from A+ to E; the A+ are timber windows

anything else?	• specify triple-glazed, timber and/or timber composite windows • avoid uPVC windows • avoid proprietary window sills/wall finishes to be delivered on site in great quantities as storage will be an issue and damage is likely to occur • it is not recommended to move the window outwards to sit flush with the external façade, to avoid specifying proprietary window sills/wall trims

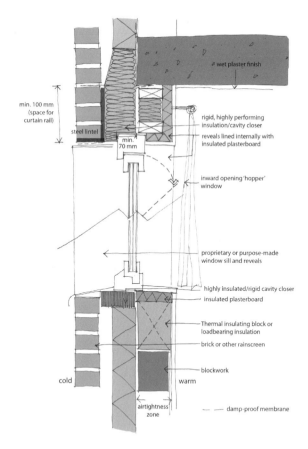

min. 100 mm (space for curtain rail)

steel lintel

min. 70 mm

wet plaster finish

rigid, highly performing insulation/cavity closer

reveals lined internally with insulated plasterboard

inward opening 'hopper' window

proprietary or purpose-made window sill and reveals

highly insulated/rigid cavity closer

insulated plasterboard

Thermal insulating block or loadbearing insulation

brick or other rainscreen

blockwork

cold

warm

airtightness zone

damp-proof membrane

Detail 6: Typical window head/sill

Detail 7: Horizontal solar shading

design considerations	• allow for maximum 100 mm above window head to fix solar shading to efficiently shade glazing • solar shading to be no more than 1500 mm deep, and normally around half depth of the window height to be effective in summer without reducing solar gain in winter • specify top inward-opening hopper window to allow for night cooling ——⟶ Jump to Section 6.6 • light-coloured and reflective solar shading is more effective • build in thermal break where fixing back to structure
advantages	• effective solar shading for south-facing windows only ——⟶ Jump to Section 6.5
disadvantages	• unsuitable for east–west orientations • shading to be installed prior to external cladding; ensure that no damage to shading element occurs while fixing external cladding • weight of solar shading requires appropriately engineered fixings • high risk of thermal bridge
suitable insulation?	• as Detail 6
thermal mass?	✓ if blockwork and exposed ceiling are wet plastered ——⟶ Jump to Chapter 6
how to minimise thermal bridges	• low k-value and robust insulation at the slab edge and where solar shading fixed
embodied energy? (based on 1 m²)	• embodied energy and carbon for precast concrete: 50 kgCO$_2$ • virgin aluminium is high embodied energy with 88 kgCO$_2$; recycled is 5% of virgin aluminium shading, but steel is highest at 214 kgCO$_2$ • use lightweight sections to lower embodied energy
BRE Green Guide	• no rating for solar shading; windows as Detail 6
anything else?	avoid proprietary solar shading to be delivered on site in great quantities as storage will be an issue and damage is likely to occur

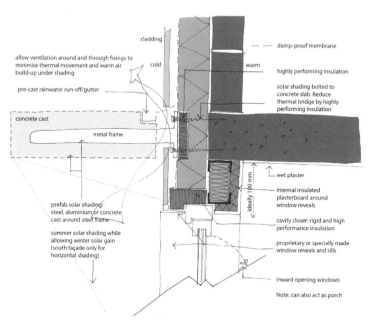

cladding

damp-proof membrane

allow ventilation around and through fixings to minimise thermal movement and warm air build-up under shading

cold

warm

highly performing insulation

pre-cast rainwater run-off/gutter

solar shading bolted to concrete slab. Reduce thermal bridge by highly performing insulation

concrete cast

metal frame

ideally 100 mm

wet plaster

internal insulated plasterboard around window reveals

prefab solar shading: steel, aluminium or concrete cast around steel frame

cavity closer: rigid and high performance insulation

summer solar shading while allowing winter solar gain (south façade only for horizontal shading)

proprietary or specially made window reveals and sills

inward opening windows

Note: can also act as porch

Detail 7: Horizontal solar shading

9.3 ROOFS

Detail 8a: Green roofs, including brown roofs

design considerations	• 2.5 to 5 times as heavy as conventional concrete or ceramic roof tiles; this extra weight needs to be incorporated into the structural design • retrofitting a green roof or placing a green roof on existing buildings is not straightforward and is not recommended unless increased structural supports are accommodated • use of recycled aggregate from the site as ballast/water retention layer of ideally no less than 80 mm depth • overhangs: minimum 7 m as vertical distance between roof surface and underside of overhanging soffit to allow for sun, rain and wind (for pollination) • fewer rainwater pipes required owing to reduced water runoff flow into rainwater downpipes; consult local T&C planning authorities and environment agencies • carry out waterproofing test of roof prior to installing insulation and layers
advantages	• reduced surface temperatures hence reduced urban heat island impacts ⎯⎯⟩ Jump to Section 4.2 • increased acoustic and thermal insulation, buffering extreme temperatures in winter and summer • protects roof surface from extreme thermal movements • some reduction of water runoff • supports biodiversity if species selected to suit ⎯⎯⟩ Jump to Sections 4.4 and 4.5
disadvantages	• increased cost, including increased structural design • thin green roofs may need irrigation, defeating their purpose • unlikely to provide major flood prevention and should be considered as part of a robust water management and flood prevention strategy including SUDS ⎯⎯⟩ Jump to Section 5.3 • if leaks or roof replacement, all layers require lifting • once saturated, green roofs behave similarly to conventional roofs, i.e. no water retention benefit at that point; saturation can be reached just 30 minutes after the start of a rainfall event[1]
how to minimise thermal bridges	• insulation laid in multiple layers with staggered overlapping layers and tightly laid near parapets and joints • take extra care at lightning conductor tapes, safe access latch-way supports, rainwater outlets, etc.
thermal mass?	✓ if exposed concrete slab ceiling with in-situ dense plaster for good internal thermal mass; good external thermal mass as soil depth increases; top floors benefit most from exposed thermal mass ⎯⎯⟩ Jump to Section 6.6

suitable insulation?	• limited choice as it needs to be tough and loadbearing to take additional weight, and needs to perform well under wet conditions in inverted roof construction (where insulation above waterproofing layer)
	• in inverted roof construction, allow an additional 25–30% insulation to account for increased thermal bridging
	• suitable for inverted roof: XPS and cellular glass if wrapped in waterproofing, and some EPS insulation – check with manufacturer with regard to thermal performance and water ingress
	• majority of insulations are suitable for warm roof constructions, i.e. waterproofing layer on top of insulation
	• high thermal lag insulation preferred to protect top floors from solar gains ────➣ Jump to Section 7.3.6
embodied energy?	• it is possible to use recycled materials as substrate, e.g. crushed bricks and inert subsoil from site demolition and excavation
	• initially the embodied energy for green roofs is higher than for a conventional roof owing to the demand for more material, but this increased embodied energy may be offset thanks to the energy savings resulting from its additional insulation qualities and protection of the roofing membrane below[2]
	• a brown roof has the lowest embodied energy and carbon, while the embodied carbon from intensive green roofs could be partially offset if used for vegetable growing – see Detail 9
irrigation?	• irrigation is only acceptable if water is taken from rainwater stored in attenuation tanks and recycled for this purpose
	• to avoid the need for irrigation, all roofs should be flat or within a 20° pitch and especially thin extensive green roofs should not face south unless substantially overshadowed
	• a deeper substrate is suitable in Regions 2 and 4 to retain more water and avoid the need for irrigation
maintenance?	• up to twice a year a maintenance contractor checks gutters and keeps them free from planting
	• at all times consideration of safe access to and from and while being on the roof is required in accordance with health and safety and CDM regulations
groundwater and rainwater harvesting considerations	• around 10–20% of rain enters the groundwater system,[3] so if this water is partially intercepted by a green roof, underground reserves cannot replenish, possibly aggravating the reduction of water available for extraction
	• rainwater can be harvested from green and brown roofs; it is usually filtered at drainage point; the deeper the substrate, the more water it will absorb and the less water available for water harvesting purposes
BRE Green Guide	roof structure: B-rating for precast concrete slabs; C-rating for in-situ concrete slabs and A+ rating where timber joists, which would be unsuitable for deeper intensive green roofs

Extensive green roof & brown 'biodiverse' roof

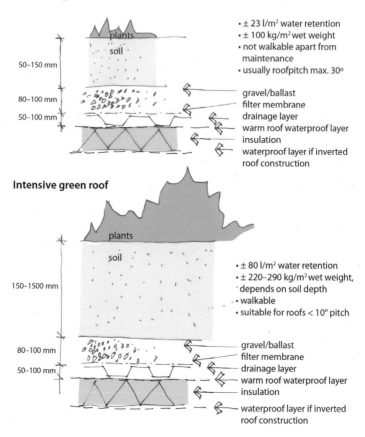

plants
soil

50–150 mm

- ± 23 l/m² water retention
- ± 100 kg/m² wet weight
- not walkable apart from maintenance
- usually roofpitch max. 30°

80–100 mm
50–100 mm

gravel/ballast
filter membrane
drainage layer
warm roof waterproof layer
insulation
waterproof layer if inverted roof construction

Intensive green roof

plants

soil

150–1500 mm

- ± 80 l/m² water retention
- ± 220–290 kg/m² wet weight, depends on soil depth
- walkable
- suitable for roofs < 10° pitch

80–100 mm
50–100 mm

gravel/ballast
filter membrane
drainage layer
warm roof waterproof layer
insulation

waterproof layer if inverted roof construction

Detail 8: Types of green roofs, including brown roofs

Detail 8b. Types of green roofs, including brown roofs

	Extensive green roof	Brown roof	Intensive green roof
soil depth mm	50–150	50–150	150–1500
total depth mm excluding structure	180–350	180–350	280–1700
cost?[4]	£165–190/m²	£140–180/m²	£175–210/m²
walkable?	X	X	✓
wet weight kg/m²	±100	±100	≥ 290
water retention l/m²	±23	±23	±80
water retention?	retains approx. 40–60% of water rainfall if less than 30 mm[5]		retains approx. 70–90% of water
supports biodiversity?	✓	✓ ✓	✓
suitable for food growing?	X	X	✓
maximum roofpitch?	roof pitch under 30°, and ideally ≤20°; if 30° pitch, counter battens required to retain soil; 'flat' roofs: 1:60 fall		≤10° pitch
embodied energy? 1 m² area	50 mm soil depth	150 mm soil depth	300 mm soil depth
	62 kgCO₂	59 kgCO₂	70 kgCO₂
compatibility with renewables?	• solar thermal and PV-T panels are unsuitable on green roofs • PVs benefit from plants' evaporative cooling effect ⟶ Jump to Section 12.5		
advantages	sedums thrive in shady areas; avoid full sun to avoid irrigation	recommended in urban areas	can be properly landscaped to provide valuable open space
disadvantages	cannot be used for leisure		heavy
	avoid in Regions 2 and 4 unless (partially) shaded place larger orders 18 months in advance to source locally grown sedum[6]	no immediate 'green' roof as plants need time to settle and grow	

259

Detail 9: Typical green roof parapet and water drainage

design considerations	• suitable for all green/brown roofs • sedum can grow up to 150 mm high; ensure that the parapet is at least 150 mm high above the sedum blanket top level • rooflights with min. 150 mm upstand above sedum blanket • higher parapets where intensive green roofs and public access (900–1100 mm) • gravel or edge trim of 500 mm required around all edges • balcony spout required for drainage of roof; proprietary products are available • parapet to slope towards roof • depth roof depends on roof build-up • waterproofing to extend from roof level to over and around parapet
disadvantages	• thermal bridging where lightweight parapet frame fixed to concrete slab
suitable insulation?	see general note, Detail 8a
thermal mass?	see general note, Detail 8a
how to minimise thermal bridges	• see previous notes, Detail 8a • a course of thermal blockwork or loadbearing insulation under the lightweight parapet structure • fill lightweight parapet wall tightly with insulation • reduced, but highly performing insulation at slab level • if concrete or concrete blockwork upstand: insulation to tightly wrap around all sides of the upstand and connect with cavity insulation and roof slab insulation
BRE Green Guide	see general note, Detail 8a

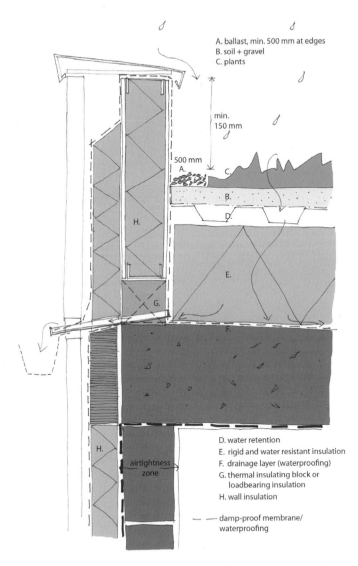

A. ballast, min. 500 mm at edges
B. soil + gravel
C. plants

min.
150 mm

500 mm
A.
C.
B.
D.

H.

E.

G.

F.

H.

airtightness
zone

D. water retention
E. rigid and water resistant insulation
F. drainage layer (waterproofing)
G. thermal insulating block or
   loadbearing insulation
H. wall insulation

— — damp-proof membrane/
     waterproofing

Detail 9: Typical green roof parapet and water drainage

Detail 10: Flush threshold with roof garden/terrace

design considerations	• to achieve level access to external terrace, the internal floor is to be built up to suit external roof build-up, mostly determined by insulation depth requirement • low k-value insulation, possibly with reduced depth, must be specified to minimise floor build-up depth to create flush thresholds • grille required along the door outer edge to divert water away from the door to avoid any water ingress • pavers/decking with gaps to allow rainfall to layers below for runoff • terrace pavers on adjustable footings to achieve flush finish with door level • check NHBC and other insurers' requirements for compliance
disadvantages	• thermal bridging where water grille and doorframe are fixed to the wall
suitable insulation?	• see general note, Detail 8a
thermal mass?	• see general note, Detail 8a
how to minimise thermal bridges	• a course of thermal blockwork under the door frame, wrapped tightly with insulation • door to overlap minimum 70 mm with insulation layer and ensure doorframe in contact with insulation • reduced and rigid, but highly performing insulation to be specified around external side of the thermal block as well as above under the water grille • pack roof insulation tightly with overlapping joints • if ceiling is insulated: loss of thermal mass
BRE Green Guide	see general note, Detail 8a

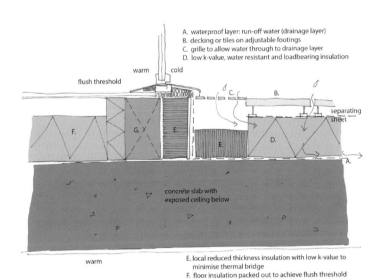

A. waterproof layer: run-off water (drainage layer)
B. decking or tiles on adjustable footings
C. grille to allow water through to drainage layer
D. low k-value, water resistant and loadbearing insulation

warm   cold

flush threshold

separating
sheet

F.   G.   E.

E.

D.

A.

concrete slab with
exposed ceiling below

warm

E. local reduced thickness insulation with low k-value to
minimise thermal bridge
F. floor insulation packed out to achieve flush threshold
G. thermal insulating block/rigid loadbearing insulation

Detail 10: Flush threshold with roof garden/terrace

Detail 11: Roof junction between roof terrace and green roof

design considerations	• suitable for all green/brown roofs • see previous notes, Details 8–9 • reduced, but highly performing insulation depth, under terrace pavers, if flush threshold is required – see Detail 10 • increased insulation depth required under green roof, where no flush threshold is required • dividing wall between terrace and green roof built from lightweight metal or timber frame • waterproofing to be wrapped around and over the parapet wall • parapet finish to slope towards green roof • terrace ideally to have separate water runoff from green roof • sedum can grow up to 150 mm high, so ensure that the parapet is at least 150 mm high above the sedum blanket level • use higher parapets where intensive green roofs and public access (900–1100 mm) • gravel or edge trim of 500 mm required around all edges
disadvantages	• thermal bridging where lightweight wall fixed to concrete structure
suitable insulation?	• see general note, Detail 8a
thermal mass?	• see general note, Detail 8a
how to minimise thermal bridges	• a course of thermal blockwork or rigid, loadbearing insulation under the lightweight structure, tightly filled with insulation • roof insulation fitted tightly against roof waterproofing • pack roof insulation tightly with overlapping joints • if ceiling insulated, loss of thermal mass • if concrete or concrete blockwork upstand, insulation to tightly wrap around all sides of the upstand and connect with roof slab insulation either side
BRE Green Guide	see general note, Detail 8a

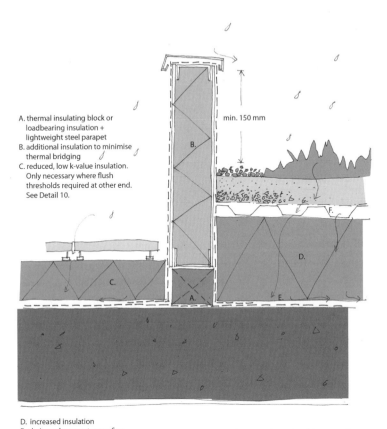

A. thermal insulating block or
   loadbearing insulation +
   lightweight steel parapet
B. additional insulation to minimise
   thermal bridging
C. reduced, low k-value insulation.
   Only necessary where flush
   thresholds required at other end.
   See Detail 10.

min. 150 mm

D. increased insulation
E. drainage layer: waterproofing
F. retention layer with filtration membrane
   and ballast above

— — damp-proof membrane/waterproofing

Detail 11: Roof junction between roof terrace and green roof

Detail 12: Pitched green roof with bird/bat habitat

design considerations	• ideal roof pitch ≤20°; if 20–30°, counter battens required to keep soil in place • only suitable for extensive or brown roof • sedum can grow up to 150 mm high, so likely to be visible from street level with pitched roof • gravel or edge trim of 500 mm required around all edges • large overhanging roofs are beneficial for increased water runoff in extreme rainfall events, even from green roofs • large overhangs allow provision of bat/bird habitat space under the eaves; proprietary products may be suitable • minimum 30 × 70 mm gap or opening required • habitat space boarded with non-treated timber
disadvantages	• visible and large eaves
suitable insulation?	• mineral fibres, cellulose and other natural fibre blankets are good for tight-fitting in between the rafters/joists • high thermal lag insulation required in timber joist roof for summer solar protection • panel/board insulation is suitable for walls and over joists and above/under rafter insulation
thermal mass?	see general note, Detail 8a
how to minimise thermal bridges	• insulation to wrap tightly from wall cavity to rafter spaces • insulation between rafters and under rafters (or above) • cavity full-fill to avoid thermal bypasses; increase insulation by 25–30% if thermal performance of insulation affected by potential dampness ——⟶ Jump to Section 7.3.5
BRE Green Guide	pitched roof rating ranges from A+ to A for both timber and steel construction; higher rating likely where reclaimed tiles are used

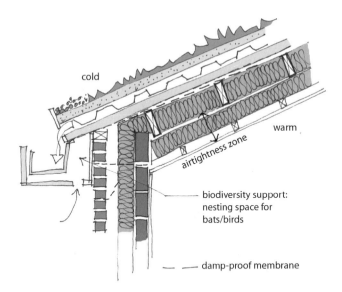

cold

warm

airtightness zone

biodiversity support:
nesting space for
bats/birds

damp-proof membrane

Note:
May need cross battening to keep soil in place at
steeper pitches.

Also for refurbishment of existing homes: ensure
structure suitable to take additional load of ± 100 kg/m²

Detail 12: Pitched green roof with bird/bat habitat

Detail 13: Pitched roof with bird/bat habitat

design considerations	• also suitable for retrofitting a building with cavity wall insulation or internal insulation, for example • if tiled roof, ideal roof pitch ≥25° • increase gutter capacity • increase density of fixing patterns for slates and tile • allow provision of bat/bird habitat space under the roof space, approx. 300 × 500 mm • habitat to be boarded with non-treated wood panels and waterproof sheeting over • minimum 30 × 70 mm gap or opening required so ventilation spacing 30 mm deep. • proprietary products may be suitable
disadvantages	• risk of thermal bypasses in service voids and in the bird/bat habitat
suitable insulation?	as Detail 12
thermal mass?	• only if internal brick/block wall in-situ plastered
How to minimise thermal bridges/ bypasses?	• insulation to wrap tightly from wall cavity to rafter spaces • insulation between rafters and under rafters (and/or above) • tight-fitting insulation with overlapping junctions and taped at joints and junctions • cavity full-fill to avoid thermal bypasses; increase insulation by 25–30% if thermal performance of insulation affected by potential dampness ——⟶ Jump to Section 7.3.5 • fill service gap with insulation around services to avoid thermal bypass heat losses
BRE Green Guide	see Detail 12

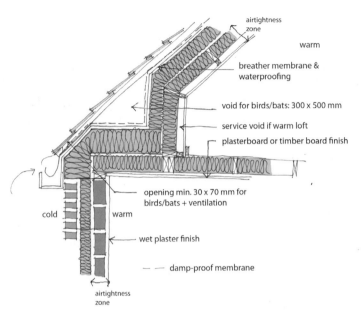

airtightness zone

warm

breather membrane & waterproofing

void for birds/bats: 300 x 500 mm

service void if warm loft

plasterboard or timber board finish

opening min. 30 x 70 mm for birds/bats + ventilation

cold   warm

wet plaster finish

— — damp-proof membrane

airtightness zone

Detail 13: Pitched roof with bird/bat habitat

Detail 14: Retrofitting a pitched roof with bird/bat habitat

design considerations	• illustrated with external wall insulation – see Detail 2 • if tiled roof, ideal roof pitch ≥25° • increase gutter capacity • increase density of fixing patterns for slates and tile • large overhanging roofs are beneficial for increased water runoff in extreme rainfall events • large overhangs allow provision of bat/bird habitat space under the eaves; proprietary products may be suitable • minimum 30 × 70 mm gap or opening required • habitat space boarded with non-treated timber • minimum 250 mm roof insulation
disadvantages	• visible and large eaves • risk of thermal bypasses in roof ventilation void
suitable insulation?	as Detail 12
thermal mass?	only if internal brick/block wall in-situ dense plastered
how to minimise thermal bridges	• insulation to wrap tightly from wall cavity to rafter spaces • insulation between rafters and under rafters (and/or above) • tight-fitting insulation with overlapping junctions and taped at joints and junctions • external insulation to tightly fit against window frames • internally, window frames to be sealed and fitted against rigid, highly performing insulation
BRE Green Guide	see Detail 12

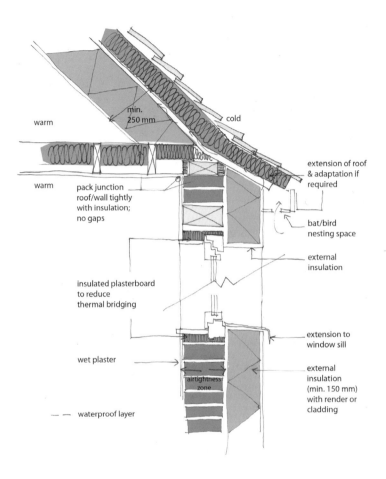

warm

min.
250 mm

cold

warm

pack junction
roof/wall tightly
with insulation;
no gaps

extension of roof
& adaptation if
required

bat/bird
nesting space

external
insulation

insulated plasterboard
to reduce
thermal bridging

extension to
window sill

wet plaster

airtightness
zone

external
insulation
(min. 150 mm)
with render or
cladding

— — waterproof layer

Detail 14: Retrofitting a pitched roof with bird/bat habitat

9.4   APPLICABLE LEGISLATION AND GUIDANCE

- AECB CarbonLite: Standards and Guidance, Volume 4 – design guidance step 1/silver standard, Volume 5 – design guidance, steps 2&3/Passivhaus and gold
  www.aecb.net/standards_and_guidance.php
- Energy Saving Trust, Enhanced Construction Details, CE297, CE302
- Liddell *et al.* (2008), Design and Detailing for Toxic Chemical Reduction in Buildings, SEDA Design Guides for Scotland: No. 3
- Morgan (2006), Design and Detailing for Airtightness, SEDA Design Guides for Scotland: No. 2
- Stevenson and Morgan (2005), Design for Deconstruction book, SEDA Design Guides for Scotland: No. 1
- Technical Booklet D (Structure) L and K, Northern Ireland
- Technical Handbooks Section 1 (Structure), Section 3 and Section 6 Scotland
- The Building Regulations 2010 Part A, F, L and J, England and Wales
- The Building Regulations Accredited Construction Details (ACDs) Part L

9.5   FURTHER READING

- Banting et al. (2005), Report on the Environmental Benefits and Costs of Green Roof Technology for the City of Toronto
- BRE, GBG 67, Parts 1 to 3; Achieving Airthightness, 2006
- BRE, Ventilation, airtightness and indoor air quality in new homes, 2005
- Building Research Energy Conservation Support Unit, Minimising thermal bridging when upgrading existing housing: a detailed guide for architects and building designers. 1996. BRECSU Good Practice Guide 183, DOE, London
- Building Research Energy Conservation Support Unit. Energy Saving Trust. Refurbishment site guidance for solid walled houses – ground floors, 2000.
- BRECSU Good Practice Guide 294, DoE, London
- Building Research Energy Conservation Support Unit. Energy Saving Trust. Refurbishment site guidance for solid walled houses – walls, 2000.
- BRECSU Good Practice Guide 297, DoE, London
- Buntain et al. (2000), External insulation systems for walls of dwellings GPG 293. Energy Efficiency Best Practice in Housing, London, Energy Saving Trust
- CIBSE Guide F
- Dunnett, N., Kingsbury, N., (2008), *Planting green roofs and living walls*, Timber Press, London
- EST, Enhanced Construction Details, CE297, CE302
- Kosareo and Ries (2006), Comparative environmental life cycle assessment of green roofs, Department of Civil and Environmental Engineering, University of Pittsburgh, USA
- NHBC, A practical guide to building airtight dwellings, 2009
- Sinn and Perry (2008), Housing, The Environment and our Changing Climate, Chartered Institute of Housing Policy
- Stirling (2001), Good Building Guide 45 Insulating Ground Floors, BRE
- Williams (2010), *Biodiversity for Low and Zero Carbon Buildings: A Technical Guide for New Build*, RIBA Publishing

Chapter 10
Energy supply and demand

Energy supply is often wrongly considered to be the most important issue in delivering low carbon buildings.

In fact, the priority is to reduce energy demand.

When considering energy supply and demand, a clear hierarchy exists:

1. Fabric energy efficiency is always the first 'renewable' to consider as opposed to trying to meet a building's large energy demand.
2. Once reduced, it is easier to meet any remaining energy demand, which should be met using efficient methods. This avoids wasting energy in transmission, even if it is energy from 'low carbon' sources.
3. Low carbon energy supply should only be considered once the above strategies have been maximised.

The preceding chapters have focused on the first point and set out strategies to reduce energy demand in buildings.

This chapter relates to operational energy and operational carbon from buildings. It summarises the energy demands of different building typologies. It investigates efficient methods of delivering energy, such as underfloor heating, use of A-rated appliances and local energy generation from district heating schemes.

 Symbol indicates relevance to the Code for Sustainable Homes, EcoHomes & BREEAM.

10.1   TYPICAL ENERGY DEMANDS

We must understand and realistically estimate a building's energy demand before we consider energy supply.

Energy demand can generally be broken down into 'regulated' and 'unregulated' energy and emissions.

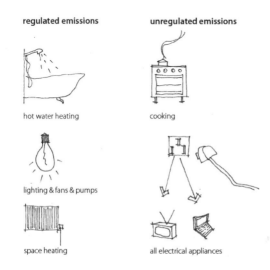

Fig. 10.1.1 Regulated vs unregulated emissions

10.1.1 What are regulated and unregulated emissions?

regulated emissions	Building Regulations 'regulate' the use of energy and its emissions in a building. This includes energy for space heating, hot water, ventilation, cooling and fixed lighting.
unregulated emissions	This includes energy for cooking, all plug-in devices and appliances such as TVs and computers. Unregulated energy use is difficult to estimate as it depends on individual user behaviour. Generally around 75% of all electricity use in a dwelling is for unregulated energy use.

10.1.2 Energy demand benchmarks for different building typologies

The following methods can be used to estimate a building's energy demand:
- Undertake software modelling (particularly useful for space heat demand).
- Use existing energy bills, where user/building known.
- Use 'good practice' benchmarks, which are usually derived from a database of different building typologies that have been monitored for energy use. These can be obtained from CIBSE Guide F, www.carbonbuzz.org; for dwellings, see also the 40% House[1] and the English House Condition Survey.

Figures for typical usage can differ quite substantially and are related to the fabric performance of the building and user behaviour. ⟶ Jump to Section 1.5. For dwellings, hot water, cooking and electricity demand are a typical average of 105 kWh/m² per year.[2] This is also the maximum for the Passivhaus standard. In most buildings, the bulk of energy is used for hot water and space heating. Space heat demand in particular can be reduced by increasing building fabric standards. ⟶ Jump to Chapters 7 & 8.

Fig. 10.1.2 Building energy demand benchmarks[3]

Building Typology	Regulated energy kWh/m² per year			Unregulated energy kWh/m² per year		Total energy demand kWh/m² per year
	space heating	hot water	lighting, fans, pumps, cooling	appliances, equipment	cooking, catering	
dwelling, Building Regulations	60–75	55	10	25	15	165–180
zero carbon dwelling	39–46	55	10	25	15	144–151
dwelling, Passivhaus (PH) standard	15	55	10	25	15	120
any building, PH standard	15	105				120
nursing home	247		44			291
typical hotel	260		42	15	23	340
office naturally ventilated	79		27	24	3	133
office air-conditioned	97		79	44	5	225
school	110		24			134
fitness centre	209		73	5	—	285
supermarket	200		915			1115

10.2   CARBON IMPACT OF THE ENERGY USED: CO_2 FUEL INTENSITIES

Different fuels have different CO_2 intensities, specific to the UK. It is important to choose the correct and most up-to-date conversion factor to avoid over- or underestimating a building's carbon impact. For business carbon reduction commitments (CRC), the Defra figures are used,[4] while for Building Regulation purposes, the SAP figures are relevant.[5] ——⇥ Jump to Chapter 1. SAP 2009 figures are those used throughout in the pocketbook calculations. Note that using biomass is not 'zero carbon', as is often assumed.

Fig. 10.2.1 CO_2 conversion factors, from SAP 2009

Energy source/fuel	CO_2 'intensity': kgCO_2/kWh[6] (SAP)	CO_2 'intensity': (Defra/Carbon Trust) kgCO_2e/kWh[7]
gas (grid)	0.198	0.185
electricity (grid) imported	0.517	0.545
electricity displaced from the grid (generated by renewables)	−0.529	−0.545
Other fuels		
wood logs	0.008	0.0189
woodchip	0.009	0.0157
biomass	0.013	—
biogas	0.018	—
wood pellets	0.028	0.0389
heat from community CHP and geothermal	0.036	—
LPG	0.245	0.214
diesel	0.291	0.253
petrol	0.306	0.241
heat from heat pump	0.517	—
electricity from CHP	−0.529	—

10.2.1 Grid electricity is the most polluting energy source

- The UK's commitment to providing renewable energy means that the CO_2 fuel intensity for electricity should decrease year on year.
- At present, reliance on electricity for heating or cooling is a bad idea. However, if there is a very low space heating requirement ($\leq$30 kWh/m²a), electrical space heating could be considered as part of future-proofing strategies. See Section 10.5.
- At present, SAP 2009 allows for greater CO_2 saving (0.529 kgCO_2/kWh) when exporting to the grid than when using from the grid (0.517 kgCO_2/kWh).
- The increased electrical usage in our buildings will be difficult to manage and supply, particularly as occupants acquire more electrical gadgets. See Section 10.4.3.

10.2.2 Different building typologies and carbon impact

A building's operational carbon footprint is obtained by multiplying the energy demand by the CO_2 fuel intensity of the fuel used:

Energy demand (kWh/m² per year) $\times$ CO_2 intensity (kgCO_2/kWh) = carbon footprint from operational energy demand (kg CO_2/m² per year). See Fig. 10.2.2 overleaf.

Fig. 10.2.2 Carbon footprints with CO_2 conversion factors from SAP 2009, gas-grid assumed for all heating requirements unless otherwise stated

A building's typical carbon footprint from operational energy demand						
Building typology	Regulated carbon emissions $kgCO_2/m^2$ per year			Unregulated carbon emissions $kgCO_2/m^2$ per year		Total CO_2 emissions $kgCO_2/m^2$ per year
	space heat	hot water	lighting, fans, pumps, cooling	appliance, equipment	cooking catering ***	
dwelling, Building Regulations	12–15	11	5	13	3/8	44–52
dwelling, zero carbon	8–9	11	5	13	3/8	40–46**
dwelling, Passivhaus standard-PH	3/8*	11	5	13	3/8	35/45
any building, PH standard	3/8*	32–37				35/45
nursing home	49			23		72
typical hotel	51		22	8	5/12	86/93
office, naturally ventilated	16		14	12	3	45
office, air-conditioned	19		41	23	1/3	84/86
school	22			12		34
fitness centre	41		38	3	—	82
supermarket	40			473		513

* Higher number if space heat demand is supplied with electrical fuel, which is common in a Passivhaus. ———➣ Jump to Section 7.5.

** Zero carbon emissions will need to be reduced further by on-site strategies and 'allowable solutions'. ———➣ Jump to Chapter 11.

*** Use lower emissions if gas cooking and higher emissions if electrical cooking.

10.3   EFFICIENT SUPPLY OF ENERGY

Before considering clean technologies to supply a building's energy demand, fuel efficiency must be maximised.

> ### Key recommendations
>
> · Prioritise energy-efficient fabric performance of buildings.
>   ⟶⟩ Jump to Chapters 7 & 8.
> · Deliver energy in an efficient manner, i.e. closest to its demand source where it can be harnessed efficiently.
> · Use efficient technologies and products. See Section 10.4.

10.3.1 Traditional energy supply

The traditional way of generating energy is inefficient:
  · Transmission losses occur between energy generation (mostly away from urban areas) and its delivery (mostly in urban areas).
  · Burning coal to produce electricity is an inefficient process.

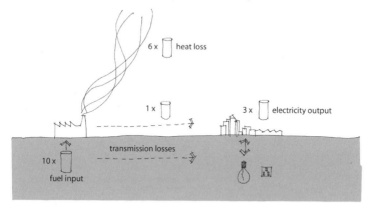

Fig. 10.3.1 Traditional energy production

10.3.2 Delivering energy efficiently: on-site energy generation

To avoid transmission losses, it makes sense to generate energy closer to where people need it. Urban areas have great potential for community energy networks and district heating/electricity generation.

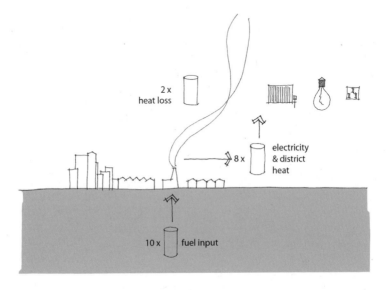

Fig. 10.3.2 District energy production

- Even where 'clean' energy is generated, the efficiency of the technologies chosen is paramount. Not even 'low or zero carbon' energy should be wasted.
- As buildings and cities utilise some 40–50% of all UK energy demand (⟶⟩ Jump to Chapter 1), it makes sense to produce energy in/on or near buildings. Local renewable energy generation works particularly well in buildings in rural areas.
- However, in urban areas, where 90% of the UK population live,[8] the application of renewable energy in buildings becomes more challenging.
- Renewables mostly rely on energy from natural elements (wind, sun) which become unpredictable and difficult to harness in urban areas.
    ⟶⟩ Jump to Chapter 12 for more information on renewables.

10.3.3 District/community heating

Community heating provides heat from a central source to one or many building blocks via its own distribution network. Heat can be supplied from conventional fossil fuels and/or through low and zero carbon technologies. Where combined heat and power (CHP) is utilised, the community plant not only generates electricity, but also captures the waste heat generated in this process for local use.

Key recommendations

- Community heating works best where there is a balance of energy demand throughout the day. This is best where domestic and non-domestic energy use is combined.
- It is suitable where buildings are located close together. This minimises transmission losses and distribution costs. Ideal density is ≥55 dwellings/ha.[9]
- For large schemes of more than 100 dwellings, using several smaller plant rooms will help to avoid distribution losses.
- Project lifetime is usually 25 years and will require a maintenance and management team to ensure smooth running and timely billing. Sometimes ESCOs are used. See Section 10.3.4.
- Existing neighbouring buildings could be connected to the community heating system but this is legally complicated where roads and properties are owned by different parties. Exporting heat may count towards 'allowable solutions' to achieve zero carbon compliance.
  ——⟶ Jump to Chapter 11.
- Using electrical cooking avoids the need to fit each dwelling with individual gas connections and flue systems. This can increase safety and reduce gas distribution costs.
- Dwellings do not require individual boilers, which can save space, and it externalises some of the maintenance regime.
- Space heating and hot water controls work in the same way as a conventional boiler but occupants cannot switch their heating supplier.
- The heating network (i.e. pipes for distribution) should be well insulated to avoid transmission losses. Pipework is usually manufactured with integral insulation, leak detection and a 30-year lifespan.
- For CHP ——⟶ Jump to Section 12.6.

10.3.4 On-site energy supply and management (ESCOs)

Whether local energy is produced by district heating schemes or low and zero carbon technologies, regular maintenance and management are required. Traditionally, energy supply is managed by the electricity and gas companies who sell energy to us. Producing energy on site requires housing developers and building managers to become energy suppliers and managing this with little or no expertise and resources. Sometimes they delegate these responsibilities to third parties such as energy services companies (ESCOs).

ESCO advantages
ESCO takes on all the design, installation, commissioning and maintenance commitments, and often also offers financial initiatives, usually expressed as a percentage or lump sum contribution to the capital cost.
ESCO carries all risk and does all the billing, instead of developer or social landlord.

ESCO disadvantages
An ESCO contract will be for the provision of heating and electricity, tying in the developer/landlord and therefore tenants for a long-term agreement.
Energy prices will be fixed and taken as an average of several other suppliers (likewise for 'extras' such as broadband and telephone provision), and so prices are not always competitive.
ESCOs are usually for-profit companies: they shoulder all the financial risks but will also seek to profit from selling energy
ESCOs are often only interested in a larger number of dwellings, usually 300–500.[10]
ESCOs should be involved from feasibility stages.
Developer loses out on profits and strategic control.

10.4   ENERGY-EFFICIENT TECHNOLOGIES AND PRODUCTS

Energy can be supplied using low or zero carbon technologies. However, the energy efficiency of heat supply and distribution and the energy efficiency of electrical appliances remain a priority for consideration. Even low and zero carbon energy should not be wasted.

- specify A+ and A++ rated electrical appliances
- consider underfloor heating
- specify heating and cooling technologies of ideally no less than COP 3. See Section 10.4.2 and ——➔ Jump to Chapter 12

 Code for Sustainable Homes (Ene 3, Ene 5), EcoHomes (Ene 4) and BREEAM credits (Ene 4 mandatory, Ene 5, Ene 7, Ene 8)

10.4.1 Energy-efficient space heating

Space heating is generally distributed through radiators. However, conventional radiators require much higher input temperatures (and therefore more energy) than, for example, underfloor heating or hot air heating.

- Underfloor heating is the most efficient way of distributing space heating.
- Certain technologies, such as heat pumps and solar thermal panels, should only be used in combination with energy-efficient space heating such as air-to-air heating, underfloor heating and low surface temperature radiators. ——➔ Jump to Chapter 12.
- Each room should have a user-friendly thermostat control, regardless of which distribution technology is used.

Fig. 10.4.1 Heating distribution systems and efficiencies

Building heating distribution system	Heat input temperatures required[11]
conventional radiators	60–90°C
domestic hot water	60–65°C
low temperature radiators	45–55°C
hot air fan coil unit	35–45°C
underfloor heating	30–40°C

A thermal store

Many technologies should only be used in combination with a thermal store, which stores excess heat. This is useful because many technologies rely on the sun to generate heat. This is most intense in summer and at midday, yet most of a building's heat demand is in the evenings and in winter. A thermal store is usually a closed container of water into which heat is 'dumped' and stored, easing daily and seasonal discrepancies. The storage tank can be underground or in the thermal envelope and the tank has to be well insulated. Usually 250 litres is the minimum tank size for a typical household.

10.4.2 What is COP (coefficient of performance)?

Coefficient of performance (COP) expresses the energy efficiency of cooling and heating technologies. COP is the useful output of energy compared to the input of energy (usually electricity) required. The higher the COP, the higher the technology's energy efficiency.

For example, a technology with COP of 3 means that for each unit of electricity, three useful units of heat are delivered.

10.4.3 Energy efficiency of electrical appliances

Only A+ and AA+ rated appliances to be specified. This can save as much as 140 kgCO$_2$ per year, more than certain low carbon technologies.
⟶ Jump to Section 12.2.6.

Fig. 10.4.2 Carbon emission reductions from A+ or A++ rated appliances

A+ or A++ rated appliances	kgCO$_2$/year reduction compared to a 1998 appliance[12]
fridge freezer	140 kgCO$_2$ per year
upright/chest freezer	80 kgCO$_2$ per year
fridge	45 kgCO$_2$ per year
dishwasher	48 kgCO$_2$ per year

10.4.4 Typical unregulated appliances and energy use[13]

A+ rated appliances	Energy consumption (watt, unless stated otherwise)	Usage (hr/day)	Estimated kWh/ year for a typical household
iron	1300	3	608
8 kg load washing machine	1.225 kWh/cycle	270 cycles per year	331
typical dishwasher	0.95 kWh/cycle	250 cycles per year	237
fridge freezer	—	—	208
tumble dryer	1.6 kWh/cycle	127 cycles per year	203
LCD TV	77	6	169
hair dryer	1000	0.2	104
vacuum cleaner	1200	1.5	94
modem WiFi	9	24	79
electric kettle	2100	0.1	77
iPod touch charging	36	4	75
microwave	900	0.2	66
four-slice toaster	2200	0.1	57
laptop	1/5 (in use/idle)	n/a	19
phone: cordless	1.7	24	15
Nintendo Wii	17	2	12
food processor	650	0.1	10
blender	500	0.1	10
mobile phone charging	3.68	4	9
inkjet printer	11	n/a	5.80

10.5   FUTURE-PROOFING

The investment required to connect buildings to the national gas grid may not make much sense in the long term, since energy demands might ultimately be met via electricity alone. However, until at least 2050, providing all energy from grid-electricity would increase a building's carbon footprint. Providing space heating via electricity will only make environmental sense when at least 60% of the national electricity grid is delivered from clean, renewable sources. The impact of grid de-carbonisation will be significant, particularly for electrical space heating options, which will become less carbon intense.

Fig. 10.5.1 Yearly CO_2 impact of gas versus electrical space heating

Standard	Space heat demand	CO_2 impact if delivery by natural gas	CO_2 impact if delivery by 2011 grid-electricity	CO_2 impact of delivery by 2020[14] (grid-electricity predicted 0.362 kgCO$_2$/kWh)
	kWh/m² per year	kgCO$_2$/m² per year		kgCO$_2$/m² per year
2010 Building Regulations dwelling	60–75	12–15	31–39	22–27
Passivhaus standard	15	3	8	5

Generally, the following future-proofing strategies should be used to assess the viability of fuel sources:

Fig. 10.5.2 Future-proofing checklist

		☑ ☒
1.	Has energy efficiency been maximised?	☐
2.	How low is space heating demand? (See below)	
	≤15 kWh/m² per year: no conventional heating system is required. Space heat demand can be met electrically. ⟶ Jump to Section 7.5.3.	☐
	15–30 kWh/m² per year: grid gas connection may be avoided; ideally, efficient heat pumps are used and/or at least 40% of space heat demand is provided by renewable technologies to offset the additional CO_2 emissions until 2050.	☐
	>30 kWh/m² per year: electrical space heating is never a good idea unless the grid de-carbonises significantly or no gas connection is available.	☐
3.	Can the building be occupied if power fails? Even if producing much of its own energy, a building still needs a backup supply in case its own technologies fail. An electricity grid connection is almost always required.	☐

10.6   ON-SITE CO_2 REDUCTION TARGETS

Low and zero carbon technologies are the final consideration in the effort to reduce carbon emissions. They should only be explored after fabric efficiency and efficient energy delivery have been ensured.

The EU requires the UK to supply 15% of all its energy from renewable sources by 2020. However, the UK has committed to a 30% clean energy production target with a 34% cut in carbon emissions by 2020 and 80% by 2050.[15]

In order to achieve these ambitious reduction targets, most UK local authorities stipulate renewable energy production requirements. This is referred to as the 'Merton Rule' and is usually at least 10% and often up to 20%, as is the case in London's boroughs.

This can either be:
- a certain percentage of the development's energy demand to be supplied by on-site renewables
- a percentage carbon reduction to be achieved from on-site renewable energy supply.

As the UK's drive towards zero carbon progresses, CO_2 reduction targets from on-site renewables will be not only embedded by town planning, but also regulated by the Building Regulations.

10.6.1 How to calculate a building's carbon footprint and how to apply the Merton Rule

This is done in four steps and starts by establishing the energy demand and CO_2 emissions of the building. These can be obtained by software modelling or from actual energy bills in existing dwellings.

For preliminary estimates, benchmark figures can also be used. See Fig. 10.1.2. A carbon footprint calculator is provided overleaf.

 For Code for Sustainable Homes, zero carbon and Building Regulations approval, use of SAP software is usually compulsory.

How to calculate a building's carbon footprint

Step 1: Calculate energy demand

Total building area (m²) =   100 m²

regulated energy	Column A	Column B
	kWh/m² per year	kWh per year (total building area × Column A results)
space heating	39	3900
hot water	55	5500
regulated electricity (cooling, ventilation, lighting)	10	1000
total regulated	104	10400
unregulated energy	kWh/m² per year	kWh per year
electrical appliances and equipment	25	2500
cooking/catering	15	1500
total unregulated	40	4000
total energy demand (regulated + unregulated)	144	14400
	kWh/m² per year	kWh per year

Step 2: Calculate CO_2 footprint

multiply the energy demand obtained in Step 1, Column B × specific fuel CO_2 intensity in table Fig. 10.2.1

regulated emissions	Column C	Column D
	CO_2 fuel intensity: gas: 0.198 kgCO₂/kWh electricity: 0.517 kgCO₂/kWh	kgCO₂ per year (Column C × Column B)
space heating	3900 × 0.198	772.2
hot water	5500 × 0.198	1089
regulated electricity (cooling, ventilation, lighting)	1000 × 0.517	517
total regulated		2378.2

unregulated emissions		kgCO$_2$ per year
electrical appliances and equipment	2500 × 0.517	1292.5
cooking/catering (gas)	1500 × 0.198	297
	total unregulated	1589.5
	total CO$_2$ emissions (regulated + unregulated emissions)	3967.7
		kgCO$_2$ per year

Step 3: On-site CO$_2$ reduction from renewable energy generation

option 1: energy reduction from on-site renewables.	apply required % energy reduction to total CO$_2$ footprint of development (= % reduction × result Step 1, Column B)	apply % reduction required: 30% × 14,400 = 4320 kWh reduction from renewables required
energy reduction to be achieved by on-site renewables		kWh per year (see above)
option 2: carbon reduction from on-site renewables.	apply required t% carbon reduction to total CO$_2$ footprint of development (= % reduction × result Step 2, Column D)	apply % reduction: 30% × 3967.7 = 1190.31 kgCO$_2$ saving from 30% of renewables
carbon reduction to be achieved by on-site renewables		kgCO$_2$ per year (see above)

Step 4: Determine suitable renewable technologies

———⟫ Jump to Chapter 12.

From the above, we can see how energy demand drives the amount of technology required, and hence the case for reducing demand as much as possible prior to considering low and zero carbon technologies. For a zero carbon calculator, ———⟫ Jump to Chapter 11.

The worked example above is based on a 100 m^2 terraced house built to zero carbon fabric energy efficiency standard. ———⟫ Jump to Section 7.5.2.

10.7 FINANCIAL INCENTIVES TO SUPPLY ENERGY FROM LOW AND ZERO CARBON TECHNOLOGIES

To encourage the uptake of low and zero carbon technologies, financial incentives have been introduced:
- Feed-in tariffs (FITs) for on-site electricity generation.
- Electricity export tariff: 3.1 pence/kWh exported to the grid.
- Renewable Heat Incentive (RHI) for on-site heat generation for non-domestic buildings. To be extended to houses in Autumn 2012.
- RHI premium payment: some technologies will be eligible for a grant to help cover the capital cost. Only applies to houses not connected to gas-grid; apart from solar thermal panels. See Fig. 10.7.2.
- The Green Deal may also provide capital grants for certain domestic technologies. ──⟩ Jump to Section 8.5.

Note that at present Northern Ireland is excluded from the incentives. Always check the latest tariffs, eligible technologies and generation scale, as they change continually. Check at www.decc.gov.uk. Eligibility of incentives is likely to be linked to minimum fabric efficiency standards from April 2012; reduced FITs may apply if those standards are not met. FITs will be adjusted on a yearly basis (usually downwards), encouraging early adoption.

Fig. 10.7.1 Electricity feed-in tariff (FIT) (figures from Autumn 2011)[16]

Technology – electricity generation	Feed-in tariff (pence/kWh)	Export tariff	years
solar PV – electricity retrofit ≤4 kW (under 30 m²)	43.3/21*	3.1 pence per kWh exported to the grid	25
solar PV – electricity new build ≤4 kW (under 30 m²)	37.8/21*		25
solar PV – electricity >4–10 kW (>30–75 m²)	37.8/16.8*		25
wind ≤1.5 kW	36.2		20
wind >1.5–15 kW	28		20
hydroelectricity ≤15 kW	20.9		20
anaerobic digestion ≤250 kW	14		20
micro CHP ≤2 kW	10.5		10

* Lower rate proposed for new installations from 2012, as announced in Autumn 2011. For latest, check www.decc.gov.uk

Fig. 10.7.2 Renewable Heat Incentive (RHI) (figures from Autumn 2011)[17]

Technology – heat generation[18]	Energy generation tariff – for 20 years (at present for non-domestic only)	RHI premium (for houses not on gas-grid)
solar thermal ≤200 kW	8.5 pence/kWh	£300 per unit for all houses
heat from small biomass boilers, including waste and biomass CHP	1.9–7.6 pence/kWh	£950 per unit
on-site biogas/biomethane <200 kW	6.5 pence/kWh	—
small water and ground source heat pumps and geothermal <100 kWh	4.3 pence/kWh	£1250 per unit
air source heat pumps	not currently eligible	£850 per unit

10.8   FURTHER READING

- Boardman et al. (2005), 40% house Environmental Change Institute, free from www.eci.ox.ac.uk/research/energy/40house/index.php
- BRE Domestic Energy Fact File 2008
- BREEAM2011 Technical Manual www.breeam.org BREEAM2011SchemeDocument/
- CIBSE Guide F Energy efficiency in Buildings 2004
- Code for Sustainable Homes Technical Guide, November 2010
- EcoHomes 2006, The environmental rating for homes, The Guidance – 2006 / Issue 1.2 April 2006
- Energy Savings Trust, Community Heating – a Guide (2004)
- GLA Renewable Energy Toolkit (2004)
- NHBC, Community Heating and Combined Heat and Power (2009)
- NHBC, The Merton Rule: A Review of the Practical, Environmental and Economic Effects, (2009)
- Planning Policy Statement 22 (PPS 22) and Local Development Frameworks
- The Department for Energy and Climate Change – www.decc.gov.uk
- The English House Condition Survey, www.communities.gov.uk/housing/housingresearch/housingsurveys/englishhousecondition/
- www.bre.co.uk/sap2009
- www.carbonbuzz.org
- www.carbontruststandard.com
- www.fitariffs.co.uk
- Zero Carbon Hub (2010), Topic 2 – Carbon intensity of fuels

Chapter 11
Zero carbon buildings

$0 \; CO_2$

The zero carbon definition is still being developed at the time of writing. England has made the most progress with its zero carbon definition for housing and so it is this standard which is used in this chapter.

By 2020, all new UK buildings must meet the zero carbon standard. At present this means that 100% of a building's regulated carbon emissions are to be reduced to 'zero' over a 30-year life. This is achieved through:

1. increased fabric energy efficiency standards (FEES)
   —⇢ Jump to Section 7.5.2
2. on-site energy supply (low and zero carbon technologies)
   —⇢ Jump to Chapter 12
3. 'allowable solutions', which could be a combination of the above, or other off-site measures, and this may include payment per tonne of remaining CO_2 emissions (see Section 11.1.3)

Steps 1 and 2 are called 'carbon compliance'.
A simple zero carbon calculator is provided so that the reader may roughly estimate a development's zero carbon feasibility.

The zero carbon standard is continuously evolving, so the reader should always check for the latest updates:
Scotland: www.scotland.gov.uk/Topics/Built-Environment/
England: www.zerocarbonhub.org
Wales: www.sustainablebuildingportal.co.uk
Northern Ireland: www.theccc.org.uk/topics/uk-and-regions/northern-ireland

 Symbol indicates relevance to the Code for Sustainable Homes, EcoHomes & BREEAM.

11.1   THE ZERO CARBON DEFINITION

From 2016, all new dwellings in England are to be built to zero carbon standards. Non-domestic buildings will follow suit from 2019. Wales (2014),[1] Scotland (2016/17)[2] and Northern Ireland are also setting their own goals and definitions of zero carbon.

11.1.1 What does building to zero carbon standards mean?

The zero carbon definition has been controversial: initially it counted all energy from a dwelling, including occupants' unregulated energy use. This has since been revised and currently the UK zero carbon definition excludes occupants' lifestyles but requires every dwelling (or development of dwellings) to generate or offset all of its own regulated energy use. This is closely aligned to other EU countries. In addition:

- required for only 30 years after building handover, not for its entire designed lifespan
- definition applies to building as built, not just as designed (to be regulated by Building Control)
- 100% reduction from regulated energy is included: space heat demand, hot water demand and electricity demand for ventilation, cooling, fans and pumps
- no required reduction in unregulated energy, such as appliances and plug-in devices
- unclear whether building only approach is allowed, or whether site approach will be permitted, which will determine suitable strategies and technologies
- embodied energy is not included, but may be considered as part of 'allowable solutions'; see Section 11.1.3.

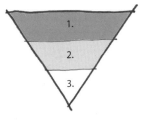

There are three parts to the zero carbon standard. The first two are referred to as 'carbon compliance'. See Section 11.1.2.

1. Fabric energy efficiency standards (FEES), dependent on building typology. Jump to Section 7.5.2

2. Provision of on-site energy production from low and zero carbon technologies

3. 'Allowable solutions'

Fig. 11.1.1 Zero carbon principles[3]

Check www.zerocarbonhub.org for latest updates.

11.1.2 Carbon compliance

To achieve 'carbon compliance', limits have been set for the amount of carbon that can be emitted in a building. This is expressed as $kgCO_2/m^2$ per year. This 'carbon limit' or 'carbon allowance' has to be achieved through:

1. minimum fabric energy efficiency standards: maximum space heat demand of 39 kWh/m^2 per year for flats and terraced houses, and 46 kWh/m^2 per year for detached houses ——→ Jump to Section 7.5.2
2. energy supply from on-site low and zero carbon technologies.

The carbon compliance limits are dependent on building typology to acknowledge limitations of each. The lower the carbon compliance figure, the greater its feasibility for on-site low and zero carbon technologies.

Fig. 11.1.2 Proposed carbon compliance, dwellings (2011)[4]

'Carbon allowance' to be achieved by energy efficiency and on-site 'clean' technologies	
detached house	10 $kgCO_2/m^2$ per year
terraced/semi-detached house	11 $kgCO_2/m^2$ per year
low-rise apartment block (≤ four storeys)	14 $kgCO_2/m^2$ per year
high-rise apartments (≥ five storeys)	tbc

Fig. 11.1.3 Proposed carbon compliance, non-domestic buildings (2010)[5]

school	8 $kgCO_2/m^2$ per year
warehouse (with or without rooflights)	9 $kgCO_2/m^2$ per year
office (shallow plan/natural ventilation)	10 $kgCO_2/m^2$ per year
office (deep plan/air-conditioning)	18 $kgCO_2/m^2$ per year
office (shallow plan/air-conditioning)	20 $kgCO_2/m^2$ per year
hotel	31 $kgCO_2/m^2$ per year
retail	39 $kgCO_2/m^2$ per year
supermarket	59 $kgCO_2/m^2$ per year

Code for Sustainable Homes credits (Ene 1–9), EcoHomes credits (Ene 1–6) and BREEAM credits (Ene 1–9). Note: CSH credits Ene 1, 2 and 7 likely to be integrated in the building regulations in the future.

11.1.3 Allowable solutions

Of the UK population, 90% live in urban areas and around 80% of urban dwellings would not be able to meet their energy demand from on-site renewables only.[6] Therefore a combination of on-site and off-site energy generation, or other 'allowable solutions', must be harnessed.

Allowable solutions can only be used to offset the remaining regulated emissions once carbon compliance has been achieved. Allowable solutions only need to be in place for the first 30 years of the building's lifespan.[7] At the time of writing, the specific allowable solutions are unconfirmed but are likely to include:

- more on-site technologies
- the building's embodied carbon ⟶ Jump to Chapter 7
- upgrade existing buildings in the vicinity
- contribute to a 'community energy fund'
- export heating to surrounding buildings
- pay £46– £200 per tonne of carbon 'left over': for example, a 100 m² terraced house, after carbon compliance, still emits 11 $kgCO_2/m^2$ per year, or 1.1 tonnes of CO_2 per year, and over 30 years this adds up to 33 tonnes of CO_2 which can be offset by paying £82.50 per year or £2475 at an illustrative rate of £75/tonne CO_2 over 30 years.

Check www.zerocarbonhub.org (England) and www.cewales.org.uk, www.scotland.gov.uk for latest updates.

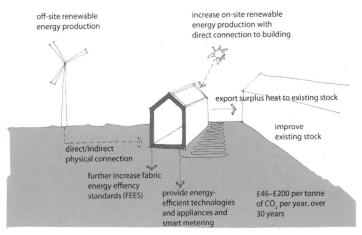

off-site renewable energy production

increase on-site renewable energy production with direct connection to building

export surplus heat to existing stock

improve existing stock

direct/indirect physical connection

further increase fabric energy effiency standards (FEES)

provide energy-efficient technologies and appliances and smart metering

£46–£200 per tonne of CO_2 per year, over 30 years

Fig. 11.1.4 Diagram allowable solutions

11.1.4 Zero carbon summary

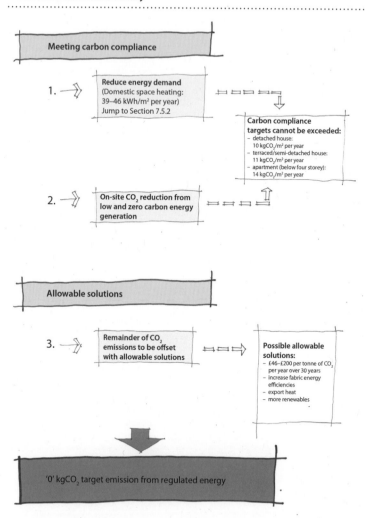

Meeting carbon compliance

1. Reduce energy demand
(Domestic space heating:
39–46 kWh/m² per year)
Jump to Section 7.5.2

Carbon compliance
targets cannot be exceeded:
– detached house:
10 kgCO₂/m² per year
– terraced/semi-detached house:
11 kgCO₂/m² per year
– apartment (below four storey):
14 kgCO₂/m² per year

2. On-site CO₂ reduction from
low and zero carbon energy
generation

Allowable solutions

3. Remainder of CO₂
emissions to be offset
with allowable solutions

Possible allowable
solutions:
– £46–£200 per tonne of CO₂
per year over 30 years
– increase fabric energy
efficiencies
– export heat
– more renewables

'0' kgCO₂ target emission from regulated energy

Fig. 11.1.5 Principles of zero carbon

11.2   ZERO CARBON CHALLENGES

The building industry is under increased pressure to be accountable for all regulated building energy demands. This requires us to change the way we design and construct buildings.

- Standards as built will need to meet design standards: care in design and building construction ——⤳ Jump to Chapter 7.
- Close monitoring of specified technologies to ensure they perform as expected/designed.
- Understanding of building occupants' impact on building performance. ——⤳ Jump to Section 1.5.
- Someone needs to be responsible for the next 30 years of energy production – the building developer traditionally 'builds and walks away' and has no long-term stake in a development, but now housing providers and developers are required to become energy providers but without any real experience. ——⤳ Jump to Section 10.3.4.
- Only the first 30 years have to be 'zero carbon', so this means a development could be zero carbon now but not in future; how this will be managed and how CO_2 emissions will be regulated beyond the 30-year timescale is unclear.
- Where energy generating systems are located on roofs of shared buildings, maintenance and legal ownership will be an issue.
- Lack of clarity on complex government policy.

11.3   THE ZERO CARBON CALCULATOR

For quick calculations, the zero carbon calculator can be used. It calculates zero carbon feasibility based on absolute energy demand figures. It can be used to gain a more detailed understanding of the zero carbon definition and to allow a quick estimation of its feasibility without having to go through onerous modelling. This allows the reader to assess and understand zero carbon feasibility even when working only with aspirational targets during the early design stages.

To determine a building's or a development's initial zero carbon feasibility, fill in the three steps in the tables provided. The first two steps fall under carbon compliance, and the third under allowable solutions. Average energy demand benchmarks can be used for preliminary estimates. ——⤳ Jump to Section 10.1.2.

**Fig. 11.3.1 The zero carbon calculator (worked example in grey, based on a 100 m²
terraced house)*****

Carbon compliance		
Step 1: Calculate energy demand and CO_2 footprint		
typical CO_2 fuel intensity for Column B and Column D calculations: gas: 0.198 $kgCO_2$/kWh electricity: 0.517 $kgCO_2$/kWh (more in Section 10.2)	**Column A**	**Column B**
	regulated energy demand	**regulated carbon emissions**
	kWh/m² per year	$kgCO_2$/m² per year (Column A results × CO_2 fuel intensity)
space heating (max. 39–46 kWh/m² per year)	39	39 × 0.198 = 7.72
hot water	55	55 × 0.198 = 10.89
regulated electricity (cooling, ventilation, lighting, pumps, fans)	10	10 × 0.517 = 5.17
total regulated	104	23.78 $kgCO_2$/m² per year
Step 2: On-site CO_2 reduction from low and zero carbon energy generation ⟶ ⇨ Jump to Chapter 12 for technologies		
List the technologies below	**Column C**	**Column D**
	energy supplied by technology (kWh/m² per year*)	**carbon reduction from technology ($kgCO_2$/m² per year*)**
technology 1: PV 5.5 m²	= 5.5 kWh per m² of development	5.5 × 0.529 = 2.9 $kgCO_2$ per m2 of development
technology 2: solar thermal 10 m²	= 50 kWh per m² of development	50 × 0.198 = 9.9 $kgCO_2$ per m² of development
total contribution from technologies	55.5 kWh per m² of development	12.8 $kgCO_2$ per m² of development

* Total energy supplied from technologies/total carbon reductions to be divided per m² of
development/building area

Final carbon compliance	
total Column B (Step 1) – total Column D (Step 2)**	*10.98 kgCO₂/m² per year:* Is carbon compliance met?**

** To be ≤ carbon compliance figures as below: (see also Section 11.1.2)

detached house:	10 kgCO$_2$/m^2 per year
terraced/semi-detached house:	11 kgCO$_2$/m^2 per year
apartment (below four storey):	14 kgCO$_2$/m^2 per year

Allowable solutions		
Step 3:	**After meeting carbon compliance, meet remainder of the carbon emissions from allowable solutions**	
Option 1	allowable solutions at £46–200 per 1000 kgCO$_2$ over 30 years sum to be paid calculated as follows: final carbon compliance figure (Step 2) × development area (m^2) × 30 × £46–£200/1000; see worked example Section 11.1.3	
	sum to be paid:	*10.98 × 100 m² × 30 × 75/1000 = £2470.5 or £82.35 per year, over 30 years*
Option 2	other allowable solutions leading to further carbon reductions (list allowable solution below)	

*** Note: This calculator is not intended to be used for any compliance or regulatory approval. The UK has approved National Calculation Methods (NCM) to assess the energy performance of buildings, i.e. SAP for dwellings and SBEM for non-domestic buildings, which are used for compliance. Software extensions may need to be downloaded for SAP zero carbon modelling.

11.4   ZERO CARBON: WHAT WILL IT COST?

The additional capital cost to meet the zero carbon standard is significant. It is estimated at around £7,000–17,000[8] per dwelling. This is dependent on dwelling typology and technologies specified.

Key recommendations

· The lower the development density, the easier and cheaper the carbon reductions, especially if <50 dw/ha. ——⇥ Jump to Section 3.3.3.
· Renewable technologies become more financially viable as incentives are introduced. In particular, solar thermal and photovoltaic electricity panels are more economical and may see up to a 25% return on their capital investment after 20 years, based on current financial incentives. ——⇥ Jump to Sections 10.7 and 12.5.
· Other technologies, such as heat pumps and communal boilers/district heating schemes, may never pay back their initial capital investment.

11.4.1 Some incentives to support zero carbon

· Feed-in tariffs (FITs) and renewable heat incentives (RHI): the owner earns a fixed income for exported energy and for every kWh of heat or electricity generated. ——⇥ Jump to Section 10.7.
· Stamp duty relief[9] on first sale only, up to sale price of £500,000, until October 2012 – Northern Ireland has some relief under its low carbon homes scheme until March 2012.[10]
· Grants/funding – financial support may be available for capital cost of certain technologies, including renewable heat incentive premium payments and the Green Deal. ——⇥ Jump to Sections 8.5 and 10.7. There may also be separate grants available in Scotland; check www.energysavingtrust.org.uk/scotland

Cost-effective zero carbon strategies for densities ≤50 dw/ha[11]

• all dwellings achieve a Fabric Energy Efficiency Standard of ≤39–46 kWh/m² per year, depending on typology	
individual building strategy	boiler with PV + solar thermal panels per unit; groundsource heatpumps suitable, but unlikely to be cost-effective
communal strategy	district heating (biomass) with communal roof PV
communal strategy (only suitable if ≥250 dwellings)	communal boiler with communal roof PV or separate building block energy centres and district heating systems

Cost-effective zero carbon strategies for densities >50 dw/ha [12]

Typology[13]	Strategies likely to be cost-effective to achieve 100% CO_2 reduction[14]
terraced/semi-detached dwelling	• Fabric Energy Efficiency Standard of ≤39–46 kWh/m² per year • gas boiler + solar panels on roof • groundsource heatpumps suitable, but unlikely to be cost-effective
four-storey apartment block	• Fabric Energy Efficiency Standard of ≤39 kWh/m² per year • small communal gas boiler + solar panels on roof; CHP suitable where mixed use development
eight-storey flat block and	• fabric standards were undefined at the time of writing, but fabric energy efficiency standards of ≤39 kWh/m² per year are likely • solar panels on roof and gas CHP • high-rise apartments will require increased technologies and are unlikely to be cost-effective

11.5 FURTHER READING

- BREEAM2011 Technical Manual www.breeam.org/BREEAM2011SchemeDocument/
- Building Research Establishment – www.bre.co.uk
- Code for Sustainable Homes Technical Guide, November 2010
- Ecohomes 2006, The environmental rating for homes, The Guidance – 2006/Issue1.2 April 2006
- Energy Savings Trust, Low carbon futures: zero carbon case studies
- EST Low and Zero Carbon Energy Sources – Strategic Guide
- Integrated Sustainable Design Solutions for Modular Neighbourhoods. Developer Guidelines, 2010, East Midlands Development Agency
- NHBC, Introduction to Feed in Tariffs (2011)
- NHBC, Zero Carbon Compendium, Who is doing what in the housing worldwide? (2009)
- The Carbon Trust – www.carbontrust.co.uk
- The Department for Energy and Climate Change – www.decc.gov.uk/
- UKGBC, Zero Carbon Task Group Report, The Definition of Zero Carbon (2008)
- Zero Carbon Hub (2009), Defining Zero Carbon Homes
- Zero Carbon Hub (2010), Carbon Compliance: Carbon Compliance For Tomorrow's New Homes – A Review of the Modelling Tool and Assumptions (Topic 1–5)
- Zero Carbon Hub (2010), 'Carbon Compliance – What is the appropriate level for 2016?' and Carbon Intensity of Fuels
- Zero Carbon Hub, Carbon Compliance, Setting an appropriate limit for zero carbon new homes, Findings and recommendations, February 2011
- Zero Carbon Hub, Allowable Solutions For Tomorrow's New Homes. Towards A Workable Framework, July 2011

Chapter 12
Low and zero carbon technologies and renewables

Renewable energy is energy that comes from inexhaustible sources. It usually originates directly or indirectly from the sun's radiation.

Not all technologies which offer significant environmental benefits over the use of conventional fossil fuels fall into this category. This is why the term 'low and zero carbon technologies' (LZC) is often used instead of 'renewable energy technologies'.

Low and zero carbon technologies are often incorrectly seen as fundamental to 'green buildings'. In fact, reducing energy demand is the priority when delivering low carbon buildings.

Suitable 'clean' energy sources should be discussed early on as part of a holistic strategy, but only utilised after maximising energy savings from passive measures and fabric efficiencies.

Symbol indicates relevance to the Code for Sustainable Homes, EcoHomes & BREEAM.

12.1 CO₂/ENERGY REDUCTION TARGETS

The EU has set legally binding renewable energy production targets. The UK has also set its own ambitious targets which were made legally binding in the Climate Change Act 2008. ⟶ Jump to Section 1.3.

	EU/UK renewable energy targets
2020	• 20% of all EU energy to be produced from renewables (already a requirement for most new buildings in London) • 15% renewable energy target in UK, which is a seven-fold increase from 2008 • the UK overall committed to a 34% cut in carbon emissions, with own target of 30% clean energy production,[1] compared to 1990 emission levels
2050	• 50% of all EU energy to be produced from renewables • UK to reduce carbon emissions by 80% from 1990 levels

 Code for Sustainable Homes credits (Ene 1 mandatory, Ene 7), EcoHomes credits (Ene 1) and BREEAM (Ene 1, Ene 4 mandatory)

12.2 LOW AND ZERO CARBON TECHNOLOGIES OVERVIEW

Before considering any renewable energy application it is crucial to understand the kind of energy that is needed:

 • to provide electricity
 • or to provide heat
 • for cooling
 • or a mix of the above

It is also important to understand the site location's constraints and how this affects the suitability of different low and zero carbon technologies. In particular, the scale and densities of the development must be taken into account, e.g. how many dwellings per hectare (dw/ha). See Figs.12.2.1. and 12.2.3.

Do remember the '2 of everything rule': a back-up of another energy supply system is required (often fossil fuel based or grid-linked) in case the primary energy supply system is not producing energy or fails.

12.2.1 Renewable energy decision-making matrix – heating

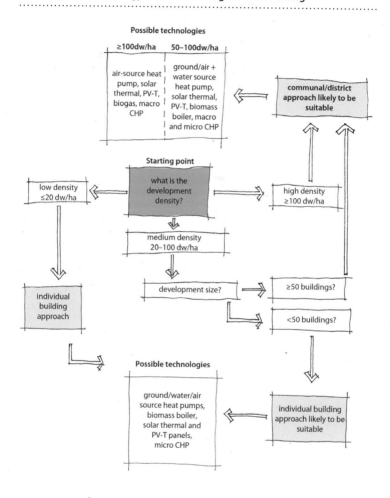

Fig. 12.2.1. Renewable energy decision-making matrix – heating

12.2.2 Renewable energy decision-making matrix – cooling

In the UK, the need for full air-conditioning is, and should remain, rare. However, a move towards active domestic cooling is predicted as the UK experiences hotter summers and as occupants get accustomed to air-conditioned spaces abroad and in their office/leisure environments.[2] Air-conditioning can increase a building's running costs and CO_2 emissions significantly. A typical air-conditioned office can increase emissions by 50–75 $kgCO_2/m^2$ per year, inhibiting any CO_2 reductions the UK has committed to.[3] If buildings are designed well the need for active cooling systems is minimised.

A hybrid of active cooling and natural ventilation methods or full air-conditioning may need to be considered:
- in hot, humid climates (where night-cooling is difficult)
- where lots of equipment/lots of people gather (large internal heat gains).
- for unpredictable wind situations where wind-driven ventilation systems are unreliable.
- in polluted inner city areas where air quality/noise is an issue.

These issues do not tend to occur in UK housing design, with the exception of the noise/security issues associated with natural ventilation, particularly at night.

Key recommendations

- Try to avoid active cooling/air-conditioning systems entirely. This can be achieved with passive design measures. ——$\gg$ Jump to Sections 6.5 & 6.6.
- Appropriate fabric design is crucial, to avoid occupants retrofitting portable air-conditioning units.
- Higher summer temperatures are predicted for the UK this century, with as much as a 5°C increase in certain regions. ——$\gg$ Jump to Chapter 2.
- While day-usage is switched on/off when needed, active night cooling is more problematic as systems tend to be left on all night.[4]

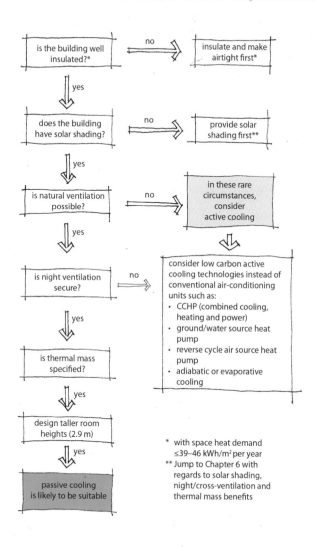

Fig. 12.2.2 Renewable energy decision-making matrix — cooling

12.2.3 Renewable energy-decision making matrix – electricity

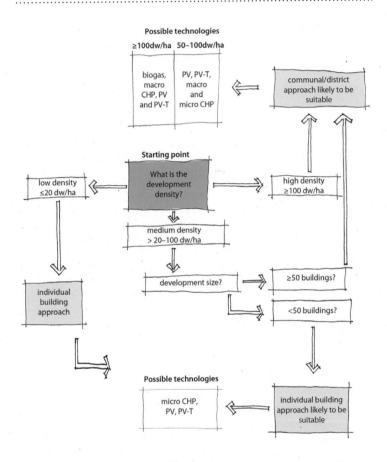

Fig. 12.2.3 Renewable energy decision-making matrix – electricity

12.2.4 Low and zero carbon energy technology summary

On-site technologies	Used for			Definition			Suitability				Financial incentive			
	Heating	Electricity	Cooling	Renewable	Low carbon but not renewable	More energy efficient*	High density?	Low density?	Small development (≤50 building blocks)	Larger development (>50 building blocks)	Feed-in tariffs?	Renewable heat initiative?	Green Deal or RHI premium?	Page reference
micro hydro		✓		✓				✓	✓	✓	✓			322
micro wind		✓		✓				✓	✓		✓			325
PV		✓		✓			✓	✓	✓	✓	✓		✓	334
PV-T	✓	✓		✓		✓	✓	✓	✓	✓	✓			337
solar thermal panels	✓			✓			✓	✓	✓	✓		✓	✓	339
micro CHP gas	✓	✓				✓	✓	✓	✓	✓	✓		✓	345
macro CHP gas	✓	✓				✓	✓			✓				348
macro CHP biomass	✓	✓			✓		✓	✓		✓		✓		348
CCHP gas	✓	✓	✓			✓	✓			✓				350
biomass boiler	✓				✓			✓	✓			✓	✓	351
biogas	✓	✓			✓			✓		✓	✓	✓	✓	358
gas-condensing boiler	✓						✓	✓	✓	✓				362
air source heat pump	✓		✓		✓		✓	✓	✓	✓			✓	366
MVHR	✓					✓	✓	✓	✓	✓				368
ground/water source heat pump	✓		✓		✓			✓	✓			✓	✓	368
geothermal piling	✓		✓		✓		✓		✓	✓				372
evaporative cooling			✓			✓	✓	✓	✓	✓				373
fuel cells/ hydrogen	✓	✓				✓	✓	✓	✓	✓				375

* Technology that should be more efficient than mains electricity or a gas boiler in its method of delivering energy.

12.2.5 Myth: 'If the energy is "clean", it doesn't matter how much I use.'

Renewable energy supply should only be considered once the building's fabric energy efficiency has been optimised. This is because:

- A building's lifespan is usually 60 years and often much longer; windows and roof surfaces are likely to need renewing two or three times during this period, but most of the building fabric will continue to perform for the building's entire lifespan. Fabric efficiencies give occupants continued thermal comfort and reduced carbon and fuel costs throughout the building's lifespan.

- Most active renewable energy systems have a lifespan of around 15–25 years, so if the fabric specification is neglected in favour of 'green' technologies, the eventual failure of the active systems will immediately increase the building's CO_2 footprint, jeopardise thermal comfort for occupants and increase fuel bills.

- At present there is no regulation which requires or guarantees the replacement of renewable energy technology if it stops working; the 2011 definition of 'zero carbon' applies for the first 30 years of the building's lifespan only. ⟶ Jump to Chapter 11.

- The embodied energy of renewables should not be neglected because the greater the energy need, the greater the renewable energy array required, which directly impacts on the embodied energy profile of the building, so even 'clean' energy should not be wasted.

12.2.6 How much low and zero carbon technology is required?

- A typical 100 m^2 terraced zero carbon house has a regulated electrical demand of around 1000 kWh per year. Regulated electricity is only a fraction of total electricity demand.

- A 100 m^2 terraced house, built to zero carbon Fabric Energy Efficiency Standards, has a regulated space heating demand of no more than 3900 kWh per year.

Tables below indicate technology sizes and carbon reductions compared to electricity grid connection or gas connection with a 90% efficient boiler. They are based on the above energy needs and CO_2 savings. For typical energy demand benchmarks, ——⇒ Jump to Section 10.1.2. For carbon compliance ——⇒ Jump to Chapter 11.

Clarification note

The CO_2 reduction figures presented here are lower than most published data. This is because:

- Manufacturers and other official bodies publish idealised commercial data, often based on theoretical performance rather than actual performance.
- Renewable technologies are often compared to low efficiency (80%) gas boilers, which would no longer pass Building Regulations anyway.[5]
- Published field trial data indicates that most technologies operate at much lower efficiencies in reality.
- Some low carbon or energy-efficient technologies rely on a high emission factor of electricity, and some technologies will no longer make sense on a decarbonised grid, while others become larger carbon savers.

Using the correct CO_2 reduction is crucial for comparing technologies. Where possible, carbon reduction and energy generation estimates are based on actual field data performance. Carbon savings are compared to a natural gas efficiency boiler of 90% at fuel intensity of 0.198 kgCO$_2$/kWh and displacement of grid electricity at 0.529 kgCO$_2$/kWh. Yet, these carbon reductions are still theoretical: they are dependent on each building's specific characteristics and the careful design, installation and commissioning of technologies. As technologies advance and as the grid decarbonises, so will their carbon reduction potential change.

💡	Technologies which generate renewable electricity per dwelling			
Technology	How much is required to meet 100% electrical demand of a 100 m² zero carbon dwelling?	How much energy is generated? (kWh per year)	What is the carbon reduction? (kgCO₂ per year)	Page
micro hydro power*	1 × 200 W micro hydro turbine	2300	1216	322
micro wind power, rural or urban ≥15 storeys	2 × wind turbines with 1.4 metre rotor diameter, wind speed 5.5 m/s	1000	500**	325
micro wind power, urban <15 storeys***	20 wind turbines with 1.4 metre rotor diameter, wind speed 2.5 m/s	1000	230–380**	325
PV panel	10 m² of PV ≈ 1.3 kW$_{peak}$ approx. six PV panels	1000	529	334

* The smallest available micro hydro unit works with minimum 35 litres per second waterflow and 1.5 m head, and its energy generation is likely to exceed yearly regulated electricity demand. If micro hydro power is an option, it will be of significant benefit to utilise it.

** Net carbon reduction, after taking into account energy used by the micro turbine; see Section 12.4.

*** Carbon reduction from electricity generation may never be offset by the embodied carbon of turbines required; see Section 12.4.

	Technologies which generate heat only			
Technology	How much is required to meet 100% space heating demand of a 100 m² zero carbon dwelling?	How much heating energy does it generate? (kWh/a)	How much carbon is reduced? (kgCO₂/a)	Page
solar thermal,* evacuated tubes	8 m² of solar thermal panels	3900	800	339
solar thermal,* flat plate collectors	13 m² of solar thermal panels	3900	800	339
biomass boiler, woodchip fuel		3900	737	351
biomass boiler, wood pellet fuel	1 × 5 kW boiler	3900	663	351
ground/water source heat pump* COP of 2.4**	For sizing, see Section 12.8 Assumed here: 100% space heat demand by heat pump with gas back-up boiler for 100% of hot water demand	3900	425	368
air source heat pump* COP of 2.2**		3900	350	366

* Ideally combined with underfloor heating, low surface temperature radiators or air-to-air heating.

** COP based on actual field trial data, which is much lower than product literature.

Micro scale technologies which generate electricity and heat at micro scale per dwelling				
Technology	How much is required to meet 100% space heating demand of a 100 m² zero carbon dwelling?	How much energy does it generate? (kWh per year)	How much carbon is reduced? (kgCO₂ per year)	Page
PV-T*	16 m² of PV-T panels	heat: 3900 electricity: 1920	1120**	337
Micro CHP***	1 kWe‡ CHP unit, 75% efficient, 6:1 heat-to-power ratio	heat: 3900 electricity: 650	165	345

‡ kWe refers to kW of electrical energy.
* Sized to meet 100% of space heat demand.
** Net carbon reduction after taking into account energy used by the PV-T heat pump; see Section 12.5.8.
*** Could probably also meet hot water demand, but not recommended for well-insulated dwellings; see Section 12.6.5.

Macro scale technologies which generate electricity and heat at macro scale				
Technology	How much is required to meet 100% space heating demand of a 100 m² zero carbon dwelling?	How much energy does it generate? (kWh per year)	How much carbon is reduced? (kgCO₂ per year per dwelling)	Page
macro CHP biomass fuel, wood pellets	1 × CHP unit 250 kWe 80% efficient, 1.5:1 heat-to-power ratio, to meet heat demand of 410 dwellings	heat: 1,600,000	1900*	348
macro CHP gas fuel		electricity: 1,100,000	612**	348
biogas	organic waste of 10,000 dwellings	total energy: 1,200,000	maximum 65***	358

* If biomass macro CHP also provides hot water, carbon savings would be around 40–60% greater; if woodchip is used as a fuel, an additional carbon reduction of 7–8% can be achieved.
** If macro CHP is used to meet hot water demand also, carbon savings are about three times as much as those listed.
*** This is difficult to calculate, and is an estimate based on electrical energy being exported only.

12.2.7 APPLICABLE LEGISLATION AND GUIDANCE

- Building Regulations: Region 2, 4: Part L; Region 1: Technical Handbook Section 6 and Region 3: Technical Booklet F.
- COSSH 1994
- GLA Renewable Energy Toolkit: pp 92–106: feasibility tables; p 107: heat/electricity demands
- Local Development Frameworks
- PPS 22, Planning Policy Statement 22, Renewable Energy
- BS EN 62075:2008 Technical energy systems – Methods for analysis, Parts 1 & 2

12.2.8 FURTHER READING

- Boardman et al. (2005), 40% House Environmental Change Institute
- BRE Domestic Energy Fact File 2008
- CAT, Zero Carbon Britain 2030
- CIBSE Chartered Institute of Building Services Engineers
- EST, Domestic Low and zero carbon technologies, 2010
- GLA Renewable Energy Toolkit
- Mackay (2008), *Sustainable Energy, Without the Hot Air*, UIT Cambridge Ltd
- NHBC, A review of micro generation and renewable technologies (2008)
- Renewables feasibility: www.retscreen.net/
- The Department for Energy and Climate Change – www.decc.gov.uk/
- www.bre.co.uk/sap2009
- www.carbontrust.co.uk – New Practice Case Studies etc.

12.3 MICRO HYDRO POWER – ELECTRICITY

12.3.1 What is it?

Energy can be derived from flowing water – for example, hydroelectricity from river damming or electricity from tidal and wave movements. Hydroelectricity harnesses energy by using height differences in the river or water course. These height differences may occur where a river flows downstream, or where there is a waterfall or man-made dam. The vertical fall of the water is referred to as 'head' (H) and is crucial to generate sufficient electricity. Small-scale hydro systems (≤100 kW) contain water at high level, then channel it down a drop of about 50 m to drive a small turbine which generates electricity. The higher the head, the greater the amount of water, and also the faster it flows, the more electricity is generated.[6] After generating the electricity, the water is diverted back into the water stream.[7]

12.3.2 Is it feasible?

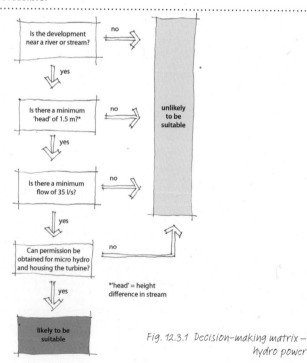

Fig. 12.3.1 Decision-making matrix – hydro power

12.3.3 Key characteristics and key recommendations

When to use? (see Fig. 12.3.1)	• near a reliable river or stream • unlikely to be suitable or relevant in urban areas • most commercially viable locations in the UK have already been exploited[8] • not where wildlife is protected or at risk • ideally near a national grid connection to export surplus energy back to the grid
Key facts and characteristics	• Q = flow rate of water and is the volume passing per second in m³/second or litres per second – ideally a minimum of 35 litres/second[9] • micro hydro systems are 60–80% efficient[10]
Key design recommendations	• a head greater than 50 m is best – ideally not less than 10 m[11] • the absolute minimum head is 1.5 m • planning permission is likely to be required for any turbine installation and the building housing it • acoustic insulation between turbine and other uses is required
How much space is required?	• 9–18 m² to house the turbine and equipment[12]
How much energy does it generate?	• this is highly site dependent, particularly on head and water flow; the greater the head and the water flow, the greater the power production • the power generated from a micro hydro scheme can be calculated as follows: P (kW) = efficiency/10 × Q (m³/s) × H (m)[13] • yearly output (kWh/year) = P × 8760, assuming the turbine works 24/7 for 365 days • to illustrate: the power generated from a 1 kW 70% efficient micro hydro scheme with flow of 40 litres per second and head of 1.5 m is sufficient to meet the electrical requirements of a typical UK household: (70/10) × 0.04 m³/s × 1.5 m × 8760 = 3679 kWh per year • a typical 10 kW micro hydro scheme with maximum head of 10 m can produce as much as 50,000 kWh per year[14]
What are the carbon reductions?	• highly site dependent; based on the above, a typical 10 kW micro hydro scheme could reduce 26.5 tonnes CO_2 per year
Cost? (including financial incentives)	• the capital cost of a 5–10 kW scheme is £10,000–30,000[15] • hydro systems ≤15 kW are also eligible to receive feed-in tariffs ——➔ Jump to Section 10.7
Any maintenance issues?	• reliable, hence low maintenance[16]

continued

Anything else?	• an extraction licence from the relevant Environment Agency needs to be obtained to extract, divert and return water into river courses[17]
	• large-scale hydro power schemes can have a large environmental impact as the damming often causes disruption to the wildlife[18]
	• tidal and wave power are also ways of generating electricity, but are unlikely to be directly applicable to the building industry

12.3.4 Applicable legislation, guidance and further reading

• Bridgewater (2008), *The off-grid energy handbook*, New Holland
• Harvey and Brown (1993), *Micro-hydro Design Manual: Guide to Small-scale Water Schemes*, ITDG Publishing
• Langley and Curtis, B (2004), *Going with the flow*, CAT

12.4   MICRO WIND – ELECTRICAL ENERGY

12.4.1 What is it?

Electrical energy can be generated by wind turbines. The wind turns the blades which drive a turbine to generate electricity. The stronger the wind, the faster the blades turn and the more electricity is produced. Micro-wind turbines are usually mounted on buildings.

12.4.2 Is it feasible?

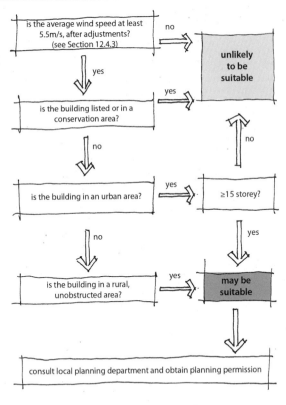

Fig. 12.4.1 Decision-making matrix – micro wind

12.4.3 Key characteristics and key recommendations

When to use? (see Fig. 12.4.1)	wind turbines should be placed where the wind is, and they require a consistent average wind speed of minimum 5.5–6 m/s (roughly the speed of a cyclist – 20 km/hour)[19]		
	urban areas ≤45 m roof height	urban areas ≥45 m roof height	rural areas
	x	may be possible	✓
Key facts and characteristics	based on 1 kW roof-mounted turbine		
	• weight distribution = 20–30 kg/m² • blade diameter of around 1–2 m • official wind speed data overestimates the actual on-site wind speeds by as much as 40%[20] • when using official wind speed rather than actual measured data, adjust official data as below[21]		
	urban areas ≤45 m	urban areas ≥45 m	rural areas
	–40% wind speed	–5% wind speed	–10% wind speed
	≈ 4.5 times less energy than predicted	≈ 1.2 times less energy than predicted	≈ 1.4 times less energy than predicted
Key design recommendations (see Fig. 12.4.2)	• before implementing this technology, take at least a full year's on-site wind speed measurements • planning permission is required • 1–2 kW[22] turbines are suitable for roof-mounting • check structural and wind loads • noise (52–55 dBA)[23] is a real issue when turbines are located on buildings[24] • life span: 10–20 years		
How much space is required? (see Fig. 12.4.2)	• a wind turbine should be twice the height of any obstructions within 10–20 m of it[25] • turbines should be distanced from other turbines and obstructions by 10 × the total turbine height (including the building it may be fixed to) • if standalone in rural areas, turbines should be at least 10 m high		

How much energy does it generate?	• a simplified wind turbine energy output can be calculated as follows: total energy generated (kWh/year) = $1.66 \times D^2 \times V^3$ where V = yearly average wind speed (m/s), D = rotor diameter (m)[26] • a typical 1 kW micro wind turbine consumes 29 kWh per year[27] to run its electronics; this equals 15 kgCO$_2$ per year, and must be deducted from any energy resulting CO$_2$ reductions • 1 kW roof-mounted micro turbine provides only 3% (low rise urban) to 23% (urban high rise/rural areas) of the electricity needs of an average UK dwelling		
	urban areas ≤45 m	urban areas ≥45 m	rural areas
	maximum 110 kWh per year[28]	maximum 800 kWh per year[29]	
What are the carbon reductions?	maximum 40 kgCO$_2$ per year (net)	maximum 400 kgCO$_2$ per year (net)	
What is the embodied carbon?	• a typical 1.5 kW micro wind turbine's embodied carbon is around 2428 kgCO$_2$[30] • the embodied carbon payback from energy generated is around six years • a micro turbine in an urban area below 15 storeys is not recommended: it would take 60 years to pay back its embodied carbon from the energy it generates,[31] i.e. much longer than the estimated 10–15 year lifespan of the turbine		
Cost? (including financial incentives)	• £1550–3000 for a 1 kW system[32] • feed-in tariffs apply ⟶ Jump to Section 10.7		
Any maintenance issues?	minimal maintenance – annual visit by manufacturer		
Anything else?	Cubic relation between power and wind speed means that if wind speed doubles, power output increases by a factor of eight.		

12.4.4 Apllicable legislation, guidance and further reading

• British Wind Energy Association, www.bwea.com
• BS EN 61400 Wind turbines
• BS EN 61400-25 series for wind turbines
• BS EN 61400-1:2005 Wind turbines, Design requirements
• EST, Location, location, location, Domestic small-scale wind field trial report, 2009
• www.bwea.com/noabl/index.html for local wind speed data
• Mackay (2008), Sustainable Energy, Without the Hot Air, UIT Cambridge Ltd. Also from: www.withouthotair.com

Most appropriate location – rural areas

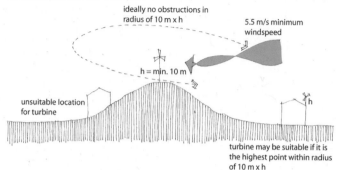

ideally no obstructions in
radius of 10 m x h

5.5 m/s minimum
windspeed

h = min. 10 m

unsuitable location
for turbine

turbine may be suitable if it is
the highest point within radius
of 10 m x h

Urban high rise area – may be suitable if ≥ 15 storeys

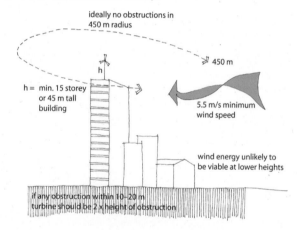

ideally no obstructions in
450 m radius

450 m

h = min. 15 storey
or 45 m tall
building

5.5 m/s minimum
wind speed

wind energy unlikely to
be viable at lower heights

if any obstruction within 10–20 m
turbine should be 2 x height of obstruction

Urban low rise location – unlikely to be suitable

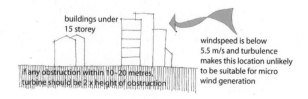

buildings under
15 storey

windspeed is below
5.5 m/s and turbulence
makes this location unlikely
to be suitable for micro
wind generation

if any obstruction within 10–20 metres,
turbine should be 2 x height of obstruction

Fig. 12.4.2 Key design recommendations – micro wind[93]

12.5   SOLAR ENERGY – HEATING AND ELECTRICAL ENERGY

12.5.1 What is it?

The sun's energy can be converted into useful electrical/heating energy for our buildings. Solar energy is seasonally and geographically dependent: it peaks in summer and around midday, so more energy is generated at these times.

There are different solar panels:
- photovoltaic (PV) panels which generate electricity only
- photovoltaic-thermal (PV-T) panels which generate both electricity and heating
- solar thermal panels (e.g. flat plate solar panels and evacuated tubes) which generate heating energy only.

12.5.2 General solar panel design implications

- ideally placed within 10° from south, although up to 30° is acceptable – see Fig.12.5.2
- should not be overshadowed by neighbouring buildings – take into account nearby chimneys, roofs and roof parapets
- reduce a flat roof's total useful area by 25% for actual placement of solar panels; this takes into account 1 m maintenance walkways around the edges and between PV rows
- allow for safe access and maintenance on roofs
- can be retrofitted fairly easily
- weight distribution of panels is around 20–25 kg/m^2
- structural weight and wind load need to be assessed for both new-build and retrofit applications
- usually allowed under permitted development in England, unless in a listed building or conservation area, where planning permission or listed building consent would then need to be obtained from the local authority

12.5.3 Solar energy: is it feasible?

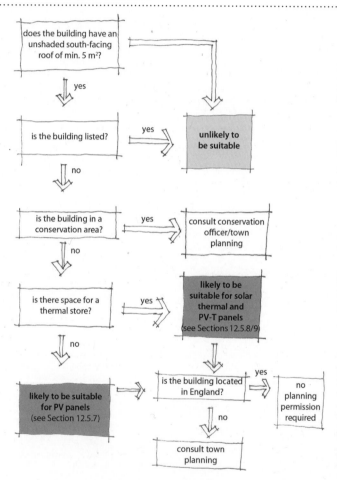

Fig. 12.5.1 Solar panel feasibility decision matrix

Note: Throughout this section, optimised conditions are assumed in calculations, unless stated otherwise, i.e. use of most efficient technologies, located south and at optimum angle. This gives the maximum energy generation and hence carbon savings. Loss factor has been taken into account as per Section 12.5.4.

12.5.4 Solar panel electrical energy calculator

- Manufacturers' literature usually gives the maximum theoretical figures for energy generation. In reality, the energy generated depends on:
  - panel orientation
  - yearly solar radiation, which depends on latitude
  - panel efficiency, which depends on technology and manufacturer – see each technology (Sections 12.5.7 and 12.5.8)
  - around 25% solar radiation is lost because of minor shading (dust, dirt collecting), snow cover, heat loss and DC–AC conversion loss,[34] so a 'loss factor' of 0.75 should be applied
  - tilt factor: this is the angle of the roof or surface on which the solar panels are mounted. See Section 12.5.5.

A more realistic electricity generation figure can be calculated with a simple formula:

Electricity (kWh) generated per 1 m^2 of PV/PV-T per year = yearly solar radiation (kWh/m^2 per year) × panel efficiency (%) × 0.75 (loss factor) × tilt factor (%)

Yearly average solar radiation in UK regions	
Based on solar radiation per m^2 ground surface per year	
Region 1 – Scotland	865 kWh/m^2 per year
Region 2 – north England and north Wales	960 kWh/m^2 per year
Region 3 – Northern Ireland	920 kWh/m^2 per year
Region 4 – south England and south Wales	1030 kWh/m^2 per year

12.5.5 Tilt factor: effect of tilt and orientation on energy output

Optimal positioning leads to tilt factor of 100%.

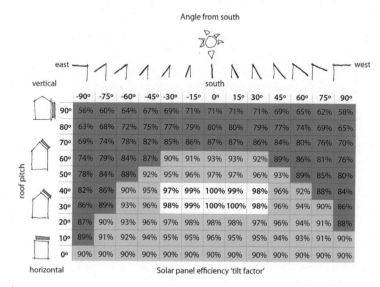

roof pitch		-90°	-75°	-60°	-45°	-30°	-15°	0°	15°	30°	45°	60°	75°	90°
	90°	56%	60%	64%	67%	69%	71%	71%	71%	71%	69%	65%	62%	58%
	80°	63%	68%	72%	75%	77%	79%	80%	80%	79%	77%	74%	69%	65%
	70°	69%	74%	78%	82%	85%	86%	87%	87%	86%	84%	80%	76%	70%
	60°	74%	79%	84%	87%	90%	91%	93%	93%	92%	89%	86%	81%	76%
	50°	78%	84%	88%	92%	95%	96%	97%	97%	96%	93%	89%	85%	80%
	40°	82%	86%	90%	95%	97%	99%	100%	99%	98%	96%	92%	88%	84%
	30°	86%	89%	93%	96%	98%	99%	100%	100%	98%	96%	94%	90%	86%
	20°	87%	90%	93%	96%	97%	98%	98%	98%	97%	96%	94%	91%	88%
	10°	89%	91%	92%	94%	95%	95%	96%	95%	95%	94%	93%	91%	90%
	0°	90%	90%	90%	90%	90%	90%	90%	90%	90%	90%	90%	90%	90%

horizontal   Solar panel efficiency 'tilt factor'

Fig. 12.52 Effect of tilt and orientation on energy output[35]

12.5.6 APPLICABLE LEGISLATION, GUIDANCE AND FURTHER READING

- BRE Digest 489, Wind loads on roof-based PV systems
- BRE Digest 495, Mechanical installation of roof-mounted PV systems
- BS EN 15316-1 Heating systems in buildings
- BS EN 61215:2005 Crystalline silicon terrestrial photovoltaic (PV) modules, Design qualification and type approval
- BS EN12975 and 76, Solar thermal systems and components
- Building Regulations: Region 2, 4: Part L; Region 1: Technical Handbook Section 6; and Region 3: Technical Booklet F
- CIBSE Domestic Building Service Panel – design guide for solar water heating
- CIBSE TM25, Understanding Building Integrated PVs
- COSSH 1994
- Domestic Heating Compliance Guide, Communities and Local Government, NBS publishing
- Energy Savings Trust, CE131
- Energy Savings Trust, Community Heating – a Guide (2004)
- Energy Savings Trust, Domestic Low And Zero Carbon Technologies, 2010
- Fthenakis and Alsema (2004), Photovoltaics Energy Payback Times, Greenhouse Gas Emissions and External Costs: 2004
- GLA Renewable Energy Toolkit: pp 92–106: feasibility tables, p 107: heat/electricity demands
- Harper (2009), *Domestic Solar Energy*, Crowood Press
- HSC L8 (2000) Control of Legionella Bacteria in Waters Systems
- NHBC, A review of micro generation and renewable technologies (2008)
- NHBC, Community Heating and Combined Heat and Power (2009)
- Renewables feasibility: www.retscreen.net/
- Ross and Royer (1999), *Photovoltaics in Cold Climates*, James and James
- Solar Trade Association, www.solar-trade.org.uk
- The Green Deal: www.decc.gov.uk/en/content/cms/what_we_do/consumers/green_deal/green_deal.aspx
- TS 12977 – Solar thermal systems and components and stores
- www.carbontrust.co.uk – New Practice Case Studies etc.
- Yannas (1994), *Solar Energy and Housing Design*, Architectural Association

12.5.7 Key characteristics and key recommendations – PV

What is it?	PVs convert solar energy into electricity. Domestic electricity demand usually peaks in winter and in the evenings – when solar energy is least available. For office and school uses, electricity peaks during the day. At present, PVs are a relatively inefficient technology: 10–15% of the solar energy reaching the surface is converted into clean electricity. The rest of the sun's heat is wasted, unless a PV-T system is used.
When to use? (see Fig. 12.5.1)	in unshaded areas, facing within 10° of south

Key facts and characteristics	There are different types of PVs:		
	monocrystalline PV	polycrystalline PV	amorphous PV
	most efficient, most expensive	less efficient, but cheaper	works with diffuse light, very low efficiency.
	$1\ kW_{peak} \approx 7.5\ m^2$	$1\ kW_{peak} \approx 10\ m^2$	$1\ kW_{peak} \approx 20\ m^2$
	efficiency* 10%[36]	efficiency* 8%	efficiency* 6%[37]
	can be see-through	requires larger roof area	flexible
	lifespan of 20–25 years, but some components need replacing after 15 years		efficiencies drop towards end of life

Key design recommendations (see Fig. 12.5.3)	• ideally with tilt angle of 35–40° to suit year-round electrical production • PV panel overheating leads to a drop of up to 10% in electricity generation. To avoid overheating, allow at least 150 mm air circulation at the back of the PV panels • separate PV panels from long runs and locate on a light-coloured or green roof to help cool the surface temperature (ensure plant growth does not cast shadow) • green roof and PV panel maintenance requirements may contradict each other • grid used as a 'storage battery' for unused electricity; this can be sold back: feed-in tariffs make this attractive
How much space is required?*	• around 35 m² of PV (a 4.6 kW$_{peak}$ installation) would be required to meet/offset a typical dwelling's electrical need • for a Passivhaus with MVHR ventilation and electrical space heating, this would increase to around 41 m² or 5.5 kW$_{peak}$ • this increases with electrical cooking • many dwellings do not have such a large south-facing roof area available

How much energy does it generate?*	1 m² of monocrystalline PV produces maximum around 100 kWh of electricity per year;[38] this is a UK average, and can be adapted more accurately for each region – see Section 12.5.4.		
What are the carbon reductions?*	Each m² of monocrystalline PV will save a maximum of 53 kgCO₂ per year and displace about 1 tonne of CO₂ over its lifetime.		
What is the embodied carbon?[39]	monocrystalline PV[40, 41]	polycrystalline PV	amorphous PV
	242 kgCO₂	208 kgCO₂	67 kgCO₂
	5 year payback of embodied carbon		2 year payback
Cost? (including financial incentives)	• £950–1050 per m² of PV[42] • costs decrease if system size increases (e.g. around £750/m² for 15 m² of PV)[43] • may receive capital funding by the Green Deal from autumn 2012 • feed-in tariffs apply. ──⟶ Jump to Section 10.7.		
Any maintenance issues?	Snow clearing and inspection to remove leaves, bird droppings and dust.		
Anything else?	• storing generated electricity is a potential issue: using the national grid to export (sell) electricity will be problematic on a large scale since supply (daytime) and demand (evening) do not match • PVs are currently the most viable option to help reduce carbon emissions from electricity in urban areas		

* Based on optimised conditions, unless stated otherwise. Efficiency takes combined system losses of 0.75 into account for PV-T and PV systems. See Sections 12.5.4 and 12.5.5.

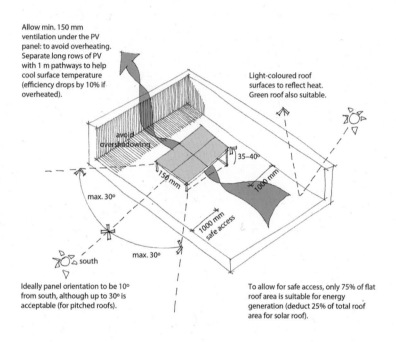

Allow min. 150 mm ventilation under the PV panel: to avoid overheating. Separate long rows of PV with 1 m pathways to help cool surface temperature (efficiency drops by 10% if overheated).

Light-coloured roof surfaces to reflect heat. Green roof also suitable.

avoid overshadowing

35–40º

150 mm

1000 mm

max. 30º

1000 mm safe access

south

max. 30º

Ideally panel orientation to be 10º from south, although up to 30º is acceptable (for pitched roofs).

To allow for safe access, only 75% of flat roof area is suitable for energy generation (deduct 25% of total roof area for solar roof).

Fig. 12.5.3 PV design considerations diagram

12.5.8 Key characteristics and key recommendations – PV-T

What is it?	PV-Ts are a relatively new technology and remain largely untested. Their potential to produce more energy from a given roof area compared to other technologies is very promising. PV-Ts utilise PV overheating by drawing heat away from the PV panel, usually with an air source heat pump. This increases a PV's capacity for electrical energy generation as well as providing heat. Some electrical energy for the heat pump is required.
When to use? (see Fig. 12.5.1)	Where there is a large and permanent heat demand, locate in unshaded areas, facing within 10° of south.
Key facts and characteristics	• typically, around 2–2.5 times more heat than electricity is produced • PV-Ts are efficient monocrystalline PV collectors with a heat pump to collect the waste heat
Key design recommendations (see Fig. 12.5.4)	• always size the PV-T array to suit heat demand, not electricity demand • do not oversize as it wastes heat which cannot be exported • always tilt the PV-T array to suit year-round electrical energy production; optimal inclination from horizontal roof surface: 35–40° • combine with efficient space heating technologies such as air-to-air heating, but underfloor heating or low surface temperature radiators may also be suitable • if heat is be used for a wet underfloor heating system or for hot water demand, provide a thermal store/water tank: provide 50 litres per m² of PV-T panel, with minimum of 250 litres per dwelling, and insulate pipework (25 mm) and water tank (100 mm)[44] • water must be regularly heated to 60°C to stop legionella build-up, particularly in winter when water temperature otherwise falls to 40°C • use dark roof surface area to increase heat-harnessing efficiency • do not combine with green roofs
How much space is required?*	• 16 m² of PV-T would be required to meet 100% of a 100 m² zero carbon standard dwelling's yearly space heating demand – this could meet around 60% of the total electrical needs • around 22 m² of PV-T is required to meet 100% of the hot water demand of a typical domestic building
How much energy does it generate?*	1 m² of PV-T produces around 120 kWh of electricity per year and around 250 kWh of useful heat,[45] with an efficiency of 12% electricity and 25% heat generation.

* Based on optimised conditions, unless stated otherwise. Efficiency takes combined system losses of 0.75 into account for PV-T and PV systems. See Sections 12.5.4 and 12.5.5.

continued

What are the carbon reductions?	1 m² of PV-T saves around 70 kg of CO_2 per year (CO_2 reduction takes account of the electricity used by the heat pump to extract the heat and its associated CO_2 emissions) – each m² of PV-T will displace about 1.8 tonnes of CO_2 over its lifetime. Total embodied carbon is unknown.
Cost? (including financial incentives)	• £1,000–1,500/m² • costs decrease if system size increases – around £1000/m² for 15 m² • feed-in tariffs may apply for the electricity generating component → Jump to Section 10.7
Any maintenance issues?	Snow clearing and inspection to remove leaves, bird droppings and dust, and refrigerant needs replacing and requires yearly access.

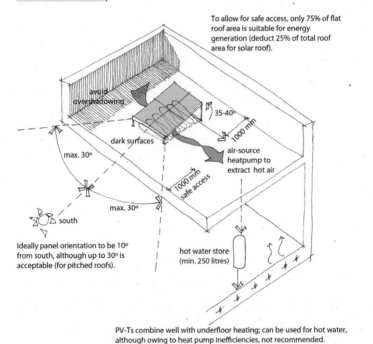

To allow for safe access, only 75% of flat roof area is suitable for energy generation (deduct 25% of total roof area for solar roof).

avoid overshadowing

35-40°

1000 mm

dark surfaces

max. 30°

air-source heatpump to extract hot air

1000 mm safe access

max. 30°

south

Ideally panel orientation to be 10° from south, although up to 30° is acceptable (for pitched roofs).

hot water store (min. 250 litres)

PV-Ts combine well with underfloor heating; can be used for hot water, although owing to heat pump inefficiencies, not recommended.

Fig. 12.5.4 PV-T design considerations diagram

12.5.9 Key characteristics and key recommendations – solar thermal

What is it?	Solar hot water or solar thermal panels convert energy from the sun into hot water. They can provide heat for space heating and hot water. As we build to higher fabric efficiency standards, CO_2 emissions from heating water become proportionally more significant.
When to use? (see Fig. 12.5.1)	Suitable in most applications, as long as good access to solar gain and within 10° of south.

Key facts and characteristics	There are two different types of solar thermal panels:	
	flat plate collectors	evacuated tubes
	less efficient, so larger surface area required	more efficient, more expensive
	efficiency* ≈ 30%	efficiency* ≈ 50%
	lifespan 20–25 years	lifespan 25–30 years[46]
	antifreeze needs replacing after 5–10 years	

Key design recommendations (see Fig.12.5.5)	flat plate collectors	evacuated tubes
	for hot water only: optimal inclination: 35–40° tilt angle	can be positioned flat on the roof
	for hot water and space heating: optimal tilt angle 50–60°	
	50 litres thermal store per m² of panel[47]	70 litres thermal store per m² of panel[48]

- size array to suit hot water demand – normally sized to meet 50–70% of a household's hot water needs, but do not oversize as this wastes heat
- use dark roof surface area to increase heat-harnessing efficiency, but do not combine with green roofs
- around 20% of winter hot water needs are met and 100% in summer, but a 'top-up' from another heating source is still required; water must be regularly warmed to 60°C to prevent legionella
- the 'top-up' heating source should be an efficient gas-condensing boiler instead of an electrical immersion heater, unless electrical carbon emissions are offset with renewables
- combine with efficient space heating technologies such as underfloor heating or low surface temperature radiators
- water will be around 90°C in summer and 40°C in winter, so an interseasonal thermal store is required: minimum 250 litres per dwelling
- insulate pipework (25 mm) and water tank (100 mm)[49]

continued

How much space is required?*	• 5 to 6 m² of evacuated tubes are required to meet 50% of the hot water demand in a typical dwelling • 10 m² of evacuated tubes is required to meet 50% of a zero carbon house's combined hot water and space heat demand • these areas increase by around 1.5 times when specifying flat plate collectors	
How much energy does it generate?*	flat plate collectors	evacuated tubes
	1 m² of flat plate collector produces around 300 kWh of heat per year	1 m² of evacuated tubes produces around 500 kWh of heat per year
What are the carbon reductions?*	60 kgCO₂ per m² of panel per year reduction	100 kgCO₂ per m² of panel per year reduction
What is the embodied carbon?	Around 120 kgCO₂e per m² of panel[50] (carbon equivalent) so it would take up to two years to pay back the embodied carbon.	
Cost? (including financial incentives)	• £750–1250 per m² of panel • costs decrease if system size increases • evacuated tubes are around 30% more expensive per m² than flat plate collectors, but this is usually offset as they produce around 30% more heat • may receive capital funding by the Green Deal from autumn 2012; a £300 renewable heat initiative premium may also apply • RHI applies ———➔ Jump to Section 10.7	
Any maintenance issues?	Snow clearing and inspection to remove leaves, bird droppings and dust.	
Anything else?	Solar hot water panels are a low-cost option to reduce carbon emissions from space heating/hot water demand.	

* Based on optimised conditions, unless stated otherwise.

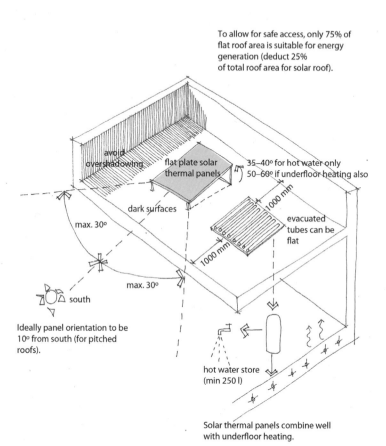

To allow for safe access, only 75% of flat roof area is suitable for energy generation (deduct 25% of total roof area for solar roof).

avoid overshadowing

flat plate solar thermal panels

35–40° for hot water only
50–60° if underfloor heating also

dark surfaces

1000 mm

1000 mm

evacuated tubes can be flat

max. 30°

south

max. 30°

Ideally panel orientation to be 10° from south (for pitched roofs).

hot water store (min 250 l)

Solar thermal panels combine well with underfloor heating.

12.5.5 *Solar thermal design considerations diagram*

12.6 ENERGY-EFFICIENT DELIVERY METHODS – HEATING AND ELECTRICITY

12.6.1 Combined heat and power (CHP): what is it?

A CHP plant – also referred to as co-generation – is a form of decentralised energy production. A CHP plant burns fuel to produce electricity and utilises the waste heat to provide space heating (or cooling) and hot water. Its energy generation is 75% efficient compared to 40% efficiency of the electricity grid. This is because CHP avoids the grid's transmission losses by producing energy near the point of use and utilising the waste heat generated.[51] CHPs are generally divided into large-scale macro CHPs and small-scale micro CHPs for individual buildings. The larger a CHP plant, the more efficient its electricity production and the greater the CO_2 reductions. Its viability towards zero carbon compliance also increases proportionally.[52]

12.6.2 Applicable legislation, guidance and further reading

• Building Regulations: Region 2, 4: Part L; Region 1: Technical Handbook Section 6 and Region 3: Technical Booklet F
• Carbon Trust, Introducing Combined Heat and Power and Technology Fact Sheet
• CHPA, Community Energy: Planning, development and delivery (2010)
• Clean Air Act
• Energy Saving Trust, Domestic Low and Zero Carbon Technologies (2010)
• GLA Renewable Energy Toolkit
• HSC L8 (2000) Control of Legionella Bacteria in Waters Systems
• NHBC, A review of micro generation and renewable energy technologies (2008)
• NHBC, Community heating and combined heat and power (2009)
• Pollution Prevention and Control
• SAP 2009, Appendix N

12.6.3 Is it feasible?

CHPs are only suitable where there is a large space heating and hot water demand, such as in leisure centres, hotels and existing housing stock where space heating demand cannot be reduced. See Fig. 12.6.1.

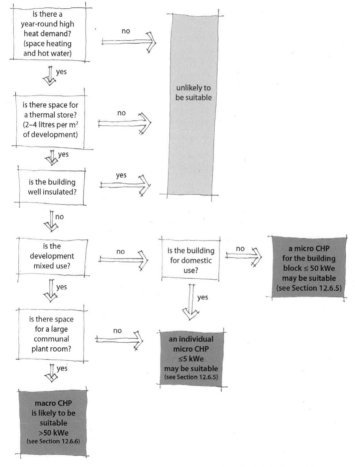

Fig. 12.6.1 CHP decision matrix

12.6.4 General CHP design considerations

- CHPs are only viable where there is high demand for space heating, cooling and hot water – around 12 hours per day throughout the year.[53]
- Ideal for hotels, leisure centres, care homes and hospitals.
- CHPs are usually unsuitable for new housing developments, such as well-insulated dwellings to zero carbon fabric efficiency standard or better, because the total heating demand is too low.
- A CHP plant needs to be correctly sized to avoid 'dumping' heat that cannot be used
- When there is no need for heat, the CHP suspends operation and does not produce electricity.
- CHPs usually run on natural gas, which is a fossil fuel, but they can reduce CO_2 emissions compared to a conventional gas-condensing boiler.
- Other cleaner fuels are available, which could reduce CO_2 emissions by 3–7 times compared to a conventional gas-condensing boiler, but technologies such as biomass, hydrogen and fuel cell technologies are less mature.[54]
- CHPs always need a thermal store for generated heat; a thermal store allows a CHP plant to operate more continuously and eases seasonal discrepancies; the water storage tank must be well insulated and can be housed underground.
- Size of the thermal store = 2–4 litres per m^2 of development and 250 litres minimum per dwelling; some CHP units come with an integral hot water storage tank.
- CHP ratio of heat and power generation is expressed as a heat-to-power ratio – the closer to 1:1, the greater the CO_2 reductions; CHP units with a heat-to-power ratio above 5:1 should not be specified, to ensure that carbon savings are delivered (5:1 means that for each kW electricity generated, 5 kW of heat is captured; this is not very efficient).
- Overall CHP efficiency percentage relates to the efficiency of burning the primary fuel, usually gas; CHP units with efficiencies lower than 90% should not be specified.

12.6.5 Key characteristics and key recommendations – micro CHP

Read in conjunction with general design notes, Section 12.6.4. above

When to use? (see Fig. 12.6.1)	Micro CHPs are usually specified for single building uses with a large heating demand throughout the year (note that kWe refers to kW of electrical energy)	
	micro CHP 5–50 kWe	micro CHP <5 kWe
	for small, single non-domestic uses	for single dwellings only; should run for minimum 4 hrs per day
	for example, small leisure centre, care home, nursery	suitable if dwelling ≥100 m² and/ or heat demand ≥20,000 kWh per year
		not suitable for well-insulated dwellings, e.g. zero carbon standard or where space heat demand ≤ 5000 kWh per year
		good for existing housing which is difficult to insulate (e.g. with listed building status)
Key facts and characteristics	micro CHP 5–50 kWe	micro CHP ≤5 kWe
	back-up boiler required	replaces conventional boiler
	building block plant	individual dwelling installation
	likely to contribute to zero carbon compliance; good combined with PV	published large CO_2 reductions are at present unverified; can actually increase CO_2 emissions[55] (see more under 'What are the carbon reductions?' section)
Key design recommendations	• size the system based on typical autumn/spring hot water and heat demand, rather than yearly electrical demand; regard electricity as a by-product[56] • install within the thermal envelope • specify units of minimum 15% electrical efficiency or heat-to-power ratio of 4:1 or better (note: such efficient units are in their infancy; most units on the market are far less efficient) • always combine with a thermal store: 2–4 litres per m² of development and 250 litres minimum per dwelling	

continued

How much space is required?	micro CHP 5–50 kWe	micro CHP ≤5 kWe
	separate plant room required, depending on CHP size and fuel used; for biomass fuels, additional storage space is required: see Sections 12.7.3. and 12.7.5.	most units are the size of a washing machine, or are the size of a standard gas-condensing boiler and can be wall-mounted
How much energy does it generate?	energy generated depends on each unit, the heat-to-power ratio and the overall CHP efficiency	
	micro CHP 5–50 kWe	micro CHP ≤5 kWe
	thermal CHP efficiency: 75–90%	thermal CHP efficiency: 75%
	typical heat-to-power ratio 2.5:1	typical heat-to-power ratio of a 1 kWe system is 6:1, and it generates 8000 kWh of heating energy and 1330 kWh of electricity per year[57]
	fuel cells may achieve 1.5–2:1 heat-to-power ratio,[58] but are untested at present	
What are the carbon reductions?	• carbon reductions are dependent on building typology, CHP specification and energy demand • published theoretical CO_2 reductions do not seem to match actual CO_2 reductions, and may even increase CO_2 emissions[60] • CO_2 emission reductions presented here are based on actual field trial data for a typical ≤5 kWe gas-fuelled CHP • maximum 260 kg CO_2/year per dwelling[61] if an old uninsulated or large dwelling • <100 kgCO_2 per year for a well-insulated dwelling • may even increase carbon emissions if electrical efficiency <15% or heat-to-power ratio is ≥6:1;[62] more efficient units of 2.5–3:1 heat-to-power ratio are being piloted • CO_2 reductions can be 2–2.5 times as great if woodchip and wood pellets are used[64] • if the grid decarbonises, burning gas to produce electricity will no longer make sense unless micro CHPs' current heat-to-power ratio significantly improves; otherwise, utilising a micro CHP would increase CO_2 emissions compared to a conventional gas boiler[65]	

Cost? (including financial incentives)	micro CHP 5–50 kWe	micro CHP ≤5 kWe
	5.5 kWe CHP plant = £13,000[66]	1 kWe = £5500 installed[67]
	FIT/RHI unlikely to apply; small biomass CHP to receive up to £950 per unit capital RHI premium. ——⟶ Jump to Section 10.7	Feed-in tariffs apply. ——⟶ Jump to Section 10.7
	2.5 times more expensive than conventional boiler/biomass stove[68] but may receive capital funding by the Green Deal from autumn 2012.	
Any maintenance issues?	An annual inspection and maintenance check, which includes a planned shutdown of the system.[69]	

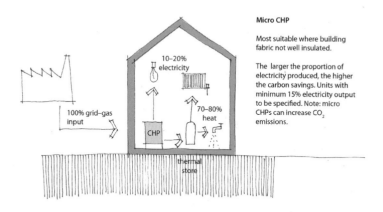

Micro CHP

Most suitable where building fabric not well insulated.

The larger the proportion of electricity produced, the higher the carbon savings. Units with minimum 15% electricity output to be specified. Note: micro CHPs can increase CO_2 emissions.

10–20% electricity

70–80% heat

100% grid–gas input

CHP

thermal store

Fig. 12.6.2 Micro CHPs

12.6.6 Key characteristics and key recommendations – macro CHP

Read in conjunction with general design notes (see Section 12.6.4).

When to use?	• macro CHPs are usually specified for large non-domestic single uses or combined with housing in large mixed-use developments • suitable if ≥4500 hrs of space heat/cooling/hot water demand per year (around 12 hrs/day) • suited to hotels, leisure centres and swimming pools, university halls, hospitals and care homes
Key facts and characteristics	• usually these are large installations of ≥50 kWe • often part of community/district heating strategies ⟶ Jump to Section 10.3.3 • total efficiency can be as low as 75%, which means that for each 100 units, 25 units are 'wasted'
Key design recommendations	• for system sizing, use the yearly electricity needs • for largest carbon reductions, specify CHP plant with heat-to-power ratio as close as possible to 1:1 with total efficiencies of 85–90% and electrical efficiencies of 25–30% • back-up boilers required in case of failure • pipework/connections are expensive and represent the majority of the capital cost • there may be legal issues where connecting across roads which are not owned • no planning permission is required • woodchips and wood pellets can be used in specifically designed CHP plants, but technology is less mature, and there are issues associated with biomass supply – see Section 12.7.3 • biomass usage will need to be approved in smoke-control zones, such as London • always provide a hot water store of 2–4 litres per m² of development • systems are noisy so need to be installed in an acoustically separated plant room
How much space is required?	• for 50 dwellings + nursery, a 50 m² plant room is typically required • for biomass fuels, additional space for biofuel storage is required – see Sections 12.7.3 and 12.7.5
How much energy does it generate?	• heat-to-power ratio is 1.5–2:1[70] which means that 1.5–2 units of heat are generated for each unit of electricity generated

What are the carbon reductions?	• reduction of up to 415 kgCO$_2$/year per dwelling as part of a communal scheme[71] • reduction of 1550 and 1700 kgCO$_2$/year per dwelling for wood pellets and woodchip respectively[72] • in urban areas, macro CHP is a feasible option for zero carbon compliance when combined with a communal roof PV array
Cost? (including financial incentives)	• 100 kWe macro CHP system = £900 per dwelling[73] • 250 kWe, including pipework and connections which are majority of cost: £2500–3000 per dwelling[74] • capital cost of a biomass CHP, pipework not included: 50 kWe = £150,000[75] • RHI: likely to be only applicable if a biofuel is used. ⟶ Jump to Section 10.7 • unlikely to receive FIT or RHI/Green Deal capital grants
Any maintenance issues?	• technical assistance and maintenance required for fine-tuning and regular upkeep • may be suitable under an ESCO agreement ⟶ Jump to Section 10.3.4

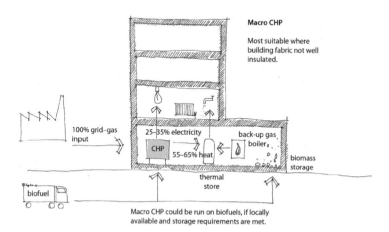

Macro CHP

Most suitable where building fabric not well insulated.

100% grid-gas input

25–35% electricity

CHP

55–65% heat

back-up gas boiler

biomass storage

biofuel

thermal store

Macro CHP could be run on biofuels, if locally available and storage requirements are met.

Fig. 12.6.3 Macro CHPs

12.6.7 A snapshot: combined cooling heat and power

- Combined cooling heat and power (CCHP) is tri-generation. Three useful types of energy are generated: cooling, heating and electricity. Like CHP, the fuel burned to provide heat and power now also provides cooling.
- It is a counter-intuitive process: hot water can drive absorption chillers to provide cool water for use in buildings. Absorption chillers use a heat pump to turn waste heat into cooling energy. This is more efficient than conventional air-conditioning.
- Useful for schemes which have offices, supermarkets, etc. that require cooling.
- Suitable for community schemes and larger mixed-use developments with a large winter heating demand.
- Particularly suited to urban areas.
- Should be combined with air-to-air/underfloor heating for both space heating and summer cooling.

12.7 ENERGY-EFFICIENT DELIVERY METHODS WITH BIOFUELS

12.7.1 Biomass – what is it?

Biomass is fuel derived from burning or gasification of trees or plants which have absorbed CO_2 during their lifetime. When timber burns or rots, this captured carbon is released back into the atmosphere. Hence, timber is best used as a building material, keeping the CO_2 locked in for decades if not centuries.

Sometimes, however, it may be appropriate to burn biomass such as waste wood cuttings/chips as fuel. This biomass may come from woodland management and sustainably grown, short rotation coppice plants such as willow or miscanthus. These are usually made into wood pellets.

The principle of short rotation coppice is that they are grown for short periods (1–5 years) before being harvested. New crops are grown simultaneously to absorb the CO_2 emissions released from biomass burning. Biomass crops need to be processed, so the fuel derived is not entirely carbon neutral. This is reflected in SAP 2009 fuel CO_2 intensity figures. ⟶ Jump to Section 10.2.

Biomass can be burned in a biomass boiler or gasified in CHP systems. This is not yet a mature technology.

12.7.2 Applicable legislation, guidance and further reading

- Biomass Energy Centre: www.biomassenergycentre.org.uk/
- Building Regulations (Conservation of fuel and power and combustion of appliances and fuel storage systems)
- Building Regulations: Region 2, 4: Part L; Region 1: Technical Handbook Section 6 and Region 3: Technical Booklet F
- Clean Air Act
- DD CEN/TS 15234:2006 Solid biofuels, Fuel quality assurance
- DD CEN/TS 15359:2006 Solid recovered fuels, Specifications and classes
- DD CEN/TS 15400:2006 Solid recovered fuels, Methods for the determination of calorific value
- DD CEN/TS 15440:2006 Solid recovered fuels, Method for the determination of biomass content
- EST, Biomass heating, A practical guide for potential users, 2009
- HSC L8 (2000) Control of Legionella Bacteria in Waters Systems
- Pollution Prevention and Control
- SAP 2009, Appendix N

12.7.3 Biomass: is it feasible?

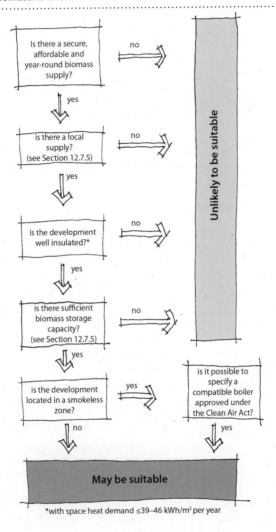

Fig. 12.7.1 Renewable energy decision matrix – biomass fuel

12.7.4 Key characteristics and key recommendations – biomass

What is it?	• a biomass boiler works pretty much like a conventional gas boiler; it is hooked up to a central heating system but burns wood instead of gas • a biomass CHP plant can also provide electrical power; the technology is still immature but carbon savings could be significant • a wood stove can heat a well-insulated small building or 3/4 bedroom house
When to use? (see Fig. 12.7.1)	• in well-insulated buildings with low heat demand, e.g. zero carbon standard or better • when there is a local, secure and sustainable supply of biomass • where approved boilers can be specified to comply with the Clean Air Act[76]
Key facts and characteristics	• wood stove: ideal for a small building, typically 6–12 kW with efficiency of 70%, using wood logs or pellets • biomass boiler: ideal for large communal schemes, efficiency 90%, uses wood pellets or chips – characteristics below:

woodchip	wood pellets
waste product, cheaper to buy, usually UK sourced	more processed and often imported from abroad
better suited to community schemes (≥25 kW)	ideal for single dwelling 3/4 bedroom: 8–15 kW

Key design recommendations	• communal systems would need other energy-efficient gas boilers as back-up • biomass boilers and wood stoves are ideally sized for winter space heating demand • solar power can provide hot water heating in summer, so the biomass boiler can be switched off from May to September • never import biomass from overseas, but source locally to reduce 'embodied' carbon; see Figs 12.7.2–4 • specify automatic pellet/chip feeders for communal systems • take into account fuel delivery and lorry access to storage area/ plant room (maximum distance from road to storage space to be 15–30 m) • provide hot water thermal stores – minimum 250 litres per dwelling

continued

	• technologies should comply with smoke control zones where applicable, but at present only limited technology is approved in urban smoke control zones such as London (Clean Air Act) • beware 'planning scam': biomass boilers are often the most economic means to comply with the Merton Rule (———⟫ Jump to Chapter 10) and zero carbon compliance[77] (———⟫ Jump to Chapter 11). In the past, biomass boilers have been specified and installed but never commissioned, owing to security or cost of supply. This 'planning scam' will be more difficult once carbon compliance certificates are required for 'as built' and not at design stages.
How much space is required?	Not very efficient, so large storage areas are required. See also Figs 12.7.2–4.

woodchip	wood pellets
$6-8$ m³ minimum	typically $1.5-2$ m³

How much energy does it generate?	• using wood as a heating source is inefficient: 3.6 m² of biomass growing land area is required to provide 1 kWh of heat per year[78] • to illustrate this: around 4.5 ha of biomass growing land is required to meet a typical dwelling's space heating and hot water demand • this reduces to 2.7 and 2 ha for zero carbon and Passivhaus standards respectively, so biomass should only be used in well-insulated dwellings • a typical 20 kW biomass pellet boiler can meet a dwelling's space heat and hot water demand

woodchip	wood pellets
1 m³ of woodchip (200 kg) generates 800 kWh giving 150 $kgCO_2$ reduction	1 m³ of wood pellets (650 kg) generates 3000 kWh giving 500 $kgCO_2$ reduction

What are the carbon reductions?	• compared to a 90% gas-condensing boiler: – wood pellets: CO_2 reduction of 0.17 $kgCO_2$/kWh of delivered heat – woodchip: CO_2 reduction of 0.189 $kgCO_2$ per kWh of delivered heat • a dwelling built to zero carbon standards with hot water and space heat demand met by a biomass boiler will reduce CO_2 emissions by: – 1600 $kgCO_2$ per year – wood pellets – 1880 $kgCO_2$ per year – woodchip

What is the embodied carbon?	Wood pellets are often imported from abroad which significantly increases the embodied carbon, and there are also ethical issues if biomass is imported from regions where tropical rainforest or agricultural land has been cleared for fuel crops for faraway regions.
Cost? (including financial incentives)	• wood stove: around £2500[79] • biomass boilers: £6000–14,000[80] • biomass pellet boiler: £10,000 providing 8000 kWh/yr (includes flue pipe and fully automated pellet feeder)[81] • biomass boilers may receive capital funding by the Green Deal from autumn 2012 and up to £950 from the renewable heat premium • RHI applies. ——→ Jump to Section 10.7

woodchip	wood pellets
1 tonne of woodchips = £80[82] or 2.3p/kWh,[83] which is cheaper than current gas prices	1 tonne of wood pellets = £185 or 3.9p/kWh,[84] which is similar to natural gas prices

Any maintenance issues?	Biomass systems require a higher user input than other technologies and this may be as much as 1.5 days per month.[85]
Anything else?	• competing demands for biomass/fuels in other sectors, such as the car/transport industry • mono-cultural crops may threaten biodiversity • land intensive – if all UK arable land were cultivated for biomass, it would still only meet the hot water and space heat demand for around 2.5 million typical dwellings – around 10% of the current housing stock (or for 6 million dwellings if built to zero carbon standards)[86]

12.7.5 How far to import biomass from?

Biomass fuels should always be sourced locally to minimise transportation CO_2 emissions. The larger the heating energy requirement, the more frequent the deliveries, unless sufficiently large storage areas are provided. This is illustrated in Figs 12.7.2–4.

The Biomass Energy Centre has a list of suppliers for England, Wales and Scotland.

Typical zero carbon house – woodchip

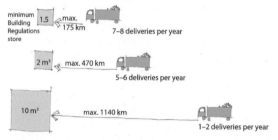

Typical zero carbon house – wood pellet

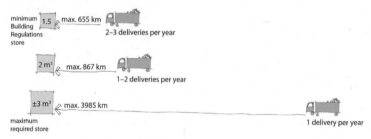

Fig. 12.7.2 Maximum recommended sourcing distances of biomass for heating energy requirements of zero carbon house

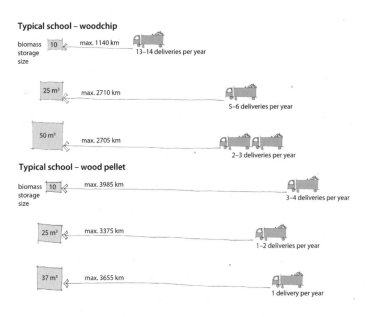

Typical school – woodchip

biomass storage size: 10 — max. 1140 km — 13–14 deliveries per year

25 m³ — max. 2710 km — 5–6 deliveries per year

50 m³ — max. 2705 km — 2–3 deliveries per year

Typical school – wood pellet

biomass storage size: 10 — max. 3985 km — 3–4 deliveries per year

25 m³ — max. 3375 km — 1–2 deliveries per year

37 m³ — max. 3655 km — 1 delivery per year

Fig. 12.7.3 Maximum recommended sourcing distances of biomass for heating energy requirements of typical school

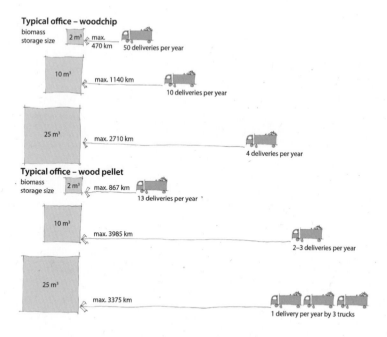

Fig. 12.7.4 *Maximum recommended sourcing distances of biomass for heating energy requirements of typical office*

12.7.6 Anaerobic digestion/biogas – what is it?

Energy can be derived from waste. Each person in the UK generates around 250 kg of organic waste[87] which can be collected, put into sealed tanks and heated to generate biogas. This process is called anaerobic digestion.

Biogas, which is mostly methane and CO_2, results from the anaerobic decomposition of organic materials (kitchen, garden and paper waste). This biogas is used as fuel for a boiler or CHP plant to produce heat and electricity, both to run the biogas plant (30–40% of heat generated) and to export the surplus energy generated (60–70%).[88]

Anaerobic digestion makes it possible to dispose of municipal waste, reduce odours, deal with humid waste and produce high-quality compost which can be sold. However, a lot of waste is required for relatively modest energy production.

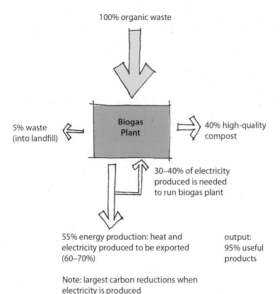

100% organic waste

Biogas Plant

5% waste (into landfill)

40% high-quality compost

30–40% of electricity produced is needed to run biogas plant

55% energy production: heat and electricity produced to be exported (60–70%)

output: 95% useful products

Note: largest carbon reductions when electricity is produced

Fig. 12.7.5 Biogas diagram

12.7.7 Applicable legislation, guidance and further reading

Building Regulations: Region 2, 4: Part L; Region 1: Technical Handbook Section 6 and Region 3: Technical Booklet F.

- England and Wales
  - Environmental Permitting Programme (integrating the previous Waste Management Licences and Pollution Prevention Control)
  - Animal By-product Regulations
- Scotland
  - Waste Management Licences or Pollution Prevention and Control Permit
  - Animal By-Products Regulations
  - Proposed Zero Waste (Scotland) Regulations 2011
  - Scottish Planning Policy (SPP) Anaerobic digestion
- N. Ireland
  - Waste Management Licence
  - Pollution Prevention and Control
  - Animal by-product Regulations

12.7.8 Biogas: is it feasible?

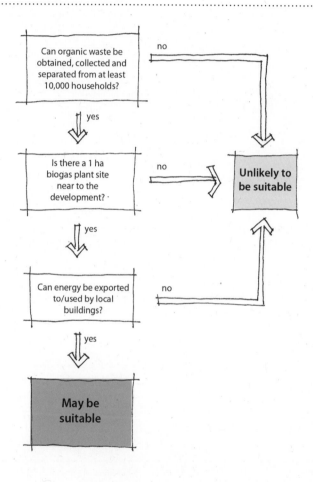

Fig. 12.7.6 Renewable electricity decision-making matrix – biogas

12.7.9 Key characteristics and key recommendations – biogas

When to use? (see Fig. 12.7.6)	• biogas is only suitable for district heating/community plant to provide a holistic solution to municipal waste • ideally heating and electrical energy can be used nearby • particularly suitable near farms and industry with high organic waste output
Key facts and characteristics	• a lot of waste is required for modest energy returns • heat distribution to the community must be energy-efficient
Key design recommendations	• to significantly reduce CO_2 reductions, plant should be sized to maximise electricity production
How much space is required?	• the plant requires a large amount of space and a large number of households to provide the organic waste • ideally plant is sized to process organic waste from at least 10,000 households/dwellings • a 1 ha site is required to deal with the organic household waste of around 92,000 households; this could meet 100% of the typical electrical needs of 3200 dwellings/households
How much energy does it generate?	• 10 kg waste generates around 2 kWh of useful net energy • organic waste collection from 10,000 dwellings could meet 3.5% of the same community's typical electrical energy needs
What are the carbon reductions?	This is difficult to calculate, as it depends on the proportion of useful heat and electricity exported: • if all of the useful waste heat is exported as electricity, then 10 kg waste = 1 $kgCO_2$/year reduction[89] • only an estimated 25 $kgCO_2$ reduction per year per dwelling if waste heat is exported as space heating without accounting for transmission losses[90] • CO_2 emissions reductions[91] are an estimated 65 kg CO_2/year per dwelling if the biogas is mostly converted and exported as electricity
Cost? (including financial incentives)	May be eligible both under RHI and FIT. ——⟶ Jump to Section 10.7.
Any maintenance issues?	Regular maintenance to avoid/check for contaminants and corrosion of pumps.[92]
Anything else?	100% of the waste input is converted into energy with 5% waste for landfill and 40% high-quality compost to be sold.

12.8 ENERGY-EFFICIENT DELIVERY METHODS – HEATING AND COOLING

12.8.1 Gas-condensing boiler

A gas boiler burns gas to heat water for personal washing and space heating systems.

Old gas boilers are non-condensing and work on efficiencies as low as 55–80%. This means that there are large losses in converting fossil fuel into useful heating energy.

UK regulations require condensing boilers of at least SEDBUK 88% (Seasonal Efficiency of a Domestic Boiler in the UK) but they can be as high as 91%, based on field trial data.[93] Condensing boilers achieve this by recovering any useful heat from the outgoing water vapour. In old boilers the heat is lost with the flue gases.

Gas-condensing boilers are easy to install but require:
- an external connection to allow the condensate to drain away
- external flue to allow water vapour to escape; the water vapour is 50–60°C instead of 120–180°C in a non-condensing boiler[94]
- where boilers combined with other low and zero carbon technologies, ensure that the boiler system and/or thermal store allows the input of other heat sources
- they operate most efficiently when switched on for 2 hours or more at a time, and when return temperature ≤ 55°C

12.8.2 Heat pumps – what are they?

A heat pump extracts heat from one location (the 'source'), upgrades the heat and then moves it to another location (the 'sink'). The source of heat can be the ground, water or air.

The temperature gained is lower than with other technologies and a heat pump requires electricity (or gas) to convert harvested heat into useful heating. The electrical energy used for the pump can be offset by renewable energy sources such as PV.

12.8.3 Heat pumps: are they feasible?

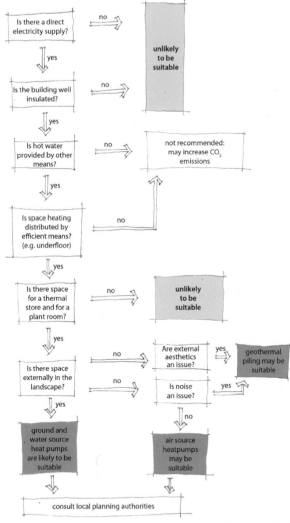

Fig. 12.8.1 Renewable energy–decision matrix –
air/ground/water source heat pumps

12.8.4 General design considerations – heat pumps

When to use? (see Fig. 12.8.1)	Heat pumps are appropriate for meeting part of the space heating demand in well-insulated and airtight dwellings (at least zero carbon fabric energy efficiency standard).
Why?	• 45–50°C is the maximum temperature that can be obtained from heat pumps – this can be much lower for air source heat pumps; however, this is likely to be improved in the future. • additional energy is required to 'top up' the source temperatures; in some situations, this increases carbon emissions (e.g. where electrical immersion heaters are used as top-up/back-up boilers and where heat pumps are used for hot water supply)
What to avoid?	• not recommended for hot water supply, as this is likely to produce higher carbon emissions than a conventional gas-condensing boiler • avoid conventional radiators as they require heat input of around 60°C • avoid electrical immersion back-up/top-up heaters • using heat pumps for hot water provision with a back-up electrical immersion heater would increase emissions by about 1 tonne CO_2 per year
What is recommended?	• size the heat pump to meet around 85–95% of the annual space heat load demand • heat pumps should only be used with low-surface temperature heating systems – these require 30–45°C heat input 　——⟶ Jump to Section 10.4 • renewable energy could offset the heat pump's electrical energy • if possible, the back-up/top-up boiler should be biomass or an efficient gas-condensing boiler instead of an electric immersion heater • specify a heat pump with a theoretical COP >3; manufacturers' data suggests theoretical COP to be around 2–4, but in practice heat pumps operate at 20–25% less efficiency than claimed[95] • Seasonal Performance Factor (SPF) expresses the COP during heating season, i.e. when the heat is required, from autumn onwards – this is to reflect that COP falls in the winter season due to colder source temperatures[96] • weather compensation controls recommended: an outside temperature sensor signals the required output temperature for the heat pump • to optimise efficiencies, opt for straight running pipework and minimise bends and junctions
How much space is required?	• 60 litres per person with a minimum of 250 litres per dwelling; a heat store keeps the efficiency of the heat pump high – some systems come with an integral heat store • always seek specialist advice on using heat pumps

Cost? (including financial incentives)	Ground and air source heat pumps may receive capital funding by the Green Deal from autumn 2012, but they are unlikely to qualify for payback incentives under the Renewable Heat Initiative. ⟶ Jump to Section 10.7.
Anything else?	• regularly heat water to ≥60°C to prevent legionella • heat pumps can be run in reverse to meet cooling requirements, but this is expensive and leads to lower winter efficiencies – see Section 12.8.6. • combines well with solar thermal panels to meet year-round hot water demand • as the grid decarbonises, the CO_2 reduction potential of heat pumps significantly increases, and this also means that hot water provision from heat pumps is likely to become more viable

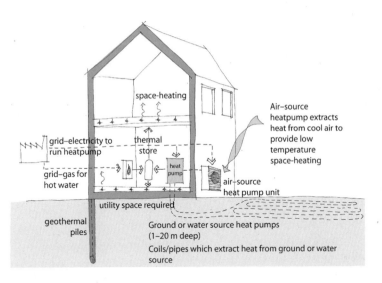

Fig. 12.8.2 Heat pumps

12.8.5 Key characteristics and key recommendations – air source heat pumps (ASHP)
Read in conjunction with general design notes (Section 12.8.4).

What is it?	Air source heat pumps extract heat from the air even when outside temperatures are low. They are less efficient than ground source heat pumps since the external air is cooler than the ground. The air source pump is least efficient in winter which is exactly when space heat demand peaks.
When to use? (see Fig. 12.8.1)	• most suitable in urban areas; external units have noise and aesthetic implications • unlikely to be suitable in Region 1 (Scotland) owing to low air temperatures and snow cover • recommended with low surface temperature heating systems ———➣ Jump to Section 10.4.1 • not recommended for hot water provision • not recommended where the building does not achieve high energy efficiency standards such as zero carbon or Passivhaus ———➣ Jump to Section 7.5
Key facts and characteristics	• a theoretical COP of 2–3 performed closer to a COP of 2.2 for space heating with an air source heat pump[97] • the COP lowers to 1.6 where used for hot water[98] as more electricity is needed to boost the source temperature • when temperatures go below 5°C, the COP efficiency falls to below 1,[99] and more electricity is needed than heat harvested – this jeopardises overall CO_2 reductions • noise of the external heat pump unit: 65dBA at 10 m, although those below 42dBA at 10 m are favoured by Building Regulations • 15–20 year lifespan • air-to-water heat pumps transfer heat to a thermal store, and this heats water which is connected to a central underfloor heating system • air-to-air heat pumps produce warm air which is circulated by fans for space heating
Key design recommendations	• using air from a passively solar heated area (conservatory/solar space) will boost efficiency (COP), and the heat can be used to warm water or air for underfloor or air-to-air heating • consider the noise aspect during design and planning stage • consider visual impact • place external heat pump away from any activity-triggered security lights • place bushes around heat pump protecting from cold winds to increase efficiency and reduce defrosting cycles

How much space is required?	• external heat pump component around 700 mm × 150 mm × 350 mm wide – similar to air-conditioning units to be placed externally • external heat pump requires clearance of 1 m in front + 200 mm around sides for air intake • electric heater and thermal store required internally • some air source heat pump systems have an integral thermal store. A thermal store is essential, otherwise the ASHP cools the space during a defrost cycle (60 litres per person, with a minimum of 250 litres per dwelling)
How much energy does it generate and what are the carbon reductions?	• can meet 80–100% of the space heating demand in southern UK regions • for each kWh of electricity used, around 2.2 kWh of space heat are gained (COP 2.2) • heat load demand of 3900 kWh, delivered by ASHP, decreases CO_2 emissions by 350 $kgCO_2$ per year (with a gas boiler for all hot water needs and as backup) • emissions increase by about 1 tonne per year if heat pumps are used for 50% hot water provision and 80–100% space heat demand (with electrical immersion heater as backup) • from 2020, if the grid decarbonises as expected, greater overall CO_2 reductions could be achieved
Cost? (including financial incentives)	• £6,000–10,000[100] • ground and air source heat pumps may receive capital funding by the Green Deal from autumn 2012, if minimum efficiencies are met (COP ≥2.9) • possibly up to £850 capital funding from the renewable heat premium ——⟩ Jump to Section 10.7
Any maintenance issues?	• winter de-icing; specify unit with defrost control • manual removal of snow • ice can form at temperatures as high as 7°C, and the ASHP will then defrost itself, 'reversing' the heat cycle and drawing from the heat store to do so – this lowers its efficiency[101] • low maintenance with an annual need for safety checks

12.8.6 A snapshot: reverse cycle air source heat pump

- Most heat pumps are reversible to provide cooling in summer, including air-to-water and air-to-air heat pumps. The technology is rarely used in the UK.
- It will reduce heating efficiency in winter.
- PV-T technology includes a heat pump which can turn the waste heat into useful cooling, but this is untested. ——➤ Jump to Section 12.5.8.

12.8.7 MVHR

MVHR (mechanical ventilation with heat recovery) is not a heat pump but an air-to-air heat exchanger which uses hot internal air as its source to heat fresh colder air. It can provide all the ventilation and, with a top-up heating source, the space heating demands of a well-insulated dwelling (to Passivhaus standard). See also ground ducts. ——➤ Jump to Section 6.7.

12.8.8 Key characteristics and key recommendations – ground source heat pumps (GSHP) Read in conjunction with general design notes (Section 12.8.4)	
What is it?	Throughout the year, soil temperatures 10 m deep are fairly stable at 10–14°C. This 'base heat' or 'coolth' can be harvested by a GSHP. Pipework is inserted into the soil horizontally, vertically or with 'slinky coils'.
When to use? (see Fig. 12.8.1)	• suburban and rural locations are most suitable as GSHPs require a lot of space; good in clay soil but unsuitable in chalk • GSHP is often not a viable option in urban areas where other services already compete for ground space • not recommended without underfloor heating or low surface temperature radiators ——➤ Jump to Section 10.4.1 • not recommended for hot water provision • not recommended in buildings without high energy efficiency standards such as zero carbon or Passivhaus. ——➤ Jump to Section 7.5
Key facts and characteristics	• a theoretical COP of 3–4 can perform closer to a COP of 2.4 for space heating[102] • the COP lowers to 1.8 where used for hot water heating[103] as more electricity is needed to boost the source temperature; hence not recommended for this purpose • ground source heat pumps work best with a sink temperature of 25–45°C, hence they work well with underfloor heating ——➤ Jump to Section 10.4 • 30–50 year lifespan for external pipework

Key design recommendations	• ideally located in areas where solar gain is maximised • can be installed under dark surfaces such as playgrounds to obtain more heat • trenches should be 3–5 m apart • no visual impact • pipework limits landscaping opportunities and is disruptive • where extensive landscaping is taking place anyway, the capital cost of ground source heat pumps may be reduced • horizontal and slinky coils are installed at 1–2 m depth so they are more influenced by seasonal extremes
	Vertical GSHP – based on 5kW heat pump
	• around 35 m of pipe per kW installed capacity, i.e. 175 m pipework run at depth of 15–20 m • more expensive but requires less space; its depth makes it more seasonally stable • typical house would have one or two boreholes with one or two pipes in each borehole • pipework is usually liquid based • can be included in building foundations; see Section 12.8.10
	Slinky coils – based on 5kW heat pump
	• most compact: 10 m pipe required per kW capacity; around 50 m run of pipework required
	Horizontal GSHP – based on 5kW heat pump
	• pipework laid in trenches, with around 50 m of pipework per kW, i.e. 250 m pipework required • in air-based systems, horizontal ducts are 150–500 mm wide and buried at least 2 m deep;[104] see also ground ducts ⟶ Jump to Section 6.7 • approximately the same external area required for pipework as the internal floor area
How much space is required?	• a heat pump is approximately standard boiler size but depending on capacity can be to 1 m × 1 m × 0.5 m • heat store of 60 litres per person, with a minimum of 250 litres per dwelling • around 150 m² of open, unbuilt land is required per dwelling. This is not only to accommodate pipework but to allow the soil to recharge in solar heat year to retain source temperatures year on year. (Excess summer solar thermal heat could be used to raise the soil's ground temperature, but this area is experimental at present.)

continued

How much energy does it generate? And what are the carbon reductions?	• a 5 kW GSHP can meet 80–100% of the space heating demand of a zero carbon dwelling • for each kWh of electricity used, around 2.4 kWh of space heat gained • heat demand of 3900 kWh, if delivered by a GSHP, decreases CO_2 emissions by 425 kgCO_2 per year if gas boiler used as back-up and for all hot water • emissions increase by almost 1 tonne per year if heat pumps are used for 50% hot water provision and 80–100% space heat demand (with an electrical immersion heater as back-up) • from 2020, if the grid decarbonises as expected, greater overall CO_2 reductions could be achieved
Cost? (including financial incentives)	• capital cost of a ground source heat pump is £6000–17,000 • ground and air source heat pumps may receive capital funding from the Green Deal from autumn 2012 and up to £1250 under the RHI premium • RHI applies to ground source <100 kW ⟶ Jump to Section 10.7
Any maintenance issues?	• low maintenance with an annual need for safety checks[105]
Anything else?	• ground source heat pumps are often incorrectly referred to as 'geothermal energy', but while heat pumps harvest heat from the soil at shallow depths, geothermal heating extracts heat from underground aquifers at depths of hundreds of metres • heat pumps can be reversed to provide cooling; see Section 12.8.12

12.8.9 Water source heat pump and solar ponds

Water source heat pumps work in a similar way to ground source heat pumps (see section 12.8.8) but the medium is a body of water rather than soil. Ideally, the body of water is a solar pond.

A solar pond maximises direct solar gain which increases heat pump efficiencies. With around 200–300 kg/m³ salt[106] in the pond, water temperatures can be as high as 48°C in summer and 13°C in winter.[107]

- suitable in rural/coastal areas with abundant open space to accommodate a pond without overshadowing
- electricity could, in theory, be obtained from solar ponds but this is not feasible with the UK's low temperatures
- should only be considered for space heating
- pond should be 3–5 m deep[108] and around 4.5 m diameter
- for CO_2 reductions, use GSHP figures, although efficiencies and carbon emission reductions are likely to be higher

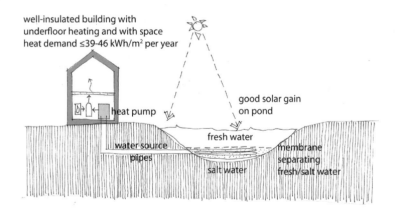

Fig. 12.8.3 Solar pond diagram

12.8.10 Geothermal piling – what is it?

Geothermal piles work on the same principle as vertical ground source heat pump pipes (see Section 12.8.8). Instead of being inserted into the ground, the pipework is incorporated into the structural concrete foundation piles. The concrete piles have a high thermal mass and transfer the base heat or cooling temperatures to the heat pump.

12.8.11 Key characteristics and key recommendations – geothermal piling	
When to use?	• where substantial groundworks and pile foundations are specified • in well-insulated buildings with energy-efficient space-heating distribution systems such as underfloor heating, low surface temperature radiators
Key facts and characteristics	• flexible pipes of 20–32 mm, which contain water as a medium, are incorporated within the pile reinforcement cages[109] • the pile should not be allowed to freeze; usually water is mixed with antifreeze • the piles' structural performance is not usually adversely affected by the heating and cooling of the pipes[110] • see ground source heat pumps
Key design recommendations	• early agreement between designer, client, contractor, structural and M&E engineers to be undertaken • can be at lower depths than traditional vertical ground source pipes,[111] although the deeper the pipes, the more efficient the system • do not specify a heat pump system with COP <3 • see ground source heat pumps, Section 12.8.8
How much space is required?	See ground source heat pumps, Section 12.8.8.
How much energy does it generate?	• 30 W of heating and cooling energy per metre depth[112] • one 33 m deep precast pile is enough to heat and cool a well-insulated 4 m × 4 m room[113]
What are the carbon reductions?	See ground source heat pumps, Section 12.8.8.
Cost? (including financial incentives)	• unclear whether it will be classified as GSHP for RHI purposes ——⟩ Jump to Section 10.7 • three times more expensive than a gas-condensing boiler and traditional radiators – typically £11,000–12,000 for a well-insulated three-bedroom dwelling[114]
Any maintenance issues?	low maintenance

12.8.12 A snapshot: earth cooling

- Earth cooling can be an effective way to provide base cooling through bypassing the heat pump. In winter, the GSHP can provide base heat and in summer, the same underground temperatures of 10–14°C can provide cooling through an existing underfloor/hot air-heating system. For ground ducts, ——→ Jump to Section 6.7.
- Suitable for smaller developments and for suburban/rural locations with lots of outdoor space. These locations tend to benefit from good cross-ventilation, so prioritise passive cooling.

12.8.13 A snapshot: evaporative cooling

- Hot air from outside is continuously moved over water-soaked pads. Heat is consumed by the evaporation process and lowers the surrounding temperature. Cooler air is moved into the building space.
- It consumes water and pushes hot air outside, exacerbating the urban heat island effect.
- The unit is located on the roof or an external wall and draws in hot air with electrically driven fans. However, it consumes less energy than air-conditioning units.
- Evaporation is reduced when the hot air has a high relative humidity. This is why evaporative cooling is most suitable in hot, dry climates. The UK has high relative humidity of 50–75% in summer months.[115]
- A maximum evaporative cooling effect of around 5°C could be achieved,[116] but as the cool air is 80–90% humid this may actually decrease thermal comfort as temperatures will feel warmer.
- Limited application to achieve thermal comfort in UK heatwaves.
- Health concerns are related to possibly insufficient air/pollution filtering and increased humidity.

For adiabatic cooling and passive cooling measures, ——→ Jump to Section 6.7.

12.8.14 Applicable legislation, guidance and further reading

- Bridgewater (2008), *The Off-grid Energy Handbook*, New Holland
- BS EN 14511 Air conditioners, liquid chilling packages and heat pumps
- BS EN 15316-1 Heating systems in buildings
- BS EN 378 Refrigeration systems and heat pumps
- BSRIA TN18/99, Ground source heat pumps: a technology review
- Building Regulations: Region 2, 4: Part L; Region 1: Technical Handbook Section 6 and Region 3: Technical Booklet F
- Efficient design of piled foundations for low-rise housing, Design guide – Arup, NHBC Foundation, 2010
- Energy Savings Trust, Domestic low and zero carbon technologies (2010)
- EST, Domestic Ground Source Heat Pumps: Design and installation
- EST, Getting warmer: a field trial of heat pumps, 2010
- HSC L8 (2000) Control of Legionella Bacteria in Waters Systems
- NHBC, Ground source heat pump systems: Benefits, drivers and barriers in residential developments (2007)
- SAP 2009
- The Heat Pump Centre (www.heatpumpcentre.org)
- The UK Ground Source Heat Pump Association – www.gshp.org.uk/

12.9 EMERGING TECHNOLOGIES

12.9.1 Fuel cells and hydrogen (electricity and heat) – what is it?

An electric current sent through water (H_2O) can split it into hydrogen gas (H_2) and oxygen (O_2). This process is called electrolysis. Fuel cells reverse this procedure to produce electricity, with water as a by-product. If the fuel cells' hydrogen compound is obtained through renewable instead of fossil fuel processes, then they are able to produce electricity efficiently, quietly and with much lower pollution outputs. This could make fuel cells a renewable fuel. The heat is a waste product which the building industry is able to use.

12.9.2 Is it feasible?

- Obtaining hydrogen must first become more efficient. Although 1 kg of hydrogen can produce 40 kWh, at present it may require up to twice as much electricity to obtain the hydrogen in the first place.[117]
- Fuel cell technology is currently at the development stage. It is expensive and has limited commercial application in the building industry.
- Where used in CHP plants, fuel cells lead to more favourable heat-to-power ratios in CHPs, i.e. 1.5:1. This creates significant carbon reductions and opens CHP up to a wider range of applications (not just for high heat demand).

12.9.3 Key characteristics and key recommendations

When to use?	In the UK, there are very few examples of installed CHP fuel cells – mainly demonstration projects or field trials:
	• Woking Park fuel cell CHP: the 200 kWe fuel cell CHP provides electricity for lighting and heat for the swimming pool; it is combined with a thermal store, and PVs are included.[118]
	• Hydrogen Mini Grid System, Yorkshire,[119] uses a wind turbine to obtain hydrogen from electrolysis and stores it in fuel cells, which can then be used for hydrogen-fuelled cars and electricity for homes.
	• Current micro CHP field trials are exploring the potential to significantly increase micro CHPs' heat-to-power ratio.[120]
Key design recommendations	• use fuel cells as CHP fuel
	• size the fuel cell based on combined electrical, cooling and heating demand
How much space is required?	Similar to micro/macro CHP plus hydrogen storage.
What are the carbon reductions?	Manufacturers claim[121] an estimate of 40–50% CO_2 reduction of a typical UK home.
Anything else?	Storage issues: hydrogen is difficult to contain, and leakages can lead to combustion/explosions, particularly in closed buildings with electrical ignition.

12.9.4 Applicable legislation, guidance and further reading

• Bridgewater (2008), *The Off-grid Energy Handbook*, New Holland
• Efficient design of piled foundations for low-rise housing, Design guide – Arup, NHBC Foundation, 2010
• Energy Savings Trust, Domestic low and zero carbon technologies (2010)
• www.ukhfca.co.uk/the-industry/hydrogen/
• UK Hydrogen and Fuel Cell Association (UK HFCA)
• BS EN 62282-2:2004 Fuel cell technologies, Fuel cell modules
• BS EN 62282-3-2:2006 Fuel cell technologies, Stationary fuel cell power systems, Performance test methods

Notes

Chapter 1

1   Called the troposphere, to be exact.
2   Mackay (2008), *Sustainable Energy, Without the Hot Air*, UIT Cambridge Ltd, p.15. From primary source: Emission database for global atmospheric research (http://themasites.pbl.nl/en/themasites/edgar/index. html).
3   ibid.
4   ibid, pp.15, 16.
5   ibid, pp.16, 17 and calculated with directgov.transportdirect.info and www. mapcrow.info.
6   Edwards (2010), *Rough Guide to Sustainability*, RIBA and www.decc. gov.uk/assets/decc/Statistics/climate_change/1215-2009-final-uk-ghg-emissionsdata-tables.xls.
7   www.willmottdixongroup.co.uk/assets/b/r/briefing-note-14-embodied-energy.pdf and Developing a strategic approach to construction waste 20 year strategy draft for comment – 2006 www.bre.co.uk/filelibrary/df/rpts/waste/ConstructionWasteReport 240906.pdf.
8   IPCC (2007), *Zero Carbon Britain 2030*, CAT, p.39, UKCIP 09, p.09.
9   ibid.
10   UKCP 09, *Climate Projections for UK and Zero Carbon Britain 2030*, CAT, pp.1,2.
11   Jennings and Hulme (2010), UK newspaper (mis) representations of the potential for a collapse of the Thermohaline Circulation, *Area*, vol 42, 4, pp.222–456.
12   ibid.
13   ibid.
14   ibid, vol 42, issue 4, pp.444–456, December 2010 and Seager Richard, www.ldeo.columbia.edu/res/div/ocp/gs/.
15   Stern Review (2007), *The Economics of Climate Change*, Cambridge University Press; and CAT (2010), *Zero Carbon Britain 2030*.
16   CAT, *Zero Carbon Britain 2030*, p.2.

17   The term 'carbon' is used as a short form of CO_2, instead of the chemical compound carbon (C).
18   Climate Change Act 2008, Department of Energy & Climate change, www.decc. gov.uk; and UK Low Carbon Transition Plan (2009). Cuts based on 1990 levels.
19   Mackay (2008), *Sustainable Energy, Without the Hot Air*, UIT Cambridge Ltd; and https://spreadsheets. google. com/ccc?key=t8CL0fnzBR6 VLhRwsh-QZTw#gid=1 and http://en.wikipedia. org/wiki/List_of_ countries_by_carbon_dioxide_emissions.
20   Mackay (2008), *Sustainable Energy, Without the Hot Air*, UIT Cambridge Ltd, pp.15,16; and *Zero Carbon Britain 2030*, CAT, p.54, respectively.
21   Highlighted by research by the author and Stephen Choi.
22   *Building*, 4 Nov 2010, Low-carbon homes underperform, says report.
23   Boardman *et al.* (2005), *The 40% House*, Environmental Change Institute; Hadi & Halfhide (2010), *The Move to Low Carbon Design: Are designers taking the needs of building users into account?* BRE Trust; and Stevenson & Leaman (2010), 'Evaluating housing performance in relation to human behaviour: new challenges', *Building Research & Information*, 38: 5, 437–441.
24   www.guardian.co.uk/environment/2007/jun/19/china.usnews.
25   spreadsheets.google.com/ccc?key=t8CL0fnzBR6 VLhRwsh-QZTw#gid=1.
26   Climate Change Act 2008.
27   www. green.sustainablehomes.co.uk and www.breeam.org/page.jsp?id=86.
28   From CCC (2009), Chapter 1 Technical Appendix: Projecting global emissions, concentrations and temperatures, p.6.
29   Sassi (2006), *Strategies for Sustainable Architecture*, Taylor & Francis, p.7.
30   Edwards (2010), *Rough Guide to Sustainability*, RIBA/Earthscan, pix.

31 BRE + Royal Townplanning Institute, www.rtpi. org.uk.
32 Edwards (2010), *Rough Guide to Sustainability*, RIBA/Earthscan, pix.
33 www.corporatewatch.org and www.illegallogging. info/uploads/ FERNspecialreportlL.pdf.
34 Edwards (2010), *Rough Guide to Sustainability*, RIBA/Earthscan, pix.
35 Sassi (2006), *Strategies for Sustainable Architecture*, Taylor & Francis, p.7.
36 Based on comparison of EST data in CE 317, *Domestic Low & Zero Carbon Technologies*, 2010, p.10.
37 Zero Carbon Hub (2010), *Carbon Compliance – What Is The Appropriate Level for 2016?*, fig. 4.
38 Stevenson & Leaman (2010), 'Evaluating housing performance in relation to human behaviour: new challenges', *Building Research & Information*, 38: 5

Chapter 2

1 UKCP09: UK Climate Projections, July 2009. www. ukcip.org.uk http://ukcp09. defra.gov.uk/.
2 ibid.
3 ibid.
4 ibid.
5 ibid.
6 ibid.
7 Depending on sources, estimates range from 360 mm to 1–3 m or more by the end of this century.
8 Town and Country Planning Association (2007), *Climate Change Adaptation by Design*.
9 UKCP09, p.21; and July 2009 briefing seminar.
10 Based on UKCP09 data, taking into account medium and high emission scenarios, representing any lower or higher values respectively. Where only one figure, averages taken.
11 ibid.
12 ibid.
13 ibid.

14 Stern Review (2007), *The Economics of Climate Change*, Cambridge University Press.
15 ibid., pxv.

Chapter 3

1 Sustainable Neighbourhoods, Methodology-LDA design, 2005, www.plymouth.gov.uk/cd28_ methodology_sustainable_ neighbourhood_studies.pdf.
2 Randall (ed.) (2003), *Sustainable Urban Design, An Environmental Approach*, Spon Press, pp.21–22.
3 Barton & Tsourou (2000), *Healthy Urban Planning*, Taylor & Francis Ltd.
4 ibid.
5 derived from CLP, Live tables on land use change statistics www.communities. gov.uk/planningandbuilding/ planningbuilding/planningstatistics/ livetables/landusechange/; and www. doeni.gov.uk; www. birmingham.gov. uk; www.plymouth.gov.uk; http:// cardiff-consult.limehouse.co.uk/portal/ ldp/devplan/ldp; www.edinburgh. gov.uk; www.glasgow. gov.uk; www. highland.gov.uk; www.london.gov. uk/thelondonplan; http://manchester. limehouse.co.uk/portal.
6 Research by Pelsmakers, Borna and Konadu, 'Technologies for Sustainable Development Conference', Lausanne, 9 Feb 2010: 'Zero carbon Housing in dense urban areas: Can it be done? (and if so, how?) Case studies in UK, Kumasi (Ghana) and Teheran'. Also Choi, S., personal communication (2010–2011).
7 Derived from author's own research and from *Integrated Sustainable Design Solutions for Modular Neighbourhoods Developer Guidelines*, 2010, East Midlands Development Agency.
8 Wilson & Navaro, 'Driving to Green Buildings: The Transportation Energy Intensity of Buildings', 1 Sep, 2007, greenbuilding.com.

9   Based on, Llewellyn–Davies (2007), *Urban Design Compendium*, English Partnerships/The Housing Corporation, www.urbandesigncompendium.co.uk/and Jan Gehl (2008), *Life Between Buildings: Using Public Space,* Danish Architectural Press.

10 Jan Gehl (2008), *Life Between Buildings: Using Public Space,* Danish Architectural Press.

11 Llewellyn-Davies (2007), *Urban Design Compendium*, English Partnerships/The Housing Corporation, www.urbandesigncompendium.co.uk/.

12 Based on Crawford (2002), *Carfree Cities*, International Books; Llewellyn-Davies (2007), *Urban Design Compendium*, English Partnerships/The Housing Corporation, www.urbandesigncompendium.co.uk/and Jan Gehl (2008), *Life Between Buildings: Using Public Space*, Danish Architectural Press.

13 Derived from DEFRA UK 2009 final GHG emissions database, www.decc.gov.uk/assets/decc/Statistics/climate_change/1215–2009-final-uk-ghgemissions- data-tables.xls.

14 Sassi (2006), *Strategies for Sustainable Architecture,* Taylor & Francis, p.27.

15 Moughtin *et al.* (2009), *Urban Design: Health and the Therapeutic Environment*, Architectural Press, p.24.

16 Mass *et al.* (2006), Green space, urbanity & health: how strong is the relation? *Journal of Epidemiology and Community Health* 60 (2006):587–592; and Tzoulas (2007), 'Promoting ecosystem and human health in urban areas using green infrastructure: a literature review', *Landscape & Urban Planning* 81, Elsevier, pp.167–178.

17 Natural England's Accessible Natural Green Space Standard (ANGSt).

18 Llewellyn-Davies (2007), *Urban Design Compendium*, English Partnerships/The Housing Corporation, www.urbandesigncompendium.co.uk/

19 The Environment Agency, Science Report SC20061/SR6, The social impacts of heat waves, 2007; and BRE, Cooling buildings in London: overcoming the heat island, 2001

20 BRE, *Cooling buildings in London: overcoming the heat island,* 2001

21 ibid.

22 Dunster *et al.* (2008), *The ZEDbook*, Taylor and Francis, p.179; and Pelsmakers' own modelling

23 Littlefield (2007), *Metric Handbook*, Planning & design data, Thermal Environment pp.39–27.

24 Dunster *et al.* (2008), *The ZEDbook*, Taylor and Francis.

25 Littlefair, Santamouris *et al.* (2000), Environmental Site Layout Planning, BRE.

Chapter 4

1   CABE (2008), *Does Money Grow On Trees?*

2   Erell (2011), *Urban Microclimate: Designing the Spaces Between Buildings*, Earthscan Ltd, p.170.

3   ibid.

4   After research by Santamouris (2000), *Energy and Climate in the Urban Built Environment*, James & James Ltd; and Erell (2011), *Urban Microclimate: Designing the Spaces Between Buildings*, Earthscan Ltd.

5   After research by Ward (2004), *Energy and Environmental Issues for the Practising Architect*, Thomas Telford; Santamouris (2000), *Energy and Climate in the Urban Built Environment*, James & James Ltd; and Erell (2011), *Urban Microclimate: Designing the Spaces Between Buildings*, Earthscan Ltd.

6   www.livingroofs.org.

7   After research by Ward (2004), *Energy and environmental issues for the practising architect*, Thomas Telford; and Santamouris (2000), *Energy and Climate in the Urban Built Environment*,

James & James Ltd; and Erell (2011), *Urban microclimate, designing the spaces between buildings*, Earthscan Ltd.

8   Bache & MacAskill (1984), *Vegetation in Civil and Landscape Engineering*, Granada Publishing.

9   ibid.

10 ibid.

11 After research by Ward, *Energy and Environmental Issues for the Practising Architect*; and Santamouris (2000), *Energy and Climate in the Urban Built Environment*, James & James Ltd.

12 Beer & Higgins (1999), *Environmental Planning for Site Development*, Taylor & Francis, p.115.

13 After *Agroforestry Journal*, 'Trees as noise buffers', www.agroforestry.net.

14 ibid.

15 Erell (2011), *Urban Microclimate, Designing the Spaces Between Buildings*, Earthscan.

16 After research/text by Vernon *et al.* (2009), *Landscape Architect's Pocketbook*, Elsevier; Erell (2011), *Urban Microclimate, Designing the Spaces Between Buildings*; and Austin Williams 'The distance at which trees can affect buildings is quite significant', *The Architects' Journal*, 07.12.06, pp.44–46.

17 Defra (2008), *Populations of Butterflies in England*; and Defra (2008), *Populations of Wild Birds in England*.

18 Di Giulio (2009), 'Effects of habitat and landscape fragmentation on humans and biodiversity in densely populated landscapes', *Journal of Environmental Management* 90 (2009): 2959–2968.

19 Goddard (2009), 'Scaling up from gardens: biodiversity conservation in urban environments', *Trends in Ecology and Evolution*, Elsevier; and Cornelis 'Biodiversity relationships in urban and suburban parks in Flanders', *Landscape & Urban Planning* 69 (2004): pp.385–401.

20 Savard (2000), 'Biodiversity concepts and urban ecosystems', *Landscape & Urban Planning* 48, Elsevier pp.131–142;

and Bryant (2006), 'Urban landscape conservation and the role of ecological greenways at local and metropolitan scales', *Landscape & Urban Planning* 76: 23–44.

21 Baines (2009), *Ecobuild Talk*.

22 ibid.

23 Dearborn & Kark (2009), *Motivations for Conserving Urban Biodiversity, Conservation Biology*, vol 24. no 2: 432–440.

24 Williams (2010), *Biodiversity for Low and Zero Carbon Buildings: A Technical Guide for New Build*, RIBA Publishing.

25 www.greenspec.co.uk/building-products/batroost- bird-boxes/and Williams (2010), *Biodiversity for Low and Zero Carbon Buildings: A Technical Guide for New Build*, RIBA Publishing.

26 www.froglife.org/livingwater/.

27 www.froglife.org/documents/ CountrysideSurvey-PondsReport2007. pdf.

28 BARS action plans.

29 Brenneisen, S., Space for Urban Wildlife: Designing Green Roofs as Habitats in Switzerland. www. urbanhabitats.org/ v04n01/wildlife_full.html and www. urbanhabitats.org/v04n01/london_pdf.

30 www.livingroofs.org.uk/ index. php?option=com_ content&view=article&id=46.

31 www.foxleas.com/PDF/sparrows_07.pdf.

32 www.d4b.org.uk/keyConcepts/ birdBricks/index.asp.

33 Williams (2010), *Biodiversity for Low and Zero Carbon Buildings: A Technical Guide for New Build*, RIBA Publishing.

34 ibid.

35 www.greenroofs.com/projects/pview. php?id=549.

36 www.blackredstarts.org.uk/pages/ otherbirds. html.

37 Williams (2010), *Biodiversity for Low and Zero Carbon Buildings: A Technical Guide for New Build*, RIBA Publishing.

38 ibid.

39 BARS action plans.

40 www.urbanhabitats.org/v04n01/ london_pdf and www.livingroofs. org.uk/index. php?option=com_ content&view=article&id=46.

41 www.blackredstarts.org.uk/pages/ otherbirds. html.

42 Williams (2010), *Biodiversity for Low and Zero Carbon Buildings: A Technical Guide for New Build*, RIBA Publishing.

43 www.rspb.org.uk/wildlife/birdguide/ name/s/swallow/encouraging.aspx.

44 Williams (2010), *Biodiversity for Low and Zero Carbon Buildings: A Technical Guide for New Build*, RIBA Publishing.

45 ibid.

46 ibid.

47 ibid.

48 ibid.

49 www.rspb.org.uk/wildlife/birdguide/ name/s/songthrush/threats.aspx.

50 Williams (2010), *Biodiversity for Low and Zero Carbon Buildings: A Technical Guide for New Build,* RIBA Publishing, p.10.

51 ibid.

52 www.d4b.org.uk/keyConcepts/ birdBricks/index.asp; and Williams (2010), *Biodiversity for Low and Zero Carbon Buildings: A Technical Guide for New Build*, RIBA Publishing.

53 Williams (2010), *Biodiversity for Low and Zero Carbon Buildings: A Technical Guide for New Build*, RIBA Publishing.

54 http://lwt.elmbrook.eu/Species/Bats/ tabid/111/Default.aspx.

55 www.kentbatgroup.org.uk/.

56 Williams (2010), *Biodiversity for Low and Zero Carbon Buildings: A Technical Guide for New Build*, RIBA Publishing.

57 www.d4b.org.uk/keyConcepts/ birdBricks/index.asp.

58 Williams (2010), *Biodiversity for Low and Zero Carbon Buildings: A Technical Guide for New Build*, RIBA Publishing.

59 ibid.

60 www.britishhedgehogs.org.uk.

61 Williams (2010), *Biodiversity for Low and Zero Carbon Buildings: A Technical Guide for New Build*, RIBA Publishing.

62 www.d4b.org.uk/keyConcepts/ birdBricks/index.asp.

63 www.livingroofs.org.uk/ index. php?option=com_ content&view=article&id=46; and www.livingroofs.org.uk/bees-green-roofs.html.

64 Gaston (2005), 'Urban domestic gardens (II): experimental tests of methods for increasing biodiversity', *Biodiversity & Conservation* 14 (2005): 395–413.

65 Goddard (2009), 'Scaling up from gardens: biodiversity conservation in urban environments', *Trends in Ecology and Evolution*, Elsevier.

66 Nowak *et al.* (2002), Effects of urban tree management and species selection on atmospheric carbon, *Journal of Arboriculture* 28:3 (May 2002).

67 ibid.

68 Trees for the Future, 'How to calculate the amount of CO_2 sequestered in a tree per year', www.plant-trees. org.

69 Calculation method from US Department of Energy, 'Method for calculating carbon sequestration by trees in urban and suburban settings'; also supported by CAT, *Zero Carbon Britain 2030*, Land Use. Research courtesy of Nick Newman.

70 Calculation method from US Department of Energy, 'Method for calculating carbon sequestration by trees in urban and suburban settings'; also supported by CAT, *Zero Carbon Britain 2030*, Land Use. Research courtesy of Nick Newman and Dr Federico Calboli.

71 Rowe (2010), *Green Roofs as a Means of Pollution Abatement*, Elsevier.

72 ibid.

73 Press release: 'London's food "carbon footprint"', 2009, www.london.gov.uk.

74 ibid.

75 Food quantities based on 'Purchased quantities of household food and drink by Government Office Region and Country', Nov 2010, Defra, and on worst

case scenario travel distance and mode (air), to each city location. Research courtesy of Georgia Laganakou.

76 Yields documented from a north London allotment plot over two years by author.

77 ibid.

78 Tesco supermarket was chosen as typical supermarket. Each vegetable/fruit was allocated a journey from country of origin, to UK depot centre to sub-depot centre to city centre supermarket. Defra CO_2 emissions from transportation were used.

79 Based on research by author in a north London allotment, over two years. Food mile calculations courtesy of Georgia Laganakou.

80 www.north-herts.gov.uk/the_food_we_waste_wrap_report-3.pdf, Food waste report v2.

81 www.recycleforyourcommunity.com/where_you_live/havering/compost/in_your_garden.aspx.

82 www.homecomposting.org.uk/composting/buy_bin.php

Chapter 5

1 www.communities.gov.uk/planningandbuilding/planningbuilding/planningstatistics/livetables/landusechange/.

2 RIBA, ICE (2010), 'Facing up to Rising Sea Levels', http://buildingfutures.org.uk/events/facing-up-to-risingsea- levels.

3 'Revised Statement of Principles on the Provision of Flood Insurance', www.abi.org.uk/Publications/revised_statement_of_Principles_on_the_Provision_ of_Flood_insurance1.aspx.

4 *The World Factbook*, https://www.cia.gov/library/publications/the-world-factbook/geos/uk.html.

5 *Planning Policy Statement 25: Development and Flood Risk* (2010), www.communities. gov.uk/documents/planningandbuilding/pdf/planningpolicystatement25.pdf.

6 *Planning Portal: Paving Your Garden*, www.planningportal.gov.uk/permission/commonprojects/pavingfrontgarden/.

7 CLG, 'Improving the flood performance of new buildings, Flood resilient construction' May 2007, Consortium managed by CIRIA, London www.planningportal.gov.uk/uploads/br/flood_performance. pdf.

8 Adapted from Randall (2003), *Sustainable Urban Design: Environmental Approach*, Spon, p.38.

9 ibid., p.44.

10 ibid., p.40.

11 ibid.

12 ibid.

13 ibid.

14 Metered water usage figures derived from www.ofwat.gov.uk (England and Wales), www. watercommission.co.uk (Scotland) and www.niwater. com (Northern Ireland), average occupants per household: 2.4 persons; Northern Ireland unmetered figures used.

15 Fidar *et al.* (2010), *Environmental Implications of Water Efficient Micro Components in Residential Buildings*, Elsevier; and www.water.org.uk/home/news/press-releases/sustainable-water/sustainability2008.pdf. The carbon footprint of this water usage is around 0.97 gCO_2 per litre of water used.

16 Clarke *et al.* (2009), *Quantifying the Energy and Carbon Effects of Water Saving: Full Technical Report*, EST/EA, p.35.

17 From the author's own calculations based on 55 kWh/m^2a hot water demand, and usage of 0.060 kWh/litres of hot water (but only for showers and baths) from Critchley and Phipps (2007), *Water Efficient Showers*, Liverpool John Moores University for United Utilities, p.5.

18 Adapted from www.waterwise.org.uk and the author's own use (taking into account 5-min shower and

foot-bathing), and similar to Clarke *et al.* (2009), *Quantifying the Energy and Carbon Effects of Water Saving Full Technical Report,* EST/EA.

19 The author's own estimate based on actual water use figures after 5-min shower. Bath water use adapted to account for higher number of showers.

20 www.waterwise.org.uk – adapted from daily water consumption, average of 0.39 baths per person per day.

21 Calculated from 1–3 litres savings when using a bag from www.dry-planet.com and a hippo bag (www. hippo-the-watersaver.co.uk) respectively.

22 Assuming five flushes per day.

23 Such as www.roca.com.es and www. sanlamere. co.uk. Around 30% of flush water comes from hand wash basin.

24 Vacuum toilets: www.evds.org.uk.

25 Related to water consumption from the mains and removal to treatment plant.

26 Uses around 4 litres per min.

27 Uses around 6 litres per min (mixer).

28 From SAP(2009), *C3.2 Energy for Pumping.*

29 Environmental Change Unit (1997), *Energy and Environment Programme,* 2 MtC Report, University of Oxford, p.97, www.eci.ox.ac.uk.

30 www.eci.ox.ac.uk/research/energy/downloads/2 mtc.pdf.

31 Based on average performance and water usage between three washing machines – Hotpoint WT965, AEG LL1620, John Lewis JLWM1604.

32 Environmental Change Unit (1997), *Energy and Environment Programme,* 2 MtC Report, University of Oxford, p.79, www.eci.ox.ac.uk.

33 Based on average performance and water usage between three dishwashers: Neff S5453, Siemens SE60T392GB, Miele G1552 SC.

34 Based on average 250 cycles/year, Environmental Change Unit (1997), *Energy and Environment Programme,* 2 MtC Report, University of Oxford, p.22.

35 Based on operational energy for dishwasher and water heating for hand washing.

36 Based on water supply, treatment, water heating and operational energy.

37 Hassel, C., (2008), Water and the Code for Sustainable Homes, *Green Building Magazine* Autumn 2008, pp.26–30

38 www.water.org.uk.

39 Kwok *et al.* (2007), *Green Studio Handbook,* Elsevier.

40 www.cat.org.uk.

41 BS 8525-1:2010 Greywater Systems. Code of practice.

42 Based on each system operational intensities kWh/m3 adopted from: Parkes *et al.* (2010), 'Energy and carbon implications of rainwater harvesting and greywater recycling', Environment Agency, www.environmentagency. gov. uk.

43 www.wwuk.co.uk/grow.htm.

44 Clarke *et al.* (2009), *Quantifying the Energy and Carbon Effects of Water Saving Full Technical Report,* (EST/EA), p.51.

45 CIRIA C539 (2001), *Rainwater and Greywater Use in Buildings,* p.71.

46 Data adapted from supplier: Pontos Heatcycle http://pro.hansgrohe-int.com/assets/global/pontos_ heatcycle_en.pdf.

47 Derived from Kinkade-Levario (2007), 'Design for water', *New Society,* pp.190–191.

48 Based on each system's operational intensities kWh/m³ adopted from: Parkes *et al.* (2010), *Energy and Carbon Implications of Rainwater Harvesting and Greywater Recycling,* Environment Agency.

49 ibid.

50 Adapted from CIRIA C539 (2001), *Rainwater and Greywater Use in Buildings.*

Chapter 6

1   Based on Julia Park (2010), *Levitt Bernstein's Easi-Guide to Good Housing Practice*.

2   ibid.

3   Based on EcoHomes and Code for Sustainable Homes requirements.

4   www.hse.gov.uk/temperature/thermal/explained.htm and BS EN ISO 7730.

5   ibid.

6   CIBSE Guide B, Heating, ventilating, air conditioning and refrigeration, 2005, pp.2–15.

7   ibid.

8   Littlefield(2008), *Metric Handbook: Planning and Designing Data*, Architectural Press.

9   CIBSE Guide A, Environmental design 2006.

10 Hacker *et al.* (2005), *Beating the Heat: Keeping UK Buildings Cool in a Warming Climate*. UKCIP Briefing Report, UKCIP, Oxford, p.8.

11 Laurence *et al.* (2000), 'Saving lives during extreme summer weather', *British Medical Journal*; and Vandentorren *et al.* (2006), 'August 2003 Heat wave in France: risk factors for death of elderly people living at home', *European Journal of Public Health*, 16(6), pp.583–591.

12 Hacker *et al.* (2005), *Beating the Heat: Keeping UK Buildings Cool in a Warming Climate*. UKCIP Briefing Report, UKCIP, Oxford, p.17.

13 CIBSE TM 36, Climate change and the indoor environment: impacts and adaptation, 2005; and CIBSE Guide A Environmental design, 2006.

14 Vandentorren, *et al.* (2006), 'August heat wave in France: risk factors for death of elderly people living at home', *European Journal of Public Health*, 16(6), pp.583–591.

15 Building Regulations 2010, Conservation of fuel and power, Approved Document L: Criterion 3, England and Wales; Scotland; Technical Handbooks 2009 – Domestic Energy Section 6, Scotland; and DFP Technical Booklet F1: 2006 – Conservation of fuel and power in dwellings, N. Ireland.

16 Graves *et al.* (2011), *Cooling Buildings in London: Overcoming the Heat Island*, BRE 2001, p.21.

17 Based on research by Jessica Eyers and Hastings *et al.* (2007), *Sustainable Solar Housing, Volume 2, Exemplary Buildings and Technologies*, Earthscan.

18 V. Olgyay (1992), *Design with Climate: A Bioclimatic Approach to Architectural Regionalism*, Van Nostrand Reinhold, New York.

19 Derived from Erell *et al.* (2011), *Urban Microclimate, Designing the Spaces Between Buildings*, Earthscan London.

20 Sun data www.gaisma.com/en/location/belfast.html and http://aa.usno.navy.mil/data/docs/AltAz.php Astronomical Applications Dept. U.S. Naval Observatory, Washington, DC 20392–5420.

21 BS 8206–2:2008 Lighting for buildings – Part 2: Code of practice for Daylighting, BSI 2008.

22 2010 L1a (new dwellings) From L1a.

23 BS 8206–2:2008 Lighting for buildings – Part 2: Code of practice for Daylighting, BSI 2008.

24 CIBSE, Guide F Energy efficiency in Buildings, 2004.

25 Thermie Programme of the European Commision DGXVII (1999), *A Green Vitruvius: Sustainable Architectural Design*, James and James Science Publishing.

26 BS 8206–2:2008 Lighting for buildings – Part 2: Code of practice for Daylighting, BSI 2008, Table A.1 Approximate values of the reflectance of light, p.33.

27 Stevenson and Williams (2007), *Sustainable Housing Design Guide for Scotland*, Communities Scotland.

28 Dye and McEvoy (2008), *Environmental Construction Handbook*, RIBA Publishing.

29 Comfort (2006), CIBSE Knowledge Series.

30 Hacker *et al.* (2007), 'Embodied and operational carbon emissions from housing: a case study on the effects of thermal mass and climate change', *Energy and Buildings* 40(2008), pp.375–384, Elsevier, 2007.

31 Smith (2006), *Architecture in a Climate of Change*, Architectural Press.

32 Derived from Martin & Goswami (2005), *Solar Energy Pocket Reference*, Earthscan.

33 Hacker *et al.* (2007), 'Embodied and operational carbon emissions from housing: a case study on the effects of thermal mass and climate change', *Energy and Buildings* 40(2008), pp.375–384, Elsevier, 2007.

34 Zero Carbon Hub (2010), *Carbon Compliance for Tomorrow's New Homes*, Topic 3, Future climate change.

35 www.concretecentre.com/online_services/design_tools/dynamic_thermal_m.aspx.

36 www.woodforgood.com/the_facts.html.

37 Hacker *et al.* (2007), Embodied and operational carbon emissions from housing: a case study on the effects of thermal mass and climate change, *Energy and Buildings* 40(2008), pp.375–384, Elsevier, 2007.

38 Building Regulations England and Wales (2010), 2000- Ventilation, Approved Document F.

39 Randall *et al.* (2006), *Environmental Design: An Introduction for Architects and Engineers*, Taylor & Francis.

40 BS 5925: 1991Code of practice for ventilation principles and designing for natural ventilation.

41 Feist *et al.* (2007), *Passive House Planning Package*, Passivhaus Institut.

42 Code for Sustainable Homes, *Impact assessment*, Dec 2009; CIBSE Guide B, *Heating, ventilating, air conditioning and refrigeration*, 2005; and CIBSE TM23: *Testing buildings for air leakage*, 2000.

43 Adapted with SAP 09 fuel intensity figures, from a CarbonLite Information Paper, 2009, Comparing energy use and CO_2 emissions from natural ventilation and MVHR in a Passivhaus House.

44 be.passive 05, autumn 2010, p.37.

45 C. Yu and D. Crump (2002), VOC emissions from building products, Sources, testing and emission data, Centre for Safety, Health and Environment, BRE Environment Division.

Chapter 7

1 Dunster, B., (2003) *From A to ZED*, Realising Zero (fossil) energy developments, Surrey, www.zedfactory.com

2 Willmot Dixon 2010, Embodied Energy Briefing Note.

3 Including energy needed for MVHR, compared to Scottish building regulations and based on a typical 100 m^2 house; and based on a CarbonLite Information Paper, 2009, Comparing energy use and CO_2 emissions from natural ventilation and MVHR in a Passivhaus house.

4 Sartori *et al.* (2007), 'Energy use in the life cycle of conventional and low energy buildings, a review article', *Energy and Buildings* 39(2007), pp.249–257, Elsevier.

5 2010 Guidelines to Defra/DECC's GHG Conversion Factors for Company Reporting Produced by AEA for the Department of Energy and Climate Change (DECC) and the Department for Environment, Food and Rural Affairs (Defra) Version 1.2.1 Final Updated: 06/10/2010, Annex 7 – Freight Transport Conversion Tables.

6 R Evans, R Haryott, *et al.* (1998), *The Long Term Costs of Owning and Using Buildings*, Royal Academy of Engineering, p.6.

7 Based on Lazarus (2003), *Beddington Zero (Fossil) Energy Development, Construction Materials Report, Toolkit for*

Carbon Neutral Developments – Part 1, BioRegional Development Group, 2003.

8 Practical solutions for sustainable construction, Reclaimed building products guide: A guide to procuring reclaimed building products and materials for use in construction projects, Waste and Resources Action Programme, www.wrap.org.uk/.

9 Hurley *et al.* (2001), Deconstruction and reuse of construction materials, BRE 2001.

10 Practical solutions for sustainable construction, Reclaimed building products guide: A guide to procuring reclaimed building products and materials for use in construction projects, Waste and Resources Action Programme, www.wrap.org.uk/.

11 Institute of Civil Engineers (ICE) (2008), *Demolition Protocol*.

12 Practical solutions for sustainable construction, Reclaimed building products guide: A guide to procuring reclaimed building products and materials for use in construction projects, Waste and Resources Action Programme, www.wrap.org.uk/.

13 ibid.

14 ibid.

15 ibid.

16 Hurley *et al.* (2001), *Deconstruction and Reuse of Construction Materials*, BRE.

17 Institute of Civil Engineers (ICE), *Demolition Protocol*, 2008.

18 BRE (2007) *Modern Methods of Construction (MMC) in Housing: Designing for Manufacture*.

19 Berge (2009), *The Ecology of Building Materials*, Elsevier.

20 Consumer Protection (2003), No. 271, *The Creosote (Prohibition on use and marketing) Regulations 2003*.

21 'Executive summary: Fire safety in London, Fire risks in London's tall and timber-framed buildings', Dec 2010 from www.london.gov.uk/who-runslondon/the-london-assembly/publications/housingplanning/fire-safety-in-london.

22 Hammond and Jones (2011), 'Inventory of Carbon and Energy (ICE)', version 2 database, Bath University.

23 www.bbacerts.co.uk/PDF/S029PS1i3.pdf.

24 Bevan and Woolley (2008), *Hemp Lime Construction: A Guide to Building with Hemp Lime Composites*, IHS BRE Press 2008.

25 www.limecrete.co.uk/.

26 www.limetechnology.co.uk/hemcrete.htm.

27 www.limecrete.co.uk/.

28 www.limecrete.co.uk/.

29 www.limetechnology.co.uk/hemcrete.htm.

30 Berge (2009), *The Ecology of Building Material*, Elsevier.

31 ibid.

32 Baker Laporte *et al.* (2001), *Prescriptions for a Healthy House: A Practical Guide for Architects, Builders and Homeowners*, New Society Publishers, Canada.

33 Berge (2009), *The Ecology of Building Materials*, Elsevier.

34 Practical solutions for sustainable construction, Reclaimed building products guide: A guide to procuring reclaimed building products and materials for use in construction projects, Waste and Resources Action Programme www.wrap.org.uk/.

35 All embodied carbon data from Hammond and Jones (2011), 'Inventory of Carbon and Energy (ICE)', version 2 database, Bath University.

36 www.bfrc.org/pdf/GGF%20calculations%20leaflet.pdf.

37 www.greenspec.co.uk/glossary-r.php#reflective.

38 Ward (2004), *Energy and Environmental Issues for the Practising Architect*, p.74.

39 ibid.

40 www.greenspec.co.uk

41 Hastings *et al.* (2007), *Sustainable Solar Housing, Volume 2, Exemplary Buildings and Technologies*, Earthscan.

42 ibid.

43   Built performance vs. design performance – from Topic 4 – Zero Carbon Hub.

44   Feist *et al.* (2007), *Passive House Planning Package*, Passivhaus Institut.

45   Courtesy of Brian Murphy, www. greenspec.co.uk.

46   Courtesy of Brian Murphy, www.greenspec.co.uk.

47   CAT, Energy Efficiency in the Home, www.cat.org.uk.

48   Paul Jennings, 'Airtightness for Passivhaus', Student Passivhaus Conference, UEL, Paul Jennings, Air Leakage Detailing and Awareness Services, October 2010.

49   Derived from CIBSE Technical Memoranda TM23:2000.

50   EST(2006), *Energy Efficient Ventilation in Dwellings: A Guide for Specifiers*.

51   Assessment of Energy Efficiency, Impact of Building Regulations Compliance, BRE/EST, 2004; and Zero Carbon Hub, *Carbon Compliance for Tomorrow's New Homes*, Topic 4, Closing the gap between designed and built performance.

52   Hastings *et al.* (2007), *Sustainable Solar Housing, Volume 2, Exemplary Buildings and Technologies*, Earthscan.

53   Heath (2009), *Green Building Magazine*, 44–45.

54   Paper submitted to PLEA 2011: 'Cost of retrofitting to Passivhaus standards' (Baeli, Pelsmakers).

55   IPHA, *Active for More Comfort: The Passive House*, 2010 and personal communication with bere: architects.

Chapter 8

1   *RIBA Climate Change Toolkit*, 01 Climate Change Briefing, p.9.

2   Boardman *et al.* (2005), *40% House*, Environmental Change Institute.

3   *RIBA Climate Change Toolkit*, 01 Climate Change Briefing.

4   The English House Condition Survey, www. communities.gov.uk.

5   EST and the Energy Efficiency Partnership for Homes, 2009.

6   www.energysavingtrust.org.uk/business/Business/Housing-professionals.

7   The English House Condition Survey, www. communities.gov.uk.

8   Results average of typical Victorian terraced house as modelled in different UK regions in PHPP by author. This also correlates with English House Condition Survey, which found from actual surveys that pre-1919 houses have 480 kWh/(m²a) total energy usage, of which around 90–110 kWh/(m²a) is for electricity/hot water and cooking (40% house and EST), and this brings space heat demand to around 370–390 kWh/(m²a).

9   46 kWh/(m²a) for semi-detached and detached dwellings is allowed as maximum heatload – Zero Carbon Hub.

10   EnerPHit standard is a Passivhaus Institute standard for building refurbishment.

11   The carbon intensity for Passivhaus heatload has been calculated with 0.517 kgCO₂ per kWh/(m²a) of heatload as the heatload may be met through electricity.

12   ibid.

13   Research undertaken by author using UKCIP climate predictions for eight locations – results averaged across UK.

14   Estimated by author, based on Gulf Stream cutting out and comparing UK city locations with other northern European climates near coast which are not as favourably influenced by Gulf Stream, for example Manchester vs Hamburg.

15   Marion Baeli, Pelsmakers, (2010), 'The cost of retrofitting to Passivhaus standards', UEL, paper PLEA conference 2011.

16   ibid.

17   Adapted from research at MA sustainability and design, UEL, by Paschal Volney, 2010.

18 Location factors in costing have not been allowed for as these are unpredictable, but the BCIS *Greener Home Price Guide* (p.17) asserts that prices in Wales are cheapest (0.96) and those in Greater London most expensive (1.14); costs are based on 100% or a factor of 1 or towards the upper end – i.e. Greater London used as a basis as case studies used are based there.

Chapter 9

1   Peter Acteson Rook (2006), 'Green roofs', Thesis Research, University of East London.
2   Kosareo and Ries (2006), *Comparative Environmental Life Cycle Assessment of Green Roofs*, Department of Civil and Environmental Engineering, University of Pittsburgh, USA.
3   McLarenet *et al.* (1998). *Tomorrow's World*, Earthscan.
4   Hutchins (2011), *UK Building Blackbook: The Cost and Carbon Guide, Small and Major Works*, Franklin and Andrews.
5   Banting *et al.* (2005), *Report on the Environmental Benefits and Costs of Green Roof Technology for the City of Toronto*, p.20.
6   Dunster (2009), *The Zedbook*, Taylor & Francis.

Chapter 10

1   www.eci.ox.ac.uk/research/energy/40house/index.php.
2   Research derived from *40% House* (pp.41, 61) and EST, *Domestic Low and Zero Carbon Technologies*, p.10, energy uses based on Part L 2006 and average UK electricity consumption of 4700 kWh per year.
3   Domestic energy benchmarks based on *40% House*, English House Condition Survey and energy modelling by author; non-domestic energy benchmarks based on CIBSE Guide F.

4   www.carbontruststandard.com/pages/Assessment-criteria and www.decc.gov.uk/en/content/cms/what_we_do/lc_uk/crc/crc.aspx#more_ about_CRC.
5   SAP fuel CO_2 intensity methodology questioned in Zero Carbon Hub (2010), Topic 2 – Carbon intensity of fuels.
6   SAP (2009), *The Government's Standard Assessment Procedure for Energy Rating of Dwellings*, p.157.
7   Fuel factors can be found from Defra/DECC www.defra.gov.uk/environment/business/reporting/conversion-factors.htm. Also referred to as carbon dioxide emission factor. Other EU countries' emissions can also be obtained and many more fuel factors.
8   Office for National Statistics, UK.
9   Energy Savings Trust (2004), *Community Heating: A Guide*.
10 Author's own experience and NHBC (2009), *Community Heating and Combined Heat and Power*.
11 Based on SAP (2009), *The Government's Standard Assessment Procedure for Energy Rating of Dwellings*.
12 www.energysavingtrust.org.uk/Energy-savingassumptions and www.energysavingtrust.org.uk/Home-improvements-and-products/Home-appliances. Carbon emissions adapted to SAP 2009 CO_2 electricity intensity.
13 Table courtesy of Cristina Blanco Lion.
14 Towards a low carbon future, DECC.
15 DECC, *The UK Low Carbon Transition Plan*.
16 www.fitariffs.co.uk/eligible/levels/.
17 www.decc.gov.uk/en/content/cms/news/PN2011_023/PN2011_023.aspx.
18 www.biomassenergycentre.org.uk

Chapter 11

1 http://wales.gov.uk/topics/ sustainabledevelopment/design/ zerocarbonhub/?lang=en

2 Recommended in the Sullivan Report (2009), *Zero Carbon Homes: An Introductory Guide for House builders*, NHBC, p.19 (2016/17: CSH level 5 and zero carbon by 2030).

3 Courtesy Stephen Choi.

4 From Zero Carbon Hub (2010), *Carbon Compliance: What is the appropriate level for 2016?* Interim Report.

5 Zero Carbon Hub (2010), *Carbon Compliance for Tomorrow's New Homes: A Review of the Modelling Tool and Assumptions* – Topic 5, How the performance standard should be expressed, p.25.

6 UKGBC, Zero Carbon Task Group Report (2008), 'The Definition of Zero Carbon', unpublished research by Pelsmakers and Choi.

7 Page 61 of the consultation document: www.communities.gov.uk/ publications/planningandbuilding/ futureofcodeconsultation,.

8 Zero Carbon Hub (2011), *Carbon Compliance: Setting an Appropriate Limit for Zero Carbon New Homes, Findings and Recommendations*; summarised from East Midlands Development Agency (2010), *Integrated Sustainable Design Solutions for Modular Neighbourhoods Developer Guidelines*, pp.63–81, and similar figures for zero carbon from Zero Carbon Hub (2010), *Carbon Compliance: What is the Appropriate Level for 2016?*, Fig. 4.

9 Detailed guidance from. www.hmrc. gov.uk/sdlt/reliefs-exemptions/ overview.htm#14.

10 www.nidirect.gov.uk/index/property- and-housing/buying-selling-and- renting-a-home/selling-your-home-1/ index/information-and-services/ property-and-housing/rates/help-with- paying-yourrates/zero-and-low-carbon- homes.htm.

11 Summarised from *Integrated Sustainable Design Solutions for Modular Neighbourhoods Developer Guidelines, 2010*, East Midlands Development Agency

12 ibid.

13 Approximate densities derived from Levitt (2010), *The Housing Design Handbook: A Guide to Good Practice*, Routledge, pp.75–76.

14 Zero Carbon Hub (2010), *Carbon Compliance: What is the Appropriate Level for 2016?*; and East Midlands Development Agency (2010), *Integrated Sustainable Design Solutions for Modular Neighbourhoods Developer Guidelines*.

Chapter 12

1 DECC, *The UK Low Carbon Transition Plan*.

2 BSRIA, compiled by AM Holley, B Hirst and A Giles (1998), *Future Market Potential for Small Scale Air Conditioning in the UK*, Building Services Research and Information Association, Bracknell, Nov 1998; Pathan *et al.* (2008), *UK Domestic Air Conditioning: A Study of Occupant Use and Energy Efficiency*.

3 CIBSE Guide F (2004), *Energy Efficiency in Buildings*, Section 7.2.

4 Pathan *et al.* (2008), *UK Domestic Air Conditioning: A Study of Occupant Use and Energy Efficiency*.

5 Often LZC technologies are compared to the lowest efficiency boilers (which no longer meet building regulations) and are compared to this to then calculate carbon savings. This is unrealistic and deceptive. A 90% efficient boiler has been used for the purposes of the calculations in this pocketbook.

6 www.energysavingtrust.org.uk/ Generate-yourown- energy/ Hydroelectricity.

7   The British Hydropower Association, A
    guide to UK mini-hydro developments,
    January 2005 www.british-hydro.org/
    mini-hydro/infopage862f. html?infoid
    =359.

8   Energy Savings Trust (2010), *Domestic
    Low and Zero Carbon Technologies*, p.19.

9   Bridgewater (2008), *The Off-Grid Energy
    Handbook*, New Holland.

10 The British Hydropower Association, A
    guide to UK mini-hydro developments,
    January 2005 www.british-hydro.org/
    mini-hydro/infopage862f. html?infoid
    =359.

11 ibid.

12 Kwok *et al.* (2006), *Green Studio
    Handbook*, Architectural Press.

13 British Hydropower Association, 'A
    guide to UK mini-hydro developments,
    January 2005' www.british-hydro.
    org/mini-hydro/infopage862f.
    html?infoid=359.

14 Energy Savings Trust (2010), *Domestic
    Low and Zero Carbon Technologies*, p.19.

15 ibid.; and www.energysavingtrust.
    org.uk/Generate-your-own-energy/
    Hydroelectricity.

16 www.energysavingtrust.org.uk/
    Generate-yourown-energy/
    Hydroelectricity.

17 www.therenewableenergycentre.co.uk/
    waveand-tidal-power/.

18 ibid.

19 Mackay (2008), *Sustainable Energy,
    Without the Hot Air*, UIT Cambridge Ltd,
    pp.66, 268.

20 Warwick Wind Trials, Final Report,
    2008, Official NOABL wind speed data
    used. SAP 2009 also has wind speed
    reduction factors, p.81.

21 ibid.

22 '1 kW turbine' means that it will
    produce 1 kilowatt of power at a
    specific wind speed, usually greater
    than 10 m/s; this wind speed will never
    be achieved in an urban area – hence
    the 1 kW turbine produces much less
    than 1 kW!

23 Kwok *et al.* (2007), *Green Studio
    Handbook*, Architectural Press, p.204.

24 Warwick Wind Trials, Final Report, 2008,
    www.warwickwindtrials.org.uk/2.html.

25 www.bwea.com.

26 Adapted from Kwok *et al.* (2007), *Green
    Studio Handbook*, Architectural Press.

27 Warwick Wind Trials: Final Report, 2008,
    www. warwickwindtrials.org.uk/2.html.

28 Averages obtained and derived from
    Warwick Wind Trials, Final Report, 2008;
    mean electricity production = 94 kWh/
    year at mean urban wind speeds of 2.5
    m/s and typical 130 kWh/year at 3 m/s
    from Carbon Trust CTC738, p.10.

29 Average of around 800 kWh/year from
    Hall, *The Green Building Bible, Volume 1*,
    p.329 (750 kWh/year); Warwick Wind
    Trials, Final Report, 2008 (869 kWh/
    year); and Energy Savings Trust, (2010)
    Domestic and Low Carbon Technologies,
    p.18 (750 kWh/year for rural 1 kW
    turbine).

30 Carbon Trust CTC738, pp.10, 16.

31 BRE (2007), *Micro Wind Turbines in Urban
    Environments: An Assessment*.

32 Hutchins (2011), *UK Building Blackbook:
    The Cost and Carbon Guide, Small and
    Major Works*, Franklin and Andrews.

33 www.bwea.com.

34 Fthenakis and Alsema (2004),
    *Photovoltaics Energy Payback Times,
    Greenhouse Gas Emissions and External
    Costs: 2004*.

35 Adapted from www.solsticeenergy.
    co.uk/photovoltaics.htm.

36 DTI (2006), *PV Domestic Field Trial, Final
    Technical Report*, p.93.

37 Boxwell (2010), *Solar Electricity
    Handbook*, Green Stream Publishing,
    p.58; and Harper (2009), *Domestic Solar
    Energy*, Crowood Press, p.50.

38 Based on author's own calculations;
    similar figures from p.200, Feilden
    Clegg Bradley, *Environmental Design
    Handbook*, and *PV Domestic Field Trial,
    Final Technical Report (2006)*, p.94,
    DTI (798 kWh/kWp – roughly 106

kWh/m² with 1 kWp = 7.5 m²); *Green Building Magazine*, 'Zero Carbon in the City', p.17 (Winter 2010) and *Green Building Magazine* (Autumn 2009), 'Electricity from solar – a full year of data', Jerry Clark, p.41 – measured output 1060 kWh/m²a for 10 m² of PV (author derived PV area from Sanyo manufacturer).

39   Hammond (2011), ICE version 2.

40   ibid.

41   Averages derived and adapted to UK scenario from Fthenakis and Alsema (2004), *Photovoltaics Energy Payback Times, Greenhouse Gas Emissions and External Costs* and 'PV FAQ', What is the Energy Payback for PV?, US Department of Energy Office of Energy Efficiency and Renewable Energy.

42   Hutchins (2011), *UK Building Blackbook: The Cost and Carbon Guide, Small and Major Works*, Franklin and Andrews.

43   www.aweenergy.com/solar.php and BICS, The Greener Home Price Guide.

44   www.greenspec.co.uk.

45   Calculated based on 20% increased efficiencies from PV as reported by New Form Energy. Similar to research by Santbergen *et al*. Detailed analysis of the energy yield of systems with covered sheet-and-tube PVT collectors, Netherlands, 2010 (Table 2, p.6: 110 kWh/m²a electrical energy and 266.5 Kwh/m²a thermal energy).

46   Hutchins (2011), *UK Building Blackbook: The Cost and Carbon Guide, Small and Major Works*, Franklin and Andrews.

47   www.cibsejournal.com/cpd/2009–02/.

48   ibid.

49   www.greenspec.co.uk.

50   Hammond *et al*. (2008), 'Integrated appraisal of micro generators: methods and applications'. *Proceedings of the Institution of Civil Engineers – Energy*, 161 (2), pp.73–86.

51   Carbon Trust, *Technology Fact Sheet*.

52   Zero Carbon Hub, www.zerocarbonhub.org

53   Carbon Trust, *Technology Fact Sheet*.

54   www.greenspec.co.uk/biomass.php.

55   Carbon Trust, *Micro-CHP Accelerator* + own calculations.

56   Carbon Trust (2007), *Micro-CHP Accelerator: Interim Report*.

57   Carbon Trust, *Introducing Combined Heat and Power*.

58   Energy Savings Trust (2010), *Domestic Low and Zero Carbon Technologies*, p.28.

59   Hexis.com.

60   Carbon Trust (2005), *Micro-CHP Accelerator, Impact of Micro-CHP Systems on Domestic Sector CO_2 Emissions*, Peacock and Newborough (2005) and *Effect of Heatsaving Measures on the CO_2 Savings Attributable to Micro Combined Heat and Power (mCHP) Systems in UK Dwellings* (2007); and author's own calculations.

61   Based on author's own calculations and similar to findings by Carbon Trust (2007), *Micro-CHP Accelerator: Interim Report*, when adjusted to new SAP 2009 fuel intensity data and in line with Peacock and Newborough (2005), and *Effect of Heatsaving Measures on the CO_2 Savings Attributable to Micro Combined Heat and Power (mCHP) Systems in UK Dwellings* (2007).

62   ibid.

63   Carbon Trust, *Micro-CHP Accelerator, Impact of Micro-CHP Systems on Domestic Sector CO_2 Emissions*, Peacock and Newborough (2005), *Effect of Heatsaving Measures on the CO_2 Savings Attributable to Micro Combined Heat and Power (mCHP) Systems in UK Dwellings* (2007); and author's own calculations.

64   Large CHP units run on woodchips; typical plant from www.biomasschp.co.uk. Smaller CHPs usually on wood pellets, determined by storage facilities.

65   Calculations based on 30% electricity from renewables by 2020 – so 0.239 kgCO₂/kWh.

66   Energy Savings Trust (2010), *Domestic Low and Zero Carbon Technologies*, p.32.

67 ibid., p.28.

68 BCIS, *The Greener Home Price Guide*.

69 http://chp.decc.gov.uk/cms/reliability/.

70 Carbon Trust (2010), *Introducing Combined Heat and Power* (CTV044).

71 Based on author's own calculations: 415 kgCO₂/dwelling based on 500 dwellings and 80% efficiency with heat-to-power ratio 1.5:1, compared to gas boiler efficiency of 88–90% and taking SAP 2009 heat distribution losses into account at 0.036 kgCO₂/kWh of heat.

72 Large CHP units run on woodchips; typical plant from www.biomasschp.co.uk; smaller CHPs usually on wood pellets, determined by storage facilities.

73 Energy Savings Trust (2010), *Domestic Low and Zero Carbon Technologies*, pp.27,37.

74 ibid.

75 Adapted to 2010 costs from GLA Renewable Energy toolkit, £2730/kWe (2004 prices).

76 Defra Technical Guidance: Screening assessment for biomass boilers 2008, http://uk-air.defra.gov.uk/reports/cat18/0806261519_methods.pdf.

77 Zero Carbon Hub, www.zerocarbonhub.org.

78 Estimates based on Energy Savings Trust (2010), *Domestic Low and Zero Carbon Technologies*, p.20.

79 www.buildingforafuture.co.uk/autumn03/wood_pellets_page_2.php.

80 BCIS, *The Greener Homes Price Guide*, RICS.

81 Energy Savings Trust (2010), *Domestic Low and Zero Carbon Technologies*.

82 www.biomassenergycentre.org.uk.

83 Prices dated Dec 2010; for latest prices go to www.biomassenergycentre.org.uk.

84 ibid.

85 www.carbontrust.co.uk/SiteCollectionDocuments/Various/Emerging%20technologies/Current%20Focus%20Areas/Biomass%20Heat/Biomass%20end%20user%20guide.pdf.

86 Estimates based on Energy Savings Trust (2010), *Domestic Low and Zero Carbon Technologies*, p.20.

87 www.wasteonline.org.uk/resources/informationsheets/wastedisposal.htm and www. statistics.gov.uk.

88 Brecht II Dranco – Anaerobic digestion facility (Belgium), from www.docstoc.com.

89 Author's calculations derived and based on Brecht II Dranco – Anaerobic digestion facility (Belgium), from www.docstoc.com.

90 ibid.

91 ibid.

92 www.sac.ac.uk/mainrep/pdfs/pgad.pdf.

93 www.sedbuk.com/pages/sap2009.htm.

94 Energy Saving Trust (2003; revised 2006), *Domestic Condensing Boilers: The Benefits and the Myths* CE52.

95 Energy Saving Trust (2010), *Getting Warmer: A Field Trial of Heat Pumps*.

96 www.icax.co.uk/gshp.html.

97 Energy Saving Trust (2010), *Getting Warmer: A Field Trial of Heat Pumps*.

98 ibid.

99 David Strong, Air source heat pumps, *AECB Green Building Magazine* 09, Autumn issue, p.29.

100 The Energy Saving Trust (2010), *Getting Warmer: A Field Trial of Heat Pumps*.

101 David Strong, Air source heat pumps, *AECB Green Building Magazine* 09, Autumn issue, p.29.

102 The Energy Saving Trust (2010), *Getting Warmer: A Field Trial of Heat Pumps*.

103 ibid.

104 Kwok and Grondzik (2007), *The Green Studio Book, UK* – Architectural Press, 0164.

105 http://ceo.decc.gov.uk/en/ceol/cms/process/stage_4Project/ground_source/ground_source.aspx.

106 Unsworth, *et al.* (1985), 'A salt gradient solar pond for solar heat collection and long-term storage'. Commission of the European communities and www.solarponds.com/; and Zangrando,

Observation and analysis of a full-scale experimental salt gradient solar pond. The University of New Mexico, 1979.

107 Unsworth, *et al.* (1985), 'A salt gradient solar pond for solar heat collection and long-term storage'. Commission of the European communities.

108 Akbarzadeh (2009), Examining potential benefits of combining a chimney with a solar gradient solar pond for production of power in salt-affected areas, Elsevier.

109 Arup- NHBC Foundation (2010), *Efficient Design of Piled Foundations for Low-Rise Housing*, Design Guide, www. nhbcfoundation.org/LinkClick. aspx?fileticket=Sm7 AAf2jPJk%3Dandtabid=339andmid =774andlanguage=en-GB.

110 ibid.

111 The concrete society www.concrete.org. uk/services/fingertips_nuggets. asp?cmd=displayandid=922.

112 ibid.

113 ibid.

114 Arup- NHBC Foundation (2010), *Efficient Design of Piled Foundations for Low-Rise Housing*, Design Guide, www.nhbcfoundation.org/LinkClick. asp x?fileticket=Sm7AAf2jPJk%3Dandtabid= 339andmid =774andlanguage=en-GB.

115 From BBC weather data.

116 Estimated by the author based on typical UK temperatures and relative humidity, using a psychometric chart.

117 http://en.wikipedia.org/wiki/ Hydrogen_economy.

118 www.woking.gov.uk/environment/ Greeninitiatives/sustainablewoking/ fuelcell.pdf.

119 www.hydrogen-yorkshire.co.uk/ documents/HMGS_Flyer.pdf.

120 www.cerespower.com/store/ files/231- Field%20Trial%20 commencement%20010211.pdf.

121 Ceres Power Ltd, 2 June 2009, www. publications.parliament.uk/pa/ cm200910/cmselect/cmenvaud/ 159/159we23.htm.

Index

C

M